EMPIRE AND IRELAND

Empire and Ireland

The Transatlantic Career
of the Canadian Imperialist
Hamar Greenwood, 1870–1948

ROY MACLAREN

McGill-Queen's University Press
Montreal & Kingston • London • Ithaca

ISBN 978-0-7735-4548-9 (cloth)
ISBN 978-0-7735-8222-4 (ePDF)
ISBN 978-0-7735-8227-9 (ePUB)

Legal deposit second quarter 2015
Bibliothèque nationale du Québec

Printed in Canada on acid-free paper that is 100% ancient forest free
(100% post-consumer recycled), processed chlorine free

This book has been published with the help of a grant from the
Henry N.R. Jackman Foundation.

McGill-Queen's University Press acknowledges the support of the Canada
Council for the Arts for our publishing program. We also acknowledge the
financial support of the Government of Canada through the Canada Book
Fund for our publishing activities.

Library and Archives Canada Cataloguing in Publication

MacLaren, Roy, 1934–, author
  Empire and Ireland: the transatlantic career of the Canadian imperialist
  Hamar Greenwood, 1870–1948 / Roy MacLaren.

  Includes bibliographical references and index.
  Issued in print and electronic formats.
  ISBN 978-0-7735-4548-9 (bound). – ISBN 978-0-7735-8222-4 (ePDF). –
  ISBN 978-0-7735-8227-9 (ePUB)

  1. Greenwood, Hamar Greenwood, Viscount, 1870–1948. 2. Cabinet
  officers – Great Britain – Biography. 3. Ireland. Chief Secretary – Officials
  and employees – Biography. 4. Ireland – Politics and government – 1910–1921.
  5. Great Britain – Politics and government – 1901–1936. I. Title.

  DA566.9.G74M33 2015   941.083092   C2014-908492-7
                                               C2014-908493-5

This book was typeset by Interscript in 10.5/13 Baskerville.

For Alethea

Contents

Acknowledgments

There are four people and one institution whom I wish to thank for their assistance during the gestation of this book.

The first is the late Major Alexander Greenwood, the co-executor of the estate of Lady Greenwood, who, although no direct relation of either Lord or Lady Greenwood, knew intimately the course of their lives together. In my conversations with him and his wife, Shirley, Alex Greenwood was always candid, amusing, and helpful. I am most grateful for his readiness to share with me his first-hand knowledge of Lady Greenwood's remarkable life.

The second is Mark Abley, the proficient and knowledgeable editor at McGill-Queen's University Press who is himself a notable author. His learned observations and wry suggestions never failed to improve the story of the Greenwoods.

The third is Elsie del Bianco, the research librarian at Trinity College in the University of Toronto, who was unfailing in the quest for material and references. Her energy and perseverance were, moreover, always informed by gentle humour.

The fourth is my late son, Ian MacLaren, who with his remarkable technical skills launched the manuscript on its otherwise uncertain course.

The institution is the Rockefeller Foundation's Bellagio Center, a retreat of beauty, order, and solace on the shores of Lake Como in Italy. To the Rockefeller Foundation and its highly competent staff at Bellagio, I am indebted for the time afforded me to contemplate and reflect upon a turbulent imperial world of a century ago.

Studio portrait of the Greenwood family ca. 1887, Whitby, Ontario. *Left centre*, father, John Greenwood (1824–1902); *right centre*, mother, Charlotte Churchill Hubbard Greenwood (1846–1902). The youngest daughter, Gladys Cecil Hamer "Sadie" 1886–1966), is seated between her parents. *Front row left*, Margery Virginia Victoria "Ulla" (1883–1947); *centre*, Isabella Rachel Letitia (1874–1887); *right*, Adeliza Florence Louise "Bryddie" (1879–1975). *Back row, from left*, Mary Harriet (1866–1953), Thomas Hamer ("Hamar") (1870–1948), William Hamer "Billy" (1872–1923), and Charlotte Jane (1868–1936).

Lieutenant Thomas Hamer Greenwood of the 34th Battalion (later the Ontario Regiment) of the Canadian militia, complete with the *de rigueur* military waxed moustache. He enlisted as a private in 1886 and was commissioned in 1890, aged twenty, following four summers of training at the militia camp at Niagara-on-the-Lake, Ontario.

Hamar Greenwood, member of Parliament for York, ca. 1908. He was an ardent supporter of the pre-war Liberal governments of Sir Henry Campbell-Bannerman and H.H. Asquith. As a radical Liberal MP, he was a tireless temperance advocate, a vocal supporter of the budgets of Lloyd George and of Home Rule for Ireland. Copyright National Portrait Gallery, London.

Margery (Margo) Spencer, Lady Greenwood, ca. 1915. The daughter of the affluent Reverend Walter Spencer, she displayed an intense interest in politics and was an intimate of Lloyd George and "the strong right arm" of her husband. She played a significant part in shaping the thinking of Lloyd George about Ireland during the troubles of 1921–22.

British Prime Minister David Lloyd George (in bowler) at an inspection in Downing Street of "Black and Tans" reinforcements of the Royal Irish Constabulary in November 1920. Below, Greenwood is on Lloyd George's right and Bonar Law is on his left.

The ability of the IRA to pass unnoticed amidst civilian crowds imposed upon the Crown forces the need to search constantly for concealed weapons on pedestrians, cyclists, and vehicles.

THE KINDEST CUT OF ALL.

WELSH WIZARD. "I NOW PROCEED TO CUT THIS MAP INTO TWO PARTS AND PLACE THEM IN THE HAT. AFTER A SUITABLE INTERVAL THEY WILL BE FOUND TO HAVE COME TOGETHER OF THEIR OWN ACCORD—(ASIDE)—AT LEAST LET'S HOPE SO; I'VE NEVER DONE THIS TRICK BEFORE."

A cartoon from *Punch* in 1920, sceptical of Lloyd George's Government of Ireland bill to partition Ireland by establishing parliaments in both North and South, linked by an Irish Council.

The Munster Arcade and William Egan's maintain a presence in Patrick Street in the aftermath of the burning of Cork city centre by Crown forces in December 1920. Photograph courtesy of the *Irish Examiner*.

Funeral passing through Patrick Street shortly after the burning of Cork, 12 December 1920. Photograph courtesy of the *Irish Examiner.*

Thomas Hamar Greenwood, studio portrait by Bassano, 14 October 1924. Having survived repeated threats on his life, Greenwood had become the Conservative Member of Parliament for Sunderland, following the collapse of Lloyd George's coalition government in late 1922. For some, the photograph reflected Northcliffe's comment in mid-1921 that he understood that Greenwood "has become an ancient man in the last three or four months." Copyright National Portrait Gallery, London.

Margo Greenwood in a studio portrait by Bassano, 14 October 1924.

Lord Beaverbrook, ca. 1930, one of the most eminent and mischievous of the many Canadians in the British Parliament. Greenwood declined Beaverbrook's invitation to head his controversial Empire Crusade in 1930. He was always wary of the wayward and erratic initiatives of his fellow Canadian, but they remained friends until Greenwood's death in 1948, each always assessing how to use the other. Copyright National Portrait Gallery, London.

John Amery, the elder son of Leo and Bryddie Amery, on 27 April 1932, shortly after his twenty-first birthday. At the age of twenty, in Athens, still a minor, he had married Una Eveline Wing, a Piccadilly prostitute. His support for Hitler across occupied Europe during the Second World War resulted in his execution for treason in London in 1945. Copyright National Portrait Gallery, London.

The Hon. Deborah Greenwood, at age eighteen, with her mother, the Viscountess Greenwood, on 21 June 1935, before Deborah's presentation at court. Copyright National Portrait Gallery, London.

Canadian Prime Minister William Lyon Mackenzie King, in a studio
portrait by Bassano during King's visit to London in November
1936. King and Greenwood, having collaborated closely on the
student protest at the University of Toronto in 1895, remained
life-long friends, although never finally agreeing about what a
liberal, constructive British Commonwealth could become.
Copyright National Portrait Gallery, London.

The Greenwoods and their second daughter, Deborah, winter of 1940–41, on the West Pier at Brighton, where the Greenwoods had a second home. Deborah is in the uniform of the Women's Auxiliary Air Force (WAAF), "an efficient officer," in her father's proud view. Whitby Public Library collection, Ontario.

Greenwood and Sam McLaughlin, founder of the McLaughlin Motors and later president of General Motors (Canada), at Oshawa, 4 September 1938, during Greenwood's visit to Canada to receive an honorary doctorate from his alma mater, the University of Toronto. Michael (Eric) Greenwood is to the rear right. Greenwood's visit followed a difficult and controversial strike the year before. Whitby Public Library collection.

A late, undated oil portrait of her husband by Margo Greenwood.

Lady Greenwood and Princess Elizabeth at a Pilgrims dinner at the Savoy in London in 1952, following the unveiling of the monument to President Roosevelt in Grosvenor Square.

EMPIRE AND IRELAND

Introduction

In February 1921, from the south of France, Clementine Churchill wrote to her husband, Winston, who four days before had been moved by Prime Minister Lloyd George from secretary of state for war to secretary of state for the colonies. In reviewing his various cabinet colleagues, she described Sir Hamar Greenwood, the chief secretary for Ireland, as "nothing but a blaspheming, hearty, vulgar, brave, Knockabout Colonial."[1]

I chanced on Clementine Churchill's letter while writing another book. With a little digging, I soon learned that although today he is almost forgotten, Hamar Greenwood was in his lifetime a well-known and controversial public figure, one who transformed himself from a boy in a small Ontario town to a cabinet minister in London, a liberal imperialist at the height and heart of the British Empire, a life-long advocate of a collaborative Commonwealth of equals. But however dismissive the words of Clementine Churchill, they would have been too flaccid for militant Irish insurgents during "the troubles" of the early 1920s. They would have said that she was being far too charitable about a chief secretary for Ireland whom they execrated for being ultimately responsible – short of Prime Minister Lloyd George himself – for the brutal excesses of the Black and Tans and Auxiliaries, the deeply feared and hated English reinforcements for the beleaguered Royal Irish Constabulary.

Greenwood may have been something of what Clementine Churchill wrote, but a later description offered by her husband was certainly contrary to hers. Both agreed that Greenwood was brave, but Winston Churchill went on to describe his former parliamentary private secretary in terms quite different from those of his wife. Toward the end of the Irish turmoil, he concluded a salute to his intrepid fellow Liberal as "always hoping that the day would dawn when a reconciliation could be effected between the two islands. No one welcomed that day more than you, and no man more proudly wrote his name across the great Treaty which in the mercy of God may yet draw a curtain of blessed oblivion across the long and sombre past."[2]

It is impossible to delineate a public figure adequately with a phrase or two, and so I set out on my own *Quest for Corvo* to learn who Hamar Greenwood was. I gathered together as much material about him as I was able to find in Canada and the British Isles and attempted to impose some order upon its random character. The fact that most of the personal papers and diaries of Greenwood and his wife, Margo, were destroyed in the London Blitz of 1940 makes problematic any later depiction of him as a man, or of his relations with his entrepreneurial wife and their four assorted children, his siblings, relatives, and friends, as well as his colleagues, including Churchill, Lloyd George, and Mackenzie King. There is, for example, little material extant that reflects what Greenwood thought or felt in later years – other than his unchanging commitment to an evolving British Empire – and no indication of whether at the end of his life he looked back with anger or delight, pride or regret. A friend who read this biography in manuscript expressed surprise that I could take as a subject a man whom I appeared neither to like nor to dislike (he himself dismissing Greenwood in a neat phrase as "Lloyd George's eternal patsy"). I dissented, believing that it is indeed possible, although certainly not easy, to attempt an impartial account of someone who was the subject of major controversy during the Irish conflict of ninety or more years ago. As in much civil strife, one man's freedom fighter is another man's terrorist, so I have attempted to describe how Greenwood and his wife ("my strong right arm") saw and reacted to events and trends of the day, rather than simply accepting the depictions of them by either diehard Conservative-Unionists or Irish Republicans.

As his own life was ending, Greenwood deplored the end of the British Empire. In his eyes, Kipling's apprehensive "Recessional" had broadly come true, the lamentable result of the sterile thinking of Conservatives who merely wanted to conserve. (A notable exception in Greenwood's mind was his Conservative brother-in-law, Leo Amery, who had long been in the vanguard of those few in Britain who attempted to think through how to reconcile dominions with imperialism.) Throughout his decades in the United Kingdom, Greenwood sought an Empire that would be in a permanent state of reform, constantly engaged in adaption and innovation. As did Sir Robert Borden, the prime minister of Canada for the decade embracing the First World War, Greenwood saw the Empire as a community of interests in which the Dominions and India and in time all the colonies – no Anglo-Saxon racist he – could better realize their individual potential. He strove to see the Empire and later the British Commonwealth affirm responsible self-government within a liberal, constructive tradition. As we shall see, he did not develop detailed thinking about the nature of that perpetual reform, but he was quite certain that it should originate at least as much in the Dominions and India as in Britain itself, where an unholy combination of Little Englanders and intransigent Conservatives militated against such liberal speculation and implementation.

Unlike Mackenzie King and some of those around him, Greenwood was not haunted by imperial centrists supposedly bent upon retaining in London all meaningful imperial lead strings. Many earlier Canadian historians, some influenced by romantic perceptions of the American War of Independence, interpreted the history of Canada as a similar (if decidedly more laggard and insipid) progression from abject dependency to splendid autonomy, a straight-line story from colony to nation. For them, the continuing imperial connection was a hindrance and not a help in the realization by the Dominions and India of their true potential. A decade or so ago, a serious reassessment of such historiography began, with one imperial historian recording, "Anyone who calls for a re-assertion of the significance of the imperial relationship is dismissed as an imperial apologist, a reactionary who wishes to wallow in imperial nostalgia. This is patent nonsense." Equally obviously, those instances that have been offered by historians as evidence of conflict between Canada and Britain are "not necessarily how those events were viewed by contemporary Canadians."[3] Certainly Greenwood, never simply "a blaspheming, hearty, vulgar, brave Knock-about Colonial," regarded throughout his life the occasional points of imperial abrasion as arising naturally from the introduction of responsible government in the Dominions and India, but capable of resolution by consultation and reform, not least in the United Kingdom itself.

Today's historians no longer view two centuries of Canada's development in yesterday's simplistic terms. They recognize that Canada benefited from its steadily evolving place in the Empire, and the Empire's steadily evolving place in Canada. Certainly the advantages to Canada within a progressive, reformist Empire were evident to Greenwood.

He strove to make them real to others, including apathetic Englishmen. His life, uneven though it was, should be seen by imperial historians of today and tomorrow as joining with others in offering additional refutation of the now hoary idea that wary if not downright hostile colonials had forced a reluctant Britain to surrender first economic and then political hegemony. It was never that simple – and certainly not to Greenwood.

Canadian Origins, 1870–1895

The future Viscount Greenwood of Holbourne was born Thomas Hubbard Hamer Greenwood on 7 February 1870 in the small county seat of Whitby in the Province of Ontario, fifty kilometres east of Toronto and two or three kilometres from the flat shores of Lake Ontario. Less than three years before his birth, four of the British North American colonies had come together in the new Confederation of Canada, apprehensive as they were of the ambitions of those in a now imperialist United States that espoused a "manifest destiny" to take over the whole of North America following its predatory Mexican wars and the conclusion of its long and bloody Civil War. Apprehensions in Canada only increased a year later with the embarkation of the last British regiment, except for the dockyard garrison in Halifax. Canada was a British colony, a large and important one, but many "Little Englanders," including some in the cabinet of Liberal Prime Minister William Gladstone, would have been happy enough to see any colony either out of the Empire or, as in the view of Benjamin Disraeli, strictly paying its own way.

Greenwood was born about the time that long-standing Liberal "Little Englanders" began to be matched by Conservative imperialists led by Disraeli, who abandoned his earlier scepticism about the Empire "as a millstone around our necks." He recognized that the newly enfranchised working class took pride in the Empire as it evolved from primarily a commercial enterprise to an imperial romance of bugles of the Thin Red Line with their call to duty for queen and country. But Canada remained something of an imperial nuisance throughout, placed precariously as it was on a five-thousand kilometre porous border with the United States. Led by Sir John A. Macdonald, Canada's first prime minister, most Canadians, even French-Canadians for their own reasons, consistently sought to remain a self-governing part of the British Empire, the threats and blandishments of the post-Civil War United States notwithstanding. Independence was stubbornly refused, since Canadians sensed it would soon lead to absorption by their burgeoning neighbour. Britain was Canada's big brother, its role model, and its protector. Although some in London would have been happy to see Canada depart the Empire of its own volition and thereby remove real and potential frictions with the United States, Britain always opposed annexationist ambitions in Washington as a threat to the honour of the crown. The great thing was to continue to reduce or eliminate points of abrasion.

From adolescence, Greenwood was himself convinced that imperialists in the colonies understood what the Empire was and what it could become better than the British in the British Isles. What Richard Gwyn has written about the attitude of Sir John A. Macdonald applies equally to Greenwood: "His was fiercely loyal, of course; but there was no deference in his posture. Macdonald was exactly the kind of colonial ... who could break through English reserve and snobbery simply because there was not a trace of colonial cringe about him."[1] Canada and the Empire were so co-mingled in Greenwood's mind that Stephen Leacock's memorable self-definition – "I am an imperialist because I refuse to be colonial" – was equally applicable to him.

Greenwood is generally accounted in England as a Nottingham or Yorkshire name, but Hamar Greenwood's family was solidly Welsh. His great-grandfather, John (1754–1842), was a tenant smallholder on the hills of Radnorshire. His son, William (1793–1872), married Mary Hamer (1795–1838), whose modest circumstances were only marginally superior to his. Mary died young, their short married life marked with no material advance. In Wales, the decade of the 1840s was marred by severe economic depression. For many, the only escape from rural poverty was either urban slums or emigration, chiefly to North America. To emigrate was a difficult decision at any time, especially given the likely prospect of no return. In the case of William Greenwood's son, John, it was made a little easier by the presence in Canada West of Hamer relatives.

A tall, strong, young man, John Hamer Greenwood (1829–1902) emigrated from his Welsh hills in 1850 at the age of twenty-one, to be welcomed by his uncle John Hamer (1787–1872) of Hamer's Corners near Whitby. Said to have been "unable either to read or write a word of English," John Greenwood, like many immigrants, readily took whatever jobs he could find.[2] For example, by 1853 he was employed mixing mortar and carrying bricks for the construction in Whitby of the new courthouse for Ontario County. His limited leisure hours he spent improving his education, including his English. On the basis of his early schooling in Wales and what he had since taught himself, he was eventually accepted, in accordance with the rather informal proceedings of the day, as a local schoolteacher. The small income from this position was just enough to allow him to begin concurrently the study of law as an articling student in Whitby.

In 1860, ten years after his arrival in Canada West, John Greenwood was admitted as a solicitor by the Law Society of Upper Canada. During the 1870s, he was a senior partner in the Whitby firm of Greenwood and McMillan, barristers and solicitors, public notaries, and land conveyancers, appearing in the courthouse that he had helped to build. Between 1872 and 1875, he was also president and part-owner of the Canada Clock Company which, when it failed, almost dragged him into bankruptcy, a calamity that would have been fatal for both his emerging law practice and his local political ambitions. He nevertheless continued to speculate in various small entrepreneurial ventures, but none met with much success. An obituary would sum him up "as a financier who could always wiggle out of a hole, but his enterprising and speculative nature pulled him back into the hole as fast as he could struggle his way out."[3] His reported excessive drinking may also have hindered his strivings (certainly his elder son, Thomas, later became a life-long teetotaller and noted temperance advocate).

John Greenwood's law practice, uneven although it was, finally gave him the confidence to marry. In 1865, five years after his admission to the Law Society of Upper Canada as a solicitor, he married, at the age of thirty-six, the nineteen-year-old Charlotte Churchill Hubbard of Brougham, a hamlet a few kilometres west of Whitby in Pickering Township. In the 1770s Charlotte Hubbard's great-grandfather had taken his discharge from the British army in Virginia. Following the American War of Independence, his descendants, with many others loyal to the crown, departed the thirteen rebellious colonies for Nova Scotia or the new colonies of Upper Canada and New Brunswick. Charlotte Hubbard was all her life proud of her loyalist heritage as expressing an allegiance to the British Empire. In turn she inculcated this pride in her children, several of whom later lived in Britain and, in the case of one son and two daughters, died there. She was equally proud of her grandfather, a Brougham Township councillor and a magistrate who had nevertheless supported the Rebellion of 1837, striving for the liberal traditions of British civil society to be equally evident in the colonies. In 1917, the elder of her two surviving sons, Thomas (by then known as Hamar), would proclaim proudly to the British House of Commons, "I am the great grandson of a rebel in Canada, a fine old citizen, who took twelve sons with him into the rebellion for Home Rule [in Upper Canada]. He took nearly his whole family. They were fine men in those days."[4]

Charlotte Greenwood bore ten children, seven daughters and three sons, in the twenty years between 1866 and 1886, the last when she was forty years of age. Three died in infancy or early childhood. The seven surviving children, as we shall see, all later achieved some greater or lesser recognition, but it is the third child and elder surviving son, Thomas Hamer Greenwood, who is the subject of this biography. In memory of his paternal grandfather, "Hamer" was included in his name when he was christened in 1870 at All Saints Church in Whitby. (Decades later, he would donate a stained-glass window to All Saints in memory of his parents.) The Greenwoods soon moved to "Spencerwood" at 210 Henry Street, a two-storey white clapboard house with a small garden, a sign of some modest affluence in Whitby.

Charlotte Greenwood kept an annual diary with careful household accounts, but the only volume extant is for the year 1871 when she was twenty-five. She begins with loving references to baby Tom, then approaching his first birthday, as well as to his two sisters, all "sweet little creatures," but later adds despondently, "G. [her husband, John Greenwood] is not in until late. He has nothing to say. I go to bed early for I have not rested for so long. I would give all we are worth if we could see and think alike. I go to bed with a heavy heart. I only live for my babies, sweet creatures." Whatever were these deeply unsettling differences between Charlotte and her husband, the diary for 1871 as a whole records an uneventful existence. She noted her husband's frequent absences in Toronto to attend, among other things, "railway meetings"; her cleaning of his office in their house (not a task to be entrusted to the two maids); his late returns home and her solitary attendance at All Saints. Surprisingly, on the last day of the year, again pregnant, Charlotte completed her 1871 journal with a prayer of contrition: "Help me to be a better wife to one of the best husbands ... Watch over my dear husband in all his undertakings. Give him strength to bear his troubles. May I train my little ones up for the lambs of Thy fold." Baby Tom, she records, "is trying to talk. He knows all we say to him ... any mother should be grateful to Heaven for such a gift. May I train his young mind aright and may he grow to be an honour to his father and mother."*

Tom always recalled his schooling if not his entire childhood in Whitby as near idyllic. Later in Britain he recorded that if he had a son, he would insist upon his spending his childhood in Canada, "a boy's Paradise." No poisonous and pervasive class system hindered any student there. By contrast to the stultifying, stunting, thwarting system he observed in England, "in all our Colonies the boys and girls have an equal chance."† In Whitby, Greenwood attended a nearby elementary school of one room, a "dame school" in earlier parlance. In 1881 he entered the much more formal Whitby Collegiate Institute.

When Tom was a boy, his father was town councillor and the mayor of Whitby from 1872 to 1875 and again from 1883 to 1886. A noted partisan Liberal, John Greenwood worked closely with W.T.R. Preston, the aggressive general secretary of the Ontario Liberal Association, and with the local Liberal member of the Ontario Legislature, John Dryden. By the time of his father's second term as mayor in 1883, Tom was old enough to observe how election campaigns, however modest, were conducted and to absorb a little of their distinctive rhetoric. He learned platform eloquence by listening to his father, widely regarded as the best orator in Whitby. At the national level the year before, Tom had welcomed, somewhat precociously, the resolution of Edward Blake, the Liberal leader of the opposition in Ottawa, urging Home Rule for Ireland. Later, "he always acclaimed Edward Blake's Home Rule speech in the Canadian House of Commons as the high-watermark of statesmanship."[5] Such admiration for Blake's support of the persistent efforts of Gladstone to enable the Irish to govern themselves must have put the Greenwood family at loggerheads with some of their neighbours and Tom's schoolfellows. Adherents of the Orange Order, descendants of fanatical anti-popery Ulstermen, were everywhere in southern Ontario, forming the backbone of the Tory Party. Whitby was no exception, the Liberal Party being regarded by some as the "Catholic party." Undeterred

* Charlotte Greenwood's journal for 1871 was in the possession of the late Major Alexander Greenwood. She does not specify what her husband's troubles were.
† In the event, Hamar Greenwood sent neither of his two English-born sons to school in Canada, presumably because the first was mentally disabled, and the second was sent to Eton to meet his parents' social ambitions.

by such bigotry, the Greenwoods remained consistent in their advocacy of Home Rule for Ireland within the British Empire.

During the summer of 1885, Tom, then fifteen, made his first transatlantic crossing, accompanying his father who had somehow saved sufficient funds to pay for their visit to Britain. Where they went, whom they saw, or what they did in or beyond their ancestral homeland of Wales is unrecorded, except for a chance recollection that for some reason father and son called upon Lord Rodney "of racing fame."* They must have been everywhere aware of the greatly heightened imperial enthusiasms of that year 1885 when at its beginning "Chinese" Gordon was killed in Khartoum, despite the forlorn effort of the British army – Canadian volunteers included – to save him. Equally evident was the seemingly endless turmoil in Ireland and its impact on the fortunes in England of both the Liberal and Conservative parties, the latter habitually hostile to reforms that might loosen the ties of the Irish with Britain. Nevertheless, in the year of the Greenwoods' visit, the sizeable Irish Nationalist faction in Parliament, in exchange for a pledge to end coercion in Ireland, briefly abandoned their traditional friends, the Liberals, and joined with their traditional foes, the Conservatives, in defeating Gladstone's second government. In the new, short-lived government of Lord Salisbury, the Irish viceroy was Lord Carnarvon, who, having guided the British North America Act through Westminster in 1867, advocated granting Ireland devolved powers similar to those of a province within the Canadian federation. Salisbury and his cabinet colleagues rejected such liberal thinking on the part of a viceroy, a negative attitude that the Greenwoods, *père et fils*, would certainly have noted during their visit to Britain.

Whether the Liberal mayor of Whitby, John Greenwood, called upon the Conservative high commissioner in London, Sir Charles Tupper, is unknown, but given his long support for Home Rule for Ireland, Greenwood would have been well aware of the speeches of Tupper's predecessor, Sir Alexander Galt, in Liverpool, Glasgow, and Edinburgh as well as in London, extolling controversial resolutions of the Canadian House of Commons in favour of Irish Home Rule. During Galt's three-year tour in London (1880–83), he had been indefatigable in promoting large-scale Irish emigration as a joint Anglo-Canadian project. The Parliament at Ottawa had voted substantial sums for famine relief in Ireland and had vainly recommended to London joint Anglo-Canadian

* Lord Rodney's second son, Major Simon Rodney, was to marry Greenwood's youngest sister, Gladys – or "Sadie" – in London almost forty years later in 1922.

funding for large-scale emigration: "There is no other way of making the west of Ireland support its 600,000 souls than to take half of them away."[6] But the British government always eschewed providing direct financial support for emigration from the United Kingdom. In Ireland itself as well as in Toronto and Winnipeg, Galt had worked to foster private support for Irish emigration, but the Roman Catholic hierarchy was uneasy about the future of the faithful in a distant, sparsely populated colony, and in any event regarded emigration as a placebo rather than a remedy for Ireland's ills. Galt's persistent efforts did have an unexpected but ultimately unproductive echo in the British election of 1886, the year following the Greenwoods' visit to the United Kingdom. When out of office, the Conservative leader Lord Salisbury had proclaimed that if the British "could only emigrate another million of the Irish people ... to Manitoba, the result would be magical upon the social conditions of the Irish people."[7] Once in office, however, he exhibited no more enthusiasm for government financing of Irish emigration than did Gladstone before him. Amidst these continuing debates, when Tom Greenwood returned to his school desk that autumn, he took with him – among other things imperial – a first-hand acquaintanceship with the continuing impact of Ireland on political debate in Britain.

At Whitby Collegiate Institute, Tom was well respected by both his fellow students and teachers. Tall, athletic, and notably articulate, he was elected in 1887 head of school. Three decades later, in 1924, his elementary school teacher recalled for the *Toronto Daily Star* that he was "one of the finest boys I ever had ... He was a smart boy and withal a nice boy with the other scholars. He was always ready and willing to help out the other boys when they got into trouble." He was remembered by a less articulate but equally enthusiastic classmate as "clever ... you bet he was ... in debates and school exercises ... he was always counted on to do the best talking. Most of the boys were too afraid of ourselves when we did have to get on our feet, but not [Tom] ... it just came natural to him ... He would never stand for any bullying and he had the physical strength to make what he said go. [He] was a fine speaker ... it was natural that he should be for his father before him was one of the most gifted orators I ever heard ... [Tom] was eloquent, and he could go on a platform and handle about any subject that came along. There's no doubt [he] gets his ability as a speaker from his father." He became president of his school's debating society, distinguishing himself on one occasion by speaking especially eloquently in favour of the motion that "intemperance, as regards the use of liquor, opium, and tobacco, has caused more misery than war." On the other hand, his contributions to choral eucharists at All Saints were marked "with more vim, I'm afraid, than piety."[8] As an athlete, he was outstanding. In addition to being a skilful boxer, he was a talented cricketer. At age sixteen, being large and agile for his age, he was chosen for the "International Cricket Team ... comprised [of] the best cricketers in Canada, who were matched against the pick of the United States."[9]

In 1904 Sara Jeanette Duncan of Brantford, Ontario, a hundred or so kilometres west of Whitby, published her fourteenth novel, *The Imperialist*, its title reflecting her understanding of a general sentiment then abroad in the province. Tom Greenwood could have been the model for her liberal hero, Lorne Murchison, the aspiring young lawyer from "Elgin." The collegiate institute in the fictional town is uncannily like Whitby's: "The Collegiate Institute took in raw material and turned out teachers, more teachers than anything. The teachers taught, chiefly in rural districts where they could save money, and with the money they saved changed themselves into doctors, Fellows of the University, mining engineers [and lawyers]."[10] And the collegiate institute in "Elgin," as in Whitby, was at the centre of a community that was quietly and confidently both British and Canadian, since to be an English Canadian was, quite simply, to be British also.

When Tom graduated from Whitby Collegiate in the late spring of 1887, he hoped to enrol that autumn in the University of Toronto, but his father wanted him to article at his firm as a first step in a legal career. School-teaching, however, beckoned, as it had to his father before him. A year or two of teaching would give him more time to reflect on his plans for the future, as well as providing some savings for his university expenses. His emerging ambitions had the encouragement of one of his collegiate teachers, Anson Henderson, who became something of a mentor to him. Henderson "was the greatest teacher of history I ever heard of. He inspired me with a desire to make history. He inspired me to a serious study of history and geography – the two subjects of which there is the greatest need to bring a realization of the greatness of the Empire."[11] Upon receiving his junior matriculation certificate in June 1887, Tom enrolled in the teachers' training course at the small Whitby model school. Not long after the term had commenced in September, he learned that the crossroads hamlet of Manchester, twenty or so kilometres to the north, urgently needed a teacher for the few pupils who came from the surrounding farms to the one-room schoolhouse. He promptly decided that was the job for him, teaching certificate or not. Almost thirty years later, the *Canadian Magazine* would recall, "with that tenacity and determination which have always characterized him, he wheedled one of the Collegiate masters [Anson Henderson] into supporting him, wormed a permit from the county inspector, and got the appointment. At the end of the Model [School] term he returned to Whitby and passed the examination with flying colours."[12]

Now equipped with the necessary certificate, Greenwood spent a total of four years (1887–91) as schoolmaster at Manchester. Although barely seventeen when he began, he soon played a leading part in the life of the village, happily engaging in lively conversation and informal debates in the clapboard township hall. There was no tavern in the county following the prohibition of alcohol by local referendum, a decision welcome to Tom, who was already a confirmed if precocious temperance advocate. He also sang in the choir of the small Primitive Methodist church (there being no Church of England in the vicinity) and helped with the Sunday school. Despite his youth, he was "godfather at all christenings, best man at all weddings, and no funeral was complete without me because I was the only man in the township who possessed a plug [top] hat." Funerals were not considered "sad enough and respectable enough unless he looked his 'glummest' in the first buggy behind the hearse." At the graveside of the departed, he was expected "to deliver a touching and overwhelming laudatory oration ... This was no great strain on the sense of accuracy, but it well-nigh exhausted the fund of pleasing adjectives in the English tongue."[13] In later life he would also regale dinner parties with his recollection of "the buxom farmer's daughter of 22, a front-row pupil when at the age of 17 he kept school, who stayed behind each day in 'the dinner break' [i.e., midday] and proposed to him."[14]

Anson Henderson, Tom's mentor at Whitby Collegiate, was also a captain (eventually lieutenant colonel) in the 34th Battalion of the militia (later the Ontario Regiment). At his prompting, Tom, when sixteen, had enlisted as a private, having mastered elementary drill in the collegiate cadet corps (latterly as cadet captain). The 34th Battalion, initially the Highland Rifle Company of Oshawa and Whitby, had had as its first major ceremonial duty to provide the honour guard for Edward, Prince of Wales, when he passed through Whitby en route to Toronto in 1860. It had also served during the Fenian Raids of 1866 and provided volunteers for the North West Rebellion of 1885 and eventually for the South African War of 1899–1902.

Tom, like many other young men in Ontario, expressed his commitment to the Empire by volunteering for militia service as one expression of the imperial enthusiasm – even jingoism – that was common through much of the province. The descendants of United Empire Loyalists cherished their heritage; the omnipresent Orange Order, with its Protestant roots deep in Ulster, proclaimed its unshakeable allegiance to the crown; and imperial federalists searched for new ways of fostering the unity of the Empire while keeping a wary eye on the United States from whence the ill-conceived and ill-conducted armed raids by the Irish Fenians had come. First from Whitby in his last year of school and then from the hamlet of Manchester, Tom did his required annual training during the dog days of summer at Niagara-on-the-Lake, the well-equipped training camp for as many as sixteen militia battalions at one time. An enthusiastic soldier, he won his commission as second lieutenant in 1890 at the age of twenty, following four years in the ranks.

His commitment to the militia was such that several stories remain of his part-time military service. One such story, which has several variants, has Lieutenant Greenwood hurriedly seeking recruits in Toronto for the 34th Battalion. The battalion had been sharply reduced in a recent militia reorganization by the discharge of deadwood: laggards, delinquents, and incompetents. One result was that directly before the annual summer camp, two of its companies fell short of their authorized levels. Thirty volunteers were urgently needed. The recently commissioned Greenwood, ordered to find them as far afield as Toronto if necessary, was advanced a total of thirty dollars to pay for the men's rail fares to Whitby. One account has Greenwood hiring Huron Street Hall near the University of Toronto, successfully haranguing thirty or so young men on their duty to queen and country and assigning fifteen to each of the two depleted companies, before marching them down Yonge Street to the rail station to entrain for Whitby. Another account adds that before rounding up his thirty recruits, Greenwood went first to visit a military tailor in Toronto to have his hand-me-down uniform as a lieutenant refurbished and refitted at the sizeable cost of almost thirty dollars. Accordingly, on the train to Whitby, Greenwood is said to have grandly informed the intimidated conductor, "I'm an officer of the militia. I have orders to take these men to the camp at Whitby. The transportation will be paid. You needn't worry."[15]

Decades later, the solecism of Greenwood on a militia officers' training course at Stanley Barracks in Toronto under the command of Lieutenant Colonel William Otter (of North West campaign fame) was also recalled. "His interpretation of military law and regulations apparently led to his detection of some things in connection with the administration [of Stanley Barracks] which he did not approve. Instead of reciting his grievances through the ordinary channels, he went over the heads of the others [including Otter] and sent his communication to the Minister [of Militia, Mackenzie Bowell, the future prime minister] at Ottawa. He got 'in Dutch' over this breach of established rule, the communication being sent back to the commanding officer [Otter]. Greenwood got off with a reprimand, and he more than evened up matters by coming off with flying colours in his final [militia] exam."[16]

As a junior officer at summer camp at Niagara-on-the-Lake, the teetotaller Greenwood was assigned the command of a night picket to apprehend soldiers out of bounds, especially any who had crossed the Niagara River to Youngstown, New York, to visit its several notorious taverns. The regulations had hitherto been laxly enforced, but he "posted sentries along the [Canadian] bank of the Niagara River to watch small boats crossing from Youngstown. The result was that the number of prisoners the young lieutenant marched into camp far exceeded the number of his picket and established Greenwood on a high pinnacle as a disciplinarian."[17]

For Greenwood and many of his contemporaries in late Victorian Ontario, they clearly belonged to the British Empire, and the British Empire equally clearly belonged to them. They were British just as much as were those British who continued to live in the British Isles. They benefited from and were protected by the imperial power of John Bull – as Sir John A. Macdonald frequently affirmed – and they had a duty to their sovereign and their Empire as the loyalists had sacrificed to fulfil a century before. "Responsible government," as conferred by the British North America Act, was seen as perpetuating the British connection, not ending it. In short, for them, to be Canadian was to be British. One of Macdonald's ministers, the irrepressible Sir George Foster (unlike Macdonald but like Greenwood a pronounced temperance advocate), had long since recognized that "there has arisen [in Canada] ... the sense of power to be exercised within the Empire, of responsibility to imperial duties, of attachment to imperial ideals, and of co-operation in the achievement of imperial destinies."[18]

Foster well summarized the ethos of imperial Canada in which Greenwood grew up. In Greenwood's case, the unquestioning attachment to imperial ideals was compounded by his mother's cherished loyalist heritage and her emotional pride in the repulse of invaders during the American War of Independence, the War of 1812, and the Fenian raids of 1866. Greenwood was an impressionable fourteen years old when a centenary celebration of the arrival of the loyalists was held across Ontario and the maritime provinces. Further, from the militia camp on the Niagara River, he knew well the nearby Fort George and Queenston Heights where Major General Sir Isaac Brock (after whom the high street of Whitby was named) had been killed eighty years before, repelling American invaders – and where forty years before a disaffected Irishman had dynamited the tall column erected in memory of Brock's heroism.

Greenwood was still teaching at the hamlet of Manchester when in March 1891 the ailing Macdonald won his last election. Eighteen months later, in October 1892, when Greenwood entered the University of Toronto, Macdonald was dead. His last election campaign was already seen as a high point in defining Canada's place in the Empire, he having roundly proclaimed in the face of the alleged Liberal subservience to the United States, "As for myself, my course is clear. A British subject I was born – a British subject I will die. With my utmost effort, with my latest breath, will I oppose the 'veiled treason' which attempts by sordid means and mercenary proffers to lure our people from their allegiance." From Greenwood's loyalist heritage and lifetime devotion to a liberal British Empire, one may suppose that he cried amen to that ringing declaration. Throughout his life, he clung to the few simple notions of loyalty to a self-governing Canada in a cooperative Empire on which he had been nourished. His monochromatic commitment to the Empire – not to be confused with a devotion to Britain alone – echoed the straightforward thinking of his near-contemporary, Conrad's Lord Jim: "Hang ideas! They are tramps, vagabonds, knocking at the back door of your mind, each taking a little of your substance, each carrying away some crumb of that belief in a few simple notions you must cling to if you want to live decently and would like to die easily."

His four years of teaching at Manchester completed, Greenwood matriculated at the University of Toronto in October 1891. He registered not as Thomas Hubbard Hamer Greenwood but as Hamar Greenwood, having for some reason decided to drop Thomas and his mother's family name and to alter the spelling of his father's family name from Hamer to Hamar.* When he arrived at university as Hamar Greenwood, he was already twenty-two years old, four years older than

---

* Most of the Greenwood siblings changed their given names. In addition to Tom becoming Hamar, Florence became Bryddie; Gladys became Sadie; Margery became Ulla; and, more prosaically, William became Billy. Greenwood's wife, Margery, became Margo, and her sister Muriel became Molly. Eric, the second son of Hamar and Margo, became Michael. Whether this epidemic of name-changing arose from the fact that they simply did not like their names or from a more bizarre desire to reinvent themselves at some fundamental level can now be only a matter for speculation.

most freshmen. He was more mature, purposeful, and confident, as well, having not only taught school for four years but also having served for more than six in the militia, recently as an officer. His initial academic record at the university was adequate but not outstanding. His Latin, French, and German marks were seldom more than a pass, but in English literature he did consistently better. In geology and psychology he did just well enough. It was only in his third and fourth years, when he was able to concentrate on political science, economics, and law, that his marks took a decided upward turn.

Greenwood was always prominent in extracurricular activities. Having emulated his father in oratory, he readily adapted to the stage. He and another member of a scratch cast in the hamlet of Manchester had "collaborated in the writing of a melodrama of the genuine blood-and-thunder variety, Greenwood took the role of hero and the other youth that of the villain, and the drama was produced at Manchester before a great audience."[19] A later account reverses the roles. Greenwood and another young teacher from the nearby hamlet of Utica had written a melodrama, *Down the Slope*, which they staged in the small village hall. In this version of the story, Greenwood played the dastardly villain. Yet another newspaper story describes how, in his third year at university, having completed his summer militia training, he organized a tour through southwestern Ontario for a troupe of undergraduates: "Greenwood was himself advance agent and heavy tragedian of the company. The striking figure he made when he struck a new over-night stand, with his silk hat, very long-skirted Prince Albert coat and bright patent leather shoes is still remembered after twenty-five years in many an Ontario town."[20] The troupe's summer repertoire included *Uncle Tom's Cabin* (especially popular in those towns where the Underground Railway from the United States once had termini) and their own acclaimed *Down the Slope*. Yet however well received the plays, the theatre tour was not a commercial success. At Kincardine on the shores of distant Lake Huron, it came to an abrupt end. Stranded more than 250 kilometres from Whitby, Greenwood telegraphed his father for the rail fare home. He received the unsympathetic reply that he could walk back, the weather being fine.

Despite the financial failure of the troupe, Greenwood's dual role of manager and player contributed to his greater self-confidence and self-discipline. He taught himself to use his booming voice to convince audiences that he was in fact either a true-born hero or a deep-dyed villain. Later he would deploy those same oratorical and thespian skills to convince audiences of the virtues of temperance or the blessings of the

British Empire. His theatrical ambitions presumably gave rise decades later to slurs that he had toured with a circus as a barker or, according to Lord Birkenhead, that he had "started life selling tin watches for silver ones at a fair in Toronto."[21] Neither story is true.

At the University of Toronto, one fellow student later recalled "the curiosity that his advent excited. He was tall, good-looking and fashionably dressed. As he strode through the halls, his lordly manner compelled attention."[22] Yet he lived abstemiously – he was a life-long teetotaller – having little more than what he had been able to save from the pittances paid for teaching and militia service. Some slight financial relief came from John Dryden, the former reeve of Whitby Township who, with the support of John Greenwood and soon thereafter of W.T.R. Preston, the Ontario Liberal Party organizer, had begun a term of twenty-six years in the Ontario legislature, nine as minister of agriculture. Not only did John Greenwood assist Dryden in his election campaigns but both his sons, Tom and William, stumped for him. That the two boys were also active temperance advocates was an added recommendation to the teetotaller minister. Reward from Dryden eventually came in the form of part-time employment for Tom (now Hamar) while at university.* The Public Accounts for the Province of Ontario for 1893 list him as having been paid a total of $72 as "an extra clerk compiling returns" (statistics). In his third year at the university, he received $48 for "services re bulletins, etc."[23] He also began to write occasionally for local newspapers and journals, notably the *Toronto Daily Star, Saturday Night,* and *Wide World,* on a range of topics including "ice sports in Canada."

In the summer of 1894, following his annual militia training, Greenwood travelled to Chicago where a bitter strike at the nearby Pullman works was paralyzing much of the rail system in the United States. President Cleveland, over the protests of the governor of Illinois, sent in federal troops to force the end of the strike. At least twelve people were killed before the strikers capitulated in the first week of August. Why Greenwood was in Chicago is unrecorded, but at a later Ontario Royal Commission hearing, according to Greenwood's contemporary, Hector Charlesworth,† the hostile counsel for the University of Toronto

---

* In 1906, John Dryden would be appointed by the British government to a royal commission on agricultural conditions in Ireland, the same year that Greenwood was elected to the British House of Commons. Whether Greenwood had anything to do with the nomination of his erstwhile mentor is unknown.

† Charlesworth was a near classmate of Greenwood and Mackenzie King and participated with them in the 1895 student boycott at the University of Toronto.

"tried to show that Greenwood was by nature an 'agitator' and to force admission from him that he had busied himself in a great railroad strike that had occurred in Chicago two years before – imputations which Greenwood emphatically denied."[24] Whether he denied that he had "busied himself" in some way in the Pullman strike or asserted that he had simply been in Chicago by coincidence is now unclear. There is evidence that he had earlier worked as a stevedore for several months in nearby Buffalo, then a bustling inland waterway port, to observe at first hand labour developments there.

Just two months before the Pullman strike, W.T. Stead, the British social activist who was the controversial publisher of the *Review of Reviews*, had returned to London following a tumultuous four-month visit to Chicago and its world's fair. During those four months in the spring of 1894, he had also briefly visited Toronto and Ottawa, staying at Rideau Hall with the avowed Liberal governor general, Lord Aberdeen, and his ambitious wife, Ishbel. In Toronto, Stead spoke at a public meeting chaired by the mayor and later gave an address at the university. At each, he advocated both temperance and Home Rule for Ireland, warmly acclaiming the 1892 election of Edward Blake, the former Liberal leader in Canada, as an Irish Nationalist member of Parliament at Westminster. (Blake nevertheless remained a transatlantic chancellor of the University of Toronto until 1900.) Greenwood, as president of the political science club, would have heard from Stead something of the volatile labour scene in Chicago.

Beyond an interest in the contentious field of labour relations – in which his fellow student, William Lyon Mackenzie King of Berlin, Ontario, would in time take a decided if more arm's-length interest – Greenwood's extracurricular activities at university included amateur theatricals, the student newspaper, and the debating society, where he frequently joined forces with Mackenzie King. Since their first months at the university, both young men had pursued their political and partisan collaborations and joined in organizing cricket matches. Each took pride in the roles of their ancestors in the Rebellion of 1837. In their fourth year, along with James Tucker, the editor of *The Varsity*, they would become known not only throughout the university but well beyond as a result of a major campus controversy in which all three became embroiled.

In the autumn of 1894, Greenwood helped organize a debate with students from McGill University on the abolition of the Senate, but much of his leisure time was taken up by his presidency of the political science club and the furore that arose around a professor of political economy at the university, James Mavor. Greenwood wrote to a fellow undergraduate that he was "more interested in the outcome of the Mavor muddle than in social events at the University. Should not he be kicked out? The only inspiration either you or I or anyone else ever got from his nibship was an inspiration to sleep. The more I think about that man's imbecility, the more indignant I feel, indignant to think of such a creature being the head of the largest and, in my humble opinion, the best course in the University. Prepare yourself for the fray that's bound to take place."[25]

Traditional courses in classics and theology were giving way to political science, sociology, and economics. Six years earlier, in 1888, the Ontario government, then closely associated with the university, had created a chair of political economy and constitutional history. The first incumbent, an Oxonian, departed for Harvard in 1892, and was succeeded by James Mavor of Glasgow, "a mercurial Scots adventurer who in the course of his life believed in many things and nothing long."[26] During a lengthy academic career, Mavor was at one time an advocate of socialism and at another an opponent, and as an advisor to the Liberal minister of the interior, Clifford Sifton, a promoter of Doukhobor immigration. King had written in his diary enthusiastically about Mavor, but he ignited latent unease among other students. His various shortcomings and prejudices added fuel to more complex student discontents arising from, *inter alia*, the uneven quality of several other professors, the parsimonious attitude of the government towards the provincially funded university, and the rivalry between the vice chancellor, William Mulock, and the president, James Loudon, who was backed generally by Chancellor Edward Blake.

In December 1894, shortly before Greenwood wrote his letter speculating on the "fray that's bound to take place," Mavor attempted, supposedly at the behest of the president and the board of governors, to exclude two labour speakers from a debate organized by the political science club, on the grounds that permission had not been first obtained. As president of the club, Greenwood, "a young man of spirit," is said to have "challenged Mavor, in the presence of the President of the University, to a bare-knuckle fight on a point of honour."[27] Mackenzie King, of a strict teetotal family – but certainly no pugilist – was another leading club member. Both he and Greenwood were also on the editorial board of *The Varsity*, which gave full wind to the accusations of interference in free speech by the stiff-necked president and the administration. The myriad allegations and counter-allegations and protests at the university were gleefully picked up by newspapers across the province.

In response to the university's veto of the two "dangerous" socialist speakers, Greenwood rented a hall off campus in February 1895 so that the club meetings could be held as scheduled. In the days following, a popular young lecturer in Latin was expelled for his public allegations of nepotism in academic appointments and curtailment of the freedom of *The Varsity* to print what it liked. A mass meeting of students then voted on a motion put by Mackenzie King – whose blood "fairly boiled" – seconded by Greenwood, who, according to newspaper accounts, was the outstanding speaker. The vote was unanimously in favour of immediately "abstaining" from all lectures (a move, some alleged, that was backed by Mulock in his continuing differences with Chancellor Blake and President Loudon). The subsequent strike, in which "Greenwood was unquestionably the leader," was successful to the degree that it effectively brought the university to a halt, with only a few students – among them another future prime minister, Arthur Meighen – not actively supporting the fortnight boycott.* In meetings with the president, a student negotiating committee of fourteen headed by Greenwood and King finally recommended to the students that they suspend their boycott pending the conclusion of negotiations. Influenced by Greenwood, they agreed.[28]

Responding to questions in the legislature, Premier Mowatt announced, ostensibly at the prompting of the university administration, the appointment of nothing less than a Royal Commission on Discipline in the University of Toronto, chaired by the chief justice of Manitoba, to investigate the root causes of the student unrest. The strike had become a matter of interest to, variously, the labour movement, the legal profession, academia, the legislature, and, more broadly still, the evolving civil society of Ontario. Pending the commission's report, Greenwood and King organized more meetings at Wardell (later Broadway) Hall on Spadina Avenue near College Street. After examining Greenwood,

---

* Robert Blackburn, in his introduction to a 1949 memorandum of H.H. Langton, registrar of the University of Toronto at the time of the student boycott fifty-four years before, cited several student witnesses who despised Mackenzie King for having moved the boycott resolution and then attended lectures himself. He did so, they said, at the behest of his father, who was then a member of the university senate (Langton, "Mackenzie King," 503).

Arthur Meighen, a year behind King and Greenwood, took no notable part in the boycott, but was a member of the debating society, arguing on one occasion that a republican form of government was superior to a monarchical (*Varsity*, 15 November 1893). Other contemporaries of Greenwood and King included Thomas White, minister of finance in Borden's government from 1911 to 1919, George Henry, premier of Ontario from 1930 to 1934, and Charles Cross, the first attorney general of Alberta from 1905 to 1910 and from 1912 to 1918 and a Liberal member of Parliament in 1925.

King, and other student leaders, the commission mildly cautioned the university's administration for its poor relations with the undergraduate body, but it confirmed the expulsion of *Varsity* editor James Tucker, whom King regarded "as the most brilliant man of our year." (A fund raised by undergraduates (although some believed, largely contributed to by Mulock), enabled Tucker to complete his degree at the then little-known but recently richly endowed Stanford University in California.) King recalled that "Greenwood and I did the talking," with the result that they were, in King's word, "blacklisted."[29] King, following graduation that same year, failed to receive his anticipated teaching fellowship at Toronto, his erstwhile mentor and now nemesis, Mavor, speaking against him. After some vacillation, he took himself off instead to the University of Chicago, vowing that "I will make Toronto University sorry for having refused me."[30]

Greenwood was given "private advice" that, considering the general hostility amidst the Ontario legal community and the Toronto establishment more generally to the student strike, his leading role in it had effectively closed the Ontario bar to him. "He had antagonized the academics who might otherwise have helped him and he had been branded as a socialist."[31] He was fully aware that members of the royal commission and some in the broader Toronto community – thanks partly to the extensive press coverage – regarded him, the great-grandson of a rebel of 1837, as a radical liberal or even a socialist. Rumours still circulated that he had been in Chicago at the time of the Pullman strike, alongside communists, anarchists, and other socialist riff-raff. And Mavor pursued him as much as he did Mackenzie King. All in all, it was a record that would make it difficult, if not impossible, for Greenwood to seek an early professional – especially legal – career in Ontario. Consequently, he "found it wise to make his career in Great Britain."[32]

British Beginnings, 1895–1906

Upon graduation from the University of Toronto and completion of his annual militia training in the summer of 1895, Greenwood, now twenty-five, made his second crossing to Britain. This time it was in that lowest but time-honoured role of the impecunious student, mucking out the livestock decks of a cattle boat as the wretched animals staggered to keep their footing. He arrived in Liverpool dirty and virtually penniless. From his visit with his father ten years before, he was aware that of his several Welsh relatives, the only one who might be able to help him, even marginally, was his aunt Adeliza. The story of his penury being a good foil to his eventual affluence, family lore has it that upon arriving in Liverpool with only five dollars, he went first to the Welsh border town of Knighton where aunt Adeliza, the wife of the town grocer, John Clee, gave him a little money.

Someone, perhaps another relative, also arranged for Greenwood to be a speaker at a Knighton public meeting. He shared the platform with three Liberal members of Parliament who had been re-elected two months before in a general election that had returned the Conservatives, led by Lord Salisbury, to power. The three opposition MPs, David Lloyd George and his two Liberal colleagues, were in Knighton under the aegis of Cymru Fydd, the Welsh nationalist federation. Among its aims were support for Welsh culture, disestablishment of the Church of Wales, and a greater measure of local self-government. It was on this occasion that Greenwood first met Lloyd George, seven years his senior, the member for Caernarvon Boroughs. Lloyd George was then at the height of his promotion of Welsh nationalism embodied in a federation of the British Isles, or "Home Rule All

Round," Ireland included.* Part of the rally was conducted in Welsh, which Greenwood did not have, but his speech in English about "Canadian Home Rule" attracted attention from Liberal worthies. As he later recalled, he was for the next decade "actively engaged on Liberal platforms throughout the Kingdom. Took part in all bye-elections [*sic*] and spoke for very large number of Liberal candidates and Members."[1]

To cross the Atlantic to Britain was for Greenwood and many other young Canadians not so much a question of leaving Canada as simply going to another part of the British world. The immediate challenge was finding a reliable source of income. Over the following eleven years before he was finally admitted to the bar, Greenwood had to resort to a variety of ways of earning money. He arrived in London with the ambition of becoming an actor. Before he left Canada, his former classmate, the journalist Hector Charlesworth, had introduced him to another alumnus, the actor Franklin McLeay, then playing in Toronto as a member of a touring English company. Six years older than Greenwood, McLeay, after graduating from the University of Toronto, had embarked for Britain to begin a highly successful, if brief, theatrical career with Wilson Barrett, the impresario to whom he in turn undertook to introduce Greenwood. "McLeay was interested in Greenwood because of his good looks, charm of manner, and natural eloquence … Greenwood conceived of the idea of emulating McLeay and going on the stage."† However, arriving in London, Greenwood "discovered that the theatrical outlook for a young man without means or experience was not so rosy as fancy had depicted."[2]

Greenwood was more successful as a public speaker. He built upon his temperance advocacy in Canada to draw more attention to the ravages that alcohol was wreaking in Britain, especially on labourers and other low-paid workers and their hapless families. "Temperance" had become something of a catch-all phrase, loosely embracing both those who advocated total prohibition and those who limited themselves to urging

---

* John Redmond and other Irish Nationalist MPs regarded with suspicion the idea of Home Rule All Round then being urged, *inter alia*, by the Liberal turncoat Joseph Chamberlain, by his own choice the secretary of state for the colonies in Salisbury's government. The Irish Nationalists saw themselves as being asked to forego early Home Rule for Ireland until other regions of the United Kingdom "had made up their minds to pull the present Constitution absolutely to bits."

† Franklin McLeay died in 1900 at age thirty-six while playing in London with the company of Sir Herbert Beerbohm Tree.

tighter enforcement of licensing regulations.* Whatever their precise formulations, all temperance champions added weight to the mounting demands for legislation to ban or severely limit the sale of liquor.

In Canada, a temperance act of sorts had been adopted by the Canadian Parliament ten years after Confederation, but it had failed to meet the demands of its more militant promoters. The government of Sir John A. Macdonald had remained unsympathetic to their appeals, but by the time that Greenwood had become a temperance activist, Ottawa could no longer ignore the growing clamour. Delegates to the 1895 Liberal convention (the first of its kind) as well as Liberal candidates in the 1896 election were bombarded with petitions, letters, pledge cards, and resolutions adopted by mass meetings, all intended to elicit from the Liberal Party – and especially from such prohibitionist stalwarts as Sir George Foster and Newton Rowell – a commitment to act promptly if a Liberal government were elected. In March 1895, four months before Greenwood embarked for Britain, a royal commission had recommended in six volumes that Parliament delay no longer in enacting total prohibition. But when Wilfrid Laurier came to office as Canada's first French-speaking prime minister in 1896, he quietly ignored the commission's recommendations, deftly sidestepping temperance with all its church overtones. The concurrent and more threatening Manitoba school question offered him political challenge enough. Later, in 1899, Laurier, again as quietly as possible, set aside the results of a national plebiscite – itself something of a stalling tactic – that had reflected support for prohibition in most of Canada except in Quebec, on the grounds that the plebiscite vote was too small to be considered decisive.

* The temperance movement, already active in Britain and the United States, became a significant political and social force in Canada from the middle of the nineteenth century through the First World War. (There was, more or less, prohibition in Canada from 1915 to 1919.) In partisan terms in both Canada and Britain, the movement was regarded as having a distinct Liberal (or eventually Labour) and certainly a non-conformist hue, the Conservatives and by extension the established church being seen as under the influence of distillers and brewers. Drawing upon a number of temperance organizations, the Dominion Alliance, formed in 1876, mirrored and collaborated with the United Kingdom Alliance. The two sister alliances shared their experience of direct political action in attempting to persuade hesitant or sceptical local or national governments of the necessity of total prohibition or, at the least, of "local option" in the terms of licences for the sale of alcohol. In 1893 additional impetus came from the United States in the form of the Women's Christian Temperance Union, which also had the unexpected result of opening a way for women into politics.

By then, Greenwood had sailed for Britain, taking with him an intimate knowledge of the methods, rhetoric, and vocabulary of temperance advocacy. Further, the temperance Dominion Alliance had introduced him as a seasoned campaigner to the United Kingdom Alliance, with the result that he was soon offered payment for his lectures, thanks to the early support of two leading British advocates, Sir Wilfrid Lawson, MP, and Thomas Whittaker. Whittaker was to die within four years of Greenwood's arrival, but not before he had helped Sir Wilfrid Lawson launch the young Canadian on his career as a popular temperance speaker. Born in poverty, Whittaker knew personally the violence, mayhem, and deprivation that alcoholism could spawn. A Yorkshire man long active in Liberal politics and newspapers in northern England, he addressed to alcoholics a consistent message of hope, confidence, and self-reliance. He achieved his temperance fame from the bottom up; by contrast, Lawson's was from the top down. Lawson's secure place in the hierarchy of English society and politics made him an influential mentor for Greenwood. He was known nationally as an amiable and mildly eccentric land and mine owner in the north of England who, like his father before him, was a radical Liberal MP, widely admired for his unending concern for the poor. From his first election in 1859, he had become a devoted follower of Gladstone, persistent in urging reform and opposing coercion in troubled Ireland, policies intended to assist Gladstone to achieve his great goal of Home Rule for John Bull's other island or even – as Joseph Chamberlain was advocating – "Home Rule All Round." The four parts of the United Kingdom as well as the Dominions would have greater autonomy and responsibility in local matters, thereby conferring on Ireland Home Rule by the back door. If applied to the Empire as a whole, Home Rule All Round was also seen by some in Britain, Canada, and elsewhere in the Empire as a more certain way of fostering voluntary mutual assistance in a commonwealth, an appealing policy to imperial enthusiasts like Greenwood.

In parallel with their advocacy of self-government for Ireland, Lawson and other like-minded members of Parliament continued to urge temperance, bringing forward annually private members bills at Westminster to promote moderation in the consumption of alcohol, including measures intended to curtail the freewheeling Conservative support of distillers and publicans. Wilfrid Lawson was always on the watch for promising young men of Liberal leanings to speak at temperance meetings across Britain, offering one pound plus expenses for each lecture. Eager to earn any honorarium, Greenwood was soon making as many as three speeches a week, as well as becoming acquainted through Lawson with various other Liberal members of Parliament. Decades later, a privately published history of the Greenwoods described how the "Contemporary newspapers spoke well of him ... he was in big demand. He developed a temperance style of his own and his most successful lecture, given many times, bore the title of 'The Manliness of Teetotalism'. This was a new approach. Hitherto beer swilling had been associated with manly pursuits. Tom [i.e., Hamar] turned the tables and argued that a man without alcohol was twice the man he would have been with it."[3]

Lawson and Whittaker had good reason to be pleased with their new acolyte. At the imposing Free Trade Hall in Manchester, Greenwood, following speeches by two bishops, urged the Sunday closing of pubs as a step towards the suppression of the liquor trade altogether.[4] A correspondent of the *Spectator* hailed his presence on the platform: his "fine figure, gay manners, witty speech with its transatlantic tang ... won over many audiences."[5] In East Anglia, the *Ipswich Journal* of 3 February 1900 reported that "in conjunction with the Suffolk Temperance Council, a lecture and a recital was given ... by the popular Canadian advocate and reciter, Mr. Hamar Greenwood, B.A., of Toronto, Canada." Supported by clergymen from the local Anglican, Presbyterian, and Wesleyan churches, Greenwood, in a lecture entitled "Stumbling Blocks," praised the Sunday closing acts in Wales, Scotland, and Ireland and called for similar limitations in England. So impressed were Liberals – at least, temperance Liberals – with his oratorical and advocacy talents that he was introduced to the National Liberal Club in London.

More significantly, only eighteen months after his arrival in England, although still near penniless and living largely by his wits, Greenwood, at age twenty-seven, had also been admitted to Gray's Inn on 20 January 1897, supported by the required references from two barristers of the Inn. The study of law was then more informal than it later became. He was required to keep a minimum of twelve terms and pass both oral and written examinations in Roman and English law. Once admitted to the Inn, however, candidates studied independently, setting their own pace. They sat examinations only when they felt themselves ready. Many were delayed by other commitments or simply by a lack of funds. In Greenwood's case, nine and a half years separated his admission on 20 January 1897 from his call to the bar on 27 June 1906, a period that embraced the death of Queen Victoria, the accession of King Edward VII, the South African War, and the Conservative governments of Lord

Salisbury and of his nephew Arthur Balfour and the Liberal government of Henry Campbell-Bannerman – and in Canada two terms of
Liberal Prime Minister Wilfrid Laurier.

How exactly Greenwood sustained himself over almost a decade
remains partly a matter for speculation. Occasionally he contributed to
British and Canadian newspapers and periodicals, notably *Saturday
Night* where James Tucker, home with a degree from Stanford University,
was now employed as assistant editor. In July 1897, for example, *Saturday
Night* published Greenwood's description of Queen Victoria's grand
Diamond Jubilee procession a month before. In what David Cannadine
has called "an uncharacteristic fit of imperial presence of mind," the
Jubilee reflected the fact that Britain was the world's banker and inves-
tor. With *Saturday Night's* audience in mind, Greenwood reported enthusiastically that "Everywhere there were cheers for Sir Wilfrid Laurier ...
head and shoulders above all other Colonial Prime Ministers ... What
an Empire is ours! ... It was a great day for our country, and if our statesmen are wide awake and take the tide of British sentiment at the full,
the Dominion ought to reap some material benefit from the splendid
showing made by her sons."[6]

The money Greenwood earned by such occasional articles was limited, but the once would-be actor did receive an incidental if minor
additional benefit by being designated by Tucker as *Saturday Night's*
London theatre critic (free tickets were provided by theatres to accred-
ited critics). *Saturday Night* described Greenwood as having done "considerable journalistic work ... He has covered important assignments
for the *Daily Mail*."[7] More income came from his role of "advertising
manager" for Stead's popular *Review of Reviews*. Stead, having been the
radical liberal imperialist editor of the controversial and influential *Pall
Mall Gazette,* had launched the *Review of Reviews* in 1890, subsidized in
part by that ardent but very different advocate of imperial unity, Cecil
Rhodes. American and Australian editions of the *Review of Reviews* were
soon added, all three consistently calling for the union of English-
speaking peoples (i.e., the United States and a federation of the British
Empire, with Home Rule All Round), the peaceful progress of the world
depending upon the progress of a transcendental British Empire.

By 1896, when Greenwood joined it part time, the *Review of Reviews*
was notably successful. In such circumstances, he as "advertising manager" (or more simply an advertising agent) cannot have found his new
appointment demanding. His remuneration would have turned largely
upon commissions for space sold. He became something of a protégé of

Stead,* contributing anonymously to his periodicals and participating in his domestic entertainments in Wimbledon (for example, at a garden party on 4 July 1896 to mark the independence of the United States, Greenwood entertained the other guests with dramatic recitations).[8]

Other regular and more substantial income eventually came to Greenwood in the form of part-time employment as a promoter of emigration to Canada. Lord Strathcona, the octogenarian high commissioner whom both Laurier and Borden retained in office, was ostensibly non-partisan, but he was widely regarded as an unreconstructed imperialist, an unacknowledged Conservative, and a major financial supporter of Joseph Chamberlain. Although he held onto office until his death in 1914 at the age of ninety-four, the universe did not unfold quite as Strathcona had hoped. Laurier gave Clifford Sifton, his young and dynamic minister of the interior, the task of peopling the great lone lands of the Northwest. If promotion of immigration from the British Isles failed, Sifton would then do the unthinkable and seek immigrants from central and eastern Europe. To open those gates, one of Sifton's priorities was to remove from Strathcona the supervision of Canadian immigration agents across Europe. The aging high commissioner, always sensitive about his prerogatives, protested both to Sifton and to Laurier, but in the end he was told bluntly by the minister that it would be "quite impossible to make any fixed rule which would preclude me from having direct communication with an Agent when I consider it advisable."[9] Compounding Strathcona's continuing unease, Sifton appointed in January 1899 W.T.R. Preston, the former general secretary of the Ontario Liberal Association, to be the first Canadian commissioner for emigration for Europe, based in London. Preston's assignment included the introduction of some unwonted dynamism into emigration promotion in the United Kingdom. He soon opened an office on Charing Cross Road, separate from the dingy, crowded high commission chancery on Victoria Street. He invited to Canada promising MPs – in the event, most seemed to be Liberal, such as Lloyd George – to see for themselves something of what Canada offered the immigrant. Travelling across Europe, Preston recruited more local agents to help bypass local emigration embargoes.

---

* Later Stead joined Leader of the Opposition (and future Prime Minister) Sir Henry Campbell-Bannerman, Lloyd George, and other Liberals as an outspoken opponent of the war in South Africa. Stead passed suddenly out of Greenwood's life when he drowned in the sinking of the *Titanic* in 1912.

From his first days as minister, Sifton introduced aggressive advertising, offering "free farms of 160 acres" amidst a land of plenty (*not* a land of ice and snow). Preston spent money enthusiastically. His annual advertising budget in 1904 reached a staggering $4 million, all of it intended to attract farmers – city folk need not apply – to western Canada. Exhibition wagons distributed free promotional atlases and other publications, and lecturers in market towns extolled the virgin lands awaiting homesteaders. One such recruit to Preston's list of promotional speakers was Hamar Greenwood. According to Preston's recollection many years later, he received in October or November 1899 an unexpected visit from "a young Canadian who wished to see me as soon as possible":

> I saw a tall, well-dressed figure, frock coat, top hat, a clean-shaven, manly and friendly face, frank and attractive eyes, and a voice said: "You're Mr. Preston. I'm Greenwood of Whitby. Often heard you speak and I'm introducing myself because I'm in trouble." After my comment that his general demeanour rather belied the suggestion that the trouble could be serious, I swung my chair around to listen. At my invitation he sat down and said: "Well, I flipped a penny at your door to help me decide whether I'd borrow some money from you or go on down the street and enlist for the South African War. Heads it was, and here I am." Of course, one had to laugh at the frankness and candour that was so evident. This broke the ice or reserve on either side. The inquiry was natural: "How came you here and when? What are you doing? When are you going home?" The story Greenwood told will never be forgotten and he has no need to be ashamed of it even now. It was a tale of earnestly expended energy, of an ambition that was boundless, to succeed if he could get half a chance. But at the moment there was nothing in sight but the midnight darkness of disappointment and despair.[10]

Basically, Greenwood had found that "it was impossible to make ends meet, although at that time one could live in London probably cheaper than anywhere else." Over luncheon, Preston was so impressed by his articulate and imposing young visitor – whose father he had long known in Whitby as an enthusiastic Liberal – that he promptly added him to his roster of speakers, given his "active connection with the public press." Thereafter, "we were very intimate and I found his judgment useful in all the problems which arose in connection with the emigration propaganda. We lunched together every day."[11] Preston also introduced his protégé to the Canada Club, the oldest dining club in London, which in time Greenwood was to value as a platform for furthering both his political and commercial ambitions.

Preston's recollection was that Greenwood had first called upon him "shortly after Paul Krüger issued that historic ultimatum which made war inevitable between Great Britain and the Transvaal." Krüger's ultimatum was made on 9 October 1899, seven months after Preston's arrival in London. Accordingly, Preston was placing his initial meeting with Greenwood in late October or early November 1899. However, records of the Department of the Interior indicate that Preston did not put Greenwood on its payroll until May 1903, four years later.* Why did Preston err by four years? Possibly because if he had recalled accurately the date of May 1903, rather than the fanciful one of October 1899, his anecdote about how he had saved the despairing Greenwood from volunteering for the war in South Africa would have been seen as the nonsense that it was. When Greenwood began to receive his regular monthly payment of £10 from Preston, the South African War had in fact been over for a year. Further, by 1903, at the age of thirty-three, he had already sustained himself for seven years in Britain and had been a student at Gray's Inn for six. That Preston's memory was so faulty may have arisen from a desire to claim the credit for providing crucial support to a fellow Canadian – and a Liberal – who by 1920 (the year of Preston's newspaper article) had risen to be a member of the British cabinet.

From 1903, Greenwood's annual emigration promotion stipend of £120 – plus free lunches – was substantial for part-time work, when craftsmen received as little as £100 annually for their full-time work. In any event, Preston was well satisfied with his indigent protégé. Greenwood remained on his speakers' roster even after the wrathful Strathcona had in mid-1906 finally succeeded, through his repeated protests to Laurier, in forcing the departure of the ever-pugnacious Preston from Britain. Preston was first assigned temporarily to Cape Town (where he began a vitriolic biography of Strathcona) to determine how Canada's voluntary participation in the South African War could be exploited to win it lucrative reconstruction contracts. From

---

* "Acting under the instruction of the Minister of the Interior [Sifton, who had visited London that spring] I put T. Hamar Greenwood on the staff of this office at £10 per month" (Preston to Chief of Immigration Service, Ottawa, 20 May 1903, LAC, RG76, vol. 288, file 259109).

there he was posted as trade commissioner to Japan (where amidst end-less conflict with English commercial agents and the British minister, he completed his biography of Strathcona).

In January 1906, six months before Preston's departure for South Africa and Asia, Greenwood, as will be seen, was elected to the British House of Commons. Not surprisingly, upon Preston's embarkation for Cape Town, immigration officials in London promptly recommended the termination of Greenwood's part-time employment: "His increased responsibilities and duties [in the House of Commons] ... have evi-dently rendered it difficult if not impossible for him to give us the value formerly received."[12] His four-year association with emigration promo-tion was duly terminated in February 1907, more than a year after he had been elected an MP. (In other words, for one year he was on the payroll of the Canadian government while at the same time a member of the British Parliament.)

However irregular Greenwood's employment, Preston certainly got his money's worth, as had Lawson in the case of temperance lectures. His voice more than filled the halls in which he spoke, and his notable oratorical and acting skills were equally well employed. To take but one example: six months after Greenwood had joined Preston's speakers' roster, the *Southport Visiter* (*sic*) reported that he had given a lecture sponsored by the YMCA in the Chapel Street Congregational School-room in Southport. "Applause was enthusiastic" when Greenwood, fol-lowing a brief if idiosyncratic history of Canada, including a nod toward his mother's United Empire Loyalist ancestry, praised it as the preferred destination of emigrants since "the loyalty of Canadians [was] absolutely undoubted and absolutely true." He so tailored his lecture to the local audience that it took him for a fellow non-conformist, he having assured them that the English-speaking provinces of Canada provided free, non-denominational schools. They did not waste public funds on building cathedrals. In a wide digression amidst his enthusiastic advocacy of Canada as the glorious destination of all right-thinking emigrants, he decried *en passant* the continuing British embargo on the import of Canadian cattle, a persistent irritant in Anglo-Canadian relations.[13] He was not alone in his impatience: Lloyd George and other Liberal MPs, upon their return from their expense-paid visit to Canada arranged by Preston, had also condemned the unjustified cattle embargo. But Greenwood's attack no doubt carried greater immediacy from his per-sonal knowledge gained from mucking out the cattle decks on his trans-atlantic crossing eight years before.

The end of Greenwood's financial difficulties – if such there had continued to be – came unexpectedly but certainly not agreeably. London newspaper accounts of an accident that ensured his later solvency differ in detail, but all at least agree that one day he was riding on the open upper deck of a horse-drawn omnibus when it suddenly overturned, pitching him into the street. He was so severely concussed that he remained in a coma for some time. When eventually he recovered, he won a substantial settlement from the London Omnibus Company (according to one account, as much as £1,000). Some details are more or less common to later newspaper accounts of the accident, but they differ greatly as to when it happened. For example, the *Toronto Telegram* of 8 April 1920, twenty years after the accident, places it "one day in 1899." The *Toronto Globe* of the same day has the accident occurring six years later, shortly before the 1906 election. The *Globe*'s story was by the ubiquitous Preston, who seemed to have difficulty with dates. At least he could be counted upon to provide a lively if imaginative account of how he himself had played a central role in the rescue of his fellow Canadian:

On my way to the office one morning I read with dismay in the paper that a Canadian named Greenwood had been carried to King's College Hospital in an unconscious condition the previous night as the result of an omnibus overturning near Charing Cross. I hurried to the hospital only to find an unconscious figure stretched out on his cot. The medical attendant told me that he had been in that condition for nearly twelve hours, and that he feared concussion of the brain. While we were sitting beside his bed there came a sudden gleam of intelligence in his eyes, and looking around, he said: "What's the meaning of this?" Following a quiet suggestion not to be uneasy, I found his mind was a blank from the hour that he had lunched with me the previous day. He remembered nothing from that time. His progress at the hospital was not encouraging. One of the doctors, who took a warm interest in him, removed him to his clinic on Harley Street. But notwithstanding the most attentive care for several weeks the outlook was far from bright. Having to leave for Canada on important official business I went up to bid him good-bye. The doctor … said that he had been hopeful that Greenwood's magnificent constitution would pull him through, but he was disappointed in the improvement not being more speedy. I asked him why should he not be sent to some quiet place in the mountains where he would see no one except the friend who might accompany him and eat and sleep giving nature full scope. His reply was: "That's his only chance." When I went in to Greenwood, he inquired, "What's the verdict?" I told him. Taking a coin out of his pocket, he said: "Will you tell me how I can do that with only this?" I hurried off to the bank where I kept my small account and told the manager I wanted a stated sum of money, and also gave him the reason why. He hesitated and then initialled my cheque. We packed Greenwood off to the hills and when I saw him three months later it was the old Greenwood back again. His temperate habits, clean life and good constitution had pulled him through.[14]

With Preston's support and the financial settlement by the London Omnibus Company, Greenwood recovered completely. He also became sufficiently solvent to pursue, among other things, his long-standing militia commitment. On 18 February 1902, he became a lieutenant in the 4th County of London Imperial Yeomanry (King's Colonials), a cavalry regiment of the reserve, called into being the year before. It was composed of four squadrons of colonial volunteers resident in London: "British Asians" (Englishmen from the Indian Empire), Canadians, Australasians, and South Africans. The creation of such a territorial regiment reflected one of the many hard lessons that the War Office had learned in the recently concluded South African War: the Dominions and India should henceforth be invited to join in any conflict in which the Mother Country was seriously threatened. To that end, a postwar royal commission, chaired by the Montreal-born Lord Elgin, the former viceroy of India, had been assigned the challenge of identifying the shortcomings of "Military Preparations and other matters concerned with the War in South Africa." Among the members were both the Australian and the Canadian high commissioners (Strathcona had raised a cavalry regiment at his own expense as a personal gesture of imperial solidarity). In the aftermath of the war, a new cavalry regiment incorporating volunteers from across the Empire would not only reflect the findings of the royal commission but more broadly might provide impetus to thinking in Britain and Canada about expanded military collaboration. For Greenwood, service with a cavalry regiment entailed not only that: it also meant considerable personal expense. Neither Gray's Inn nor his territorial army activities brought income – they were, in fact, both continuing expenses – but together they helped in his efforts to penetrate the upper reaches, or at first the middle reaches, of Edwardian society.

In 1904, having completed training at the cavalry school at Aldershot, Greenwood was confirmed in his transition from an infantry to a cavalry officer. The following year, he did required training in musketry, including the Maxim machine gun, and shortly thereafter, at the age of thirty-five, was promoted to captain and commander of the Canadian squadron of his regiment, which had in the meantime been retitled the King's Colonials Imperial Yeomanry. He continued to be associated with the regiment even when he became a British member of Parliament, leaving only on 28 March 1913 when he was appointed a captain in the General (Regular) Reserve of Officers, seventeen months before the beginning of the First World War. By then the regiment had taken yet another name under which it was to serve – without Greenwood – throughout the war: King Edward's Horse (the King's Overseas Dominions Regiment). With dominion usage gradually replacing colonial, the new name of the regiment reflected the evolving status of the self-governing members of the Empire.

Greenwood's route to the House of Commons at Westminster was convoluted. His dynamic temperance and emigration advocacy had brought him into contact with Liberals everywhere across Britain. Concurrently he exploited his long-standing family commitment to the Liberal Party of Canada. In 1905, for example, at the same time that with the assistance of Preston he had begun to solicit work from Laurier's government, he covered his bets by "showing every attention" to the visiting Sam Hughes, the thrice-dipped Conservative and Orange member of Parliament for the Ontario constituency of Victoria-Haliburton (a few score kilometres north of Whitby). Hughes, a schoolteacher and ardent militia officer, claimed that during a visit to London in 1905 he was offered by the Conservative Central Office "an absolutely safe seat" (as Preston had earlier claimed that Liberal Prime Minister Campbell-Bannerman had offered him). Having first met Greenwood during annual militia training at Niagara-on-the-Lake, Hughes was enthusiastic about him, despite his Liberal allegiance. He described to Robert Borden a small dinner party in his honour that Greenwood had given in London. At the dinner, speaking highly of Laurier, Greenwood had also praised the leaders of the Conservative Party – of whom Sam Hughes considered himself as one of the more eminent. Greenwood defined Borden, leader of the Opposition from 1901, "as a young, untried man, and thus far he stood before the people absolutely clean, absolutely capable." In a way of recommending Greenwood to Borden over Donald Macmaster, also a Canadian, a barrister and the Conservative member for Chertsey, Hughes added enthusiastically, "I owe nothing to Hamer [*sic*] Greenwood except that I have always found him in Canada and in Britain a most courteous, capable gentleman and lawyer, willing to oblige a friend and always treating his opponents with courtesy."[15] Greenwood's life-long commitment to Home Rule for Ireland appears to have been overlooked by the doughty Orangeman.

Greenwood had been so successful as an orator at by-elections and as the author of speeches for Liberal candidates that as early as 1900 he had been sounded about letting his name go forward as a prospective Liberal candidate in Grimsby in Lincolnshire for the "khaki election" of that year (the same election in which Preston claimed that he had himself rejected a Liberal nomination). Still without steady income and almost six years from his call to the bar, Greenwood had declined the offer, but he did continue in his advocacy of temperance, Home Rule for Ireland, and other Liberal causes in his orations across Britain. *Saturday Night* later described him as "blessed with supreme confidence in himself; at ease in any circumstances in which he was placed; never at a loss for the right word or the correct action."[16]

During 1904, the Liberals, led by Campbell-Bannerman, attacked vigorously a watered-down Conservative public house licensing bill on the grounds that it did little or nothing to advance the temperance cause. Lawson, Greenwood, and other activists joined Lloyd George in again urging a local veto on the sale of liquor, with no compensation for publicans whose annual license had not been renewed. Their efforts failed to persuade the Conservatives to strengthen their flaccid temperance bill, but their advocacy across the British Isles contributed to Liberal Party unity, still strained by differences over the South African War and Home Rule for Ireland. And it brought Greenwood even more to the notice of the party, both as a popular and effective speaker and as an undoubted Liberal partisan. While he intermittently pursued his legal studies at Gray's Inn, his partisan advocacy in Wales in 1903 and 1904, especially "stumping in the Liberal interest in Radnorshire," had been particularly noted by Lloyd George. Although not yet called to the bar, Greenwood had become a leading prospective candidate in the general election foreseen for early 1906. Grimsby being no longer on offer, he was sounded on the unpromising constituency of York, even though there was already a prospective Liberal candidate in the offing. The constituency was, however, not altogether hopeless. Although Lawson had died in 1906, the local support of the Earl of Durham (grandson of "Radical Jack") and that of Joseph Rowntree, the Quaker temperance activist and flourishing chocolate manufacturer, would be decisive. Rowntree had long been an associate of Lawson and, like all Quakers, was a teetotaller. It is entirely likely that it was Lawson who had, before his death, recommended to the Rowntrees the merits of Greenwood as a strong Liberal and temperance candidate.* Writing sixteen years later, the always imaginative Preston has Greenwood despatched to York as early as 1904 by the Liberal Central Office to address a meeting called "to confirm the nomination of a distinguished Knight [Sir Henry Cotton, a retired Indian civil servant whose family had served with distinction in India for more than 150 years] who had been selected by the Central Office in London as the Liberal candidate ... Greenwood's speech on behalf of the candidate took the meeting by storm, but not in the way it was officially intended. Mr. Rowntree, the great Quaker chocolate manufacturer, and the most prominent Liberal, proposed that the young man ... should be the candidate, instead of the gentleman who had been decided upon by the heads of the Party in London."[17] The meeting enthusiastically agreed.

Preston's lively account of the nomination in York is, unfortunately, as flawed as are his other accounts of his collaboration with Greenwood. Following the York meeting, he says, a local delegation went to the Liberal Central Office in London in 1904 (in fact it was in 1903) to inform Gladstone that they would have Greenwood or no one as their candidate. (Presumably Preston had in mind Herbert Gladstone, since his father, the prime minister, had been dead for six years.) Such ambiguity leaves one again wary of Preston's memory, but he did record with greater plausibility that Rowntree undertook to meet Greenwood's election expenses and that "it was not until about two years had elapsed [before the election] that the Central Association accepted the situation. This controversy between the Liberals of York and the party whip

---

* Preston says that this was in 1904, but Greenwood, in a sort of curriculum vitae of 1917, states that it was in 1903 that "he accepted the nomination to stand for York." In winning the nomination, he also had the commitment of Joseph Rowntree's son, Seebohm, his near contemporary. Seebohm Rowntree's hero remained Lloyd George throughout his long life, which was in good part devoted to the eradication of poverty as well as to enlightened commercial management. (He was, for example, a close collaborator of Lloyd George in his "land campaign" of 1913–14). His book, *Poverty, A Study of Town Life*, was soon recognized as a major text in the emerging discipline of sociology. Winston Churchill, then under-secretary for the colonies, wrote a favourable seven-page review in which, *inter alia*, he deplored the effects of poverty on the physical fitness of recruits for the British army.

gave Greenwood considerable publicity, and also enhanced his popularity as a public speaker."[18]

A more accurate account is by Hector Charlesworth, a classmate of both Greenwood and Mackenzie King, in his *More Candid Chronicles* of two decades later. Charlesworth portrays Preston as drawing upon his extensive campaign experience in Ontario to help Greenwood to victory in York in January 1906. Greenwood "was put up as a 'forlorn hope' in order that the seat should not go to the [Conservative-] Unionists by default ... and he proceeded to give [York] something it had never known before, a campaign organized on lines similar to those long familiar to electors in his native Canada. Mr. W.T.R. Preston, formerly organizer for the Liberal Party in this country, and a well-qualified expert in methods of 'bringing out the vote', willingly lent his assistance, and after the polling the returns from York amazed the executives of both the Liberal and Conservative Parties."[19]

Of additional help to Greenwood was his endorsement by the chancellor of the exchequer. To a meeting in York of an estimated eight thousand, Lloyd George, in castigating Joseph Chamberlain's scheme for an imperial tariff preference on the familiar grounds that it would increase the cost of food, praised Greenwood as "coming from the colonies and representing the right kind of colonial preference. Mr. Greenwood has a sense of humour and nothing is more useful than that for piercing sham." The *Toronto Daily Star* reported that when Greenwood "went up against the stronghold of Toryism in York it seemed the foolhardy performance of an inexperienced youth." (In fact he was thirty-five.) "But he fought bravely and won. To win in York for a Liberal, a Nonconformist" (in fact he was an Anglican) "and a Canadian was itself to get into the political limelight."[20]

Greenwood was one of four candidates in the two-seat constituency of York. In the Liberal landslide, one of the largest in British history, he headed the poll, followed by one of the two Conservative-Unionist candidates. From Ottawa, Mackenzie King was prompt in his telegraphic felicitations, but in his diary he was more nuanced. After rejoicing that John Burns, the radical MP, would be in the new Liberal cabinet, he added, "It is hard to regard Greenwood as other than a self-advertiser. This may be unfair. It reveals too what unlimited nerve will do."[21] Certainly King saw himself as having nervous problems. Throughout his long political career he was seized before making a speech with what he called "the terror complex," whereas rather enviously he saw Greenwood as fearing "neither God nor man when speaking."[22]

3

House of Commons, 1906–1910

The 1906 election in Britain resulted in 401 Liberal, 157 Conservative, 83 Irish Nationalist, and 29 Labour members. The new prime minister was Sir Henry Campbell-Bannerman, a minister in Gladstone's previous two governments, and already a sick man. Campbell-Bannerman set his new government on a decidedly liberal track, appointing Asquith chancellor of the exchequer and Lloyd George president of the Board of Trade. But he gave little priority to Home Rule for Ireland, partly by inclination and partly as a result of his preoccupation with restoring party unity following his and Lloyd George's controversial opposition to the South African War. Further, his majority was so large that he was not dependent on the Irish Nationalists MPs for the survival of his government. And by setting aside Home Rule, he avoided a major clash with Conservative-Unionists over an issue he did not consider of paramount current importance.[*]

With Greenwood now embarked on his parliamentary career and with Campbell-Bannerman as his leader, here is a place to summarize how Greenwood got where he did by 1906. In an Empire of equal parts, a liberal, collaborative Empire, he could, if he played his Canadian cards effectively, hope to win a leading place as readily as a candidate born in the United Kingdom. And Greenwood did play his limited hand well. As we have seen, before his departure from Canada he had arranged for the temperance Dominion Alliance to recommend him to the Liberal-associated United Kingdom Alliance and, in time, to the

[*] Greenwood, an admirer of Campbell-Bannerman, was eager to associate himself with him whenever possible, For example, in December 1907 he invited the prime minister to join Balfour as a patron of the annual Scottish concert in York (Greenwood to Campbell-Bannerman, 20 December 1907, British Library, Ms. 41240, f 175).

Quakers influential in York. Perhaps at his prompting, relatives in Wales had arranged for him to be included on the Liberal platform at Knighton with Lloyd George. The former Liberal Party organizer in Ontario, W.T.R. Preston, when resident in London as the enthusiastic promoter of emigration to Canada, had responded to Greenwood's plea for financial and (later) campaign support. In London Greenwood sought additional financial help from the radical W.T. Stead of the *Review of Reviews*. None of this progress and support was fortuitous – except the near-fatal omnibus accident. Greenwood obviously exploited every opportunity that came his way.

Greenwood arrived at Westminster a radical, a Wilfrid Lawson, Lloyd George, John Burns radical, but not a socialist. A temperance advocate on the left side of the Liberal Party, he was a critic of the stultifying effects of the English class system, including the gross inadequacies of education for the poor. In time he would contend for the "democratisation" of Parliament and the army as well as the education system. An outspoken advocate of Lloyd George's radical budget and social program of 1909–10, "he was kept busy by the Whips, speaking in the country in support of Government policy and bills, especially the budget of 1910." During the First World War he was to call repeatedly for improved pensions for war widows, orphans, and the wounded. A staunch supporter of Home Rule for Ireland – and later for India – it was only with the strange death of the Liberal Party, following the fatal wartime divisions between Asquith and Lloyd George, that he was eventually forced in his political progress to make a choice between the socialist Labour Party and the capitalist Conservative.

Summarizing thus Greenwood's political evolution might raise the objection that to do so at the outset of his many years in both houses of Parliament allows for no development in his later political thinking, but in his case there was in fact no major change. During the four decades that he was in one house of Parliament or the other, he remained a constructive imperialist. To be sure, events later changed the circumstances of his parliamentary career. Eventually with his political ambitions modified by electoral circumstances, he moved from his long membership in a hopelessly divided Liberal Party to the Conservative, but his basic commitment to a liberal British Empire never faltered. In a sense, he saw himself not as the member for York – or later for Sunderland or East Walthamstow – nor even as one of the dozen or more "Canadian MPs" customarily at Westminster. He saw himself more as a "Member for the Empire."

Greenwood esteemed the Empire – at least as he, a Liberal, conceived and described it. For him it provided the essential framework for the benign if not beneficial evolution of societies across the globe. And those societies were not only in the settlement colonies. Never in his days as chief secretary for Ireland or during his later days on Indian constitutional reform did he betray any belief in the racial superiority of the Anglo-Saxon. Not for him was the Conservative leader Bonar Law's dismissive definition of the Irish as "an inferior race" or Winston Churchill's condemnation of Indians as being incapable of governing themselves. The rule of law was in itself a basic imperial legacy; it also provided the sure foundation for economic enhancement. For Greenwood the Empire was not only a political incubator: it was also an economic self-help club of like-minded members.

Greenwood's childhood in Ontario was spent amongst what were later to be described as constructive imperialists, including descendants of United Empire Loyalists and the rebels of 1837 and advocates of Home Rule for Ireland. For him, the pageantry of Victoria's Diamond Jubilee and the coronation of Edward VII were not jingoist celebrations of dominion over palm and pine but affirmations of a global mission. The question of what an evolving Empire, acquired in a fit of absent-mindedness or otherwise, should be had occupied the minds of few – surprisingly few – thinkers in both the United Kingdom and the Dominions during Greenwood's student years. Throughout the latter decades of the nineteenth century and the first of the twentieth, John Seeley, Charles Dilke, James Froude, and Joseph Chamberlain in the United Kingdom and George Parkin, George Grant, and George Denison in Canada were prominent among those attempting in various ways to think through what the Empire meant and what it could become.[*] The Imperial Federation League (1884–93) and later the Round Table, active both in the Dominions as well as in Britain, were leaders among the intellectual ginger groups that grappled with the fundamental challenge of reconciling colonial nationalism with an effective global structure to render a liberal Empire secure and prosperous in a world

---

[*] The imperial musings of the three Georges, Parkin, Grant, and Denison, must have been familiar to any political science student at the University of Toronto, but perhaps *The New Empire* by Oliver Howland, a member of the Provincial Legislature and soon to be mayor of Toronto, best summed up Greenwood's thinking as he embarked for Liverpool: "The free men of the Empire [claim] equal imperial citizenship, whether our homes are in Great Britain, Canada or Australia." Howland also wrote *The Irish Problem* (London 1887).

increasingly divided both militarily and economically. All in all, however, the evolution of the Empire and its potential received little real attention in either government or the universities.

Winston Churchill, the newly appointed under-secretary of state for the colonies, aware of the imperial commitments of the neophyte member from "the senior Dominion," invited Greenwood when Parliament met in February 1906 to be his parliamentary private secretary.* The post was unpaid and in the gift of the minister (without formal reference to the prime minister, but generally with the agreement of the whip). The role of a PPS was simply to be as helpful as possible to his minister. Beyond that, he could make of it what he could. From his place in the House directly behind Churchill, Greenwood was expected to be readily accessible to other backbenchers, conveying their comments and messages and offering his minister his assessments of the mood of the House. A PPS had also more opportunity to participate in debates, at least in matters pertaining to his minister's portfolio. If a backbencher shone in that unofficial role, a more formal appointment often followed as a stepping stone on the way to a ministerial appointment and eventually to the cabinet.

During the first two of the four years between Greenwood's election in January 1906 and his defeat in the election of January 1910, Liberal fortunes flourished under the benign and measured – if not spectacular – leadership of Campbell-Bannerman until fatal illness forced him from office in April 1908. Greenwood wrote later that during those four years, he was a frequent advocate of Lloyd George's radical Limehouse program. Additionally, he began an avocation – he hoped – as an interlocutor between the Canadian and British governments that he would pursue for the next eight years, the final eight years of Strathcona's record term as high commissioner. In employing Greenwood in several assignments that a high commissioner might have been expected to do, Laurier simply bypassed Strathcona rather than confronting him, only correcting him courteously in his several imperial excesses when absolutely necessary.

From Greenwood's first days as a candidate in York, he consistently described himself as a Canadian. He drew upon his Canadian background in his untiring advocacy of Home Rule for Ireland, imperial

---

* Winston Churchill, four years younger than Greenwood, was born in 1874, the same year as Mackenzie King. By 1906 he was a Liberal MP, despite having told his mother that he would never consent to Home Rule for Ireland, his father having proclaimed that it would "plunge the knife into the heart of the British Empire."

military collaboration, and full fiscal autonomy for the Dominions. He soon became as well an unfailing host for Canadians visiting London. For example, when the celebrated Mohawk poet Pauline Johnson of Vancouver was making in 1906 one of her several successful speaking tours of the United Kingdom, Greenwood invited her to tea on the terrace of the House of Commons. The all-Canadian gathering included another visiting Canadian poet, Wilfred Campbell; the attorney general of Manitoba; and two Canadian Irish Nationalist MPs, Greenwood's boyhood hero Edward Blake and Charles Devlin.*

At Laurier's request, Greenwood undertook specific tasks that in other circumstances the high commissioner would have been expected to do. Seven weeks after the Commons assembled following the January 1906 election, Greenwood in his maiden speech argued the case for lifting the long-standing British embargo on the import of Canadian cattle. Amendments to the Diseases of Animals Act (1896) would have returned to the Board (i.e., Ministry) of Agriculture discretionary power to decide upon any protectionist proposals, away from the partisan and other local preoccupations of members of Parliament. It was hardly the type of stirring subject that other ambitious neophyte MPs might have chosen for their maiden speech. For example, three weeks before, speaking from the opposition backbenches, the barrister F.E. Smith (the future Lord Birkenhead) had ignored the convention that maiden speeches should not be controversial. He electrified the House with his sardonic debut, wittily excoriating the Liberals. Greenwood, however, chose to follow convention by limiting himself to the cattle embargo, that durable irritant in Anglo-Canadian economic relations, an intervention that he knew would be welcome to Laurier and his colleagues in Ottawa, if not to many at Westminster itself.

* Greenwood overlapped briefly with the two Canadian Irish Nationalists MPs: Edward Blake of Toronto (1833–1912) and Charles Devlin of Ottawa (1858–1914). Blake was first elected for South Longford in Ireland in 1892. He was re-elected in January 1906, but before resigning for health reasons in August 1907 he overlapped with Greenwood for eighteen months (see Banks, *Edward Blake*). Devlin, after serving in the Canadian House of Commons, was the first Canadian trade and immigration agent in Dublin, from 1897 to 1903. He was elected to the British House of Commons in 1903 as an Irish Nationalist but resigned three years later to return to the Canadian House of Commons.

As in every British election between Confederation and the Second World War, in the January 1906 election a number of Canadians were elected. They included the radical Joseph Martin, who had set some sort of record by being a minister in the government of Manitoba, a premier of British Columbia, and a member of Parliament in both Ottawa and London (McEwan, "Canadians at Westminster," 522–38).

From the early 1880s, the import of Canadian live cattle had been prohibited on the grounds of alleged disease. In 1883, the newly arrived high commissioner, Sir Charles Tupper, an Edinburgh-trained surgeon, had gone hurriedly to the Liverpool docks to dissect three randomly chosen cattle from a Canadian shipment, demonstrating before the disconcerted local health inspectors that they had erred grossly in their diagnosis of pleura-pneumonia. Nevertheless, the prohibition remained in place, reflecting the continuing conviction at Westminster that, given the numbers of Irish Nationalist members in the House of Commons, the trade in cattle from Ireland, so important to Irish farmers, had to be protected from lower-cost imports, whether from within the Empire or without. To the government of the day, it seemed like a small price to pay to help keep Irish members on side. Despite Tupper's efforts, an offer from Strathcona to fund an independent commission to make a definitive scientific assessment, and repeated protests from Ottawa, the prohibition was to remain a problem in Anglo-Canadian relations for more than fifty years.

In his maiden speech, Greenwood spoke in vain against the cattle embargo, but he spoke ably as a barrister, rehearsing its long history and marshalling his arguments to an ineluctable conclusion. The small staff of the High Commission had briefed him in advance, but the order and vigour of his presentation at Westminster was his alone. He demonstrated that imports from Canada lowered the cost of beef, that "essential article of diet in this country, and would remove a long-standing injury and insult to 6,000,000 of our loyal countrymen" (i.e., Canadians). The embargo was, in any case, scientifically unwarranted. During the three years beginning in 1892, "over 2,000,000 head of cattle had been shipped abroad from Canada ... they had been examined by veterinarians ... and in not one case had there been symptoms of any of the disease." In short, those urging the continuation of the embargo were wrongly accusing "the Canadian Government and people of [being] desirous of dumping into this country diseased animals." In his great voice, Greenwood set upon the opponents of the amendments, recognizing with regret that Irish Nationalist members were in their vanguard:

> One of the most regrettable things about the debate was the fact that the Irish Party was against this Bill ... The profits made by Irishmen ... were artificially high ... the Irish Party for the first time ... was opposed to one, and indeed the greatest, of the self-governing Colonies ... [the amendments] were opposed [also] by some of the

Imperialists who believed in closer commercial union [but only] when it could be got at the expense of some other industry ... It was also opposed by some free traders [who said] ... this was a preferential Bill ... [and] those men who called themselves Imperialists, but who on the first opportunity they had of doing an Imperial and just act to a great colony, intended to vote against it ... It ill became this Imperial House to refuse this opportunity of granting a tardy measure of justice to 6,000,000 loyal kinsmen who did not cost this country a penny; and in granting that tardy act of justice to the Canadians they would be carrying out the principles of free trade.

Greenwood was opposed by the Irish Nationalist M Ps, who pleaded that "if men shut their eyes to the difficulty in Ireland ... they would be furnishing a very dangerous argument to those who perhaps already had argument enough as to the fatal results of the present union." On the other hand, he was joined by several English farm members, "Canadian MPs," and several members who had visited Canada. Despite their efforts and the strong support of Prime Minister Campbell-Bannerman, the amendments to the 1896 act were defeated, as is so often the case, by local rather than national interests. Greenwood "regretted that he could not carry with him ... those men who called themselves Imperialists but who on the first opportunity they had of doing an imperial and just act to a great colony intended to vote against it." [1]

On 27 June 1906, six months after his election and shortly after his maiden speech, Greenwood was finally called to the bar. Normally he would then have been required to spend a year in "pupillage" under the supervision of an experienced barrister. The facts that he was already thirty-six, that eleven years had passed since he had first gained admittance to Gray's Inn, and that, above all, he was now an MP, perhaps induced the Inn to waive its final requirement. Greenwood soon sought to launch his practice by confirming to Laurier that now as both a barrister and a Liberal member at Westminster he could, from that privileged position, act formally or informally as a counsellor to the Canadian government (a role normally that of the high commissioner). He was far from being the only Canadian who was a member of the British Parliament, but Laurier would have been well aware of Greenwood's recent election victory in York. Certainly Preston, who always claimed to be both a confidant of Laurier and a mentor of Greenwood, would have joined Mackenzie King in drawing the prime minister's attention to the surprising election results. King, appointed by Laurier as Canada's first deputy minister of labour, saluted the electoral fortunes of his former fellow agitator at the University of Toronto with a congratulatory telegram: "delighted to read ... you were returned as a Member ... for such a historic constituency as York and with such a handsome majority."[2]

After the House of Commons rose in July 1906 for its long summer recess, Greenwood sailed for Canada, returning there for the first time since his cattle-boat crossing of eleven years before. His parents had died within months of each other in 1902, when he could not afford a transatlantic crossing, but he now spent some time in his hometown of Whitby as well as in Montreal, Toronto, and Ottawa. Everywhere he spoke, he partly based himself on a long letter from Churchill who, as under-secretary for the colonies, was aware from his own earlier visit to Canada that Laurier's government and Canadians generally would be uncertain about the thinking of Campbell-Bannerman's government regarding the British Empire. The enlightened policies of the new prime minister had done much to reconcile Boer leaders, especially Botha and Smuts, to the inclusion of the new dominion, the Union of South Africa, into the Empire. Churchill intended to build on that precedent in his search for closer collaboration with Canada within the ever-expanding Empire.

Before Greenwood embarked for Montreal, he sent the "Canadian blood and bone" a letter of 20 August 1906 in which he acknowledged that for the past two decades "imperial administration" had been associated with the Conservative Party. However, with the election of Campbell-Bannerman's government, it was timely to reassure Canadians about the Liberal commitment to the Empire.[*] Churchill asked Greenwood to "try to do as far as may lie in your power ... to convince your friends and kinsfolk in Canada that this change in England, great and far-reaching though it has been, does not imply any weakening in the affection of the British people towards their kith and kin across the sea ... in so far as you can make your friends in Canada realize that in a Liberal ministry in England they will find true comradeship and faithful, unrelaxing service whenever they have need of it, you will be doing good work in a good cause."[3] Churchill and Greenwood shared the conviction that the Empire was held together by a fundamental belief that more progress

---

[*] Sir James (later Lord) Bryce, the British ambassador to the United States and a future chief secretary for Ireland, had carried the same message to Toronto in October 1904: "The Liberals in England were just as desirous of maintaining political connection with the Colonies as English Tories aimed to be" (Hyman, *Elgin and Churchill*, 319).

was to be gained by each component, however diverse and distant, by remaining within the Empire than without. Accordingly, Greenwood was eager to make extensive use of Churchill's letter not only in attempting to reassure Laurier about the good imperial intentions of Campbell-Bannerman's Liberal government but also as a reflection of his own standing at Westminster. In addition to drawing upon the letter in speeches, he had no difficulty in persuading his brother, Billy, the editor of *Toronto World*, and James Tucker at *Saturday Night* to publish it.

Before boarding the train in Whitby for Toronto, Winnipeg, and Vancouver, Greenwood mailed to Churchill a letter with newspaper clippings. "My visit here has been quite a triumphal progress. Your letter was published throughout the broad Dominion ... [and] was received with positive enthusiasm by all sections of the press." Churchill's letter had, in short, achieved what he had sought: "You have brought the country to view our Government as the true friend of all self-governing colonies and you have made yourself solid with the Canadians."[4] Having seen Laurier and Sir William Mulock, the postmaster general (who as vice-chancellor of the University of Toronto had conferred Greenwood's bachelor's degree upon him), his only regret was that Churchill himself had not made another visit to Canada where a big welcome awaited him.

While in Canada, Greenwood received from Laurier his first assignment to assist in a Canadian matter at Westminster: the passage of an amendment to section 118 of the British North America Act (in effect the Canadian constitution, then amenable only via an address of the Canadian Parliament to the British). The amendment would reorder federal fiscal transfers to the provinces. The high commissioner, Lord Strathcona, as a member of the House of Lords, could have assisted its passage, but he almost never went to Westminster and was, in any event, increasingly inactive. Greenwood, as parliamentary private secretary to the under-secretary of state for the colonies, could, by contrast, play a central role. To see the innocuous-sounding legislation through Parliament appeared in both London and Ottawa to be a straightforward undertaking. It soon proved to be anything but. In fact, the question of how much money the Dominion government should allocate to the provinces, including to the new provinces of Alberta and Saskatchewan, beyond that provided in the British North America Act, was to complicate and frequently embitter federal-provincial relations for the next century.

Greenwood was in at the beginning. At Laurier's invitation, he crossed the Atlantic a second time in 1906, to be an observer at an interprovincial conference in October in Ottawa "for the purpose of considering the financial subsidies to the Provinces." He attended the meetings of the prime minister with the nine premiers as well as their dinners and a luncheon offered by the leader of the opposition, Robert Borden. At the interprovincial conference itself, Sir Richard McBride, the premier of British Columbia, eager among other things to distract attention from irregularities in his own government, demanded "distinct and separate relief" in the form of a greater fiscal transfer than was provided for the other eight provinces. He made a vigorous plea that British Columbia, a late entrant to Confederation, had special financial needs. He threatened that if they continued to go unrecognized, he would withdraw from the conference. The chairman, Lomer Gouin, premier of Quebec, supported by James Whitney, premier of Ontario, rejected his proposal for an independent investigation, promoting instead a unanimous resolution offering British Columbia an additional $1 million spread equally over ten years. McBride left the conference dissatisfied. There the matter stood for the winter of 1906. It would be rejoined in the spring of 1907.

Upon his return to Westminster, Greenwood gave more substance to Churchill's offer of "unrelaxing service" to the Dominion by assisting Mackenzie King in his London visit as Canada's deputy minister of labour. In November 1906, King arrived to learn more about British legislation intended among other things to eliminate fraud among independent emigration operators. Greenwood asked Churchill to facilitate his visit and later provided him with material relating to the relevant Merchant Shipping bill. Upon his return to Ottawa, King sent his thanks. In reply, Greenwood urged "my dear boy" not to "spend your vigorous life in the civil service. Bide your time but at the right time, take the pulse and go into politics. No one knows your abilities better than I do ... [to] fight for the first position in Canada."[5]

Greenwood now gave an additional dimension to his imperial commitments – and escaped the worst of the English winter – by sailing in the last week of December 1906 from Bristol to Kingston, Jamaica, with five other members or former members of Parliament, several agronomists and horticulturalists led by the eminent scientist Sir Daniel Morris, and three Manchester cotton mill owners, all guests of Sir Alfred Jones, a Welshman who had flourished in Liverpool shipping and had become a noted philanthropist. The purpose of the month-long journey was to attend Jones's conference of more than one hundred experts, investors, and planters to ascertain whether the soil and climate of the British West Indies was suitable for large cotton plantations, earlier adverse

advice of post-Civil War émigrés from the United States notwithstanding. The new member for York, although no expert in tropical crops,
may have been included for any or all of three reasons: like Jones, he
was of Welsh descent; he was from Canada, which had long-standing
commercial ties with the seriously impoverished islands; and, above all,
he was parliamentary private secretary to the under-secretary of state for
the colonies.

Several weeks into the visit, on 14 January 1907, Jamaica was struck by
one of the worst earthquakes in its history. In the afternoon it destroyed
most of Kingston, killing an estimated eight hundred people. Fire
destroyed whatever wooden shops, warehouses, and banks had been left
standing. The few surviving telegraph lines were reserved for official
traffic. Amidst the fires, Greenwood sent an immediate message to
Churchill: "[Fire] Brigade helpless from the start; no water; trains top-
pled over; poles crashed across roads; everyone felt sickening helpless-
ness; people kneeling, crying 'O God, save us!' impossible to quiet
them; heartbreaking wailing."[6] The governor, Sir Alexander Swettenham
(the older brother of Sir Frank Swettenham, governor of the Malay
States), sent a message to the British minister in Havana seeking help
"at cost of colony." Two days later a US Navy torpedo boat arrived from
Guantanamo Bay bringing some basic medical supplies, followed the
next day by a flotilla, including two battleships, under the command of
Rear Admiral Davis.

Greenwood knew that he could earn a sizeable fee by scooping all
other London newspapers if he could supply a first-hand account
for Cecil Harmsworth's *Daily Mail*, for which he had written occasionally in the past. He set about contriving a way to send the story,
even though the telegraphic lines were closed to commercial traffic.
Presenting himself to US naval officers as no less than the parliamentary private secretary to the under-secretary of state for the colonies,
he asked them to transmit his message to London from the nearest
cable station in Cuba. They arranged for a cutter to take it to their
base at Guantanamo Bay for onward telegraphic transmission. For his
scoop, a welcome cheque from Harmsworth awaited Greenwood upon
his return to England.

Shortly after the US Navy flotilla arrived in Jamaica, Rear Admiral
Davis received from Swettenham a request "to re-embark the working
party and all parties which your kindness prompted you to land." The
governor's unspoken apprehensions about armed work parties of US
Marines may have arisen from misgivings about the supposed Caribbean

ambitions of the United States in the aftermath of the Spanish-American War, its support for Venezuela in a border dispute with British Guiana, and its recruitment of Jamaicans as low-paid labourers on the chaotic construction of the Panama Canal. The admiral who chaired the US Isthmian Canal Commission had mused that Washington should simply take over Jamaica as part of the projected canal's outer defences. A rumour even had it that Britain and the United States would exchange Jamaica and the Philippines. Nevertheless, the governor's letter was a clumsy one, and the offended admiral promptly saw to it that it was widely publicized. At the Colonial Office, Churchill described it as "plainly indefensible and wantonly insulting." He recommended that if Swettenham did not publicly apologize, he should be recalled, especially "in view of Root's mission to Canada" (Elihu Root, the US secretary of state, was expected to visit Ottawa imminently). Churchill was also annoyed that the governor had sought disaster relief "at cost of colony" when such relief was the "proper subject of [the non-governmental] Mansion House Funds."[7]

Greenwood, however, continued to assess favourably Swettenham's actions in a Jamaican context. Writing some months later in *Saturday Night*, he praised the governor (who had in the meantime resigned in the face of Churchill's threat of dismissal) for having risen "to the occasion, and by splendid example and a cool genius for organisation, he brought order out of chaos ... The American Admiral, with the best and most generous impulses, was a worry, not a help, with his armed sailors. The dark population of Jamaica detests the American nation because it stands for all that is horrible in the persecution of the African race, and the black Tommies of the West Indian Regiment share this antipathy. The crisis called for one strong man, and the Governor proved himself that man."[8]

Even before the earthquake, the ambitious agricultural conference in Jamaica had accomplished little. As forewarned, it came to recognize that cotton and the British West Indies were incompatible (although Sir Alfred Jones before his death in 1909 did establish a shipping line to carry bananas from Kingston to Bristol). But for Greenwood, the delegation had an unexpected positive result. In the gardens of the Constant Spring Hotel five miles from Kingston, he met Margery Spencer, the twenty-year-old daughter of the Reverend Walter Spencer of Fownhope Court in Herefordshire, who with her uncle and aunt, Major and Mrs Mcgillicuddy of Kerry, Ireland, had survived the earthquake by sheltering in the gardens of the hotel. Four years later, Greenwood and she would marry.

Once back in London from Kingston, Greenwood had before him again the challenge from the year before of how the Laurier government could best embody an additional fiscal transfer to British Columbia. In April 1907, Sir Wilfrid and Lady Laurier crossed to Britain to attend Laurier's third Colonial Conference and to conclude the fiscal question. Under the chairmanship of the secretary of state for the colonies, the Earl of Elgin, the focus of the Colonial Conference was on possibilities of additional imperial collaboration. The under-secretary, Churchill, was only thirty-three but was already noted for his loquacious pleas for the greater unity of the British Empire in the face of the rising industrial powers across the globe. Mackenzie King wrote that Canada "makes it very clear that she intends to be a factor in world politics in alliance with the Motherland," but he stressed that "it will be an alliance, not a merger."[9] Laurier continued to oppose closer imperial military collaboration; the searing French-English controversy in Canada over even voluntary participation in the South Africa War was less than ten years behind him.

Laurier rejected Joseph Chamberlain's goal, elaborated in 1903, of an imperial *Zollverein*, a customs union to unite the Empire, which Strathcona had promoted and surreptitiously helped to finance. Chamberlain, who had left Gladstone's Liberals over Home Rule for Ireland, had been sent as a newly minted Conservative to Canada and the United States to help negotiate an agreement over disputed fishing rights in the Gulf of St Lawrence. Having seen something of the two thriving federations, he had returned to London convinced that an imperial federation was the way forward for a dynamic British Empire (although the place therein of India and non-white colonies remained vague). He recognized that "the British Empire is not an Empire in the sense in which that term has been applied before. The British Colonies are no longer Colonies in the sense in which that term was originally applied to them ... We are sister States in which the Mother Country by virtue of her age, by virtue of all that has been done in the past, may claim to be the first, but only first among equals."[10]

However appealing Chamberlain's daring rhetoric – and it won interest in both Britain and the Dominions – Asquith, Lloyd George, Churchill, and other free traders, both Liberal and Conservative, identified an insurmountable problem: any imperial trade preference presupposed first the imposition of a general tariff, which would increase the costs in Britain of imported foodstuffs. The call of the opposing free traders for no "stomach taxes" had greater popular appeal than any advanced theories of an imperial customs union or other economic collaboration. In Canada, Laurier and his anglophile minister of finance, W.S. Fielding, having introduced unilaterally in 1897 a preferential tariff for Britain (as did later Australia and New Zealand), regarded the tariff as something for Canada alone to decide. Further, the infant manufacturing industries of Canada, as in the other Dominions, sought protection against lower-cost and often higher-quality imports from the United Kingdom. In brief, Laurier declared himself broadly content with the constitutional place of Canada in the Empire, knowing that for the time being any alternative would be unwelcome to either English or French-Canadians or both. He made this position clear both at the conference and at a speech at the end of April to the Canada Club – with both Churchill and Greenwood present.

By then, Laurier was ready to revive Ottawa's address to the British Parliament regarding Dominion fiscal transfers to the provinces and British Columbia's plea for "distinct and separate relief." He concurred in the recommendation of Quebec and Ontario of the year before that British Columbia receive an additional amount of $1 million over ten years, but he now included the qualification that such a transfer should be defined as "final and unalterable" in the address. In Victoria, Premier McBride strongly objected, not to the amount but to the "final and unalterable" clause. He informed the press that if the limiting phrase was not dropped, he would himself "take the case of his Province to the seat of the Empire and try to get justice done there." First, however, he appealed by telegram to Churchill and Elgin and also sought the assistance of his new friend, the parliamentary private secretary to the undersecretary of state for the colonies. Greenwood found himself on both sides of the dispute, attempting somehow to reconcile Laurier's demand for the inclusion of the "final and unalterable" phrase with McBride's adamant opposition to it. For his part, Laurier made it clear to Elgin, Churchill, and Greenwood that the limiting phrase must remain, and asked that the draft legislation be sent to him for review while on holiday in France.

On 30 May 1907, Greenwood wrote to Laurier in Paris that the necessary amending bill would be introduced by Churchill within days, the Conservative Opposition having pledged its support. "No discussion is likely … the Colonial Office has decided that it cannot interfere on behalf of any Provincial Premier" (i.e., McBride).[11] It was, as Churchill observed, "British Columbia (like Athanasius) *contra mundum.*"[12] A week later, Greenwood added that Fielding, the minister of finance, would arrive in London to "settle details." He told Laurier that "the words 'final and unalterable' will probably be dropped on the grounds that no statute can bind the sovereign parliament and that therefore the words are meaningless and redundant."[13] Churchill accordingly eliminated the offending phrase from the bill presented to the House. Laurier, however, wired Elgin from Venice reaffirming opposition to any amendment by Westminster to what had already been adopted by both houses of the Canadian Parliament in their address to the British. On 13 June, immediately following a Lunacy (Ireland) bill, Churchill sought leave of the House "to make further provision with respect to the sums to be paid by Canada to the several provinces of the Dominion ... which was not of great importance to the people of this country, but which had excited a great deal of interest in Canada."[14]

The legislation did not proceed quite so effortlessly. The essence of the bill, as Churchill explained to the largely empty Commons, was that, as section 118 of the British North America Act of 1867 set forth, the Dominion paid certain prescribed sums to the provinces in aid of their local expenditure. Churchill introduced the newly agreed scale. But a problem still remained for British Columbia over "final and unalterable." On 15 July, McBride telegraphed to Greenwood that he had learned that "it is intended in Lords [where Elgin sat] to replace [place?] words final and unalterable in [the amendment to the] BNA Act. Cannot accept this seriously in view assurances Colonial Office letter June fifth and Churchill's statements in Commons would create serious situation here. If necessary [I shall] return to London at once. Am cabling Elgin and Churchill."[15] The following day Greenwood sent a note to "Dear Mr. Churchill," informing him that he had already sent a reply to McBride, pointing out to him "that words 'final and unalterable' are not in the Act but in its schedule. I hope you will cable him ... so that he will not feel that he has been badly treated. His friendship for the Government is a mighty influence for our good in Canada [i.e., the good of both the Liberal Government and the Empire] and a cable from you will be inestimably valued by him."[16]

Churchill, as government spokesman for colonial matters in the House of Commons, had a score or more of much more difficult questions confronting him – especially those relating to postwar South Africa. He sought to be rid of the fiscal problems of Canada by having Greenwood do any detailed work necessary to speed the passage of the bill, but at Greenwood's prompting, he did send a cable to McBride on 17 July. He reconfirmed that the words "final and unalterable" would appear only in the schedule to the bill, as expressing the "intention of the Act ... to give effect to the purposes of that address [of the Canadian Parliament] so far as can be done by law. All other assertions on either side appear to me as a layman to be matters of political controversy in Canada and no authoritative pronouncement on behalf of His Majesty's Government would be possible or proper. We are responsible only for legal effects of document which is not affected by Schedule."[17] Laurier was not pleased with Churchill's effort to placate everyone. From Venice on 11 June, he wrote to Elgin, protesting against the relegation of "final and unalterable" to the schedule, "unless Fielding has agreed."[18]

In the second reading debate on 21 June, Greenwood took a leading part, supporting Churchill and speaking as a Canadian in attempting to accelerate the passage through the British Parliament of what Churchill had originally described as an inconsequential bill. Greenwood declared that "these most difficult and complicated negotiations were conducted with sympathy and hearty goodwill with the result that the Under-Secretary for the Colonies [Churchill] had been enabled to bring the bill before the House ... the Dominion of Canada and the Prime Minister of that greatest Colony of the Crown had shown a good example in the way they had dealt with the matter among themselves and with the Home Government."[19] Despite "the sympathy and hearty good-will" in the House, which Greenwood welcomed, one member quite understandably asked Churchill why the matter needed to "come here at all." Churchill explained that the "British North America Act is the fundamental act governing the constitution of the Dominion of Canada, and the different Prime Ministers [i.e., provincial premiers] of Canada voluntarily entered into that union. Adherence to the union was something in the nature of a treaty and when an alteration in the basis of the treaty is made ... it was felt desirable by all the Prime Ministers in conference that such matters should be ratified by the Imperial Parliament in the most formal way." Churchill was carefully saying that the bill, a mere formality, was at the initiative of the Government of Canada and not of the imperial Parliament. The bill, having been read a second time, proceeded through the final stages as an amendment to the British North America Act and was passed without debate by the House of Lords.

McBride reluctantly accepted Elgin's reinsertion in the Lords of the offending phrase in the schedule on the grounds of Greenwood's assurance that "final and unalterable" there would have no real effect. He despatched gifts of thanks of bearskins and moose heads to Elgin and Churchill. To Greenwood, in way of additional gratitude, he included a confidential recommendation to purchase a salmon

cannery at Hayesport, near Prince Rupert, BC. The hitherto impecunious Greenwood somehow managed to put together a small syndicate
that raised the necessary funds through a London financial house in
which a Canadian, Edward Peacock, played a leading part. Four years
later, in 1911 Greenwood would arrange for his brother Billy to resign
as managing director of *Toronto World* "to manage a fish packing company in the interests of British capital."*

Despite his desire to keep Britain out of Canadian domestic affairs,
Laurier while in London in June 1907 continued to show his deep interest in British domestic affairs, specifically proposals for Irish Home Rule
(as his predecessor, Edward Blake, had also demonstrated). Following
Laurier's speech to a Canada Club dinner, Greenwood informed him
that an Irish Council bill would be introduced by Campbell-Bannerman's
intellectually distinguished but erratic chief secretary for Ireland,
Augustine Birrell. The Conservative leader Arthur Balfour, both a
former chief secretary for Ireland and a former prime minister, and
John Redmond, the leader of the Irish Nationalist MPs, would follow.
"Knowing how desirous you are of hearing this debate, I ... hope you
may come in, if only for a half hour."[20] Laurier replied on 3 May that he
would "be more disappointed than I can say if I am unable to avail
myself of it [the invitation], but I am crowded with engagements."[21]

Following the Liberal landslide of 1906, a further effort at devolution
of powers from London to Dublin was being made. Birrell, a committed
Home Ruler, had inherited an inadequate Irish Council bill from his
Conservative predecessor, James Bryce. Much strengthened although it
was from Joseph Chamberlain's original ideas of devolution, Birrell's
expanded bill still left the United Irish League convinced that the idea
of an Irish council of one hundred was Home Rule by instalments,
intended to bury or at least further delay early Home Rule itself. With his
eye on hostile Unionists, Campbell-Bannerman, himself a former chief
secretary for Ireland, publicly offered the bill only as the first instalment
of a limited form of self-government. As he wryly described it in a speech
in Manchester, it was "a little, modest, shy, humble effort to give administrative powers to the Irish people." Whether or not it was quite as
simple as that, it was rejected by the Irish Nationalist MPs, who valued

---

* During the First World War, when Billy was employed in Ottawa as director of publicity
for the Canada Food Board, the Hayesport cannery flourished, thanks in part to Major
General A.D. McCrae, a leading Tory from Vancouver, who, as quartermaster general of
the Canadian Army Overseas, arranged for substantial orders to be placed with it.

their continued parliamentary support at a much higher price. The prime minister added to the king that the rejected bill had been "an honest attempt to improve the system of administration by enlarging the powers and enlisting the direct help of the Irish people and if it did not please them the Government have no desire to proceed with it."[22]

Laurier regretted greatly the Irish rejection of what he at least had seen as a promising step in a gradualist progression through continuing devolution to full Home Rule. On 3 June he wrote to Greenwood from Rome (Lady Laurier and he were spending a month in Italy and Switzerland before returning to Canada): "I follow British affairs as closely as I can [from Italy] and I cannot help expressing to you my disappointment that the Irish bill has met such a fate. It seems to me a mistake on the part of our friends [the Irish Nationalist MPs, Blake included], though I would not like to express a final opinion until I have had an opportunity of talking the matter over with some of them." With the experience of Canada in mind, he added, "They must, however, realize that they have nothing to gain except by compromise and conciliation."[23]

In late August 1907, the House having risen, Greenwood travelled again to Ottawa in search of more Dominion or provincial legal work and to speak to the Empire Club in Toronto. In the first days of September he visited his friend Premier Richard McBride in Victoria before returning to Toronto to speak on 13 September on the unresolved subject of Canada's role in the foreign affairs of the British Empire.

In Victoria, Greenwood would have seen what he already well knew: local opposition to further Asian immigration was nearing a flashpoint. As PPS to the under-secretary of state for the colonies, he would also have already been made aware by the India Office of the imperial problem that had arisen from the resentment in India at the various exclusionary efforts of British Columbia. For its part, the Foreign Office made Elgin, Churchill, and Greenwood fully aware of the troublesome reaction of Japan, Britain's valued trading partner and maritime ally in the Pacific. China was also a problem, but less so. Laurier wrote to an MP from British Columbia, "The Japanese has adopted European civilisation, has shown that he can whip European soldiers [in the Russo-Japanese War of 1905], has a navy equal man for man to the best afloat [i.e., the Royal Navy] and will not submit to be kicked and treated with contempt as his brother from China still meekly continues to."[24]

On 7 and 8 September, a day or two after Greenwood left Vancouver for Toronto, anti-Asian riots spread through the streets of east

Vancouver in violent reaction to the recent increased arrivals of Chinese, Sikh, and Japanese. In the case of Japan, immigrants had increased to an annual rate of eight thousand in 1907 from about a thousand a few years before. Knowing how little the indispensable Chinese temporary labourers had been paid in the hazardous building of the Canadian Pacific Railway through the Rockies, local opponents had promoted provincial legislation to limit further Asian immigration sharply so as to preserve jobs at "white men's wages." In 1906, however, Laurier's government, partly at the prompting of the colonial secretary, Joseph Chamberlain, and of the Japanese consul general in Ottawa, had taken the rare step of instructing Lieutenant Governor James Dunsmuir to disallow two acts of the British Columbia legislature. The two disallowances contributed to the mounting discontent of organized labour and all others who were convinced that their livelihood was being threatened by the arrival of what the BC Trades and Labour Congress called "cheap peoples." Prominent local citizens vigorously echoed labour's demands for the total exclusion of Asians. Premier McBride, the "People's Dick," who called for "Mongolian exclusion," travelled again to his beloved London in the hope that Britain could somehow be induced to stop or at least sharply curtail the flow of Asian immigrants at their source. He did so against the background of statements by Robert Borden, the Conservative leader of the opposition (and future prime minister), that "the Conservative Party stands for a white Canada" and by R.B. Bennett, the Conservative MP for Calgary (and another future prime minister), "We must not allow our shores to be overrun by Asiatics and become dominated by an alien race. British Columbia must remain a white man's country." [25]

The numbers of Asian immigrants had been increasing despite such obstacles as the imposition of a substantial head tax on Chinese arrivals. The animosity towards them reflected both popular and labour union fears about the "yellow peril" to wages and living standards. Such fears were fanned by the Asiatic Exclusion League, first active along the Pacific coast of the United States but now with the support of the BC Trades and Labour Congress, with a chapter in Vancouver as well. During the autumn of 1906, Mackenzie King, deputy minister of labour, had travelled to London to explore a range of issues, including ways in which the mounting opposition in British Columbia to Asian immigration might somehow be contained. In discussions in London with Elgin, Churchill, and Greenwood, King attempted to escape the clear responsibility of Ottawa to resolve the issue and, in the best colonial tradition, to attempt to place the onus on Britain. London's response was, not surprisingly, if you now want us to help solve your domestic problems, you will in turn need to suppress local racism in the interests of an overriding imperial foreign policy.

Elihu Root, the US secretary of state, understood that there was no effective way to close the highly porous Canadian-US border to Asian immigrants. He sought instead to induce Ottawa to exclude their entry to Canada. And he had no doubt where he could best apply pressure to that end. In Ottawa during his visit in mid-January 1907, he asked that Canada join the United States in denying Asian immigrants entry. Laurier was caught in the invidious position of trying to deal with political tensions in British Columbia, imperial priorities, and Root's loaded questions. Eager to develop Asian markets for western grain, Laurier had adhered to the 1894 Anglo-Japanese Treaty of Commerce and Navigation, which *inter alia* provided for reciprocal free entry and residence. On the other hand, he was loathe to surrender whatever electoral support the Liberals retained in Conservative-dominated British Columbia. One way to do so might be to revert in this instance to a quasi-colonial stance by proclaiming that it was London that was demanding – for understandable imperial reasons – an end to racist agitation in the province. Toward that end, Laurier appointed Mackenzie King as a one-man royal commission to assess claims for Vancouver riot losses and to seek to lessen local frustrations.

When Greenwood was with McBride in Victoria during the first week of September, immediately before the Vancouver riots, he had presumably elaborated for him what he intended to say about Asian migration in his Empire Club speech in Toronto on 13 September, including the imperial concerns of the Foreign and Colonial offices (as he had done earlier in meetings in Ottawa with Laurier and King). In the event, Greenwood's speech was much more outspoken and urgent. He quickly adopted the Vancouver riots as the starting point. In doing so, he was not simply speaking to the members of the Empire Club in Toronto about more general imperial matters; he was also talking over their heads specifically to racial bigots in British Columbia. There the prejudice was most pronounced, but it was not absent elsewhere in Canada, including in Ontario, where the *Toronto News* had spoken of Asian immigrants as being a "yellow-skinned, almond-eyed, long-haired swarm of grasshoppers."

The fact that the luncheon meeting of the Empire Club was chaired by Senator Robert Jaffray, the owner of the *Toronto Globe*, ensured its detailed coverage, and Billy Greenwood made certain that the coverage in the *World* was equally comprehensive, coverage that was duly reproduced in other newspapers across Canada. In his well-publicized speech, Greenwood said, "I speak to you as a Canadian by birth and, I may say, in my democratic ideals, but I also speak to you as one who has had the privilege of spending some twelve years of a very, very strenuous life in the public affairs of the Home Country. I want to speak this afternoon from the point of view of that Home Country and of a man who views the British Empire from the royal Palace of Westminster and from the Colonial Office." Having thus set out his credentials, Greenwood launched into an attack on those Canadians so parochial in their outlook that they viewed "the Empire only from the local platform." His message to all Canadians was both direct and simple. Alexander Galt, John A. Macdonald's first minister of finance, had established the right of Canada to determine its own trade policies as part of its unquestioned fiscal autonomy. However, it did not follow from such economic autonomy that Canada had its own distinctive foreign policy.

For the Empire as a whole, there could only be one collective foreign policy. Foreign countries, in relation to any event in the Empire, could approach only the foreign secretary in London. The Committee on Imperial Defence, which had emerged from colonial participation in the South African War, was, as repeatedly stated in London, not a policy-making body; its role was advisory. It was Greenwood's purpose to illustrate why this was necessarily so by decrying the cost of "the Japanese controversy which has been uneasily followed for many months in the Foreign Office [and] has been brought to a head by some very foolish people in the beautiful city of Vancouver." Given the imperial implications, Japan had protested both to Ottawa and to the Foreign Office against the rampant racial prejudices there. "Owing to the overwhelming defeat of Russia by an Oriental power [i.e., Japan in the Russo-Japanese War two years before], the sudden rise of Japan, and, following that, the Oriental immigration question on the Pacific Coast, the Dominion suddenly came within the arena of foreign politics, and to-day you have the danger zone of the world, insofar as our own Empire is concerned, shifted from the Northwest Frontier of India ... to the Pacific Coast of this Dominion."

Greenwood stressed imperial obligations: "Is it all right for Canadians to say ... 'we will have a white's man country and no Jap need apply'? ... I believe in a white Canada. I believe in strengthening the white portions of the Empire in the interests of the Empire. But ... you must not forget you have an Imperial responsibility." Sounding like Laurier in his earlier letter to the BC member of Parliament, he added, "It is impossible to treat the subjects of the Mikado in Japan in any way that will humiliate them ... We have to change our whole idea of inferior races ... You can deal as you like with the Chinaman for he is a patient fellow. He has no great Government behind him." He concluded by extolling the unity of the Empire and the need for British subjects everywhere, Vancouver included, to avoid any action that would jeopardize that essential unity. A united Empire must develop a united foreign policy. There was no room for local malcontents and agitators who, like the brutal rioters in the streets of east Vancouver, "were making the solution of the Oriental immigration question ... [by] the Foreign Secretary of the British Empire that much more difficult."

Following Greenwood, Senator Jaffray added that "the Japanese had their ability and powers of organization, and if they joined with the hordes of China the British Empire would have a very dangerous element to deal with, and one that would tax all its strength and possibly that of the United States. As Britishers, they must do their best to curb what might endanger the peace of the Empire, and he was surprised that the people on the Pacific coast did not appear to realize that if difficulty with Japan arose, they would be the sufferers. They must do what they could to make Canada a white man's country, but it was not by riot or lawlessness that they would succeed in doing so."[26]

Many in the audience may have felt the tension between Greenwood's portrayal of the demands of a united imperial foreign policy and the anger in British Columbia at what was seen as ever-increasing cheap-labour migration. That tension contributed directly to the frustration of Premier McBride who had long been an Asian exclusion man, but now both Ottawa and London – and even his friends Churchill and Greenwood – were strongly cautioning him against any local exclusionary action. "As an ardent Imperialist and at the same time a loyal British Columbian, he found himself torn between his desire to conform in every way with Imperial policy, and the need to protect the special interests of his province."[27]

In Liberal Ottawa, Greenwood's Empire Club speech was valued, at least to the degree that it could be exploited to shift some of the onus for a solution from Ottawa to London. King noted in his diary at the time that in public speaking his university friend "has infinite assurance but carries it off so well that it is not objectionable. He has force and ability as well." But Greenwood's repeated statements about the need for a single imperial foreign policy in a constructive Empire made King vaguely uneasy. (When prime minister, he would set aside the concept of imperial cooperation and substitute instead the right of Canada to isolate itself from foreign involvement.) However, in the short run at least, Greenwood's words, accurately reflecting the then orthodox thinking in the Colonial, India, and Foreign Offices, were welcomed by Laurier in helping to modulate the racist rhetoric in British Columbia and to contain Japanese resentment at the treatment of its citizens. In the wake of Greenwood's speech, Laurier showed King a telegram from the Trades and Labour Congress "dealing in a violent way with the recent influx of Japanese and calling upon the Government to withdraw from the [Anglo-Japanese] treaty."[28]

Certainly if some understanding about limits to immigration was ever to be achieved with the Japanese government, both the foreign secretary and, under his direction, the British minister in Tokyo had central roles to play. Nothing would be gained, in the short run at least, by challenging directly the orthodox concept of a single foreign policy in those areas that transcended regional or local interests. To the contrary, Ottawa could thereby sidestep responsibility for acting against local racial prejudice by contending that the problem was essentially an imperial one. Laurier despatched his minister of labour, Rodolphe Lemieux, to Japan, where Preston (who had arrived in Yokohama as trade commissioner in March 1907) and the British minister were on hand to advise and intercede on his behalf in the conclusion of a "Gentleman's Agreement" in which Japan would not demand the full implementation of the Anglo-Japan treaty, instead voluntarily limiting emigration to Canada.*

In writing to Laurier from London on 25 March 1908 to ask for legal work, Greenwood first offered the prime minister a brief review of British politics. Since "our Campbell-Bannerman is a dying man," it was foreseen that H.H. Asquith, the chancellor of the exchequer, would succeed him, that Lloyd George would succeed Asquith as chancellor and that Churchill would enter the cabinet as president of the Board of Trade. In a few weeks, all this was to come true. Following Campbell-Bannerman's death, his successor brought to the prime ministership a formidable intellect, but he was also seen by many as aloof and occasionally lethargic. Lloyd George was the opposite: J.B. Priestley was only

---

* The Chinese Immigration Act of Dominion Day 1923 all but ended Chinese immigration until 1947. See Roy, *The Oriental Question*.

one of many impressed with how pre-eminently in the Edwardian era "his mixture of energy, ruthless decision and charm could work magic." Greenwood concluded his brief political survey by touching on the question of temperance legislation, a subject that he and Laurier had discussed. He was confident that although a Liberal bill at Westminster restricting public licensing was contributing to by-election losses, its popularity with many temperance advocates across Britain would help in the general election expected in 1910 or early 1911.

Then Greenwood came to the point of his letter. Having played a supporting role in the fiscal amendment of the British American Act and having spoken out against the racism in British Columbia, he sought legal work from the prime minister. He wished him many years in office and thanked him for his gift of a "magnificent bound set of the Dominion Statutes," especially welcome since "I hope to be fighting legally and politically [for Canada] for 40 or 50 years yet ... If you and Mr. Aylesworth [the minister of justice] would give me a junior brief in a Dominion appeal to the Privy Council, you would bring about one of my great ambitions, viz, to represent my native Dominion in the Privy Council. I have already held briefs for British Columbia, Quebec, and Newfoundland, and with success."[29]

Laurier was prompt in his reply: "At this moment we have little legislation in England; [but] I am quite sure that Mr. Aylesworth would be glad to put anything that [we] can offer in your way."[30] Turning to Greenwood's support for the Liberal temperance legislation at Westminster further restricting licensed premises, Laurier, with Quebec in mind, was cautious: "Any question affecting temperance is always a ticklish one. My impression is that you will lose more than you will gain by this legislation, but I am sure this was a duty which had to be faced, whatever the consequences."[31] The legislation at Westminster referred to was a restrictive bill that Asquith had introduced in light of the weak temperance legislation that the preceding Conservative government had adopted. It was, however, the Conservative premier of Ontario rather than the Liberal prime minister of Canada to whom Greenwood provided detailed information and comment about the bill. The premier, James Whitney, wrote in January 1908 to Greenwood (not to the high commissioner) seeking a copy of the "licence bill or at any rate a bill dealing with the question of the retail liquor traffic."[32]

Greenwood confirmed by return post that he would send a copy as soon as the bill was introduced. "There will be a good deal of amending during its course through both Houses. So that when it does emerge finally ... this will be the great measure of the session and will provoke much bitter fighting. Bishops and brewers always do fight like devils in English political life."[33] Later Greenwood sent the requested copy of the bill along with Asquith's speech introducing it. "Many consider [it] one of the best of his distinguished career ... Of course 'the trade' in this country is fighting the Government hard, but as the Liberal Party of England has not had the support of any brewer or publican for twenty years, the trade protest does not much affect the administration."[34] Upon the bill's adoption in October 1908, Greenwood sent a copy of the final text by express to Whitney along with all relevant copies of Hansard. The premier, pondering similar temperance legislation in Ontario, was in turn grateful for the time and expense that Greenwood had spent meeting his request, offering in return "to reciprocate at any time." (In the event, prohibition was not introduced in Ontario until April 1916, as a wartime measure.)

Greenwood, now president of the Canada Club in London, invited Laurier to cable good wishes on the occasion of its annual dinner on 24 May 1908, the late Queen Victoria's birthday. His greetings to "a record gathering of Canadians and pro-Canadians [would be] sincerely appreciated and will more vividly link us with you and the Dominion."* Around this time, Greenwood joined the Pilgrims, an Anglo-American friendship group founded in 1902 on a British initiative pledged to closer links among Anglo-Saxon peoples. It had among its early Canadian members Lord Strathcona and Sir Gilbert Parker, MP. Greenwood, who was soon added to its management committee, was to remain active in the Pilgrims for more than forty years. At the same time he sustained his place in the radical wing of the Liberal Party, especially with Lloyd George and John Burns, the president of the Local Government Board. In June 1908 he wished "My dear Burns" a speedy recovery from a recent illness: "You're a strenuous fighter and a hard hitter."[35] Burns was a Liberal MP from 1892, a free trader, an outspoken

---

* At the Canada Club dinner, in addition to Winston Churchill and most of the "Canadian MPs," were the Lords Aberdeen, Carrington, Durham, Brassey, and Elgin. Aberdeen, the former governor general of Canada, was then viceroy in Ireland. Durham was the grandson of "Radical Jack" of the Durham Report; Brassey had long been involved in railway construction in Canada; Elgin was the Montreal-born colonial secretary; Churchill was under-secretary for the colonies. Among "the Canadian MPs" were the future Conservative prime minister of Britain, Bonar Law; the future minister of labour, Thomas Macnamara; and MPs Harry Brodie, Alexander Boulton, Sir Charles Rose, Allen Baker, and the novelist Sir Gilbert Parker.

opponent of the South African War, a supporter of Home Rule for Ireland, and, again like Greenwood, a temperance advocate who had acquired his considerable oratorical skills on the platform; he was an early parliamentary mentor of Greenwood to whom he remained a life-long icon.* The same was not true of Asquith. He was a distant figure, although something of a hero for having introduced, with the coopera-tion of Botha and Smuts, self-government for the Union of South Africa. Certainly for Greenwood the swift creation of another Dominion expressed the "new imperialism." During Asquith's eight years as prime minister, however, there is no evidence that he ever regarded Greenwood as more than a loyal backbencher.

Undeterred by Laurier's statement that currently there was no legal work available, Greenwood crossed to Canada again in September 1908, the third time in three years. Possibly he hoped to upstage the Conser-vative MP from Ontario, Donald Macmaster, who was still seen in Lon-don as a more eminent Canadian barrister. Greenwood saw Mackenzie King in Ottawa and visited friends in Whitby, Toronto, and Montreal. In Vancouver and Victoria, he again spent time with McBride and those in his government who had earlier directed legal work – and a salmon cannery – to him. This time he did not need to talk much about racial violence. He had already congratulated Mackenzie King upon his report to Laurier recommending closer collaboration with London in restrict-ing Asian immigration (the next year King was also to have successful discussions in Japan). In his absence in Canada, his sister Bryddie (Florence) in London sent their congratulations to Churchill on his engagement to Clementine Hozier.[36]

Back at Westminster, Greenwood proposed – in vain – that the impe-rial question of immigrants from India be the subject of an Empire-wide conference. He also spoke about Germany's naval ambitions and the threat that they could represent to the hitherto unchallenged maritime supremacy of the Royal Navy. But in the spring of 1909, it was Lloyd George's budget that took up most of his parliamentary time. Beginning his controversial seven-year term as chancellor of the exchequer, Lloyd George launched his radical program of social reform in his "People's Budget" of April 1909 – in Roy Jenkin's words, "the most famous budget

---

* Mackenzie King visited John Burns at his London home in January 1900. It is possible that Greenwood introduced them, although there is no record that Greenwood and King called together on Burns in London in 1899–1900.

of the century." King Edward VII and the House of Lords condemned its proposals for redistribution of income through progressive taxation as "full of false statements of socialism in its most invidious form and of virulent abuse against one particular class." In a famous speech at Limehouse on 30 July, Lloyd George defended his budget "for raising money to wage implacable war against poverty and squalor." Unprecedented pensions for the aged and help for widows, orphans, the sick, and the infirm would be provided, despite mounting demands on the exchequer for the accelerated construction of dreadnoughts for the Royal Navy. Greenwood was enthusiastic in his support for the People's Budget, even managing to incorporate into his public and parliamentary advocacy of the budget repeated pleas for Home Rule for Ireland.

The successful adoption of the People's Budget by the House of Commons required Asquith to obtain a pledge from the new – and unreceptive – king, George V, to create sufficient additional Liberal peers to swamp the Conservative-dominated House of Lords if it were to be so ill-advised as to attempt to veto the budget bill. A "super tax" on higher incomes and a new tax on landholdings, and – in the name of temperance – more restrictive licensing of public houses and increased excise taxes on liquor were prominent among the budgetary provisions that so alienated the Conservative majority in the Lords that in November 1909 they committed the ultimate folly of rashly rejecting the People's Budget. King George, on the advice of his prime minister, thereupon dissolved Parliament. The ensuing Liberal victory in the "peers versus people" election of January 1910 in effect endorsed the budget (which was reluctantly adopted by the Lords in April) and curtailed the powers of the House of Lords.

In the election of January 1910, however, Greenwood came only a close third in the two-seat constituency of York, despite the Liberal victory nationally (Irish Nationalists and Labour held the balance of power). Although strongly endorsed in the campaign by both Churchill and the chief whip, he was nevertheless, in his own word, "displaced." He lost by one hundred votes to "a brewer [who] had the support of the organized drinks trade." Perhaps his three long transatlantic absences, or possibly the unexpected equivocations of Lloyd George about free trade, also contributed to his defeat. By October 1910, Lloyd George, who was plotting to head a coalition of Liberals and Conservatives, was no longer sounding as radical as Greenwood when he paid tribute to the now incapacitated Conservative Joseph Chamberlain and his campaign for "tariff reform" (i.e., tariff protection) and imperial military cooperation. The *Yorkshire Herald* noted the widening gulf between Greenwood and his vacillating erstwhile mentor. "Many Liberals will rub their eyes when they read Mr. Lloyd George's statement ... calculated to send an ardent Party man like the ex-Liberal Member for York [Greenwood] into fits."[37]

The other Liberal candidate in York came first in the polls. Earlier in 1910, the Rowntrees, who had been instrumental in securing the Liberal nomination for Greenwood in 1906, had arranged for a family member to be the other Liberal candidate in 1910: Arnold Rowntree, well experienced in the family cocoa business but a neophyte in politics.* Before the election Greenwood had written to John Burns, asking him for "a strong personal letter saying the best you can of me. Arnold Rowntree, one of the cocoa firm, is running with me and we hope to win both seats. I wish you would also endorse him."[38]

Mackenzie King did not doubt that Greenwood's furlough from Parliament would be brief. In common with Borden, Governor General Lord Grey, the premier of Alberta, and "Canadians generally," he wrote, "I regretted your defeat at York. However, we all recognized that you were up against terrific odds and that it is only a temporary affair ... an incident affording a breathing spell between battles, and that the time will be short before you again have a seat in the British House ... Each day one seems to get new light on the greatness of the opportunity which public life in Canada, and perhaps even more so in the British Empire, affords."[39] In the same letter, King asked Greenwood's advice on whether an amendment to the British North America Act of 1867 would need to be sought if he were finally able to convince his reluctant cabinet colleagues that the government should proceed with social legislation "to conduct enquiries on subjects affecting the welfare of the working classes" and, more specifically, an eight-hour day, workmen's compensation, and possibly even a national insurance program covering accidents and illness. Greenwood replied both accurately and regretfully that, given present jurisdictions, an address from the

---

* As a Quaker and a pacifist, Arnold Rowntree would later become an outspoken critic of Asquith and Grey in the months preceding the First World War. Like other anti-war members, he was defeated in the "khaki election" of December 1918, never to return to the House of Commons.

Canadian Parliament to the British Parliament seeking an amendment to the BNA Act would indeed be necessary.*

In sending his thanks for King's kind thoughts, and offering his jurisdictional advice, Greenwood added the news that he was contemplating marriage and suggested it was time that King did so as well. King, already aware from newspaper reports of Greenwood's intentions, responded simply that it was unlikely in his case.

* The accuracy of Greenwood's advice was substantiated twenty-seven years later when the Judicial Committee of the Imperial Privy Council in 1937 ruled as *ultra vires* the "New Deal" social legislation of R.B. Bennett's Conservative government regarding, inter alia, minimum wages, hour of work, and unemployment insurance.

4

A Member for the Empire, 1910–1911

Greenwood spent most of the eleven months between the two elections of January and December 1910 pursuing both his growing legal practice and his frequent platform appearances, being "kept busy by Whips ... in support of Government policy and bills, especially the budget of 1910" (when it was finally adopted by the Lords). Although he had begun to represent in London Canadian mining interests, he had to wait more than two years for a brief from Ottawa, but when it arrived, it was a major and highly visible assignment.

Churchill had been informed by the governor general in Ottawa and the British ambassador in Washington that during the visit of Elihu Root, the US secretary of state, to Ottawa in January 1910, he would seek agreement on referring the chronic Newfoundland fisheries dispute to the newly established and Carnegie-funded Permanent Court of International Arbitration in the Hague. Britain agreed on behalf of Newfoundland. Laurier, contemplating a comprehensive tariff reciprocity agreement with the United States, welcomed the opportunity for Canada to clear away as many irritants as possible in the bilateral relationship. One such was the Newfoundland dispute.

For some years a *modus operandi* had neutralized the issue, but recent action by Newfoundland to exclude foreign fishing vessels from provisioning in its ports led to the agreed reference to the Hague Tribunal, which idealists everywhere hoped would in time prove to be the universal alternative to what Laurier called "the awful arbitment of war." The tribunal began its sittings in June 1910 with members selected from Argentina, Austro-Hungary, and the Netherlands. Sir Allen Aylesworth, the minister of justice for Canada, was "agent" for Britain and Newfoundland as well as for Canada. Greenwood, to his great satisfaction, was appointed one of a long list of learned counsel, including Asquith's brilliant barrister son,

Raymond. Mary Greenwood wrote to her brother from Cincinnati where she was the director of nursing at a hospital, that she was "so glad he got a brief in the Fisheries arbitration." So was he, having made certain beforehand that Laurier and Aylesworth were well aware of his availability in London, free for the time being of commitments in the House of Commons. From the Hague Tribunal in the summer of 1910, Greenwood wrote to friends in both Britain and Canada about how satisfactorily for Canada and Newfoundland he thought that the hearings were progressing. With their successful conclusion in early September, and with each of the four parties more or less satisfied, a way had been opened to Greenwood to seek other assignments on behalf of Canada. (He could not of course foresee that Laurier's Liberals would be defeated by Borden's Conservatives in little more than a year.)

Back in London with the success of the Hague Tribunal behind him, Greenwood, still out of Parliament, "gave away" in marriage his thirty-one-year-old sister, Adeliza Florence Louise. Named for their aunt Adeliza in Wales, her sobriquet had long been "Bryddie." On 16 November 1910, she married the thirty-seven-year-old Leopold Charles Moritz Stennett Amery. Witnesses were Prime Minister Asquith and the recently appointed solicitor general, Sir John Simon (who had been elected a Fellow of All Souls the same day as Amery). Among the guests were the former prime minister, Arthur Balfour, the archbishop of York, and the imperial proconsul, Lord Milner.* One of Bryddie's three sisters wrote candidly to her that Amery "was a dear, dear man, but no presence at all. Every girl fancies for her lover a golden-haired, blue-eyed prince." He was certainly not that, being short, dark, and bespectacled, but for Greenwood, temporarily out of the House of Commons, the marriage was a matter of satisfaction. He, a Liberal MP, now had as a brother-in-law someone who was a coming man and sooner or later would be a Conservative MP. However, the *Daily Mail* in an understatement noted that the political opinions of the two men did "not quite coincide," Greenwood being a free trader and Amery "one of the most distinguished of tariff reformers" (i.e., a protectionist). Equally, on Ireland they could hardly have been farther apart, Greenwood being a persistent and unyielding advocate of Home Rule and Amery a staunch opponent. Within two years Amery was to write a series of seventeen

---

* Asquith went directly from the wedding ceremony to the king who reluctantly agreed to create the necessary Liberal peers to assure passage of the Parliament Bill through the House of Lords, thereby opening the way for the successful adoption of a much-belated Home Rule bill in 1914.

articles for the *Morning Post*, published in 1912 as a pamphlet *The Case against Home Rule*.

Three years younger than Greenwood, Amery was born in India on 22 November 1873. His father, Charles Frederick Amery (b. 1833), had gone to the Australian gold rush before joining the newly formed Indian Forestry Commission. In January 1873 in London he married Elizabeth Johanna Saphir Leitner, a Jewish Hungarian who had converted to Christianity. They had three sons of whom Leopold was the oldest.* Elizabeth divorced her husband in 1885, alleging adultery. He thereupon disappeared into Ontario where he was briefly a farmer before moving on to New York City to become co-editor of a dictionary. He died in poverty as a gold prospector in British Guiana, having had no contact with his three sons after the divorce.

Amery was a brilliant student at Harrow (decidedly more so than his near-contemporary, Churchill) and an outstanding Oxford undergraduate with notable linguistic skills. With his childhood friend F.E. Smith – the future Lord Birkenhead – he was elected a Fellow of All Souls at an unusually young age of twenty-five before joining the staff of the *Times* in 1899, just as the war in South Africa was beginning.† Having met the charismatic Lloyd George, he toyed briefly with the idea of becoming a Liberal candidate for Parliament, but instead he pursued journalism, later writing the seven-volume *The Times History of the War in South Africa* and collaborating with Lord Milner in the postwar reconstruction of the new Union of South Africa. In 1902 he became a barrister but never practised. Given his ambitions to be the editor of the *Times*, he declined Cecil Harmsworth's offer of the editorship of the *Observer*. Whatever his current occupation, he became known "as the Empire's theoretician" in the Conservative Party, always thinking positively about the future possibilities of the Empire evolving into a commonwealth.

Bryddie Greenwood, after graduating in modern languages and history from Trinity College in the University of Toronto and teaching for several years in Toronto, had suffered "a nervous collapse." Her older sister, Mary, the nurse in Cincinnati, took her to England where the two

---

* Both of Leopold Amery's brothers died in the First World War.
† As boys, Amery and Smith had sat together for the Harrow entry examination. To Smith's everlasting consternation, only Amery was offered a place, but at Oxford they became friends and travelling companions. Later, however, Smith dismissed Amery as being "always wrong" politically.

sisters and their brother Hamar were frequent quests at the London residence of Lord Stanley, the former governor general of Canada. There Bryddie met Amery. By October 1909 when he began to write to "My dear Miss Greenwood" from Canada, she was helping to prepare her brother's campaign in York for the next general election. Amery, on his third visit to Canada, accompanied the governor general, Earl Grey, to Hudson's Bay and specifically to Fort Churchill to assess its potential as a transatlantic grain port. The enthusiastic Grey, later described by Greenwood as having come to Canada as an Englishman and returned to England a Canadian, was well matched with Amery in his "enlightened imperialism." He strongly supported an imperial federation with Ireland as a member, an inchoate concept that Amery developed in speeches to the Empire Club and the Military Institute in Toronto, as well as during a few days spent at Lindsay, Ontario, with Sam Hughes, the ebullient Conservative member for Victoria-Halliburton. Everywhere, Amery enthusiastically endorsed Joseph Chamberlain's call for a united Empire underpinned by a preferential tariff and imperial defence cooperation, including "compulsory training for national defence." He returned to London in early November "to the greatest and happiest adventure of my life," his marriage to Bryddie. His singleminded goal remained the House of Commons, but within a month of their wedding came the second general election of 1910 in which Amery was again defeated.

Before that election, the Liberal chief whip had invited Greenwood to return his York seat to the Rowntrees and to stand instead in Sunderland, a Durham county industrial town noted for its heavy industry, especially shipbuilding. Three weeks after the wedding of his sister, Greenwood was duly re-elected to Parliament. His "manifest victory ..., received with great jubilation by the Liberals," was again unexpected, a reversal of Liberal fortunes that exceeded that in any other constituency and a second personal electoral triumph for Greenwood.[1] By a 1,700 vote margin he and the other Liberal candidate in Sunderland defeated both sitting Conservatives, the eccentric and evangelical teetotaller and future home secretary, William "Jix" Joynson-Hicks, and a backbencher with the memorable name of Samuel Samuel.* The national results

---

* The Conservative William Joynson-Hicks – "Jix" – had earlier been defeated by Churchill in Manchester in an equally spectacular Liberal victory. He was elected in Sunderland in January 1910, only to be defeated by Greenwood in December. A solicitor "of limited intelligence," one of his few major clients was the London General Omnibus

were similar to those of the election of January: the Liberals and Labour combined had a plurality of forty-two seats over the Conservatives. The following year, in a by-election, Amery finally joined his brother-in-law, now a veteran of five years in the House, and Churchill, his schoolmate at Harrow, already a veteran of ten.

Greenwood was hardly back in the new Parliament in February 1911, after a year's absence, before he began to speak of the urgent need for improvement to the arms and other equipment of the army. Even more, he called for an annual payment to MPs as one means of "democratising" the House of Commons, a broad subject to which he was to return several times in the years immediately ahead. He also took a major part in yet another tariff debate, having been absent during the 1910 debate. Although presented as if the 1911 debate were about the Canada-US initiative to reduce or eliminate their tariffs against each other, it was really about the proposal advanced as early as the Colonial Conference of 1897 by Joseph Chamberlain. Britain should abandon its policy of free trade (pursued since the repeal of the Corn Laws in 1846) and erect tariff walls against imports, except from the Dominions.

Many people in Britain were either ignorant of the Empire, disregarded it, or at best were vaguely in favour of it as long as it did not cost them anything. The one insurmountable problem with Joseph Chamberlain's strong tariff advocacy was that the cost of imports – above all, food – would increase with the imposition of tariffs. The elementary political understanding that higher food prices are never welcome to electorates anywhere at any time had prompted the Liberal Party to affirm its free-trade heritage unequivocally, setting its face against any policy that would increase the cost of imported grain and other foodstuffs from Russia (especially the Ukraine), Romania, or the Argentine. The popular aversion to "stomach taxes" was such that it split even the imperialist-minded Conservative Party, leaving Balfour continuing to struggle to maintain some unity between "tariff reform" imperialists and those who were convinced that "stomach taxes" were simply political suicide.

In her contemporary novel, *The Imperialist*, Sara Jeannette Duncan has her hero, Lorne Murchison, a Liberal candidate in a southern Ontario constituency, proclaim his allegiance to the greater unity of the

---

Company when it settled Greenwood's accident claim. Four other "Canadian MPs" were elected or re-elected: the Liberal Allen Baker, the Radical Liberal Joseph Martin, the Conservative-Unionist Donald Macmaster, and the Conservative Max Aitken (the Conservative Bonar Law was defeated).

Empire, but he remains sceptical of the willingness of the British people to pay more for their food in order to foster that greater imperial unity. Murchison recalls the short-lived benefits to Canada of the "Canada Corn [wheat] Bill" that in 1843 appeared to promise unparalleled prosperity. Within three years that prospect disappeared with the repeal of the Corn Laws in 1846. "The wheat of the world flowed into every port in England and the hopes of Canada ... based then, as now, on 'preferential treatment' were blasted to the root. Now [Murchison] did not blame the people of England for insisting on [tariff-] free food. It was policy that suited their interests, and they had just as good a right to look after their interests ... as anybody else. But he did blame the British Government for holding out hopes ... to a young and struggling nation, which they must have known they would be unable to redeem. In plain words ... Great Britain had sold them before, and she would sell them again, He stood before them as loyal to British connection as any man. He addressed a public as loyal to British connection as any public. *But* – once bitten twice shy."[2]

In the tariff debates of 1911 Greenwood did not parrot Murchison, but he was decidedly uncomfortable. As an active backbencher, he was seen with Prime Minister Asquith and certain others in the Liberal Party as a liberal-imperialist, but it was Asquith who, paradoxically, had in effect ruled out closer imperial diplomatic or military ties by proclaiming in 1911 that there could be no sharing in the formulation of foreign policy with the self-governing colonies, who were themselves wary of military commitments. That left only closer economic ties on the table. But the Liberals in Ottawa were now seeking a trade agreement with the United States, leaving Greenwood in the awkward position of reconciling closer imperial economic ties on the one hand with liberalized trade with the United States on the other. Murchison, the Liberal candidate in Duncan's *The Imperialist*, summed up "the present British idea" for his audience by proclaiming bluntly that it was "to secure the Canadian market for British goods, and a handsome contribution from the Canadian taxpayer toward the expense of the British army and navy in return for the offer of favours to food supplies from Canada."

As early as 1854, British North America and the United States had agreed upon tariff reciprocity, but Washington had terminated it in 1866, partly in the mistaken belief that British North America, in the aftermath of the US Civil War, was so economically reduced that it would have little option but to sue for full political union. Instead, four of the British North American colonies had come together in a confederation as the Dominion of Canada the following year. Learning to live with higher US tariffs, the new Dominion had eventually followed with its own higher tariffs in Macdonald's "National Policy" of 1879. Once Laurier came to office in 1896, he too showed little interest in Joseph Chamberlain's dramatic call for greater imperial unity by tariff preference. Fielding, Laurier's finance minister, did unilaterally give a trade preference to the United Kingdom, which earned from Rudyard Kipling the laudatory "Our Lady of the Snows," the only ode ever written to a tariff preference. Laurier's government asked nothing of the British in return, thereby underlining that Canada's fiscal policy was for Ottawa alone to define.

By 1911, when Greenwood joined the debate, Canadian exports to the United States were flourishing, despite continuing high tariffs. With American immigrants flooding into the new prairie provinces, Laurier again asserted Canada's well-established freedom to decide its own commercial policies. He negotiated a draft trade agreement with Washington that some in Canada as well as in Britain deplored as a move toward North American commercial union, which in their view would lead, *nolens volens*, to political union. At Westminster, the exponents of imperial unity on the Conservative benches seized upon the draft Canada-US trade agreement as conclusive proof that if only Chamberlain's imperial *Zollverein* had been in place, Canada would not now be risking absorption into the United States.

The debate lasted several days, following the introduction on 8 February 1911 of a motion by the "Canadian MP" from Trenton, Ontario, Allen Baker, regretting that the British government had failed "to modify the fiscal system of the country ... has deferred the closer commercial union of the Empire, and has deprived the country of the most effective method of inducing foreign countries to grant fair treatment to British manufacturers."[3] For two days, the Commons, taking as its starting point what Canada and the United States proposed to do in "tariff reciprocity," concentrated instead upon the merits – or demerits – of "tariff reform" in the United Kingdom, the Canada-US draft agreement being seen by some as the final nail in the coffin of Chamberlain's long-standing proposal for an imperial *Zollverein*. To be sure, frequent reference was made to Canada, especially by several members who had travelled in Canada or were Canadians by birth, but Canada was not what the debate was really about.

The Conservative Austen Chamberlain, the conventional son of the unconventional Joseph, began the debate by stating that, had his father's imperial scheme been adopted, Wilfrid Laurier would never have contemplated a tariff agreement with the United States. Another Conservative, however, followed a quite different tack. Alfred Lyttelton, the former colonial secretary, who had never been a supporter of Joseph Chamberlain, spoke soon after his son, emphasizing that Canadians knew very well what they were doing in contemplating again a tariff reciprocity agreement with the United States: "The national consciousness was instinctively opposed to the commercial union which was held ... to imperil national integrity. Canadians had long been taught ... that commercial union spelt political union." But, Lyttelton argued, the pending tariff agreement that Fielding had negotiated with President Taft did no such thing. Asquith followed Lyttelton in a similar vein, even welcoming the proposed Canada-US agreement: "It is alleged against us that if we had been wise enough to put a tax upon foreign food coming into this country – in other words to give what is called a preference to the Colonies – we might have stopped the conclusion of this agreement ... In whose interest were we to do that? Was it in our interest to increase the price of food to the population of this country in order that the wall of tariffs might still remain between Canada and the United States? Was it in the interest of Canada? Surely, Canada is the best judge of her own interest." The feline Arthur Balfour, leader of the opposition, as always wary of the political impact within the Conservative Party of Austen Chamberlain's filial advocacy of "tariff reform," nevertheless responded to Asquith with Joseph Chamberlain's early argument "that it would be for the benefit of the Empire as a political whole, for the benefit of the Empire as an economic whole, if we did treat our self-governing Colonies better than we treat the foreigners."[4]

In the two-day debate, Greenwood "as a Canadian" faced what he called the "bitter antagonism" of the tariff reformers. He rebutted Balfour with a staunch defence of Laurier's liberal trade policy, flatly rejecting Balfour's description of the proposed Canada-US tariff reciprocity agreement as "an imperial disaster." It was not that, he said: it was an act of statesmanship. The 1911 bill in the Canadian Parliament followed from the stillborn 1889 Bayard treaty that "was never promulgated, because the Senate of the United States ... declined to pass a treaty which had anything in it friendly either to Canada or the United Kingdom." Greenwood as a free trader condemned Balfour's suggestion that "Tariff Reformers in the Old Country should ally themselves with those [of like-mind] in the overseas colonies. I say ... the most serious thing that could happen for the integrity of the British Empire is to interfere by political organisation with the absolute self-governing integrity of the colonies over the seas ... Canada is not a Belgium, or a Holland, or some German principality ... You cannot treat growing Dominions like Canada, Australia, and New Zealand as if they were Uganda or Zululand or Burmah."

With "Bloody Balfour," the former chief secretary for Ireland, in his sights, Greenwood added a passage about Ireland: "Is not the friendliness of the United States now due to the fact that, happily, bitterness against Ireland in this realm [England] is declining, and that the political hopes of the Irish people of this country, of the United States, and of the Colonies have made it easier ... to arrange this agreement ...?" Drawing upon Hansard, the *Canadian Annual Review* summed up Greenwood's contribution to the debate: "Mr. Hamar Greenwood, M.P., expresses the following British Liberal view: 'A reasonable arrangement, including untaxed foodstuffs, between Canada and the United States, came as no surprise to those who have seen the growing determination of the democracies of both countries to decrease the cost of living by wiping out food taxes, and, secondly, to decrease the restrictions on trade by lowering and ultimately wiping out the many taxes on manufactured articles ... Of course, if this reciprocal arrangement is adopted, the bottom is knocked out of the Tariff Reform movement in England so far as the preference to Canadian foodstuffs is concerned. It would be impossible to differentiate between Canadian and American wheat if there is no tax on corn [wheat] levied by either country.'"[5]

The Conservative "Canadian MP" Donald Macmaster (and former member of the Ontario legislature) who followed Greenwood in the debate differed with him fundamentally, urging Canada's participation in an imperial *Zollverein*. But at least three other members supported Greenwood, speaking "with great knowledge of Canada, having lived or travelled extensively there," and describing in enthusiastic terms "the great Dominion which has enjoyed fiscal autonomy as well as local and political autonomy for half a century and whose record in relation to this country is one of ever-increasing devotion and loyalty." The Liberal Sir Alfred Moritz Mond, with his leading role in developing what in time would become the International Nickel Company of Canada (INCO), extolled the love of Canadians for the empire and welcomed the Canada-US provisional trade agreement "as a step toward Anglo-Saxon free trade." Sir John Simon, the barrister friend of both Greenwood and Amery, summed up for the government: "Our united wish now is that we should send from this British House of Commons to Canada the message ... we are certain that the choice which she is now going to make will make no difference to the ties of affection and devotion which now unite us." The proposal to introduce a general tariff with preferences for the Dominions was defeated by 324 to 222, but the prospect of a Canada-US trade agreement ended seven months later in September 1911, with the defeat of Laurier's Liberals by Borden's Conservatives.

Greenwood, knowing that Laurier would be in London in May 1911 for the coronation of King George V and an accompanying imperial conference and Festival of Empire – when coincidentally the Lauriers could be invited to his wedding – added to his efforts at Westminster to increase British understanding of Canada's proposed tariff reciprocity agreement with the United States. On 13 February, four days after the conclusion of the debate, Greenwood took another swipe at any food taxes, telling the London correspondent of the *Toronto Daily Star* that Canada, "the most virile of modern countries ... cannot be and ought not to be kept in leading strings in the shape of preferential tariff arrangements in the name of the Empire." In turn, at dinners of the Canada Club and the Pilgrims (Greenwood was a future president of both), Laurier went out of his way to state his allegiance to the Empire, memorably proclaiming that "I love the United States, but as much as I love them, I love Britain still more, and if our friends on the other side of the line were to come and ask us to join them, our answer would be the answer of Diogenes to Alexander: 'Move away out of our sunlight.'" Amidst this liberal imperialism, Greenwood again managed to insert an enthusiastic statement in support of Home Rule for Ireland: "The plain fact is that the great mass of our Canadian kinsmen have not, and do not, look upon Tariff Reform in England as a serious contribution to imperial unity ... The one weak link in the Imperial chain – as Sir Wilfrid has again and again emphasized – is the withholding of Home Rule from Ireland. Such a grant would make not only a contented Ireland in the United Kingdom, but would bring a wave of sentiment and support from twelve millions of Irishmen now living abroad."[6]

Three months later, on 23 May 1911, Greenwood and Margery (not yet Margo) Spencer married, four years after their first meeting in Jamaica. The bride at age twenty-four was seventeen years younger than the forty-one-year-old bridegroom.* The future bishop of Durham officiated. Sir Wilfrid and Lady Laurier attended, along with three of Laurier's ministers: Sir Frederick Borden, minister of militia; Rodolphe

---

* The *Toronto Daily Star*, while misspelling Margo's name as "Marjorie," gushed, "One of England's most beautiful women ... a member of a family of high social distinction."

Lemieux, postmaster general; and Louis Brodeur, minister of marine and fisheries. The wedding was at the fashionable St Margaret's, Westminster, the aisles lined with troopers from the Canadian Squadron of King Edward's Horse. The bride, given away by her father, the Reverend Walter Spencer, was later described by the *Toronto World*, the newspaper of her new brother-in-law, Billy Greenwood, as being "of an ancient, dignified and not impoverished family."[7] One of her sisters was a bridesmaid, as were two of Greenwood's. One of her two brothers, Robert, attended. The best man, Sir Harry Verney, was a fellow Liberal who had been assistant private secretary to his father-in-law, the earl of Elgin, secretary of state for the colonies, when Greenwood was PPS to Churchill, the under-secretary. Greenwood had invited Mackenzie King to be his best man, but King could not leave Ottawa.

At the wedding reception, Asquith, the prime minister, joined the prime ministers of Canada and New Zealand and the wife of the prime minister of South Africa. British ministers included Lloyd George, chancellor of the exchequer; John Burns, president of the Local Government Board; Herbert Samuel, postmaster general; Lord Loreburn, lord chancellor; Lewis Harcourt, colonial secretary; and Walter Runciman, minister of education. Churchill, the home secretary, sent regrets. Among the other guests were Lord Strathcona, the Canadian high commissioner, five "Canadian MPs" at Westminster, including Sir Charles Rose, the son of Sir John A. Macdonald's second minister of finance, and six other MPs, including John Redmond, the leader of the Irish Nationalists, and Greenwood's new brothers-in-law and die-hard Conservative-Unionists Leo Amery and Wilfrid Ashley. During their long engagement, Greenwood and Margery Spencer had spent time with her Mcgillicuddy relatives in Ireland where they would also go for a brief honeymoon. As political weddings go, Greenwood had certainly arrived.

Margery Spencer was the daughter of the Reverend Walter Spencer (b. 1849) of Manchester and Annie Elizabeth Hudson, the daughter of Robert Hudson of Chester, a prosperous soap manufacturer. They had five children: two sons, Robert and Geoffrey, and three daughters, Margery, Muriel, and Olive. Walter Spencer, a graduate of Cambridge, held during the thirteen years following his ordination several urban and rural livings before he retired at the early age of forty-one from his priestly vocation. In the words of his obituary, he was "a man of means ... [who] relinquished holy orders ... to devote himself to private pursuits." An enthusiastic collector of old porcelain, oak carvings, and clocks, he was also an expert horticulturist and an accomplished musician.[8]

Walter Spencer lived in considerable affluence – *Saturday Night,* perhaps with some hyperbole, described him as "a gentleman of great wealth" – but of pronounced seclusion, first at Codicote Hall and from about 1909 at Fownhope Court, both in Herefordshire. He also had a villa at San Remo in Italy. His wife, after giving birth to their five children, became increasingly bedridden. From about 1900, when their youngest daughter was still a child, she seldom left the house. She was still living as an invalid upon the death of her husband in June 1922.

The eldest daughter, Margery, was born on 20 December 1886 at Sapiston vicarage near Bury St Edmonds. She was sent to fashionable girls' schools in Eversley and Folkstone before completing her schooling in Switzerland where she became fluent in French, a capable horsewoman, and a competent painter and sculptor. During vacations at San Remo, she also became proficient in Italian. Eventually Spencer followed his wife in declaring himself a chronic invalid, taking to his bed and, like his wife, seldom thereafter leaving it. He disliked physicians and would not see them. His death on 2 June 1922 at age seventy-three at Fownhope Court was reported in the Hereford newspapers as that of a "priest who lived like a hermit," although a decidedly affluent one. Neither neighbours nor any of his five children except Margery (who had by then changed her name to the more fashionable Margo) and Greenwood attended his funeral. In his later life Spencer seldom saw his two sons. The elder, Robert, attended his sister's wedding but later resided in China. The younger, Geoffrey, sent a gold watch as a wedding gift but did not attend.

The Spencer family had become what later generations would call "dysfunctional." There is no mention of Walter Spencer in the now much depleted papers of the Greenwoods or elsewhere, other than that he gave away his daughter at her wedding. There is no record that her mother attended. Whether Margo's two sisters had, like her, been despatched to Switzerland for finishing is unrecorded, but in any case the three sisters appear in time to have seen little of each other. The marriage of Muriel ("Molly") to Rear Admiral the Hon. Arthur Lionel Ochoncar Forbes-Sempill ended in divorce. She then married Wilfrid Ashley, the Conservative MP for Blackpool, a few days before the First World War. (Ashley, like Greenwood and several other MPs of the Parliamentary Recruiting Committee, immediately undertook to raise a battalion of volunteers, in Ashley's case the 20th Battalion, the King's

Liverpool Regiment). Ashley had been first elected to Parliament in 1906, the same year as Greenwood, but they had little in common other than being married to sisters.* He was a Conservative-Unionist, a friend of Edward Carson, and hostile to Irish Home Rule in any form. A staunch anti-socialist and a landowner in Sligo, he saw Irish republicanism as part of a larger international conspiracy to undermine the British Empire.

Margo's co-executor, Alexander Greenwood, observed how, being from her schooldays of an ambitious and decidedly independent mind, she attempted to manage her husband as well as her four children.[†] She also took an intense interest in politics; her husband claimed with some hyperbole during the First World War that she "knows every Member of the House of Commons, which she attends regularly."[9] The gossip journalist Amy Stuart Menzies observed her closely: "Those who used to see [Greenwood] going up to the House for some difficult and stormy

---

* Wilfrid Ashley's first wife was "Maudie" Cassel, the only child of the financier Sir Ernest Cassel. They had two daughters, the elder of whom, Edwina, later married Lord Mountbatten. In time, Ashley, like John Amery, regarded Hitler as the saviour of Europe from Bolshevism and advocated that Britain should fight alongside Germany "in the next war"; later he modified his more vocal support for the anti-Semitic Nazi regime, his two daughters being themselves half-Jewish. He resigned as president of the Anglo-German Fellowship but only in November 1938, less than a year before the beginning of the war. Ashley served in Parliament for twenty-six years, briefly as minister of transport, before joining Greenwood in the House of Lords in 1932 as Lord Mount-Temple. Margo's youngest sister, Olive, with whom she also had few ties, married Cecil Hagg of Fownhope. She died in 1968, a few weeks before Margo.

† Author's conversation with Alexander Greenwood, 10 March 2008. In the case of their two daughters, Margo's efforts resulted in difficulties. Angela Margo Hamar Greenwood (1912–2014) married a prosperous estate agent, Edward Dudley Delevingne, and lived quietly thereafter, seldom seeing her mother. Deborah (b. 1917) married three times. Her first marriage in 1940, dissolved thirty years later in 1970, was to Group Captain Patrick de László, RAF, son of the celebrated Anglo-Hungarian portrait painter Philip de László (1869–1937) and his wife, Lucy Guinness. Deborah presumably met him while serving as a WAAF in 1940. Although each of Deborah's marriages should on the face of it have met the test of Margo's indelible social ambitions, she for some reason approved of none, becoming so alienated from both daughters that she not only excluded them from her last will but instructed her co-executors that no note should be taken even of their existence in her death notice in the *Times*. The elder son and heir, David Hamar Greenwood (b. 1914), was, in the words of Margo's co-executor, "born an imbecile" (although Margo always preferred the explanation that he had been dropped on his head when an infant). The second son, Eric (b. 1923), later Michael, conformed to her every wish, and in return was almost smothered with adoration and constant indulgence. A flamboyant homosexual, he never married and had no children.

debate knew how much it had lowered his vitality, and her approval was what he sought first and won, when the debate was over ... She used to sit night after night in the Gallery of the House watching her husband anxiously and it was often a very cold little hand that met his clasp when all was over, for the nerve strain and tension were very trying; she knew what he was up against, and how faithless were some of his colleagues. She is a wife in a thousand, and Sir Hamar is very proud of her."[10]

Women over age thirty received the vote only in 1918 (lowered to age twenty-one in 1928). The first woman MP to take her seat did so in 1919. Margo, however, like a heroine in a Trollope novel, lived her political life vicariously. She travelled with her husband everywhere, took an unusually active role in his several constituencies, and eventually faced unflinchingly the abundant dangers of Ireland, the whole time attempting to advance his political career. Before 1918 the only way that she and other wives of MPs could themselves directly experience political power was to marry politicians or to have affairs with them, especially ministers or ideally the prime minister.

When the affair between the ambitious Margo and the licentious Lloyd George (not for nothing was he known as "The Goat") began – either before or after her marriage to Greenwood – or how long it lasted is unknown. Certainly the Greenwoods spent a holiday with him on the French Riviera in January 1912. Her executor is convinced that the liaison started before 1914, when Lloyd George, then chancellor of the exchequer, hastily arranged with Asquith, the prime minister, for Greenwood to receive a baronetcy and two salaries (one as an MP and the other as Deputy Assistant Adjutant General (DAAG) at the War Office). Greenwood's qualifications for the hereditary honour were not evident, although Lloyd George was beginning even then to be noted for his largesse – profitable to himself, as well as to his followers in the divided Liberal Party – in the sale of titles (an abuse that eventually became so flagrant that it contributed significantly to his political demise in late 1922).

The affair between Margo and Lloyd George was for him – and perhaps for her – only one of many. His principal (male) secretary later wrote, "He is mental on matters of sex ... A man and a woman could not possibly in his view be friends without sexual intercourse."[11] His early affairs ranged from "the wives of his parliamentary colleagues to secretaries in his office," and his conquests "were many and varied." He was, however, always careful to carry out "his liaisons with women who had a great deal to lose and nothing to gain by exposing him."[12] He fathered the child of a Welsh widow in 1890. He had a child by a relative of his wife in 1896. The following year, he had his first recorded affair, with the wife of a Liberal MP-to-be, Timothy Davies. Later, in 1911, an affair with the American wife of another Liberal MP, Charles Solomon Henry, became uncomfortably public. Saved by the ready denials of her husband, Lloyd George induced Asquith to provide Henry with a baronetcy.

In that same year, Frances Stevenson, a twenty-three-year-old graduate of the University of London, was first employed by Lloyd George as a governess for his younger daughter, Megan, partly on the basis that she had been a school friend of his beloved late daughter, Mair. Stevenson soon became both his personal assistant and his mistress. She remained so for thirty years until their late marriage in 1943, following the death in 1941 of Margaret, his remarkably loyal and patient wife of fifty-five years. The two lovers appear somehow to have managed – more or less – to keep their long-running affair away from her. More surprisingly, during the First World War and in its immediate aftermath, Stevenson watched Lloyd George's occasional flutters with seemingly little concern; they were no threat to her own primacy. She had a daughter by him and at least two abortions.

Whether Greenwood knew of his wife's relationship with Lloyd George is unrecorded, but from as early as 1912, Margo and Greenwood were often included in his weekend house parties, organized by Stevenson.* Many were at Lympne, the opulent country house in Kent of Philip Sassoon, Lloyd George's parliamentary private secretary, and later at Chequers, following the gift of the house by Lord and Lady Lee – the American Ruth Moore – to the nation. Lloyd George's commitment to his former mistress and her husband assumed yet more substantial form than their inclusion in house parties. Alexander Greenwood recognizes that Greenwood's appointment to the cabinet as chief secretary for Ireland had several reasons, but a principal one, the ambitious Margo later indicated to him, was her affair with Lloyd George, whose gratitude for those who played the game did not stop at invitations, a baronetcy, and other preferential treatment.[13]

---

* In the first half of 1912, Margo was pregnant. On 8 July 1912, the Greenwoods' first child, Angela Margo Hamar Greenwood, was born at home at 58 Onslow Gardens, four months after her cousin John Amery.

5

Pre-War Ambitions, 1911–1914

At the wedding of Hamar Greenwood and Margery Spencer, the recently elected Conservative member of Parliament Max Aitken and Greenwood's brother, Billy, were much together. At Greenwood's suggestion, Billy, upon his return to Toronto, began a correspondence with Aitken. He congratulated him upon his knighthood, which, after only six undistinguished months in the House of Commons, had appeared to some an act of gross political cynicism. Billy's second purpose in writing was to propose what might best be done with the money-losing periodical the *Canadian Century*, which Aitken and three corporate colleagues had begun the year before. (Aitken had already invested in the *Saint John Standard* and the *Montreal Herald*.) In 1905 Billy had become managing editor of the *London Free Press* before returning the following year to the *World*. He proposed to Aitken to resign as managing director of the *World* to become general manager of the *Canadian Century*, at the considerable annual salary of $5,000. "I am a newspaper man and a man of action, physically fit and mentally matured," he told Aitken. "I rather think that I could do things as big as you can dream."[1]

The brothers Greenwood may already have been aware that no sooner had the restless Aitken won his seat in Aston-under-Lyn (near Manchester) than he began to toy with the idea of returning to Canada to seek a constituency in the national election foreseen for 1911. With the endorsement of the Conservative leader, Robert Borden, the Ontario-born (but British resident) Aitken would be a candidate in New Brunswick where he had spent his childhood. Aitken, however, abandoned the novel idea of sitting in both parliaments as quickly as he had adopted it, He later congratulated Billy for the part that he had played "in the enormous victory" of Borden over Laurier, despite the fact that earlier Billy had repeatedly used the pages of the *World* to extol the Liberals, including Mackenzie King, partly at his brother's urging.

Aitken concluded that, having decided to pursue his imperial interests from Britain alone rather than simultaneously in Canada, he did not need the failing *Canadian Century*. Impatient at its losses, he closed it in September 1911, concentrating instead upon the much more ambitious goal of acquiring control of London's *Daily Express*. Nevertheless, he wrote to Billy on 22 September 1911, "I am going to Montreal soon and will of course see you and discuss the matters we have referred to in past conversations," but nothing is in the Aitken papers about what exactly "the matters" were.[2] Soon Billy became entangled in legal proceedings arising from the collapse of the Farmers' Bank in Ontario, and the efforts of *The World* to induce the provincial government to place significant deposits with the bank to help keep it solvent. Aitken, no stranger himself to convoluted and questionable financial manoeuvrings, may have decided that he needed no more reputation as a mischief-maker and adventurer, even by remote implication. Billy departed for the salmon cannery in British Columbia.

Aitken had been born in Maple, Ontario, in May 1879, nine years after Greenwood's birth at Whitby, some sixty kilometres or so distant, but the family soon moved to New Brunswick. From there and from Montreal, Aitken had rapidly amassed a considerable fortune, but he moved hastily to Britain in mid-1910, following his unsavoury manipulations of the Canada Cement combine. At Westminster he immediately set about creating his own political network, whether Liberal or Conservative. Partly through the Conservative F.E. Smith, he became friends with – among others – the Liberals Churchill and Lloyd George as well as the Irish Nationalist MP Tim Healy.[*]

Aitken did not neglect other Canadians in London if they could be useful to him. It was he who in 1911 introduced Greenwood to James Dunn, another New Brunswicker already flourishing in the City. When Aitken first visited Britain in 1908, he had met Bonar Law, yet another New Brunswicker and the only British prime minister to come from the colonies. After Aitken decided in 1910 that it would be prudent to absent himself from Canada, he ensured that, through his thriving Royal Securities Trust Company in Montreal, Bonar Law benefited from

---

[*] Clementine Churchill disliked Aitken at least as much as she later did Greenwood. She advised her husband, "Try ridding yourself of this microbe."

a range of transatlantic investments. It was at Law's prompting and on the advice of F.E. Smith that Aitken agreed to be the Conservative candidate in Aston-under-Lyn only a fortnight before the election itself in December 1910.* It was in turn partly the result of Aitken's tireless manoeuvrings that the two principal contenders to succeed Arthur Balfour as Conservative leader, Walter Long and Austen Chamberlain, withdrew to make way in November 1911 for the habitually introspective and melancholic Bonar Law. Lloyd George was not impressed with the new Conservative leader; he was "honest to the point of simplicity ... That is the difference between Bonar Law and me. Poor Bonar can't bear being called a liar [whereas] ... I don't mind."[3]

With the free trade election in Canada in October 1911, Borden somewhat unexpectedly became prime minister and Laurier again leader of the opposition. The proposed trade reciprocity agreement with the United States died, but two fundamental questions regarding the Dominion's role in the Empire remained to the fore. Should Canada, post–South African War, undertake to play a more active part in imperial foreign and defence policy? If so, should it, like Australia and New Zealand since 1902, contribute financially to the Royal Navy from whence came its maritime security, or should it, as Laurier had first advanced in 1909, create a Royal Canadian Navy? The first question about the role of the Dominions in the formulation of imperial foreign policy was partly answered by the agreement that the Dominion premiers would meet not less than once every four years. In the interim, Dominion ministers, either resident in London as high commissioner or simply visiting, could participate in the weekly meetings of the Committee of Imperial Defence (although only on the oft-repeated British understanding that it was a consultative and not a decision-making body).

The second question, about a naval contribution, was mired in partisan politics in both French and English Canada and, at a yet more fundamental level, involved the role of Canada in the Empire. Such questions could not be readily answered, but without missing a stroke, Greenwood moved at once from explaining Laurier's draft trade agreement with the United States to endorsing Borden's policy of Canadian

---

* At the time of the naval debate of 1911, Aitken offered to pay Churchill's expenses on a visit to Canada, as he would pay for F.E. Smith in 1912 and Healy in 1914. Aitken was later to play a major if not immediately apparent role in Greenwood's life, as he did in so many others.

cash support for the further expansion of the Royal Navy. Unless countered, the expanding and increasingly efficient German navy could
deter Britain from embarking upon a land war on the continent of
Europe, partly through threatening the maritime lifelines of the Empire.
Beginning with HMS *Dreadnought* in 1906, the Royal Navy was building
a class of battleship revolutionary in design that was seen as the sure
response to growing German naval construction. Although not forsaking his Liberal roots, Greenwood found compelling Borden's formulation that if there were to be a direct financial contribution to imperial
defence by Canada, the Dominion government was entitled to a voice in
imperial foreign policy: "Canada does not propose to become an adjunct
of even the British Empire."

The first test would be what entitlements a cash contribution to the
Royal Navy would bring. Greenwood learned more at first hand of the
naval support of Australia and New Zealand as a result of joining with
other British MPs and peers of strong imperial sentiment in founding
in 1911 the Imperial Parliamentary Association. They recognized that
the settlement colonies, having become self-governing Dominions,
made additional and more sophisticated intra-imperial consultative
links desirable, given the failure of Joseph Chamberlain to create an
imperial *Zollverein*. The Committee of Imperial Defence could offer one
such consultative link. In time, shipping subsidies and Empire marketing boards would provide other possibilities. More broadly, the shared
heritage of Westminster parliamentary democracy suggested yet another
route. Accordingly, at the time of the coronation of King George V
and the imperial conference of May 1911, MPs and peers from Britain
and the Dominions created the Empire Parliamentary Association on
a motion of Amery, seconded by Greenwood. It was increasingly widely
recognized that additional consultative links were desirable. During
the next decade, Greenwood was to continue to be active in the association, using it as another platform to extol the merits of imperial
collaboration.

In parallel, Greenwood continued to preach – and his brothers-in-law
Amery and Ashley to oppose – Home Rule for Ireland. At the time of his
wedding, Greenwood had been active in support of Asquith's appeal to
the new monarch to create the necessary number of Liberal peers to
ensure the passage through the House of Lords of the Parliament Act,
which would in turn open the way for the adoption of Irish Home Rule
by both houses. In August, despite the protests of diehards, the Lords
did pass the Parliament Act, leaving some supporters of Home Rule

relieved at the end of the constitutional crisis, but others recognizing that future Home Rule legislation would in fact have been assured of a much easier passage if the additional Liberal peers had first been created.

In the wake of the constitutional crisis over the powers of the House of Lords, Greenwood was relentless in his advocacy of Home Rule. In Toronto on a visit on 9 October 1911, he spoke to the Canadian Club about the response of the British Empire to any threat to its maritime security. "The Dominions have not yet done their fair share [in naval expansion]. But I realize that the trend of thought and affairs is in the right direction." It was, however, not defence cooperation that Greenwood reserved for his peroration. It was again Ireland, as it had been with his Empire Club speech in Toronto four years before. Amidst frequent applause, he told the Canadian Club, "Home Rule for Ireland is the predominant topic in the home country. The Government is gladly pledged to it and the bill will be introduced next year without a doubt. There are 103 Irish members in the House of Commons. Of these 86 are Home Rulers, and 17, anti-Home Rulers. These seventeen represent Ulster constituencies and they are militant Protestants. There are 16 Ulster Members who are Home Rulers. The number of anti-Home Rulers has been growing smaller for years."

Greenwood then took careful aim at the Orange prejudices that marred Ontario and concluded by advocating "Home Rule All Round":

All [that] the Irish party, through its leader, Mr Redmond, asks for is a constitution similar to the constitution of the Province of Ontario. The Irish have no desire to alter the present position with reference to the Imperial foreign policy, navy, or army. They are prepared to continue paying their share of Imperial taxes. Surely this is a reasonable request. Ireland has been shamefully treated. Her population has declined by four millions the last fifty years. And yet Roman Catholic Irishmen have fought and won the battles of the British Empire, and Roman Catholic Irishmen occupy honoured positions in this Dominion and throughout the English-speaking world. Thank God, old prejudices and gross ignorance are disappearing, and now in the United Kingdom, and I hope, throughout the British Empire, the predominant feeling is that Ireland is justly entitled to local self-government. In due course, the principle of local government will, I hope, be extended to England, Scotland, and Wales [i.e., Home Rule All Round].[4]

The following year, 1912, the cool and always articulate Asquith made a show, with whatever reservations, of attempting to implement Home Rule for Ireland – or what the more imaginative were beginning to foresee as Dominion Home Rule – by introducing in April a Government of Ireland bill. The new leader of the Conservative-Unionists, Bonar Law, an Ulsterman to his fingertips despite his Canadian birth and childhood, was prompt and clear in his rejection: "We shall oppose the Home Rule Bill by every means in our power. The Lords will not pass it ... It all turns on Ulster."[5] Antagonism to Home Rule in the Conservative-Unionist Party and in the militant opposition in Ulster had so mounted that mayhem and violence in the north of Ireland were becoming a real prospect.

Asquith's bill was no doubt a topic during a holiday in January 1912 that the Greenwoods and Lloyd George spent together on the French Riviera as the guests of Max Aitken. On 19 June, Greenwood intervened vigorously in the debate on the slow-moving Home Rule bill in an attempt to foster conciliation. He followed Asquith in declaring that the parliament at Westminster would have total supremacy over an Irish parliament in Dublin. "We maintain," the prime minister had contended in introducing the bill, "unimpaired and beyond the reach of challenge or question, the supremacy, absolute and sovereign, of the Imperial Parliament."[6] Greenwood then argued, not very convincingly, that on the one hand Home Rule would give back to Ireland its own parliament, but that on the other hand that same parliament would not be very strong. Sounding like Campbell-Bannerman and Birrell in introducing their ill-fated 1906 Irish devolution legislation, he attempted to assure Irish Nationalists that the new parliament in Dublin would have real powers (as the Parliament of Canada had), while reassuring Home Rule opponents and Ulstermen that any Irish parliament would be more subordinate than any of the great parliaments "set up by this House in the Colonies."

Not surprisingly, this impossible balancing act was received with derision by Conservative-Unionists. Hecklers enquired whether Greenwood would repeat in Canada his statement that "no Parliament that can be set up by this Imperial House is equal to the Mother of Parliaments." His simplistic reply was prompt: "Any Canadian would maintain that position, and be proud to admit the supremacy of this Parliament." That bifurcated response was of course unconvincing to the opposition: "Did Sir Wilfrid Laurier maintain that proposition in London at the [recent] Imperial Conference?" Amidst the barracking, Greenwood continued undaunted his balancing act. With his eye now mainly on Ulster, he contended that the bill had explicit limitations that "make the power of the Parliament in Ireland less than the powers now enjoyed by the Parliaments of Canada, New Zealand, Australia, South Africa, or even Newfoundland." When the Canadian Sir Gilbert Parker enquired whether the powers proposed for the Irish Parliament would be less than those of even a Canadian provincial legislature, Greenwood stated that the powers of the Irish Parliament would be greater than those of a provincial legislature, but would have at the same time "much less power than any of the Parliaments of our great Dominions."

From the opposition benches, the always caustic Conservative Irish peer Earl Winterton made it clear that he for one had heard enough of Greenwood's well-intentioned attempt to reconcile advocates and opponents of Home Rule. In fact, asked Winterton, was there anyone in the House – including Greenwood – who would seriously argue that Westminster "could abridge one jot or tittle of the rights of the Canadian Parliament without the secession of Canada from this country? ... any-one who gets up and says the Canadian Parliament is not in fact inde-pendent, is a political *farceur.* No one knows that better than the hon. Gentleman opposite [Greenwood] ... The point which we want to get at ... is, are you attempting to set up [in Ireland] ... a [subordinate] parliament, or an independent parliament equal to those set up in the Dominions?"[7]

Although seldom abashed in debate, on this occasion Greenwood did not or had not time to respond to Winterton. There was, however, no question where Bonar Law, Amery, and F.E. Smith stood in their pas-sionate opposition to Home Rule. But as Greenwood struggled with the Tories over Ulster, Amery wrote with some distaste to his wife, Bryddie, about his private impression of the Ulstermen whom he was publicly supporting so ardently. "They are a solid, determined lot ... [but] no more Irish than they are Chinese and with not much more use for 'Papishes' than they have for 'Chinks' or niggers."[8]

In the new year 1913, despite the third reading of the Government of Ireland bill and support for it by John Redmond and the Irish National-ist MPs, the prospects for early implementation had receded even fur-ther in the face of the recruitment of the Ulster Volunteer Force. The Conservative-Unionist Party adamantly rejected any real compromise. Nevertheless, on 10 June 1913, before Greenwood and Margo departed on a trans-Empire voyage, he tried again, this time adding that the Gov-ernment of Ireland bill – only now, a year later, up for second reading

– carried the support of Canada and the other Dominions, as could be attested by William Redmond, MP, brother of John, who had visited Canada the year before. Greenwood said that, to his incredulity, he understood that two other members who had recently returned, one of them Walter Long, the former chief secretary of Ireland, were proclaiming that "the people of Canada are not in … sympathy with the [Irish] Nationalist Members." In keeping with parliamentary practice, Greenwood could not accuse them directly of lying, contenting himself with the charge that they were "not talking in accordance with fact." To the contrary, the fact was that the people of Canada were decidedly not in sympathy with the Conservative-Unionist visitors. For example, in Ottawa several ministers including the minister of justice, Charles Doherty, would not appear alongside the visiting Long.* "These overseas kinsmen have tried Home Rule; they believe in it as the first step towards a united Empire," Greenwood said, and then turned to Canada's southern neighbour: "There are in the United States somewhere between twelve and twenty millions of Irishmen … it is essential to the success of this country and Empire that we should be on good terms with the people of the United States … Irish power is so great and the Irish grievance is felt so keenly, that up to the present the Government of the United States have been unable to recognize officially the attempt to celebrate 100 years of peace between the United States and the British Empire." As always citing Canada as an example for imperial progress, he added, "Anyone who knows the New World knows that the grievance of Irishmen abroad is the same as the grievance of Irishmen at home … It can easily be remedied by the granting of Home Rule … which I do not believe for a moment, as one who lived amongst Catholics in the majority as they are in some parts of Canada, means religious intolerance. But I do know it means this. It will wipe out a great barrier towards international amity between us and our kinsmen in the United States – and it will make one long stride towards the federation of this Empire."

---

* Charles Doherty, a strong supporter of Dominion Home Rule and president of the United Irish League in Montreal, had nevertheless endorsed the contribution of three dreadnoughts to the Royal Navy. Eight years later, however, the representative in Washington of the Dáil Éireann (Assembly of Ireland) wrote to de Valera (20 July 1921) that Doherty now supported the Irish Republicans and was "prepared to assist you should you so desire." See Fanning et al., *Documents on Irish Foreign Policy*, vol. 1, 1919–1922, 174.

From the opposition front bench, the dour Bonar Law rejected Greenwood's arguments:

> Who says that the whole of Canada was in favour of Home Rule? ...
> I myself, who have been in Canada, who was born in Canada, and
> who is constantly meeting Canadians, can tell him that his statement
> is utterly at variance with the facts ... He [Greenwood] said that no
> Members of Mr. Borden's cabinet had taken part in anti-Home Rule
> demonstrations ... there is not one of them who is not wise enough
> to recognize that just as we have no right to interfere in their domes-
> tic affairs, so the last thing they [Canadians] have the right to do is
> to interfere in our domestic affairs ... I defy him [Greenwood] or
> anyone to obtain from the Canadian Parliament to-day any expres-
> sion of opinion on this subject. And more than that, when he says
> the Canadians approve of this Home Rule because they like their
> own, does anyone know better than the hon. Member what non-
> sense it is? Let him propose to the Canadians that one of the provin-
> cial Parliaments should be given a separate Customs House and a
> separate Post Office, and see then what Canadians think of his
> [Home Rule] scheme.[9]

Bonar Law flatly dismissed the Government of Ireland bill as beyond repair, instead praising those members from Ulster who "have deliber-ately and wisely determined to make their appeal not through the House of Commons, but direct to the people of this country and that appeal will not be made in vain.[10] There were few if any MPs more deter-mined than Law to keep Protestant Ulster out of any Home Rule, Roman Catholic Ireland. In short, his encouragement to Ulster to ignore the House of Commons as the supreme court of the land began to sound seditious.

The debate about where Canadians stood on Irish Home Rule spilled over into letters to the *Times*. Walter Long, reactionary and unswerving as always, denied Greenwood's accusation that while in Canada he had said that he had never met anyone in favour of the Government of Ireland bill. Canadians had told him of their support for a relationship between Dublin and London that would parallel that between the provinces and Ottawa. In their view, there should be a single chamber in Dublin subject in all things to Westminster. Greenwood, in a reply to the *Times*, contradicted Long: in fact neither Robert Borden, the new prime minister of Canada, nor any minister nor any provincial premier (including McBride of British Columbia and Rogers of Manitoba) had spoken against Home Rule during Long's visit to Canada.[11]

In 1912 Greenwood had also become involved in the naval debates that paralleled those over Home Rule for Ireland. Borden, convinced that Britain needed help in the face of the German naval expansion, was optimistically if vainly casting about for a naval policy acceptable across the country, including in Quebec. Laurier, with his Naval Service Act of 1910, had created a Royal Canadian Navy at least on paper, but its proposed small ships would make no difference in terms of global maritime power. In hoping to make a difference, Borden's challenge was to achieve a balance between the imperial naval forces needed to meet the perceived German threat and the political realities at home. He hoped that he might employ "technical advice" from the Admiralty to win popular support for a major cash contribution to the Royal Navy.

Borden selected Premier Richard McBride of British Columbia as his private emissary to obtain such a statement from the Admiralty. McBride had long claimed the friendship of Churchill who in October 1911 (the same month as Borden's electoral victory) had become first lord of the Admiralty. In January 1912, Borden had asked Strathcona, the high commissioner, to take McBride to see Churchill.[*] Having heard McBride outline Borden's tentative offer "to pay for two or perhaps three of the finest vessels in the world," Churchill well understood why Borden's government had repeatedly asked London for "technical advice": "When they ask for advice, [they] would like to be told authoritatively by the Admiralty [what] they could adopt, and on this they believe they could appeal to the country at a special general election with good prospects of success."[12] In short, Borden was eager to have from Churchill a public statement that would help him to sell to the Canadian electorate – although unlikely to be the case in Quebec – a cash contribution to the Royal Navy.

In the summer of 1912, Borden, on his first visit to London as prime minister, saw among others Greenwood and Churchill, but the first lord of the Admiralty was understandably cautious at being drawn into the highly controversial naval debate in Canada. Further, he was wary of any dilution of the absolute control of the Admiralty over the fleet. The Dublin-born Lord Northcliffe, the owner of the *Times* and the *Daily*

---

* Early in January 1912 the recently married Greenwoods had spent a week on the French Riviera as Aitken's guests. On 12 January, Lloyd George, then chancellor of the exchequer, dined with them and discussed the costs of the proposed naval building program.

Mail among other newspapers, welcomed what he saw as Borden's tentative steps towards cash support for the Royal Navy and wrote to Churchill in August, urging him to undertake another speaking tour of Canada: " I have been to Canada often, and, in my judgment, there are only five public men whose presence would arouse enthusiasm – the Prime Minister, yourself, Mr. Lloyd George, Mr. Balfour, and, chiefly by reason of his Canadian birth, the Leader of the Opposition in the House of Commons [Bonar Law] ... There is no more necessity for you to refer to such matters as Imperial [tariff] Preference than there has been for Mr. Borden to do so while here ... If you went after the Canadian offer [of three dreadnoughts] had been made, there could be no suggestion that you were touting for support ... There are numerous little local details that such a Canadian as Hamar Greenwood could easily arrange."[13]

At this point, James Whitney (now Sir James), the long-serving Conservative premier of Ontario, re-entered Greenwood's life briefly – unknown to him. Always a staunch supporter of a cash contribution to the Royal Navy, he praised Borden for his visit to London. He went on:

> I do not know how much there is in the suggestion that Churchill and Hamar Greenwood are coming here. I hope, however, that the report is not true. Of course a visit by a Member of the British Government might have a good effect and, on the contrary, it might have a bad effect ... People who are apparently timid fear that an impulsive man like Churchill might create an undesirable effect by urging or asking our people to do something towards the up-keep of the Navy ... the basis of this fear is that he might talk as from a pedestal and be inclined to instruct us as to our duty, etc. Further, I think that no advantage would accrue from Greenwood's presence with him ... Neither I nor any other person of whom I know have any objection to Greenwood, but we know him here simply as a Canadian who lives in the Old Country and is a Member of the House of Commons. It is thought that a man of more prominence should accompany Churchill if he comes.[14]

Four years before, Whitney had used Greenwood for his own ends, offering to reciprocate his assistance at any time. Now in 1912 he dismissed him as a person of no prominence. There was never to be any Ontario legal work for such a Liberal. However, Greenwood himself may have been as well pleased that Churchill had decided that it would be neither timely nor prudent to make a visit to Canada. Certainly, Sir George Perley, Strathcona's successor as high commissioner and at the same time the sitting member for a Quebec constituency, later cautioned Borden against such a visit as domestically inopportune, especially if he were to sail up the Gulf of St Lawrence in a dreadnought. Amidst all this conflicting advice, a wary Churchill contented himself with the simple statement: "If it is the intention of Canada to render assistance to the naval forces of the British Empire, now is the time when that aid would be most welcome and most timely."[15]

That same year, 1912, Greenwood included a passage about the naval controversy in his sole book, the appropriately entitled *Canada as an Imperial Factor*, a slim volume in the eclectic and popular series "The Nation's Library." In his preface Greenwood thanked Strathcona and the small staff of the High Commission for their assistance in its preparation, but much of the text smacks of his own emigration promotion lectures of more than a decade before. His brief survey of the history of Canada extols its remarkable resources and puffs the unparalleled opportunities offered to settlers. It is in the final chapter, "Relations between the Mother Country and the Dominion," that he strives to appear even-handed in the concurrent naval debate, committing himself neither to the proposed emergency naval grant pursued by Borden nor rejecting Laurier's concept of an embryonic Royal Canadian Navy (which gave the Admiralty forebodings about issues of command in wartime). Greenwood begins his chapter by criticizing the Admiralty for what he regards as indecisive advice, before recording the differences between the Liberals and Conservatives in Canada:

> The Admiralty have not been consistent in dealing with the problem. At first antagonistic to local Navies, it had by the Naval and Military Conference of 1909 accepted the view that Canada should provide its own Navy, and a scheme was drawn up defining its sphere. Before tenders for the necessary ships were accepted, the Conservatives defeated the Liberals, and Mr Borden assumed office. He at once consulted the Admiralty, and has produced a plan for a money grant of $35,000,000 for the purpose of providing Dreadnoughts for the British Navy. Canadian opinion is divided. The Conservatives say that the condition of international affairs is such that there is an emergency which Canada must meet. The Liberals, while maintaining the principle of a Canadian Navy, have admitted the justice of the [Borden] proposal if an emergency

exists, but deny the emergency. There is also a not unimportant body of persons who believe that there is no need for either grant or Navy.[16]

As elsewhere in Canadian affairs, Greenwood attempted, not always successfully, to bridge differences between Liberals and Conservatives, but the naval debates of 1912 at Westminster finally convinced him that there was in fact a maritime threat to the Empire from Germany. Accordingly, he split with Laurier and King and came down on the side of Borden's bill for a contribution of cash to pay for three dreadnoughts. He urged Churchill to send him to Ottawa in an effort "to get Laurier and his followers 'to line up' with Borden's contribution,"[17] but to his chagrin a wary Churchill did not take up his offer. Borden visited London in July 1913 in a further effort to gather information that could be of use in the continuing, highly partisan naval debate. Greenwood discussed with him the German naval threat as seen from London, but both Asquith and Churchill had reservations about becoming involved in Canada's partisan debate. Any naval contribution was a matter for Canada alone to decide. In any event, Britain itself would in the end pay for the further expansion of the Royal Navy. On 13 July a weary Asquith noted, "We are going to a dismal official luncheon to-day at the Palace to meet the Colonials [Borden and his colleagues] of whom I feel that I have already seen almost as much as I want."[18]

Where Laurier stood was well reflected in the thoughts of the British prime minister's daughter when she visited Ottawa. In early 1913, Violet Asquith stayed for several weeks as guest of the governor general, the Duke of Connaught. On 13 January she listened to the naval debate in the House of Commons (the quality of the debate was "an immense improvement," she said, on that of the House of Representatives in Washington, which she had just visited). Before the debate, she had dined with Sir Wilfrid and Lady Laurier. She wrote to her future husband that the thinking of the leader of the opposition was "more from a *national* point of view: a Canadian built, Canadian-manned fleet ... but as they have neither ports to build nor men to man [their ships] it looks a little impracticable. I don't think Sir W[ilfrid] is much of an imperialist."[19]

In August 1913 Greenwood embarked with Margo for Australia via the "all-red" route across Canada with a delegation from the new Empire Parliamentary Association. (They left their first child, Angela Margo Hamar Greenwood, now a year old, in London in the care of a nanny.)

Greenwood saw Laurier in Ottawa and McBride in Victoria, but to his regret not as the designated emissary of the First Lord of the Admiralty. In a private letter to Churchill before embarking for Australia from Vancouver, he offered a candid summary of the naval situation based upon his conversations in Ottawa. He confirmed that "there was no possibility whatever of the Canadian Government paying for three dreadnoughts – or any ships – for the Royal Navy before the next general election, expected in 1915 or 1916 at the earliest. Of course no one can foretell the results, but Borden will probably win re-election. A contribution to the Royal Navy does not appeal to the masses; only a raid of Japs would stir up the modern Canuck." Seeing himself as the most active "Canadian MP" then at Westminster, Greenwood again proposed himself to Churchill as the one man who could turn around Canadian public opinion. He reminded him that the previous summer, he had asked to be sent "to get Laurier and his followers 'to line up'. I think I could have done it. At any rate, I could have attended either Party's caucus and made a personal appeal. No other British MP has that *locus*. Laurier and his colleagues and others throughout the Dominion and of both Parties keep saying to me, if the Home Government wants to stir up Imperialism in Canada, why aren't you given a chance?"[20]

In his letter Greenwood described Laurier as politely adamant in stating, "I'll fight to the death against Borden's Naval Scheme. There can be no compromise now. Nothing but my own naval scheme will have my support." In addition to Laurier, Greenwood saw the former minister of agriculture Sydney Fisher, Premier Lomer Gouin of Quebec, Senator J.P.B. Casgrain, and Mackenzie King, all of whom confirmed that if, as they expected, Borden included the $35 million grant for three dreadnoughts in his next budget, the Liberal-dominated Senate would reject it (as it still had the power to do). Laurier told Greenwood, "I risked everything to bring Quebec into line for the Empire by my naval policy … Quebec will secede before she will adopt Borden's policy … if the Home Government wants to drive Quebec out of the Dominion, the Home Government's obvious endorsement of the principle of contribution [sought by Borden] is the way to do it." Greenwood's broad conclusion to Churchill was that immigration was changing the face of Canada, with the result that "the great and growing alien element in the Dominion … is generally anti-England. The spirit of Canadian nationalism is growing, and will tend toward an independent Canada." In his summation, he reported:

1) There will *never* be a cash grant in any shape or form to the Admiralty, unless the Admiralty makes a direct *ad misericordiam* appeal, and even then there will be much opposition;
2) A permanent Naval Policy must follow the Australian precedent [of small local naval forces] plus establishment of Canadian ship-building yards, etc., let the cost be what it may be;
3) Borden cannot declare for any permanent naval policy because he is personally pledged ... to his Quebec colleagues ... against any sort or kind of permanent naval policy.

Greenwood concluded where he began: there would be no financing of warships by Canada for years to come and certainly none under Borden's scheme.[21]

Having so reported to Churchill, Greenwood and Margo sailed from Vancouver in August 1913 with the first overseas delegation of the new Empire Parliamentary Association, which he had helped to create the year before. Eight other Liberal MPs, four Conservative (including Amery), and one Labour undertook the four-month journey to Australia, New Zealand, and South Africa. Although away from the endless Irish and naval debates at Westminster, they did not escape them entirely. In both Australia and New Zealand, they held meetings with the premiers, leaders of the opposition, and fellow MPs, becoming more familiar with the effectiveness of both cash contributions to the Royal Navy and the commissioning of several small naval vessels, as well as the results of compulsory service. Frequently on the long trip Greenwood took the opportunity to advocate Dominion Home Rule for Ireland, an advocacy especially well received by the large number of Irish settlers in Australia. In turn he was honoured by being called to the bars of New South Wales and South Australia.

Given the Liberal opposition in Ottawa to Borden's naval contribu-tion policy and given what he had learned in Australia of its dual policy of support for both the Royal Navy and local naval forces, Greenwood, upon his return to London in early December 1913, moved toward Laurier. Citing to King a newspaper report that there was a rumour abroad in Canada that "I am in favour of a Naval [cash] Contribution policy," he wrote that this was most emphatically not so: "I am not in favour of the Contribution policy as distinguished from the develop-ment of local navies."[22] King probably wondered at Greenwood's sud-den reversal, knowing full well that his old friend had recently supported Borden in his cash contribution policy. He did not let him off easily. In sending Greenwood a detailed statement of Liberal naval policy, he had dryly suggested, "It would be well ... to put yourself on [public] record to the contrary in a manner which will leave no room for doubt."[23] As Greenwood had predicted, Borden's naval bill was stalled by the Liberal-dominated Senate, shortly before the First World War finally determined that Canada's contribution would necessarily be soldiers and later airmen, not dreadnoughts.

Greenwood not only deplored to Churchill his own absence from any role in the Canadian naval debate but also relayed to him the more general unease of Sam Hughes, Borden's erratic minister of militia, at the sorry state of Anglo-Canadian military collaboration. "I know Hughes intimately. He's a rough diamond but a great success as a Canadian Minister of Militia. He told me the day of my landing in Quebec that he had been shabbily treated by the War Office in the summer of 1912 and he'd never again communicate with it if he could possibly avoid it." Clearly with himself in mind as an interlocutor between London and Ottawa on military collaboration, Greenwood added, "Col. Hughes agrees with me, these functions and break-away tendencies would not occur if a man who all Canadians know had a chance."[24]

Upon their return from their four-month imperial tour, Greenwood and Amery had found that that the focus of the current debate at Westminster was not on the fragile and confusing situation brewing in the Balkans but remained on Home Rule for Ireland where there had emerged a clear threat of civil war. In Ulster, Carson had proclaimed a "provisional government" with an armed Ulster Volunteer Force now said by some to number as many as 100,000, defying Asquith's government to take any action against them. Amery plunged immediately into the increasingly bitter debate alongside Bonar Law and F.E. Smith in their unbounded enthusiasm for Ulster. They attempted to force the minority Liberal government into a general election before the passage of the bill through the House of Lords in 1914 (when it would become law even if the Lords rejected it, thanks to the 1911 Parliament Act). Greenwood, in supporting Asquith, was outspoken in his attacks on those who, like his brother-in-law Amery, sought a covenant from the government that Ulster would not be coerced. Bonar Law, the chronically negative leader of the opposition, had agreed to meet with Asquith in October 1913 and again in November at Beaverbrook's country house in an attempt to resolve the fundamental question of the place, if any, of Ulster in a Home Rule Ireland, John Redmond having made it clear that he could not accept its permanent exclusion. Parallel discussions with the king and individual ministers led nowhere other than to a flat rejection by Carson of Asquith's proposals, including special powers of veto for Ulster on any act of the proposed Irish parliament that affected the Protestant counties: "Home Rule within Home Rule."

As the deadlock became yet more public, the threatening noises of the Ulster Volunteers became yet more dire. If they were to embrace the paradox of using smuggled German arms against the British army so as to remain an integral part of the United Kingdom, if they were to challenge by those arms the supremacy of Parliament, then at least Churchill among the cabinet ministers was clear about what must be done: "We are not going to have the realm of Great Britain sink to the condition of the Republic of Mexico ... 'Let us go forward and put these grave matters to the proof.'"[25] For Churchill and Greenwood, if Ulster descended into civil war, civil war it would be. The Ulster Volunteer Force, formed with the advice of the Ulsterman Field Marshal Lord Roberts, was prompted by confidential War Office information supplied to them and to the Conservative opposition by the Ulsterman Lieutenant General Sir Henry Wilson, the director of military operations – "that poisonous mischief maker," in Asquith's restrained description. That army officers in the south of Ireland might do the unthinkable and not obey orders to move against the Ulster Volunteers became evident over the weekend of 21–22 March 1914 from the actions of the Ulsterman Brigadier General Hubert Gough. He and fifty-seven of his cavalry officers based near Dublin stated that they would prefer to be dismissed from the service rather than obey orders to move northward against the Ulster Volunteers.

While cabinet ministers – other than Churchill and one or two others who spoke frankly of there being worse things than bloodshed – blundered about in response, Asquith described the Liberal members of Parliament as being "really hot and excited – more than they have been for a long time." Greenwood was among them. As soon as the House sat on Monday, 23 March, he was on his feet thundering – as he was so adept at doing – against any such seditious action as to entice army officers not to obey orders. "It is clear as possible that the Liberal Government to-day is not only fighting the sincere antipathies of people in this country and Ireland who are opposed to Home Rule but it has also weighted against it ... an attempt to seduce the British army from its allegiance." There had never been any doubt that Greenwood was an ardent Home Ruler, but with his sonorous invective there could also be no doubt that he, like Churchill, regarded Ulster's supporters in the House – Bonar Law, Edward Carson, and F.E. Smith in the vanguard – as guilty of encouraging army officers to disobey orders. But even more than that, the farcical handling of the so-called Curragh Mutiny, which had brought with it a real danger of civil war, rendered imperative the reform of the army. "There has been no question since 1906 that has so moved the progressive forces of this House, and of this country, as the recent attempt of the Opposition to seduce the army from their allegiance ... If there are officers who qualify their allegiance, officers who say, 'We are loyal to a Government of Conservatives, but not loyal when it is Liberal', I for one would back up the Government in so democratising[*] the British army that such a state of affairs would never rise again."[26]

Greenwood, to underline his commitment to peace in Ireland, marched in a procession in London organized by the Pilgrims, ostensibly to mark a century of concord between the United States and Britain (since the War of 1812). It was at least as much an expression of hope that peace in Europe – including in Ireland – would continue, despite various threatening noises.[†] Under the procedures of the new Parliament Act, the Government of Ireland bill, providing Home Rule to a divided Ireland, finally received third reading in May 1914. Arms purchased in Germany had already been smuggled into Ulster. The bill became mired in the House of Lords in mid-July. Against the back-

---

* The "democratisation" was taken up only in 1937–40 by Leslie Hore-Belisha after he became secretary of state for war.

  Given the mishandling by the War Office of the "Curragh Mutiny," Asquith shared Greenwood's disillusion with the senior officers in Ireland as well as at the War Office, particularly Generals Wilson and French, but was pleased when he met in May "General [Sir Nevil] Macready who is over from Belfast, and is certainly one of the cleverest of the soldiers. He takes a sane, level-headed view of things" (Brock and Brock, *H.H. Asquith: Letters to Venetia Stanley*, 73).

† On 10 January 1914, Sam Hughes wrote from London a typically egocentric and bombastic letter to Prime Minister Robert Borden denouncing his fellow Conservative, the Canadian MP Donald Macmaster, as "sullen, negative, haughty," but praising the Liberal Greenwood as "a most courteous, capable gentleman and lawyer, willing to oblige a friend, and always treating his opponents with courtesy." Greenwood's brother-in-law Amery "had done more for the Empire than all the gang put together." Hughes added that "Greenwood may have sneering enemies, but thousands of friends." Hughes may have earlier clashed with his fellow Conservative either in the legislature of Ontario or in the House of Commons in Ottawa where Macmaster was a member before crossing to Westminster (he was the member for Chertsey from 1910 until his death in 1922). Hughes may also have been aware of Whitney's 1912 disparagement of Greenwood to Borden, although Hughes and Whitney were not friends.

ground of adamant opposition in the Lords and the king's continuing reluctance to create enough Liberal peers to see it through the Lords, Asquith agreed to a conference of representatives of the government, the opposition, the Irish Nationalists, and Ulster Unionists to attempt to break the deadlock.

When the conference at Buckingham Palace failed to agree, the Ulster Unionists demanding the permanent exclusion of the six counties and Asquith and Redmond offering only a six-year exclusion, Irish National Volunteers in the South (the forerunner of the Irish Republican Army, the IRA) also imported arms from Germany. Civil war was narrowly averted by the arrival on 3 August of the First World War, which, in Churchill's words, cut through the "clamour of the haggard, squalid, tragic Irish quarrel which threatened to divide the British nation into two hostile camps."[27] Despite the continuing obstruction of Unionists, Home Rule – to the mute gratification of Redmond and the Irish Nationalists – was finally placed by Asquith on the statute books on 18 September 1914. Ominously, however, Beaverbrook reported that Bonar Law and Carson believed "Asquith had tricked them both by promising them that there would be no new domestic legislation during the War and then putting the Home Rule Bill through its last stages in direct defiance of his promise."[28] More ominously still, the implementation of the bill was suspended until the end of the war.

6

First World War, 1914–1918

With the declaration of war on Germany on 4 August 1914, Greenwood was one of several sitting members of Parliament already officers in the army reserve who immediately volunteered for active military service. Being a member of Parliament was not the full-time, well-paid job that it was eventually to become. (The pastoral functions of MPs were also less.) An annual stipend of £400 had been introduced in 1911, but those who were qualified still sought to supplement their income by continuing to practise law or other professions. Accordingly it was not a major disruption to the wartime Parliament to have backbenchers absent on military leave with either the War Office or the forces at the front.

Greenwood began his active military service on the day that war began. Still a captain in the General (Regular) Reserve of Officers at age forty-four, he was appointed assistant comptroller of recruiting in the small, untried, and increasingly harassed recruiting unit of the War Office. Its initial challenge was not a lack of recruits but, on the contrary, what to do with the immediate waves of enthusiastic volunteers. In August and September 1914, 300,000 and 450,000 volunteers – three-quarters of a million men in two months – placed an enormous strain on the still very limited capacities of the War Office to process them. In September, with the sudden appointment of Lord Kitchener as secretary of state for war, Amery, who had known him in South Africa, was named director of civilian recruiting, southern command, at the War Office. His first enlistment was of his brother-in-law, Greenwood, as his chief associate, "a keen volunteer officer, but above all, a man of swift decision and real drive. Between us we collected a score or more of other Members of Parliament ... This resulted in the formation of a Parliamentary Recruiting Committee."

While Margo was awaiting the imminent birth of their second child, Greenwood was writing regularly to his sister Bryddie from Room 269 in the War Office. Amery had seen Kitchener on 3 September to propose that the way to deal with "the recruits now pouring into depots, camps, etc. and overflowing into yards and fields" was to enlist them in local units, put them on sixpence a day, and return them to their work and homes until called up. Local units were the copestone of the whole recruiting scheme. Otherwise, as Amery wrote on 1 September, middle-class volunteers would object to "bedding down in the barracks next to a couple of lousy and swearing hooligans." Unless Kitchener "quickly gets this scheme into operation, we'll have riots among recruits who are massed in the thousands without clothing, without instructors, and sometimes without food. If this scheme is accepted [by Kitchener] we could enlist a million men ... Further, the Canadians are bound to follow suit. The Australians and New Zealanders [with their pre-war national service program] have already done this, in effect."[1] The committee that Amery and Greenwood created "set to work with a will. In the next few days we discovered accommodations in all sorts of unexpected places, made arrangements for housing, feeding and training recruits, unearthed new sources of supply for cloth that could be dyed khaki, for boots and equipment of all kinds."[2] It was all rather makeshift,* but it was better than nothing until Kitchener – in Amery's words "not a mental giant" – cut short its work, still believing that every priority must be given to the small professional army rather than to local Territorials. Thereafter, the monthly numbers of volunteers were roughly in the 100,000 range until the second of half of 1916, when they began to decline sharply.

Some in the cabinet and even in the War Office believed that the fighting would be over by Christmas. On at least this occasion, Kitchener was more far-seeing. He forecast three years of conflict, but nevertheless remained opposed to conscription. In light of his and other such realistic forecasts, the War Office began to ponder what to do if compulsory military service, hitherto opposed in Britain, became in time unavoidable. Amery had long urged it, Churchill had recommended it to a reluctant cabinet in the first month of the war, and Greenwood, as assistant comptroller of recruiting, soon became involved in the

---

* The Parliamentary Recruiting Committee also commissioned posters encouraging volunteers, including a famous one entitled "Women of England say 'Go!'" and, upon the U-boat sinking of the *Lusitania*, "Take up the Sword of Justice!"

planning for such an eventuality, which would be introduced only after all efforts to promote voluntary enlistment had been exhausted. The prospect of conscription remained unpopular with those who regarded it as an alien, continental practice, not in accordance with traditional concepts of British liberty, as well as those who, more prosaically, saw it as likely to reduce industrial productivity. In the winter of 1914–15 as the war on the Western Front became static, as more and deeper trenches were dug, and as attrition became the unspoken policy on both sides, Greenwood continued at the War Office, helping to devise ways in which local committees and other small groups could encourage volunteers. At the same time, he was almost daily present in the nearby House of Commons calling for increased separation allowances and generous treatment of dependents of the now mounting war dead.

From the beginning of the war, such diverse entities as the Glasgow Tramwaymen, the Football Association, and the Gentlemen Jockeys encouraged volunteering to their own units. In the case of Wales, Greenwood was well aware of the need of support from the Welsh National Committee and local chapels. When the decision was made to add several battalions to the South Wales Borderers, Greenwood arranged to be appointed on 10 December 1914 the lieutenant colonel to help raise and subsequently to command its new 10th Battalion, composed largely of South Wales coal miners (not yet a reserved category for recruits). He soon came to admire the volunteers, including a small contingent of Canadians, for their determination and fortitude. The Welsh-born Richard Marpole of Vancouver, general superintendent of the Pacific Division of the Canadian Pacific Railway, offered at the end of January 1915 to arrange free passage from Saint John to Liverpool of any volunteer for Lloyd George's cherished goal of a "Welsh Army Corps." Some of these men found their way into the 10th Battalion, SWB.

On 8 February 1915, Greenwood was made a baronet, supposedly in recognition of his efforts to facilitate recruiting. The *Toronto Globe* would later claim to reveal "for the first time" the procedure by which he had been so honoured: "Greenwood, who for many years was an intimate friend of the present British Premier, visited Lloyd George before going to the front with the Welsh battalion that he [had] raised. Lloyd George praised his recruiting efforts and asked if there was anything he wanted. 'Nothing for myself, but I have a little son [David Hamar Greenwood, born 30 October 1914] and I should be glad to hand on to him a baronetcy if I don't come back,' he replied. 'Right,' said Lloyd George,

'Wait a moment.' He went next door to No. 10 Downing where sat the then Premier Asquith ... Greenwood got the baronetcy."[3] That the reason for the hereditary honour was quite that simple seems improbable. (A decade later, Lloyd George was to sell a baronetcy for as much as £25,000.) A former classmate of Greenwood at the University of Toronto, the writer W.A. Craik, wrote of him in the *Canadian Magazine* of March 1915, "However much one may disparage him or express dislike of his theatrical manners and masterful ways, it must be admitted that the new baronet deserves a good deal of respect. It is no light thing to have risen from humble beginnings to an eminence such as he now occupies, and that without having to resort to questionable methods. Where wealth has been the customary instrument of advancement, Sir Hamar has succeeded in winning out by sheer force of will, coupled with useful oratorical and mental powers. He has been consistent in his political career and a hard worker professionally. He has lived a clean and honourable life, and if he has some rather conspicuous peculiarities, these may be very well overlooked in summing up his outstanding achievements."[4]

Through December 1914 and the spring of 1915, the now Sir Hamar Greenwood continued both as a member of Parliament and as the lieutenant colonel commanding the 10th Battalion of the South Wales Borderers as it undertook its basic training in North Wales. To the degree that his military duties allowed, he at the same time joined his old temperance mentors, Thomas Whittaker and Joseph Rowntree, as well as his fellow teetotaller Bonar Law in supporting Lloyd George, then chancellor of the exchequer, in expressing concern over the effects of excessive drinking on industrial production, particularly in areas with large ordinance factories. Something must be done at once to counter the resultant damage – more than that of "all the German submarines put together."[5] Lloyd George succeeded in first enlisting King George V in setting an example by banishing all alcohol from the royal household. But the regal precedent was not welcomed by Conservatives, Irish Nationalists, or labour, including the shipyard workers in Greenwood's own constituency of Sunderland. Total prohibition was flatly denounced by the unions. Russian and French methods of control were equally rejected. Lloyd George's sudden idea of nationalizing all distilleries and breweries was more widely received, but the cost in the midst of attempting to finance the ever-more-expensive war effort ruled out that radical approach. In the end, to the regret of Greenwood and other temperance advocates and nonconformists, Lloyd George dropped the idea.

Instead, in April 1915 he put in place a central liquor control board, which included amongst its directors Neville Chamberlain, Philip Snowden, and Lord Astor. With wide powers, it in time made some real although less dramatic progress in combating excessive drinking through reductions in the opening hours of both public houses and off-license sales.

By the end of 1915, six hundred all ranks of the 10th Battalion SWB were under Greenwood's command at Kenmell Park near Colwyn Bay.* From that vantage point, he recommended to Lloyd George, who was pressing Kitchener for additional Welsh and Irish regiments, divisions, or even an army corps, that the Liberal MP, Brigadier General Ivor Phillips, be selected "to make your concept of a Welsh Division and army a success." On a personal note he added, "My Battalion ... is doing splendidly. It is now over 800 strong and by the end of the month will be a good 1,100." However, its training with the 38th (Welsh) Division at Winchester was "greatly handicapped by being kept waiting for service rifles, without which serious training was hardly possible." The division was finally accounted ready for active service when it was reviewed by Queen Mary on 29 November 1915, immediately preceding its channel crossing on 3 December.[6]

Earlier in November Greenwood had passed a few days in northern France near Hill 60 in the Ypres salient, familiarizing himself with the harsh conditions at the front. Behind the lines at Guernes, a fortnight of final training for the battalion followed, during which it also formed part of the parade saluting Field Marshal Sir John French upon his reluctant relinquishment of the command of the British Expeditionary Force in France. Greenwood celebrated Christmas 1915 with his battalion at Robecq, turned over its command on 28 December, as previously arranged, and recrossed the English Channel to return to the House of Commons and to the War Office, where he was again involved in recruiting. He had spent a total of three weeks in France.[†] He did not hear a shot fired in anger, but as the regimental history of the South Wales Borderers notes, during the year that he commanded the

---

* At Kenmel Park four years later there occurred the worst of several postwar riots of Canadian soldiers disgruntled at the slow pace of their repatriation. They mindlessly killed five of their fellows.

† On the last day of 1915 Lloyd George recorded cryptically, "Saw Hamar Greenwood just back from France" (Morgan, *Lloyd George Family Letters*, 181). A quartermaster sergeant, W.G. Greenwood, served in the 10th Battalion, SWB, but whether he was a distant relative is unrecorded.

battalion, he had succeeded in what he had undertaken: "He had done a good work in raising and training the 10th and had the satisfaction of handing [over] a very efficient battalion."[7]

The War Office to which Greenwood returned in February 1916 was increasingly confronted with the problem of finding sufficient volunteers to provide replacements for the rapidly growing numbers of casualties, rather than its initial problem of having a surfeit of volunteers. That was only one of the major problems challenging Asquith's government. In response on 19 May he announced a coalition government, in which he managed to shuffle off the Conservative leader, Bonar Law, whom he neither liked nor trusted, to the Colonial Office, but added to the cabinet two other anti-Home Rulers, Carson and Long. Greenwood received no junior ministerial appointment, but he had received praise in *Saturday Night*: "He is the premier Canadian in the British House of Commons, having ousted Gilbert Parker from that proud position. He accomplished this by remaining as Canadian, a thing which at least fourteen out of the sixteen Members of Parliament who acknowledge Canada as their birthplace have been unable to do. Their colour ran in the wash. Almost the first thing they did was to turn themselves into Englishmen, whereas Hamar Greenwood has always maintained that what England needed was Canadian managing."[8]

In 1915 Hamar's sister, the nurse Mary, had crossed to London to provide therapy for soldiers blinded in the war. After completing her schooling in Whitby, Mary had studied nursing in the United States, becoming in time supervisor of the Johns Hopkins Hospital Dispensary at Baltimore and nursing superintendent of the Jewish Hospital (later Mount Sinai) in Cincinnati. Having become herself blind, she became a specialist in therapy for blind soldiers at the recently established St Dunstan's Hospital in London. Amery wrote later of his sister-in-law, "When what was already a remarkable career seemed cut short by blindness, she resolved to start life afresh and threw herself with undaunted zest, as one of Sir Arthur Pearson's lieutenants, into the work for blind soldiers, which he had inaugurated at St. Dunstan's [the hospital that Pearson, blind himself, had founded in 1915]. For years Mary was indefatigable in the work of teaching Braille and even more, of inspiring hope and self-confidence in these victims of the war."[9]

With the coming of Asquith's coalition government, Lloyd George moved from a tumultuous seven years as chancellor of the exchequer to the new and less than effective ministry of munitions. He promptly replaced the Canadian Sir Percy Girouard of the Royal Engineers and other senior staff with such experienced businessmen as the brothers Eric and Auckland Geddes. He also "wanted to keep skilled workers out of the trenches, and to do this he had to provide other people to go and fight." Accordingly, Lloyd George joined several others in the government in advocating conscription. A number of Liberal backbenchers, including Greenwood and Alfred Mond (who were to work together frequently in future), petitioned Asquith to impose compulsory service as early as July 1915. In response, Asquith, as always, moved cautiously. His first step had been to bring into force a National Registration Act. The names of millions of women and men between the ages of fifteen and sixty-five were recorded on cards, with a notation for those who were employed in now designated "reserved occupations" (e.g., munitions, shipbuilding, and coal mining). The names of men between the ages of eighteen and forty-one were passed to recruiting offices and committees who pressed locally for these men to volunteer.

In October 1915, after Kitchener had estimated that 30,000 were needed *weekly* to reach a "New Army" total of three million, another step toward compulsory military service was taken. The "Derby Scheme," named after Lord Derby, newly appointed by Asquith as director general of recruiting, was a last effort to rely upon voluntary enlistment alone. The Liberal prime minister's choice of the Conservative Derby, "the uncrowned King of Lancashire," was understandable. A soldier himself, Derby had been a member of Parliament from 1892 to 1906, following several years in Canada as aide-de-camp to his father, Governor General Lord Stanley (in whose London house Bryddie and Amery first met). Although a pre-war adherent to Lord Roberts's National Service League, Derby had centred his initial and notably successful wartime recruitment efforts in Lancashire on the principle, enunciated by, among others, Amery and Greenwood in the Parliamentary Recruiting Committee, that men from the same district should be encouraged to enlist, train, and fight together in locally identifiable units.

Although Derby earned the accolade from Lloyd George as "the most efficient recruiting sergeant in England," his scheme failed to produce the numbers required to fill the increasingly depleted ranks of Kitchener's New Army. In January 1916 a National Services bill providing for compulsory enlistment of single men was introduced. Many Liberal MPs were uneasy about legislation that curtailed individual liberty, but a group of thirty or so, Greenwood included, formed the Liberal War Committee, which in their weekly meetings reflected the conviction that conscription was compatible with liberalism. The January bill and a further one in May extending conscription to all males between the ages of eighteen and forty-one were eventually adopted.

On 10 February 1916, six weeks after turning over the command of his battalion in France, Greenwood was appointed deputy assistant adjutant general (DAAG) at the War Office. Again serving in a dual capacity, he received an annual allowance of £650 from the War Office additional to his annual remuneration from Parliament of £400. Now in effect on Lord Derby's staff, Greenwood plunged into the contentious issue of conscription, intervening repeatedly in the House of Commons on the need for reinforcements as casualties soared. The radical, anti-conscriptionist Labour member for Edinburgh East interrupted the increasingly annoyed Greenwood by asking him what he knew about the army and, in referring to his return from his fleeting sojourn with his battalion in France, assured him that "You always go in the wrong direction."

John Redmond, the Irish Nationalist leader in the House, had from the first days of the war loyally called for Irish volunteers. Greenwood on 17 March praised a recent speech of Redmond's brother, Captain William Redmond MP, who upon his return to Westminster from three months of active duty "brought the breath of manliness from the trenches and offered a refreshing contrast to the criticism against recruiting." Willy Redmond offered an explanation of why he had volunteered for the army at age fifty-three: "Canada and Australia and New Zealand have been our loyal friends in our hour of strife. Their Parliaments and their statesmen have pleaded our rights ... Are we to leave these people who are our friends without our aid? If we did so, we should be justly disgraced."[10] Following Parliament's vote in May extending conscription, Greenwood wrote to a correspondent in Whitby, Ontario, in early August, a little more than a month after Asquith had agreed with Bonar Law and Max Aitken on the need to move Lloyd George from the Ministry of Munitions to secretary of state for war upon the drowning of the Russia-bound Lord Kitchener. In his letter to Whitby, Greenwood praised the bravery of Canadian soldiers at the front, especially in the Somme offensive that some were now beginning to see as the disaster it was. In the wake of Passchendaele, Greenwood emphasized the commitment of Britain to winning the war: "You can take it from me, and I speak from an intimate knowledge of things as they are, that this war the Mother Country intends to fight to a finish and to bring Germany to her knees. In spite of all strikes and [other] annoyances, the people of these Islands are of one mind in this matter, and the whole race is working together for the defeat of Germany."[11] He sent to his brother, Billy, in British Columbia a copy of his letter to his correspondent in Whitby; it duly appeared in the *Toronto World*.

After seven months as DAAG, Greenwood resigned on 5 September 1916 (he was granted the rank of honorary lieutenant colonel in 1917). In his own words, he had been appointed "to assist in establishing conscription. Conscription being established ... routine work could be done by any wounded soldier and, after consultation with Lord Derby, [I] resigned."[12] Conscription in England and Scotland had been fully imposed in May, but in the face of declining rates of volunteers and the 500,000 British and French casualties on the Somme, it remained a controversial prospect in Canada, Australia, and especially Ireland. Greenwood was aware of the deep divisions in Canada, having kept in touch with – among others – the now beleaguered Sam Hughes, the controversial minister of militia; Sir George Perley MP, the high commissioner (and soon to be also minister of the overseas military forces of Canada); and Max Aitken, from 1916 the "Canadian Military Representative at the Front."

On 16 September 1916, eleven days after his resignation as DAAG, Sir Hamar embarked with Lady Greenwood for New York, leaving their two infant children, four-year-old Angela and two-year-old David, in the care of nannies. Borden was informed that Greenwood, fresh from the conscription controversies in the United Kingdom, was to visit Australia, New Zealand, and Canada for a second time in three years under the auspices of the Empire Parliamentary Association. His resignation from the War Office and his four-month tour (of which at least six weeks were taken by sea travel), all in the midst of the imposition of compulsory military service, must have been planned and cleared with the Dominions weeks if not months in advance. In the case of Canada, Greenwood's arrival date was confirmed to Borden in cipher, an elementary precaution in light of the popular conviction – not only in Quebec – that Britain was pressing Canada to introduce conscription. In time, the British and Canadian governments would join in denying that any such secret recommendations had been made, but their denials were not always believed. No records in Britain or Canada give details of the reasons for Greenwood's imperial tour in wartime, but his interlocutors in the Dominions likely queried him about the problems and sentiments that had accompanied the introduction of conscription in the United Kingdom in the face of the appalling casualties. Only in June 1917, almost a year later, did the deeply troubled Borden introduce his highly divisive Military Service Act. The difficulties in Australia were hardly less.

The Greenwoods arrived in Sydney shortly after the return from London of Australia's pro-conscriptionist prime minister, Billy Hughes. After their departure from Australia, a referendum of October 1916 (the first of two) rejected compulsory military service. Hughes blamed the rejection chiefly on the large numbers of Irish in Australia. In parallel, Greenwood for his part never missed an opportunity during his imperial tour to invite his interlocutors to increase their vocal support for Home Rule, sharing with John Redmond in early September his conviction that "the future of Home Rule depends largely upon the Colonial impetus behind it."[13]

In Ottawa on their return journey from Australia, the Greenwoods called upon Laurier (whom they found "in splendid form"), but missed seeing Mackenzie King. Before embarking for Britain in Halifax, Greenwood had written to King accurately describing how he had found "people in Canada … too optimistic about the war. The end is not yet in sight and the Germans are not beaten or starving or decisively weakened in any way. The Hun is brutally efficient and [is] fighting and organising with devlish [sic] zeal and ingenuity. We'll finally beat them, but the road to victory will be long and awful."[14] Greenwood sidestepped the fundamental question that Borden increasingly raised: what voice in the formulation of imperial foreign policy would an evolving Canada have as a result of the sacrifice of her soldiers? Borden put the question publicly on a wartime visit to the United Kingdom: "Unless Canada could have that voice in the foreign relations of the Empire as a whole, she would before long have an independent voice in her own foreign affairs outside the Empire."[15] Canadian nationalism was best expressed through the Empire, through equality in imperial institutions, not independently. Perley, the high commissioner, echoed his prime minister: "The imperial feeling is very much alive in Canada. We perhaps feel the Empire to be a more vital thing than does the ordinary citizen of England."[16] In early 1917 the Dominion premiers gathered in London for the Imperial War Conference, which adopted, much to Greenwood's gratification, Resolution IX which anticipated that at the end of the war there would be "full recognition of the Dominions as autonomous nations of an Imperial Commonwealth, and of India as an important portion of the same … [with] the right of the Dominions and of India to an adequate voice in foreign policy." The Imperial War Conference did take a first step toward a possible imperial tariff preference by the creation of tariffs to "safeguard" certain war-sensitive industries (e.g., steel), but it left unresolved how in practice several disparate Dominions and India could join with the United Kingdom in a coordinated foreign policy.

Soon after the Greenwoods had returned to London, Britain had a new government. This is not the place to attempt a description of the plotting in which Lloyd George, Bonar Law, Carson, and the ubiquitous Max Aitken engaged to force the resignation on 5 December 1916 of the *laissez-faire* Asquith and his replacement as prime minister by the more dynamic Lloyd George. Bonar Law thereupon became chancellor of the exchequer and joined Curzon, Milner, and Henderson in Lloyd George's newly constituted and exclusive War Cabinet, supported by a secretariat headed by Maurice Hankey in which Leo Amery was soon playing a prominent part. Greenwood and other members of the Liberal War Committee had absented themselves from a meeting of Liberal MPs the day before, called to express continuing confidence in Asquith. Instead they pledged their support to the new prime minister, Lloyd George. The Liberal Party was now irreversibly split, never to form a government again.

Max Aitken, having sought in vain a senior portfolio in the new government, accepted instead a peerage as Lord Beaverbrook. (Subsequently he regretted having closed the route through the House of Commons to the prime ministership, "believing myself to have lacked sound judgement when I accepted the peerage."[17]) Rumour reached Ottawa that Lloyd George's ministerial appointments would include Greenwood. Mackenzie King wired him that he was "delighted see your name mentioned Government reconstruction."[18] In fact, Lloyd George made few ministerial appointments at the time,[*] having little choice but to keep constantly in mind the Conservative-Unionists upon whose support his Unionist-dominated coalition government depended. Amery, however, arranged to have his brother-in-law included in his new project, the War Aims Committee, which struggled with what the postwar world would likely be with the disappearance of the empires of Germany, Austro-Hungary, Ottoman Turkey, and Russia, and what the British terms should be at an eventual peace conference – including the role of the Dominions. Additionally, the committee worked with Beaverbrook after Lloyd George had appointed him minister of information in February

---

[*]   Alfred Mond was among the few MPs promoted, Lloyd George making him first commissioner of works.

1918. With Beaverbrook, the committee's challenge was to define more clearly what, after more than three years, Britain was still fighting for and to display for all to see that it was winning. President Wilson had proclaimed his famous Fourteen Points in January but, while vaguely inspiring, they left many questions unanswered. The committee supported Beaverbrook in the propaganda war, concentrating on good news and elaborating on how progress was being made, despite occasional setbacks, to ultimate victory in 1919 or even 1920.

Greenwood never missed an occasion in the House of Commons to urge Home Rule as the situation in Ireland itself worsened. Lloyd George, in the face of the Conservative-Unionists' commitment to Ulster, was unwilling to give time to the distraction of Ireland amidst the perils of the war. Convinced that he would eventually be able to work miracles in Ireland, he had somehow to buy time. Irish unrest, however, only increased. On 22 March 1917, in the wake of the meeting of the imperial war conference, Greenwood spoke in the Commons in support of a motion for the prompt adoption of Home Rule, which was again stalled by Ulster intransigence and, more broadly, by the distracting demands of the war.* Given his long friendship – if not intimacy – with Lloyd George, Greenwood proposed the formation of an "illustrious committee" of the Dominion premiers, which would quickly propose modifications to the Government of Ireland bill, "according to the course of events and the lapse of time ... The predominant feeling in the Dominions ... is in favour of Home Rule."[19] Above all, there must be no further delay, three decades having elapsed since Gladstone's bills. Greenwood was not alone in recognizing that scepticism amongst the Irish about the government's good faith was steadily mounting, fuelling radicalism. Time was clearly not on the side of the moderates. On the other hand, the Empire itself was in a state of flux. In the postwar world, Ireland must be accommodated within the imperial framework foreseen in Resolution IX adopted by the Imperial War Conference in April 1917. (Its principal author, Borden, hailed it as the occasion when "a new and greater Imperial Commonwealth" had been born.) Following the end of the war, full recognition would be given to "the Dominions as autonomous nations of an Imperial Commonwealth" and to the rights of the Dominions and India to an adequate voice in imperial for-

---

* Greenwood also asked what the response of the government had been to visiting Canadian ministers when they raised the question of the continuing embargo against Canadian cattle.

eign relations, with effective arrangements for continuous consultation. Only a vague endorsement of the idea of an imperial tariff preference was added, almost as an afterthought.

In early June 1917, Greenwood was removed temporarily from the parliamentary scene by another traffic accident. A taxi cab in which he was riding during a blackout drove into a building, so injuring him that he was absent for several weeks from the House of Commons and from a service at Westminster Abbey attended by the king commemorating the fiftieth anniversary of Canadian Confederation. Greenwood completed his convalescence by spending three weeks from August 20 in Paris with Margo as the guests of Lloyd George, three weeks that Margo, in her letter of thanks, described as "the most splendid holiday in our lives." It was also a singular expression of the regard of Lloyd George, in the midst of the war, for the Greenwoods – or at least for Margo.

Despite Greenwood's cabinet disappointment and his temporary absence from Parliament, he continued to support, with Bonar Law, Walter Long, and six other MPs in the War Aims Committee, the yet more vigorous pursuit of the war – as Robert Borden urged repeatedly on his several wartime visits to London as well as in Ottawa.* Anything less than unconditional surrender would be a betrayal of the sacrifice of the war dead. In anticipation of final Allied victory, Greenwood called for greater support for war widows and orphans, needy veterans, and the poor generally. At the same time, presumably in consultation with Perley and the Canadian military headquarters in London, he was solicitous of Canadian soldiers who had contracted venereal diseases in the stews of Britain. Whitehall had not done nearly enough either to regulate or to close brothels, despite the recommendations of a pre-war royal commission and, since 1915, of a National Council for Combating Venereal Disease. During his recent trip across Canada, Greenwood had been told by parents, "We do not mind our boys dying on the field of

---

* Always attempting to keep his Canadian contacts, Liberal or Conservative, in good working order, Greenwood saw Borden frequently in London. In June 1918, Margo and he also lunched and dined with his University of Toronto classmate Arthur Meighen, Borden's minister of the interior, who had crossed to London in a final effort to induce disgruntled British bondholders to agree to terms for the nationalization of the ailing Grand Trunk Pacific and Canadian Northern Railways. Presumably Greenwood repeated to Meighen his earlier advice to McBride about provincial assistance to the Pacific Great Eastern Railway: "I say go ahead with your Railways Policy. There are a lot of weaklings going by the name of Conservative, but the heart of the people is with you and with you to the limit of your Railway Policy" (Greenwood, *Greenwood Tree*, 26).

battle for Old England, but to think that we have sent our sons to England to come back to us ruined in health and a disgrace to us, to them and to the country is something that the Home Country should never ask us to bear."[20] One element in the tardy response of the War Office – which seemed to have learned little from a similar natural phenomenon during the South African War – was unexpectedly imaginative. No longer able to ignore the growing numbers of soldiers rendered unfit for active duty by venereal disease, the War Office, hard pressed for recruits, joined with the Ministry of Overseas Military Forces of Canada in making a pioneering forty-minute silent film, *Whatsoever a Man Soweth*, for screenings in Canadian camps in the United Kingdom and behind the lines in France. It portrayed vulture-like prostitutes in Trafalgar Square successfully soliciting innocent young Canadian boys, which soon resulted in rotting hands and legs, all graphically if silently displayed. Greenwood certainly had a point: by the end of the war, almost half a million soldiers and sailors from Britain and the Dominions had been treated for venereal disease. Canada had established two military hospitals in the United Kingdom for its treatment alone.

That the ambitious Margo as well as her husband continued to feel close to the prime minister in all his various policies and understandings was evident from a letter that she wrote to him on 13 November 1918, two days after the Armistice. "You are a brick! Hamar and I value beyond measure those words that you wrote on your photograph for us. We realize too and fully appreciate the fact that you found time to write them for us in the hour of your greatest triumph. Long may you reign! That photograph will be treasured all our lives and handed on to our son [then age four], your namesake and a very promising young David too."[21]

7

Postwar Upheavals, 1918–1920

Following the Armistice of 1918 ending the First World War, and the general election the following month, Lloyd George appointed a peace-time coalition cabinet, although he had no intention of summoning it at any early date to replace his highly convenient, five-member wartime cabinet. (The full cabinet did not in fact meet for almost a year, only in late October 1919.) Greenwood was not included. His failure to win a place at the cabinet table was not for want of trying on the part of the Greenwoods, but despite their chagrin they were realistic enough to recognize that the prime minister had few places for Liberals; there were more senior and distinguished candidates than the eager member for Sunderland.

In the December election – the first since 1910 – Greenwood had again been head of the poll in Sunderland. He was one of 150 Liberal "coupon candidates," endorsed jointly by Lloyd George's Liberals and Law's Conservatives, part of the decisive electoral victory of Lloyd George's Conservative-dominated coalition. Included in its platform had again been Home Rule for Ireland, however vaguely stated, but Sinn Fein campaigned against such a limited offer and won almost all the seats in southern Ireland. Sinn Fein thereupon declined to sit in the new parliament, again asserting its collective legitimacy in Dublin as the only true government of Ireland.

On 30 December 1918 Greenwood wrote to Lloyd George, as the soldiers' votes were being counted, "In forming your new administration, I hope that you will this time give me a chance to serve you and the state." "This time" was a contrast with May 1916 when he had written to John Redmond seeking his support for his appointment as chief secretary for Ireland. What Greenwood had in mind in December 1918 was the Home Office. Edward Shortt, the current chief secretary for Ireland, was also seeking the Home Office on his way to his ultimate ambition, the bench. Lloyd George duly rewarded Shortt for his service in Ireland by making him home secretary, and as his successor appointed Ian Macpherson, who had worked closely with Lloyd George in the Ministry of Munitions. The prime minister was fully aware of the Greenwoods' ambitions to see Hamar as home secretary, but he did only what partisan political circumstances allowed. In early January 1919 he appointed him under-secretary at the Home Office.

Brother-in-law Leo Amery was likewise not appointed to the cabinet (he became parliamentary private secretary to Lord Milner, the secretary of state for the colonies). F.E. Smith, having declined the Colonial Office on the grounds that he could not afford it (he was always in debt), accepted the more remunerative lord chancellorship, taking the title of Birkenhead upon moving to the House of Lords (and thereby avoiding a by-election). At the behest of the prime minister, he made Greenwood a king's counsel before the first of the two ministerial – but *not* cabinet – posts that he would fill in 1919 and 1920.

Greenwood had been rumoured for the bigger appointment of chief whip, an influential post that at Westminster traditionally carries with it a place at the cabinet table. To that end, he had prompted a fellow Liberal member and barrister, Sir Frederick Smith (not to be confused with F.E. Smith), lately treasurer of Gray's Inn, to recommend him to the prime minister as "an old and faithful friend [who has] character, force, tact, and influence and would [as whip] brace the Party and consolidate it."[1] Sir Frederick was a solid Greenwood supporter, but unfortunately Greenwood also had a vitriolic local detractor. In a now partly illegible letter of 29 April 1919 to Austen Chamberlain (the new chancellor of the exchequer), Samuel Storey, the Conservative-Unionist agent in Sunderland, spoke of hearing rumours that Greenwood was to be made chief whip.* If so, Storey warned Chamberlain, in the mandatory by-election that automatically followed acceptance of a paid office by a MP, despite coalition understandings about candidates the

---

* Samuel Storey sat as the Liberal MP for Sunderland from 1881 to 1895. His local credentials were impressive. He had been chairman of the Durham County Council and president of the Northern Liberal Association. However, he stood in the election of January 1910 as an "Independent Tariff Reformer" (that is, he eschewed the official Liberal commitment to free trade) and in December 1910 as an "Independent Conservative." Thereafter, he became a declared Conservative-Unionist, proving again the adage that there is no zealot like a convert.

Conservatives in Sunderland would openly oppose Greenwood. "During the Ulster fracas [of 1914] he traduced the officers of the British Army; during the War he has been a sham Colonel drawing £650 a year as such; he went with his Regiment to the front, returned after eleven days, never having seen one day's fighting service; he never threw over [?] Asquith [words illegible]. He is the worst type of a politician on the make. The local feeling against him is intense."[2] Storey invited Chamberlain to show his letter to the prime minister, which he evidently did, since it is now among the Lloyd George papers. The prime minister decided against Greenwood as whip – if he had ever considered him – knowing full well that Conservative-Unionist support for his coalition government was precarious enough without alienating more Conservatives.

As under-secretary at the Home Office during the first half of 1919, Greenwood dealt with and spoke frequently in the House on such diverse questions as citizenship and naturalization and postwar problems of growing unrest in the police forces, including the unsettling prospect of a militant police union in London. In such debates, he impressed Bonar Law, who had set aside their prewar clashes over Home Rule for Ireland. As leader of the Conservative-Unionists, Law replied to Storey, "Till a year ago I had a rather poor opinion of Greenwood. At that time, however, in the absence of Lloyd George [in Paris], I had the responsibility of dealing with the strikes which were then threatened. Greenwood was Under Secretary at the Home Office. I appointed him Chairman of an important strike committee. The position was so serious that I attended myself some of the meetings of that committee. I was greatly struck with the complete grasp which he had of the situation and the sound sense with which he was dealing with it."[3] Storey in Sunderland remained unconvinced. More than a year later he would write enigmatically to Law, "I am surprised to hear that you and Lloyd George thought Greenwood your fittest man for this arduous and dangerous post [of chief secretary for Ireland] ... You must be driving a sorry team ... I thought of setting out the whole facts so that you might realize how serious are the charges, public and private, which I can make good against him, but why should I add to your embarrassments at so serious a time?"[4]

Greenwood, having not realized his ambitions to be promoted to the cabinet direct from under-secretary in the Home Office, had to content himself during a minor ministerial shuffle in July 1919 with a lateral transfer to secretary of the Overseas Trade Department of the Foreign Office. It was, at least in the eyes of Lloyd George, a logical progression. Greenwood had travelled extensively throughout the Empire as well as Europe, and, as in the case of Canadians in general, it was simply

assumed that he knew the United States, having been born on its bor-
ders.* In an undated autobiographic note (ca. 1918), he made an even
larger claim, basing himself upon his pre-war and wartime imperial travels: "I ... know personally all Prime Ministers and ex-Prime Ministers
in the Dominions. I also know leading politicians and editors in the
Dominions and the Colonies and keep in touch with them."[5] Lloyd
George was aware that he was a barrister with aspirations to become
in time an affluent businessman following at least one term as cabinet
minister. The prime minister had appointed several businessmen to
ministerial offices, believing that they would bring much-needed order
to bloated and inefficient wartime departments. For example, when
Greenwood became secretary to the Overseas Trade Department, the
formidable Auckland Geddes was president of the Board of Trade. His
brother, Eric, was first lord of the admiralty, soon to become minister
of transport.

Mackenzie King sent Greenwood a congratulatory telegram "on your
latest promotion."[6] In response, Greenwood regretted that Margo and
he had misunderstood the short duration of King's recent brief visit to
London, because they had "hoped to arrange a really slap-up affair for
you. However, the world is young for us three yet, and it is becoming so
small and all together that we shall meet each other more frequently. I
clearly see a great future for you in Canada, as indeed we did in '95."[7]
In a few weeks, Greenwood was in turn to congratulate his former classmate on becoming leader of the Liberal Party of Canada and accordingly leader of the opposition: "With you on one side and our friend,
Arthur Meighen, on the other, the political future of Canada is in good
hands. It is a great romance that we three should be in the centre of the
main political movements in the Empire. Good luck to all of us!"[8] At the
same time, despite his rhetoric, Greenwood did not lose sight of the
base of his political fortunes, as he had possibly let happen in York. He

* Certainly Greenwood continued to cultivate his ties with Canada. On the same day
that he was appointed a minister to the Board of Trade, he attended a Canada Club
Dominion Day dinner with Amery; Sir George Perley, the high commissioner; Clifford
Sifton, the sometime minister of the interior (for whom Greenwood had done immigration promotion); and Charles Doherty, minister of justice (whom he valued as one of the
more outspoken Canadian advocates of Home Rule for Ireland). They listened to
General Currie of Canadian Corps fame proclaim that "Canada must be prepared to take
her part in the responsibilities as well as the privileges of our Empire" (presumably with
the fact in mind that the last of almost five thousand Canadian soldiers – despite
Churchill's best efforts to the contrary – were then on their way home from Russia, where
they had been part of the futile Allied intervention in the civil war).

strove to keep his difficult and contentious Sunderland constituency more or less happy, telling his private secretary, George Garro Jones,* "Every letter from a constituent is a chance to make a friend. Do not forget that a friend may be made out of an opponent."9

The Department of Overseas Trade was formally part of the Foreign Office, so Greenwood was also an "additional under-secretary" at the Foreign Office. In that second capacity, he had been assigned, under the foreign secretary, responsibilities for the consular service, including its trade promotion activities. His appointment, perhaps fortuitously, coincided with a finance bill introducing specific imperial tariff preferences upon the recommendations of the Imperial War Conferences of 1917 and 1918. Other commercial matters arising from the war took him to Brussels for meetings of the Allied Supreme Economic Council, but his ministerial responsibilities also kept him for long periods in the House of Commons, answering questions about violations of human rights, ranging from massacres in Armenia, pogroms in Poland, the plight of the Kurds in Turkey and Iraq, atrocities in Hungary, and tribal warfare in Somalia and the Sudan to the protection of stray dogs in the United Kingdom and the dangers of reckless cycling on Tooting Common.

Lloyd George also had a particular task in mind for Greenwood: the restoration of trade – but not diplomatic – relations with Bolshevik Russia. In the aftermath of the revolution, London and Moscow viewed each other with deep suspicion, but both recognized the mutual value of restoring the once substantial trade between them. Amidst continuing controversy and with some difficulty, Greenwood helped to arrange in early 1920 for a delegation not ostensibly from the communist government in Moscow but from the more innocuous-sounding "Russian co-ops" to visit Britain, an approach to the Bolshevik regime that he had advocated at the Allied Supreme Economic Council in Brussels.[10] The visit led in May to the appointment of a Russian trade delegation resident in London. No one in Whitehall was clear about exactly what

---

* George Garro Jones was a Welshman who had been commissioned in the South Wales Borderers in 1914 when Greenwood was still commanding its 10th Battalion. A veteran of both the infantry and the Royal Flying Corps, he was employed by Greenwood as his additional private secretary at the end of the First World War when Greenwood was under-secretary at the Home Office. Curiously, neither Sturgis nor Macready nor other diarists mention him. Garro Jones sat as a Liberal MP for Hackney from 1924 to 1929, having defeated the Labour candidate, Herbert Morrison. He later joined the Labour Party and sat as a Labour member from 1935 to 1945. He was with Greenwood in the House of Lords from 1947 as Baron Trefgarne. Greenwood sent a copy of Garro Jones's memoirs, *Ventures and Visions*, to Mackenzie King in 1935.

policy toward Russia the prime minister was following, many suspecting that he saw trade not only of value in itself but also as a major step toward early diplomatic recognition of what was widely condemned as a regime of assassins and terrorists. In the way of attempting to demonstrate some policy balance, Greenwood also wrote to Churchill, the secretary of state for war, about commercial possibilities in the still White-controlled south Russia. None of this, however, was to the liking of many Conservatives in the coalition government, adding yet another question in the minds of some about how much longer they wanted to go on with Lloyd George.

The prime minister had another and even more immediate reason for appointing Greenwood an additional under-secretary at the Foreign Office. He charged him with helping to secure from what would soon be the British-mandated territory of Iraq a dependable supply of oil – the fuel of the future – for the Royal Navy and for British industry more generally. With oil replacing coal on a wide scale, pre-war Britain had been largely reliant on Russia, the United States, and Mexico for its needs. Strathcona, who as well as being high commissioner was a controlling shareholder in what eventually became British Petroleum (later still, BP), had played a major role in adding supplies from Persia. If the Royal Navy was to continue to rule the waves, however, additional British-controlled sources became a pressing postwar need.

The defeat of Germany provided an opportunity. Before the war, the Ottoman Empire had granted licenses for the development of the oil-rich region of Mosul, north of Baghdad, to an Anglo-German consortium, the Turkish Petroleum Company. The lease was terminated with the coming of war, and Britain simply seized the Mosul fields. Lloyd George remained unhappy with the Sykes-Picot agreement of May 1916, which had divided up the Middle East in anticipation of the collapse of the Ottoman Empire, believing that it gave too much to France and did not recognize clearly Mosul as British territory. More fundamentally, he was opposed to a French presence in the Levant. In return for British support for large French demands in the Ruhr, Clemenceau recognized in December 1918 the British claim on Mosul. At the same time, however, France sought to replace Germany in the co-ownership of the pre-war Turkish Petroleum Company. An exchange of letters of 8 April 1919 between Walter Long,* the first lord of the admiralty (which had a fundamental interest in the whole matter), and Henri Berenger, the

---

* Walter Long had been Greenwood's particular antagonist in the 1915 debates on Home Rule for Ireland.

French minister in charge of petroleum affairs and commissioner general for petroleum producers, confirmed British acceptance of the acquisition by France of part of the pre-war German interest in the company: Britain would have 70 per cent, France 20 per cent, and Iraq 10 per cent.

The agreement, duly endorsed by the Foreign Office on 16 May 1919, seemed to conclude the dispute. Clemenceau, however, opposed a parallel agreement that would have given the company two pipeline routes from Mosul across the French-mandated Syria to the Mediterranean. In response, Lloyd George promptly declared that Britain was withdrawing from the whole Long-Berenger agreement. Six weeks later, when Greenwood became parliamentary secretary to the Overseas Trade Department, he renewed negotiations with the French, assisted by Sir John Cadman, director of the British Petroleum Executive, a government agency charged with bringing coherence to postwar petroleum policy. Greenwood was frequently in Paris during the second half of 1919 as the contentious negotiation of the terms of peace treaties with Germany's allies preoccupied Allied leaders.

At Victoria Station on 30 June, Greenwood participated with Churchill and Alfred Mond in an unusual welcoming party led by King George and the Prince of Wales to greet the prime minister on his return from the peace negotiations in Paris. Further opportunities to discuss petroleum policy with Lloyd George followed immediately and again when the Greenwoods spent a fortnight in early September as his guests at a house party near Trouville on the Normandy coast. Lord Riddell had leased the Manoir de Clairfontein at Hennequeville as a retreat for the hard-pressed prime minister – and as an assurance that he himself would be included in the house party. In addition to the Greenwoods, among the guests were Bonar Law and his daughter; Eric Geddes, now minister of transport (who brought with him someone described as his "housekeeper"); Balfour, the foreign secretary; Horne, the minister of labour; Churchill, the secretary of state for war; Lord and Lady Astor; Maurice Hankey, the cabinet secretary; and of course Frances Stevenson. Riddell, who described the house party as "merry," sardonically observed, "It is amusing to note the jealousies of most Ministers and their wives of their colleagues. This is especially notable among the lesser lights like the Astors and the Greenwoods. They are all pushing hard for place and position."[11] He added later, "The Greenwoods and Mrs. Astor are hating each other ... Both parties paying court to the PM in the most ardent and unblushing way. No wonder that Kings and Prime Ministers grow to think they are divinities."[12] In the evenings, Eric Geddes sang that wistful lament evocative of the Somme, "Roses of Picardy." Greenwood, drawing upon his histrionic experience in Ontario, performed the 1890s comic song-and-dance: "Oh, my name is Solomon Levi / I am a velly good man / I'll sell you a suit of klo-ses / So sheep as ever I can / My wife's name is Rachel / She is nothing but a sham / And every time she gets a chance / She slugs me if she can." Lord Riddell, who was present, described it simply as "an exhibition of step-dancing to the tune of *Solomon Levi*,"[13] but whether with or without words, Greenwood's performance became something of a fixture at later house parties in England.*At Hennequeville, however, even Greenwood was outdone by the "very vivacious" American Nancy Astor who "performed an apache dance, which ended in [her] flinging herself, after a series of cartwheels, into the lap of Lord Riddell."[14]

Most of the major subjects discussed at Hennequeville were not international but domestic, particularly how to counter unemployment and labour unrest while at the same time reducing government expenditure. Field Marshal Lord Allenby, who in March had been appointed high commissioner in Egypt, was, however, summoned to discuss with the prime minister the increasing unrest of Egyptian nationalists intent upon achieving the same "self-determination" that they had seen promised to smaller European nationalities by the Allied leaders – especially President Wilson – during the war. In response, Allenby received from Lloyd George the challenge of first restoring law and order by employing a combination of native Egyptian police and British soldiers before contemplating government reform.

For the Greenwoods the holiday was marred by an appeal for clemency that was to have an unexpected reverberation involving his own nephew twenty-five years later.[†] The Frenchwoman who was the owner of the Manoir de Clairfontein had a son who had been convicted as a German spy and condemned to death. She asked to see Lloyd George to appeal to him to seek clemency from Clemenceau. Lloyd George left

---

* Lord Beaverbrook in his lively *The Decline and Fall of Lloyd George* (104) offers other lyrics on another occasion when Greenwood earned the prime minister's gratitude for his "high spirits and gaiety. He had a rasping though agreeable voice and he would do a gay song and soft shoe shuffle dance: 'My name is Solomon Levi; / At my store in Salem Street, / That's where you'll buy your coats and vests, / And everything that's neat. / I've second-handed ulsterettes / And everything that's fine, / For all the boys they trade with me / At a hundred and forty-nine.' Everybody joined in the chorus *Poor Solomon Levi*."
† See page 319.

it to Greenwood to tell her that the prime minister could not possibly intervene. Her son was executed the next morning.

Following Lloyd George's discussions with Greenwood of Iraqi petroleum issues, Berenger recommended to Clemenceau a renewal of the draft agreement with the United Kingdom to ensure that France was at the table when the newly reconstituted Turkish Petroleum Company began to develop further the highly productive Mosul fields. On 21 December 1919, Greenwood and Berenger finally initialled a memorandum that was similar to the Long-Berenger agreement of six months before. A French guarantee of the routes of the two proposed pipelines though Syria to the Mediterranean coast was included at the cost of increasing France's share in the company from 20 to 25 per cent. However, Greenwood ensured that the final sentence in the agreement stated baldly, "It is clearly understood that the Turkish Petroleum Company shall be under permanent British control."[15] Lloyd George and the thirsty admiralty were satisfied. Greenwood had done well, although for the time being coal would continue as the major energy source for Britain as well as a major source of labour unrest.

During the summer of 1919, a royal commission on British coal mining had recommended a major overhaul of the industry, in part to curtail the exploitation of miners by rapacious pit owners. But the once-radical Lloyd George did surprisingly little to implement its basic recommendation in light of the hostility of his Conservative coalition partners. Some of these imaginatively regarded the miners' militancy as presaging an early communist uprising in Britain itself, following the Bolshevik triumph in Russia and the formation in July 1920 of the Communist Party of Great Britain. In October 1920 the miners went on strike, and at the end of the year the Trades Union Council supported their further goal of a general strike. Industrial unrest continued to worsen as the economy worsened. Consumer prices soared. Within a year unemployment reached a record two million. Anticipating a general strike, Lloyd George wrote to Greenwood, "In connection with the possibility of serious industrial disturbances in the near future, I have been paying attention to our organization for maintaining the essential services of the country."[16] The prime minister invited Greenwood to chair an emergency supervisory committee, "you to be Chief Commissioner and to arrange to control all other committees,"[17] under the general direction of the new minister of transport, the dynamic and egocentric Scottish entrepreneur, Eric Geddes. The other members were Amery, Lord Astor, and Edward Craig, the Northern Ireland MP.

The timing of Lloyd George's appointment of Greenwood to chair the emergency supervisory committee is puzzling: it was at the beginning of the same week that he appointed him chief secretary for Ireland. Since Greenwood as a cabinet minister could not serve on the committee, Lloyd George as late as the last week of March must have been still seeking someone else to succeed the incumbent in Ireland, Ian Macpherson. It was well known that Macpherson had come to hate the job, ill as he was and said to be living in continual terror of assassination. Although long an advocate of Home Rule, he had been dutifully implementing Lloyd George's hard-line policy of proscribing Sinn Fein and declaring illegal the self-proclaimed Irish assembly the Dáil Éireann. However, by the early spring of 1920, he had more than enough. He happily disappeared into the quiet backwaters of the Ministry of Pensions.

The emergency supervisory committee on essential services had to begin its work without Greenwood as chief commissioner. The order-in-council appointing him chief secretary for Ireland is dated 4 April 1920, a few days after his short-lived chairmanship of the emergency supervisory committee.

8

Ireland, 1919–1920

The centuries of background to the Irish "troubles" of the early 1920s have been described so often and so variously in so many books that a small library could be readily compiled of the detailed histories, local reviews, partisan tracts, polemics, personal reminiscences, novels, plays, poetry, gross exaggerations, and understated reflections. This is not the place to attempt more than a brief review of the convoluted sentiments, calamities, policies, and bigotries that contributed to the breaking point in Anglo-Irish relations during the First World War and immediately thereafter.

It is perhaps sufficient to recall here the disastrous famine of the mid-1840s and Westminster's lackadaisical response, the uprising of the Fenian Brotherhood in 1867, and especially Gladstone's vain attempts to introduce Home Rule bills in 1886 and 1893, following his controversial but successful disestablishment of the Church of Ireland (Anglican) in 1871. The more moderate nationalists in seeking a new order echoed Gladstone in looking to Canada as the precedent: "Canada did not get Home Rule because she was loyal and friendly, but she became loyal and friendly because she has got Home Rule."[1] Despite his appeal to the House on his first Home Rule bill – "Think, I beseech you, think well, think wisely, think, not for the moment, but for the years to come, before you reject this Bill" – it was defeated, as was his second Home Rule bill seven years later in the House of Lords. Both bills failed chiefly in the face of the deep hostility of both Liberal and Conservative Unionists, locked in their unwavering conviction that Home Rule would undermine the integrity of both the United Kingdom and the British Empire.

Despite the defeat of Gladstone's two bills, which he had defined as offering government "strictly and substantially analogous" to Canada's status in the Empire, the Irish Nationalist members of Parliament remained wonderfully patient, however radical they may have seemed to their more reactionary fellow members. John Redmond, the leader of the Irish Nationalists in the House of Commons, echoed Gladstone when he described Home Rule as "a measure of legislative autonomy similar to that enjoyed by any of your self-governing Colonies or Dependencies. If you want an illustration, look at Canada."[2] What was special about the many Irish members was not only their temperate and patient attitude but that at several points in the latter half of the nineteenth century and in the first years of the twentieth, they held the balance of power in the House of Commons.

Gladstone's Liberal successor, Lord Rosebery, never showed more than lukewarm interest in Ireland, even when he was a minister in Gladstone's government. As prime minister, he concentrated more on reform of the House of Lords, the Imperial Federation League, and the acquisition of Uganda. The Conservative government under Lord Salisbury hoped to "kill Home Rule with kindness." His nephew, Arthur Balfour, matched harsh coercion with a modest government-funded program to help tenants buy out those English landowners willing to make holdings available to their Irish tenants, opening the way to the resolution of the long-standing land question. In late 1905 – the same year in which the radical Irish nationalist movement, Sinn Fein, was founded by Arthur Griffith – the benign Henry Campbell-Bannerman became prime minister; he had a Liberal majority that allowed him, in the wake of the South African War, to give priority to other and seemingly more pressing domestic and foreign issues. When "CB" did occasionally turn his mind to Ireland, he envisaged gradual devolution of self-government on the successful model of Canada, "the greatest triumph of British statesmanship, of broad and liberal views, and nobly instructed imagination." But no Home Rule legislation was presented.[3]

Herbert Asquith, Campbell-Bannerman's successor in 1908, was less fortunate in his total number of Liberal members and could only form a government with the support of the Irish Nationalist M Ps. With Lloyd George, his chancellor of the exchequer, at his side, Asquith finally succeeded in depriving the House of Lords of its competence to block any legislation indefinitely. The way ahead, however, remained uncertain. In April 1912 he finally introduced a Government of Ireland bill – in effect, a third Home Rule bill.

The highly divisive debate on the Ireland bill, both within Parliament and without, was rendered even more so by the hostility of an increasingly bold Ulster at the prospect of being placed under the authority of a predominantly Roman Catholic legislature in Dublin. In early 1913, as the bill was finally moving from the Commons to the Lords, the Ulster Unionist Council called into being an Ulster Volunteer Force. It soon numbered an estimated 100,000 men, eventually armed largely with rifles smuggled from Germany in April 1914. (Walter Long solicited funds from Ulstermen in Canada and Australia to help pay for "expenses.") In July 1914, with German rifles landed for the Irish Volunteers, civil war in Ireland became a real possibility. Conservative-Unionists associated themselves with Protestant Ulstermen led by the intransigent, Dublin-born former solicitor general, Sir Edward Carson. (Carson had become leader of the Ulster Unionist Council in 1910.) He moved – unsuccessfully – an amendment to exclude all of Ulster from Asquith's Government of Ireland bill, blocked any attempts at compromise, and supported the spreading conviction in northern Ireland that, paradoxically, armed resistance against British legislation might become necessary to remain British, even as Irish republicans in the south contemplated armed resistance to remaining British. Bonar Law, who regarded Lloyd George's support for the bill as that of "a dangerous rascal," spoke for many Conservative diehards when he infamously declared, "I can imagine no length of resistance to which Ulster can go in which I should not be prepared to support them."[4] The Ulsterman General Sir Henry Wilson, the director of military operations, and other senior officers, against all notions of military integrity and discipline, covertly manoeuvred to reduce the government's freedom of action in northern Ireland.

Increasingly the British government was seen as unable to rely on the British army to carry out its orders. Carson joined Law in demanding without qualification the permanent – not temporary – exclusion of Ulster from a Home Rule Ireland, if such were ever to be created. Amendments were made to the Government of Ireland bill, but in the end to little avail in placating either Conservative-Unionists on the one hand or more radical Irish on the other. Undeterred, Lloyd George attempted to reach out to some of the Tories. He had written to the Conservative-Unionist MP and implacable Ulster supporter F.E. Smith in 1913, "You know how anxious I have been for years to work with you and a few others on your side,"[5] but guarantees to Ulster of permanent exclusion from a Home Rule Ireland remained a basic problem.*

---

* Although repeatedly declaring himself a "Gladstone Home Ruler," Lloyd George did not himself know Ireland, having visited only Belfast briefly in 1907.

Following a conference at Buckingham Palace summoned by King George V in July 1914, Asquith, fearing violence, bloodshed, and civil war in Ireland and the possibility of it spilling into England, convinced even his more pronounced Home Rule colleagues that there now remained no other option but simply to exclude Ulster. By late summer of 1914 the legislative stage was finally set for a resolution. On 18 September 1914, the Government of Ireland bill was given royal assent. However, with the British declaration of war on Germany a fortnight before, implementation of the bill was suspended for twelve months or until "such later date ... as may be fixed by His Majesty by Order in Council." The hard-fought and controversial legislation was in fact never put into effect.

By May 1915, Asquith was besieged with the demands of many of his fellow Liberals as well as Conservatives to fight the war more vigorously. With Gallipoli and Mesopotamia adding to the seemingly endless carnage on the western front, he invited Conservative-Unionists to join a Liberal-dominated coalition government. Whatever benefits the inclusion of Conservative-Unionists brought in terms of more determined prosecution of the war, it introduced into the cabinet yet greater inflexibility regarding Home Rule and Ulster. The composition of Asquith's bipartisan cabinet reflected, among other things, deep divisions about Ireland. Bonar Law and Carson were committed to the permanent separation of Protestant Ulster from the Roman Catholic south. "Bloody Balfour" had attempted coercion in Ireland when he was chief secretary and later prime minister; Lansdowne, the former governor general of Canada and former foreign secretary and a major landowner in Ireland, was opposed to Home Rule. Curzon, Austen Chamberlain, and Selbourne were, to varying degrees, hardly less so. On the other hand, Lloyd George, the long-time advocate of Home Rule All Round, was at least in principle in favour. The Liberals H.A.L. Fisher, Edwin Montagu, Walter Runciman, and Reginald McKenna were even more so.

In April 1916, in the middle of the world war, when Greenwood was still at the War Office, the situation in Ireland took a decided turn for the worse. Armed insurgents proclaimed in Dublin an Irish republic. The week-long Easter Rising, estimated to involve actively as few as 1,600 men and women, left 450 dead, including 116 soldiers and 16 police. But whatever the exact numbers, the Rising never had a chance of ousting British rule. With the world war increasingly demanding sacrifice from everyone, there was little tolerance in Whitehall or in England more generally for what was seen as a stab in the back by rebels allegedly egged on and even supplied by the German enemy. For Conservative-Unionists and some Liberals, those involved in the Rising were not freedom fighters but traitorous murderers who must be dealt with harshly as an example to any other would-be insurgents elsewhere in the Empire.

Too harshly, some in England and many in the Dominions were quick to say: within ten days, sixteen of the leaders were summarily tried by court martial and executed, and four hundred others were interned in England. Wilfrid Laurier, leader of the opposition in Ottawa, wrote despondently and acutely, "What a blunder these terrible executions have been, following the foolish attempt at rebellion in Dublin. I could not put into words the feeling of horror these executions inspire, and I cannot conceive a more serious political error. That the Asquith Government should display so much severity at Dublin, while it leaves Carson in Belfast free to preach and organize rebellion with impunity, seems to me an act of the utmost feebleness." Two months later, however, he added, more positively, to the same unidentified correspondent (Greenwood?), "the government of Ireland by England for the past three centuries has been abominable. But consider the endeavours that the Liberals have been making for a century to remedy the evil and give Ireland self-government. Consider also that in a constitutional country like England, reforms are always and necessarily slow. After all, this very slowness ensures stability."[6]

Many Irish nationalists who had been rightly convinced that rebellion in the midst of a world war was, to say the least, ill advised and certain of failure, now joined the more radical Sinn Fein in the conviction that even the eventual implementation of the oft-delayed Government of Ireland bill at the end of the war could not be relied upon to accord Irishmen full rights and freedoms. From April 1916 onwards, Sinn Fein rather than more moderate Irish nationalists became the dynamic leaders of opposition to direct British rule. And Ulster, if anything, became more opposed to any governance from Dublin. Equally, those Englishmen who believed that Ireland had long been treated unfairly increasingly renounced the use of force to keep an unhappy people in a kingdom that was patently not united.

Between the Easter Rising and his embarkation for Australia and Canada in mid-September 1916 with an Empire parliamentary delegation, Greenwood was present in the House of Commons. Hansard does not record his making any intervention or comment of substance on the deteriorating Irish situation, including the Rising. A fortnight after the rebellion, however, he wrote to John Redmond, the Irish Nationalist leader and a friend, seeking his support for his own appointment as chief secretary for Ireland. Deeply troubled by any division in the empire, he was convinced that as a Canadian Liberal and a long-time advocate of Home Rule he could play a central part in introducing some form of government that would keep Ireland within the Empire.[7] Redmond does not appear to have replied, at least not on paper.

Lloyd George, who at the time of the Easter Rising was minister of munitions, had supported Home Rule All Round from the beginning of his political career when Gladstone was still prime minister, but as one of his own private secretaries later stated, "He was never, as Gladstone was, a crusader for Home Rule." Although he did not regard Home Rule as having priority over other Liberal issues, including Welsh ones, he was judged by Asquith as the colleague best equipped to attempt to resolve the post-Easter dilemma in Ireland. Asquith even saw Lloyd George as a possible secretary of state for Ireland, following the merger of the posts of viceroy and chief secretary. The wily Lloyd George declined the formal appointment, but accepted in May Asquith's more informal invitation "to take up Ireland." He did succeed in negotiating with both Redmond and the Ulster leader Edward Carson an agreement for the immediate granting of Home Rule – not waiting for the end of the war – to the twenty-six counties of Roman Catholic southern Ireland; meanwhile the six counties of the predominantly Protestant north would remain separate, at least until after the war. Then an Ireland-wide constitutional plebiscite would be held. He pledged to Redmond that he would personally stand or fall by the government's agreement to grant Home Rule without additional delay.

It was essential to implement the deal immediately before opposition to it could mobilize in both the north and south, but Asquith and Lloyd George dithered, fatally undermining Redmond's leadership. In the face of mounting Unionist obstruction in the Lords, the agreement did not stand, but Lloyd George did not fall. Various amendments were proposed, but it soon became evident to Asquith as well as to Lloyd George that the prospect of an immediate post-Easter settlement was going nowhere and that the limited Home Rule, as envisaged in 1914, was becoming an anachronism. However, with the slaughter on the Somme and its aftermath playing out in France, there was no time for the distraction of Ireland.

On 4 July 1916, Asquith, despite misgivings about the overweening ambitions of Lloyd George, appointed him secretary of state for war in the hope of strengthening his faltering government.* Thereafter, Lloyd George, with his eye on the premiership as well as on the war of attrition on the western front, had little inclination to continue "to take up Ireland," to give more time to a tiresome sideshow. Having failed to win unanimous support in cabinet for even his modest Home Rule proposals, despite the reluctant, belated acquiescence of Balfour, Churchill, and F.E. Smith, he went back on his word to the Irish Nationalist MPs. He undercut them, but he did not resign. Frances Stevenson wrote candidly in her diary,

> The Irish are angry with him: they think he should have upheld the original terms of the agreement, & I think they have reason to be angry. A large section of people think that D. [David Lloyd George] should have resigned when he failed to carry those original terms in the Cabinet; he himself told me that he would do so if the [Conservative] Unionists refused them. Now, however, he upholds the P.M. and says the Irish are unreasonable. I think he has done himself harm by his present attitude; he would have done himself less harm by leaving the Government, but it is too late now, as he has openly upheld Asquith in the House of Commons. I think he feels that he is an awkward position, & I do not know what to say to him, as I don't agree with what he has done. I don't think he has quite played the game ... His reputation in the country was so high that it would be a pity if it were spoilt by this wretched Irish business.[8]

Margot Asquith, Asquith's outspoken second wife, became convinced at the same time that "this wretched Irish business" in the midst of the Great War was an increasing threat to the longevity of her husband's government. She pleaded with Lloyd George, of all people, to help keep him in office. In fact, it was Lloyd George who, with the crucial support of Beaverbrook and Bonar Law, engineered Asquith's resignation on 6 December 1916. For the rest of his life Asquith retained a deep personal animosity toward his successor, whom he regarded as his unprincipled usurper, leaving the Liberal Party deeply divided, a division it never resolved and from which both the Conservative and Labour

---

* In succession to Lord Kitchener who, following a visit to Russia by General Sir Henry Wilson, had drowned in June 1916 en route to Britain's increasingly turbulent and unreliable ally. It is said that Lloyd George was also to go to St Petersburg, but if so, he was detained in London at the last moment.

Parties benefited. With the Liberal split, Lloyd George's coalition government became at once Conservative dominated.

Upon becoming the coalition prime minister, Lloyd George did attempt to get the Irish unrest out of the way until at least the end of the war. To that end, he declared an amnesty for the 560 prisoners still being held without trial after the Easter Rising. Before returning to the western front, William Redmond, John Redmond's brother and himself an Irish Nationalist M P,[*] wrote begging the new prime minister to head off disaster by concluding an early settlement granting full self-government. In his reply of 6 March 1917, Lloyd George stated with some hyperbole, "There is nothing that I would like better than to be the instrument for settling the Irish question. I was elected to the House [in 1890] purely as a Home Rule candidate: it was practically the only issue of the election, and I have voted steadily for Home Rule ever since. The Irish Members and I fought together on the same side in many a fierce conflict, and I have no better friends and never wish to have better friends. But you know just as well as I do what the difficulty is in settling the Irish question, and if any man can show me the way out of that I should indeed be happy."[9]

A fortnight later, on 22 March, Greenwood, once again urging early action, repeated in the House of Commons his statement made in the 1914 Home Rule debate that "the pre-dominant feeling in the Dominions ... is in favour of Home Rule because they have experienced it in various forms, always with success to themselves, and always with a growing and warmer attachment to the Imperial ideal." The essential point was to establish Home Rule in Ireland immediately. The longer the future of Ireland remained unsettled, the more difficult any resolution would become. "Do it now," he pressed. "The matter is urgent. Any action is better than drift." Representatives from the Dominions and all parts of Ireland should join with British nominees to modify the Government of Ireland Act in light of events since 1914 to make "changes necessary to meet the views of the contracting parties."[10]

Always conscious of the dependency of his coalition government on the support of recalcitrant Conservative-Unionists, Lloyd George lamented to Lord Riddell, "Take the Irish question. If I had a clear majority in the House of Commons, I could soon settle it."[11] In the

---

[*] Major William Redmond was killed in action at Messines in June 1917. In the by-election that followed, Eamon de Valera won the seat, but refused with other members of Sinn Fein to sit at Westminster.

absence of that clear majority, he knew that an intransigent Ulster, backed by variously Bonar Law, F.E. Smith, and other Conservative-Unionists, would stop at nothing to scupper a Home Rule agreement. He nevertheless attempted amidst the turmoil of the world war to make a higher appeal to Carson's well-known allegiance to the British Empire as well as to his commitment to winning the war. Lloyd George, Stevenson recorded, was

trying to persuade Carson to make concessions. He put it to him on imperial grounds. "At every stage", he said to him, "the Irish question is a stumbling-block in the conduct of the war. It ought to have been settled last year. I feel that I was a coward then not to insist upon a settlement then. It has done much harm in Australia. Hughes [the Australian prime minister] begged me last year to settle it for the sake of Australia, but I failed to do so. Twice since then he has sent me messages saying that it is essential that the matter should be settled. I have refrained from pressing the question, knowing your difficulties. But I feel that it can remain in abeyance no longer. Now that America has come in I get the same representations from that side. If we had settled it last year, we should have had many hundreds of thousands of recruits from Australia. If we do not settle it now, this Government will not be able to continue ... It is up to you and your party to agree to this, for the sake of the Empire."[12]

All to no avail. The negative Carson continued to oppose Home Rule if Ulster was in any way included. The direct route to Home Rule being closed, the prime minister, with Redmond's support, convened in May 1917 a convention of all Irish creeds and persuasions. The idea of an all-Irish convention had been pressed by – among others – Jan Christian Smuts, the South African minister of defence and a member of the War Cabinet, who had been prompted by several British friends concerned at the way in which Ireland had become increasingly alienated. The Irish – north, south, Roman Catholic, Protestant – might themselves somehow design a durable agreement or at least take up time in attempting to agree upon one, Smuts believed.[13] He saw it as a way of letting the Irish settle their differences among themselves and as an answer to the unease in the United States and the Dominions. Quite unrealistically, the prime minister specified that any agreement that the convention might reach would have to provide for "the unity of Ireland under a single legislature" as well as for the preservation of the "well-being of the Empire and the fundamental unity of the United Kingdom." Ominously, at the same time Sinn Fein convened an alternative "Irish" convention. Although boycotted by Ulster, it was another step toward a Sinn Fein parliament in Dublin.

The All-Ireland convention, under the moderate Irish nationalist but ineffective chairman Sir Harold Plunkett (Smuts having declined), met intermittently from July 1917 to April 1918. It achieved nothing. Some of the nationalists who did participate suspected that it was merely a British sop to counter demands in the Dominions and the United States for immediate Home Rule. Ulster in any case continued adamantly to oppose its inclusion in any such settlement, envisioning, if necessary, an Ireland split in two, the south overwhelmingly Roman Catholic and the north Protestant. The *coup de grâce* of the futile convention came in the spring of 1918 when any early prospect of Home Rule became entangled in the bitterness of a concurrent debate over whether to impose conscription in Ireland – as had been done two years before in England, Wales, and Scotland. At that, the convention quietly imploded, passing the intractable Irish challenge back to Westminster, now engrossed in yet another conscription debate.

Conscription had been introduced amidst considerable popular unrest in England, Canada, and Australia – as Greenwood knew intimately from his work in the War Office and from his wartime travels. It was still not generating enough men to meet the insatiable demands of a seemingly endless war of attrition, even when the age limit for recruits had been raised to fifty. He also knew from his earlier role that Irish volunteers had initially been gratifyingly numerous, reaching an estimated 150,000 to 180,000 men. As early as January 1917, Lord Derby, Greenwood's sometime mentor at the War Office, had recommended to the prime minister that conscription in Ireland must be considered.

In the spring of 1918, the Allies were as hard pressed as they had ever been during almost four years, the German army having been able to transfer an estimated one million soldiers from the eastern to the western front following Bolshevik Russia's withdrawal from the war. As resurgent German forces again neared Paris, it suddenly seemed that, after all their sacrifice, the Allies could yet lose the war. In light of ever more pressing manpower needs and lingering suspicions of Irish republican involvement with Germany, many in England agreed with Derby's recommendation. Even the conciliatory Smuts now regarded the whole complex of Irish difficulties as "a trifling matter compared to the war." Churchill, who had become secretary of state for war, supported the simple proposition that Ireland should be treated "like all the rest of us." He later recalled, "'Why,' it was sternly asked, 'should Ireland remain a favoured area full of men in their martial prime?' ... [However,] the question ... was handled in such a fashion ... that we had the worst of both worlds, all the resentment against compulsion and in the end no law and no men."[14]

John Grigg, whose father was in Lloyd George's "garden suburb" – his private office – throughout much of the war, put the best face on the prime minister's handling of the Irish conscription dilemma: "Lloyd George embraced this proposal with extreme reluctance, since he was well aware that it was militarily futile and politically lethal. But he had no choice. Not only were most Conservatives adamant that the Irish must be conscripted, he also had to reckon with the attitude of British labour, whose support for other provisions of the bill was indispensable ... He will always be open to criticism for having failed, with Asquith, to push through the settlement that he negotiated in 1916, which might just possibly have worked. But in 1918 he was faced with a choice of evils, and cannot fairly be blamed for choosing the lesser evil. Having chosen it, he defended his enforced position robustly in debate, concealing his private chagrin."[15]

Greenwood, always eager to cooperate with his leader, who alone could satisfy his cabinet ambitions, spoke with others of the Liberal War Committee in the House of Commons as early as 14 January 1918 in favour of extending compulsory military service to Ireland but linking it with the immediate implementation of Home Rule. His brother-in-law Leo Amery called upon the Irish Nationalist MPs to temper their opposition to compulsory military service by following the conciliatory attitude of Wilfrid Laurier "who, defeated on the issue of conscription in Canada, had urged all good subjects to see that the law was carried out harmoniously."[16] However, the Dominions, whatever their own losses, were unenthusiastic about imposing conscription on Ireland. Others in England, like Greenwood, argued that it should only be contemplated after an early and definite date has been set for Home Rule. Lloyd George appeared to agree, having said, "When the young men of Ireland are brought into the fighting line, it is imperative that they should feel that they are not fighting for establishing a principle abroad which is denied to them at home" (the Allies having widely portrayed themselves as the guarantors of self-determination for small nations).[17]

With or without immediate Home Rule, the prime minister decided that he had to introduce compulsory service into Ireland without additional delay. In April 1918, by extending at least in principle conscription to Ireland despite near universal local opposition, he provided Sinn Fein with a new and potent rallying cry that united many hitherto moderate Irish nationalists. He had in effect ended his half-hearted attempts to conciliate moderates centred upon an offer of Home Rule at any early date. One young Irish observer saw clearly enough what the decision to impose compulsory service unilaterally involved:

> Early in 1918 the announcement of the British Government's intention to impose military conscription on Ireland sent the temperature of the country soaring. It aroused anger and dismay everywhere; mass meetings and petitions were organised, resolutions of protest were passed by public bodies, cries of condemnation came from the press and the pulpit, men wore green, white and orange badges inscribed "Death before Conscription." Although the [Irish] Parliamentary Party's Members at Westminster bitterly opposed the proposal to conscript Irishmen, the Government's declaration came powerfully to the aid of those who had been crying out about the futility of trying to achieve anything by negotiation with England ... The separatists reminded their listeners that the men who had died in the [Easter] Rising had declared an Irish Republic and sanctified the declaration with their blood. If further Irish blood was to be shed, let it be for Ireland, they said.[18]

A cabinet committee on Ireland, chaired by the Unionist Walter Long (himself a former chief secretary for Ireland and currently secretary of state for the colonies), had concluded that prior to the implementation of the Government of Ireland legislation, the law must be enforced and, above all, "the Irish-German conspiracy which appears to be widespread in Ireland" must be put down with a stern hand.[19] To be sure, Irish insurgents were among the several foreign recipients of German clandestine largesse.* The Irish activist Sir Roger Casement, in the midst of the world war, landed from a U-boat with secret assurances from Berlin

---

* "German agents financed French pacifists, American labour organizations and Indian nationalists. They supported Russian revolutionaries, Muslim *jihadists* and Irish Republicans" (Boghardt, *Spies of the Kaiser*, 117–18).

that it would supply money and arms (which it duly did, only to be intercepted by Royal Navy Intelligence). Casement was arrested and later executed as a traitor, and Sinn Fein leaders were jailed or deported, but the armed Irish Volunteers, soon to be transformed into the Irish Republican Army (IRA), continued to gather or enforce support. With the decision to impose conscription, a desperate move strongly supported by the Liberal War Committee (of which Greenwood was a founding member), moderate nationalists lost much of whatever influence they still retained, leaving the field to the newer and increasingly aggressive if still ill-organized Sinn Fein. Ironically, after all the bitter controversy, compulsory military service was proclaimed in April 1918 but never imposed.* It was postponed on 3 June, to be revisited on 1 October. It had become evident by then that an end to the war was finally nigh and conscription was no longer deemed necessary in Ireland. But it was too late; profound damage had been done. The British historian A.J.P. Taylor, among others, regarded it as marking "the decisive moment at which Ireland seceded from the Union."[20]

Building on its increasing popular support, partly as a result of its adamant opposition to conscription, Sinn Fein set about attempting to create an alternative government for Ireland. Meanwhile, British cabinet ministers remained divided, some now becoming diverted by the revived idea of Home Rule All Round. Lloyd George's coalition government was returned with a majority of 250 in the rushed "khaki election" of 14 December 1918, but it was really a victory for the Conservative-Unionists, who won 335 seats to 133 for the coalition Liberals (63 for Labour and 28 for Asquithian Liberals). Of the 105 Irish seats in the House of Commons, Sinn Fein candidates were elected in seventy-six (thirty-six of the successful candidates were in British prisons), Irish Nationalists in seven, and Ulster Unionists in twenty-two. Three weeks later a Sinn Fein congress confirmed that its members would – to use an Irish expression – boycott the House of Commons and instead participate in their own parliament-to-be in Dublin, the Dáil Éireann. On 21 January 1919 it duly ratified a provisional constitution for the republic that had been proclaimed at the time of the Easter Rising in 1916. The following day it elected a cabinet, which began to seek recruits for the Irish Volunteers and to promote a loan in the United States and Ireland. The first ambition of the Dáil Éireann was simply stated: "We demand evacuation of our country by the English garrison."

---

* Almost fifty thousand Irish dead are commemorated on the war memorial in Dublin.

The authority of Lloyd George, the great wartime leader, had been weakened by the election results that left his coalition government even more dependent upon the support of Conservative-Unionists. At the same time, the decimation of the Irish Nationalists and the Sinn Fein boycott of Parliament did nothing to encourage expectations of an early Irish settlement. Such a settlement was not, in any event, the most pressing question before the coalition government. In the days before the polling, the government had vaguely declared in its election manifesto that it would "explore all practical paths towards the settlement of this grave and difficult question [of Ireland] on the basis of self-government." Lloyd George's plate was, however, full to overflowing, including with popular demands to hang the kaiser and to exact huge reparations from Germany, demands that continued to poison the already difficult negotiation of several peace accords. The Allied intervention in the Russian civil war, despite Churchill's enthusiasms, was proving to be as calamitous as such interventions generally are. With the collapse of the Ottoman Empire, the seemingly endless dispute between Greece and Turkey lingered on. Additionally, questions of disarmament, reparations, the boundaries of Germany and Poland, the creation of the League of Nations, the consequences of the deadly pan-European influenza epidemic, and a multitude of other postwar difficulties required the prime minister to be almost continuously in Paris.

Even more threatening for him were domestic tensions. Britain had finally won the war, but what had victory brought to the people? Widespread labour unrest and mounting unemployment produced sharpened social stress and political uncertainties. Amidst this social and political turmoil, Ireland again became a tiresome distraction in the eyes of the prime minister and most of his coalition cabinet. T.P. O'Connor, the noted journalist and only Irish Nationalist MP with an English constituency (which he held for forty-four years), was rightly convinced that "Lloyd George insists upon ignoring the Irish question as much as he can and will not touch it ... until he is forced to do so."[21]

Whatever the impatience of the prime minister when he had more pressing and important challenges before him, in the new year 1919 the unrest in Ireland began increasingly to intrude. On 21 January 1919, in the first killings since the April 1916 Rising, two Royal Irish Constabulary were ambushed by Irish Volunteers on the day of the first session of the Dáil Éireann. Violence mounted during the second half of 1919 under the direction of Michael Collins, the "minister of finance" of the Dáil. (The assembly's leader since April 1919, the Republican Eamon de

Valera, departed to raise funds in his native United States for eighteen months from June 1919 to December 1920.)

Lloyd George from Paris and Bonar Law from London continued to assure themselves that the question of good order in Ireland could be left to Dublin Castle, the traditional seat of government. Otherwise, the *Daily Chronicle* (effectively Lloyd George's own newspaper) threatened in January 1919 that murder would beget murder: "It is obvious that if those murderers pursue their course ... we may see ... the life of prominent Sinn Feiners becoming as unsafe as the prominent officers."[22] One such "counter club" was the shadowy Anti-Sinn Fein League, which Lloyd George presumably had in mind when he assured the cabinet that "a counter murder association" was the best answer to Sinn Fein murders.[23] At the same time the prime minister had no clear, dynamic policy for Ireland, other than continuing to proclaim himself anachronistically a "Gladstonian Home Ruler." He did not trouble himself to explain how Gladstone's decades-old policy could be reshaped to fit the quite different circumstances of 1919. In August he stated simply that he could "easily govern Ireland with the sword," although the required sword needed constantly to be increased in size.[24]

With an eye on the competing demands on the War Office and the exchequer posed by Iraq, Egypt, and various other corners of an Empire wider still and wider, the prime minister asked Churchill, his secretary of state for war, why it was necessary to have so many soldiers in Ireland. He received the not very enlightening reply that the War Office was simply attempting to meet the requests of the viceroy, Field Marshal Lord French. Despite the terror being inflicted on the Royal Irish Constabulary (RIC), Churchill added with remarkable optimism, the best policy in Ireland would be to do nothing. The Irish in general "were beginning to lose faith in the protagonists of Sinn Fein who had carried out none of their promises." In light of such bland optimism, the War Office reassured the prime minister, troop reductions would be possible within twelve months.

Such optimism was not reflected in confidential communications from the RIC itself. Its inspector general, Brigadier-General Sir Joseph Aloysius Byrne, soon confirmed that the "police were confronted with almost insuperable difficulties" and that demoralization – to put it at its least – was pervading the RIC.[25] One proposed solution to the police problem had been contemplated for more than a year. At a meeting of ministers as early as 1919, the idea proposed by Walter Long of a "special emergency gendarmerie" was endorsed. Ten days later, Long urged that the RIC "should recruit ex-soldiers from England to bring up its strength quickly."[26] Volunteers for special constables or auxiliary police should be sought at once from amongst the tens of thousands of veterans eager, even desperate, to find any employment anywhere.

Perhaps believing somehow that time was on his side, and in any event heavily pressed by a myriad of other compelling issues, Lloyd George declared on 5 August 1919 that it would be difficult to produce an Irish policy before the parliamentary recess: the cabinet had "as much as they could do ... to deal with profiteering, finance, and housing, as well as announcing a coal policy." For his part, Churchill agreed that "the present" was not "a good time to look for an Irish solution." Long added optimistically that the viceroy had informed him of "a considerable improvement in the temper of the country ... during the last three months." Although that "considerable improvement" had escaped most observers, such reports made more understandable the prime minister's temporizing over Ireland, to which he was already inclined, given that coalition government had other pressing matters in mind, including increasing unrest among coal miners, rail workers and even the London police. Further, "the reluctance to embark upon a policy of resolute coercion in Ireland must be seen not so much as the product of a new enlightened spirit in English attitudes to Ireland, but rather as the result of war-weariness, for the Great War had brought tragedy to millions of homes ... people could not have cared less about Ireland."[27] Lloyd George was in any case seldom available in the House and even in cabinet. During the twelve months from the armistice in November 1918 to November 1919, he never answered questions in the House, and for six months of the Paris peace talks he was only briefly in the United Kingdom.

With the end of the war in 1918, Asquith's anachronistic Government of Ireland legislation of 1914 would have automatically become law, but it was dead with the Conservative-Unionists dominating the coalition. Another cabinet committee on Ireland was struck on 7 October 1919 to recommend what should replace it. The arch-Unionist Walter Long was again in the chair; among its members were French, Macpherson, Auckland Geddes, H.A.L. Fisher, and Lord Birkenhead. Obviously much had changed in Ireland and in the British Empire during the seven years or more since April 1912 when Asquith had first introduced his Government of Ireland bill. It was again becoming clear to the cabinet – especially among the Conservative-Unionist majority – that Ulster could not and must not be coerced. There was no longer any possibility that the six more or less Protestant counties of the north could be made part of a Home Rule, predominantly Roman Catholic, Ireland. The prime minister was fully aware that such was the bottom line for his Conservative-Unionist colleagues.

Long's committee accordingly recommended in November 1919 yet another Home Rule bill to provide for separate legislatures with limited powers in both north and south – with, it was optimistically added, an all-Ireland council to serve as the link between two legislatures to promote and facilitate eventual reunification with one legislature. The cabinet having endorsed the draft legislation in November 1919, on 25 February 1920 the prime minister introduced yet another Government of Ireland bill, replacing Asquith's 1914 legislation and specifying to what degree the two parts – not one – of Ireland were to be self-governing, with a parliament in the north of fifty-two members and a parliament in the south of 128 members. Its almost year-long passage through Parliament was slow: it did not receive third reading until 23 December 1920, ten months after its introduction. The reaction across Britain, the United States, and the Dominions to the new legislation was generally positive, but the radical *Nation* speculated quite accurately that Ulster had in effect been given a veto over the proposed Irish joint council: "Without her consent, the joint council can never come into being at all. There will be two Irish provinces, but no Ireland; a Quebec and an Ontario, but no Canada."[28] Sinn Fein flatly rejected the whole approach, seeing in it confirmation of the partition of Ireland.

Both Lloyd George and Bonar Law did agree at least to the extent that the legislation would be successful only if order were first restored, but many Conservative-Unionist backbenchers – the "diehards" – remained sceptical of what they regarded as the prime minister's half-measures to restore order. Among them was Amery, who later summed up their misgivings: "All through 1919 the campaign of arson and murder continued while no really effective measures were taken to combat it."[29] Lloyd George, beset by widespread industrial unrest and preoccupied with the bewildering political and economic fallout of the war and consequently frequently absent in Paris, had little time to give to internal strife in Ireland. He asked Bonar Law to take the lead in the search for an end to the increasing violence – by the end of 1919, thirteen Irish policemen had been killed – a reflection of his recognition that there could be no settlement unless it carried the support of Conservative-Unionists. Liberals in the House were not so numerous as to allow him to go it alone.

9

New Men and New Measures, 1920

Given the widely acknowledged ramshackle civil administration in Dublin, "new men and new measures" were finally seen as essential. During the First World War, Dublin Castle had become an administrative backwater to which the exhausted, invalided, and inadequate could be banished to join long-serving and entrenched Irish bureaucrats, the more effective and sound soldiers and civil servants being employed elsewhere in the still elusive pursuit of victory. Sir Henry Robinson, a senior public servant in Dublin, wrote despondently in March 1918, "the whole staff ... have become cowed, inefficient and lacking in resource ... you would be driven mad by their slowness of action and comprehension." In January 1919, Lord Haldane, who had been Asquith's lord chancellor, visited the viceroy in Dublin and found him "very worried in the midst of some thirty-six Departments, many of them hardly on speaking terms with each other."[1]

There was unanimity among British officials that the first challenge facing Bonar Law – to whom Lloyd George had now relegated Ireland – was what to do about the senior public service in Dublin. What Walter Long had perceived in the Royal Irish Constabulary applied even more across much of the administration: officials were "either utterly incompetent or hopelessly worn out." Macready, the new general commanding in Ireland, wrote to Long that he found himself "sitting on a volcano." He was "utterly flabbergasted at the administrative chaos that seems to reign here ... the machine was hopelessly out of date." He added in his memoirs that upon arrival, "I did not expect to find anything very striking in the way of efficient organization, but before I had been in Dublin forty-eight hours I was fairly astonished at the chaos that prevailed."[2] Warren Fisher, the widely respected permanent secretary to the Treasury and head of the civil service from 1919 to 1939, reported that "the Castle Administration does not administer. On the mechanical side it can never have been good and is now quite obsolete; in the infinitely more important sphere of (a) informing and advising the Irish Government in relation to policy and (b) of practical capacity in the application of policy it simply has no existence."[3] In a letter to Lloyd George, Bonar Law, and Austen Chamberlain, Fisher dismissed even more summarily the senior public servants in Dublin: they were "almost woodenly stupid and quite devoid of imagination."[4] The new assistant secretary, John Anderson, later wrote to Greenwood that "the ordinary machinery of civil administration was practically non-existent ... the general state of this office ...was really incredible. The police forces were in a critical condition."[5] Alfred ("Andy") Cope, who was appointed assistant under-secretary, reported, "The Chief Secretary's Office is a thousand times worse than I imagined it."[6] Even the *Times* joined in the litany: "The administrative machinery of Dublin Castle has fallen into disrepair, and has long required overhauling. The strain of present conditions in Ireland has completely deranged it."[7]

Bonar Law needed no convincing. In late April 1920, he told Greenwood that the viceroy had warned him that "the administration in Ireland is ... as bad as it is possible for it to be ... Lord French has suggested that a committee of two or three Government officials should be set up and with one representative of the Civil Service in Ireland to enquire into the administration of Dublin Castle.* This seems to me a very good idea ... I shall try to have suitable members chosen."[8] In wielding the new broom, Law began by arranging for the replacement of the commander-in-chief in Ireland, whose unenviable military task was to support an increasingly demoralized Royal Irish Constabulary; the IRA had announced in April 1920 that it would henceforth boycott the police, who became their prime target. The new man to command both the army and police – if anyone could be readily found to take the combined job – would need to be sensitive to political as well as to security issues.

The first nominee was Churchill's: Field Marshal "Wully" Robertson. Robertson was, however, unacceptable to Lloyd George, who had long been in dispute with him as chief of the imperial general staff over the conduct of the war. The prime minister insisted instead on General

* The idea was in fact that of Sir Henry Robinson, the vice-president of the Local Government Board.

Sir Nevil Macready, a well-qualified but reluctant candidate to take on what was becoming seen as an impossible challenge. The son of the actor William Charles Macready (a close friend of Charles Dickens, to whom the writer dedicated *Nicholas Nickleby*), the general was a veteran of the South African War and a postwar administrator in the Cape Province. In November 1910, he had been appointed by Churchill, then home secretary, to command both the troops and the police sent to Tonypandy in South Wales, where a prolonged and bitter strike by miners in the Rhondda valley threatened possible violence. For nine months he maintained good order there, carefully avoiding being seen as taking sides in the dispute, an impartiality admired by Asquith, Churchill, and Lloyd George. Macready's success in South Wales contributed to Asquith's decision in December 1913 to send him to Ulster to attempt to help keep the lid on violent Unionist agitation there.* The challenge to Macready of countering the Ulster Volunteer Force had been formidable, especially given the ardent support for it of Bonar Law, Carson, F.E. Smith, several generals, and other Conservative-Unionists, but he again applied his rule of not taking sides, although ready to fight the Ulster Volunteers if so ordered. Later he summed up his attitude: "So far as the political government of Ireland was concerned, I was entirely indifferent, having no interest of any kind in the island. The policy I did advocate, whether applicable to the North or South, was 'govern or get out', and that is exactly what Mr. Asquith would not do."[9] The lid remained on, but only barely, until the outbreak of the First World War intervened.

During the war Macready was adjutant general to Lord French when he commanded the British Expeditionary Force on the Western Front before becoming General Officer Commanding Home Forces. Macready's immediate (and unwelcome) postwar appointment was commissioner of the Metropolitan Police in London, where he introduced such innovations as policewomen and dealt deftly with the aftermath of the unprecedented Metropolitan Police union strike of August 1918. His combined military and police experience appeared to make him especially suitable for Ireland. His personal attitude, however, was no longer "entirely indifferent." He had written to Ian Macpherson upon his appointment as chief secretary, "I cannot say I envy you for

---

* The Ulster Volunteer Force was being trained in their German arms by, among others, Captain Frank Crozier, whom Macready would encounter later as a senior British officer in Dublin during the "troubles" of 1920–22. See pages 185–6.

I loathe the country you are going to and its people with a depth deeper than the sea and more violent than that I feel against the Boche."[10]

Upon accepting the Irish appointment (formally offered on 23 March 1920), Macready asked to be left in London for three weeks to familiarize himself with the current situation in both the south and north; he also used the time to arrange a notably high salary for himself. He did not leave for Dublin until 14 April, after lunching with the king and queen. In later years, he recalled that he had disembarked in a mood of depression. Other than for the desire of his old mentor, Lord French, to see him accept the job, "nothing would have induced me to return to a country to which I was never attracted, or to take up a task which I instinctively felt would be affected by every variation of the political weathercock, and in which it was doubtful if any satisfactory result could be attained."[11] He may have had another factor in mind in accepting a dangerous appointment that no one else seemed to want: he had marital complications (as did French) easier to manage from Dublin than from London. Frances Stevenson, who had a sharp eye for such matters, noted in her diary in July 1921, "Macready is having difficulties with his spouse ... won't have her back in Ireland ... going to set up a separate establishment."[12] (Macready's wife spent the winter of 1920–21 in Egypt.) In a diary entry for 9 January 1921, Margo Greenwood had already recorded that Lloyd George had told her of his "great disappointment" with Macready's performance. "I thought the explanation was that he was unhappy in Ireland. We both agreed on the cause – a domestic one!"[13] Lord French was hardly in a happier situation. In the eyes of an assistant under-secretary, he remained "a terribly pathetic figure ... a lonely little old gentleman who has fought with his wife and his children."[14]

As for the deteriorating and beleaguered RIC, Major General Hugh Tudor was named "police advisor." However, chronic confusion over his mandate and over the relationship of the police to the army became further instances of the self-defeating uncertainties about who was responsible for what. Tudor's appointment was on Churchill's recommendation after Lieutenant General Sir Edward Bulfin, a veteran of effective police and military collaboration in Egypt and Mesopotamia, had declined on the grounds that as a Roman Catholic Irishman he would find the proposed appointment "distasteful."[15] Tudor and Churchill had been junior officers together in India and in the South African War, and Churchill had served under him on the western front in 1916.[*] Later Churchill, back in the cabinet as minister of munitions, had visited his old friend at his divisional headquarters in 1918. By the end of the war Tudor had risen to major general, the youngest in the army, but he remained junior to Macready – which later gave rise to problems. He was regarded "as a most intrepid and resourceful soldier," but his role in Ireland was never clearly defined. Having been appointed police advisor on 15 May 1920 without any clear mandate, he was finally confirmed as the chief of the RIC nine months later on 21 February 1921, only four months before the truce, which contributed to the unease reflected in the oft-repeated and justifiable lament that there was never any real unity of command in Ireland.

To conduct the urgent enquiry into the dilapidated Irish civil service, Lloyd George and Bonar Law first considered Churchill himself, but he and two other possible nominees having declined, they could not have chosen anyone better to head the urgent enquiry than Sir Warren Fisher, the young (at forty) secretary to the Treasury and hence head of the civil service. (There was something of a precedent for his appointment: a predecessor had been sent, in the wake of the Easter Rising of 1916, to enquire into the workings of Dublin Castle.) On 4 May, Fisher disembarked, along with Alfred Cope, also of the Treasury. They arrived fully aware from a meeting with Law and his colleagues of the conviction in Whitehall that Ireland desperately needed "new men and new measures."[†] Although himself burdened with a multitude of postwar problems at the Treasury, Fisher was both timely and succinct in his recommendations. They were more or less implemented, but their benefit was reduced by the confusion that was never eliminated from the command structure. It remained unclear who, if anyone, was in charge of the whole show.

For the key role of joint permanent under-secretary of the Irish Office – or more simply assistant secretary for Ireland – Fisher nominated Sir John Anderson, one of the most promising, if not *the* most promising,

---

[*] The chief of British Intelligence in Ireland, the unconventional Colonel Ormonde de l'Épée Winter, had served with Tudor in the Royal Artillery in India and in the First World War on the Western Front (see Winter, *Winter's Tale*).

[†] G.C. Duggan, of the Finance Division in the chief secretary's office, summed up his understanding of the motives behind Whitehall's appointment of the new men: "They desired peace and they hoped to obtain it by placing in power officials who had no axe to grind, no stake in the country, and whose future careers did not lie in Ireland, and who could afford to act independently" (Duggan, *Last Days*, 148).

of the younger civil servants. The Edinburgh-educated Anderson had already served in the Colonial Office, the National Insurance Commission, the Local Government Board, and as secretary to the wartime Ministry of Shipping. From the Ministry of Health he had been promoted to the chairmanship of the Board of Inland Revenue, where Fisher had confirmed for himself that Anderson had the potential to be one of the greatest British public servants of the twentieth century. Having "a mind of very great gasp and reach" as well as imperturbable courage, he was to play a pivotal role in Ireland (despite having to sustain at the same time the sudden death of his beloved wife).[16]

Along with Fisher, Lloyd George himself had been involved in the selection of Alfred Cope as, ostensibly, assistant under-secretary. The prime minister's ever fertile and opportunistic mind had recognized the need for a trusted undercover interlocutor with Sinn Fein and the IRA, someone who could pass covertly between the two sides, with his personal safety guaranteed by both. The IRA, through informal channels, soon gave its guarantee. Both sides were killing each other, but they knew that secret *pourparlers* could prove indispensable. Cope was a former detective in Customs and Excise, a bachelor, and a trusted colleague of Fisher who had him transferred to Dublin Castle from the Ministry of Pensions (where Macpherson had just gone as minister). In him, as well as in Anderson, Fisher had nominated well.

A third inspired nomination by Fisher – although clearly different in character from Anderson and Cope – was Mark Sturgis, an English civil servant who was to act as Anderson's surrogate in Dublin during his frequent absences in London. Sturgis would also supplement Cope's central role in talking with and helping to interpret each side to the other. A product of Eton and Oxford, and in his leisure time a congenial fishing and racing enthusiast, he had married into and moved easily among the landed gentry. An assistant private secretary to Prime Minister Asquith in 1908–10, he was "more detached ... more cognizant of the great world outside" than others at Dublin Castle. As Anderson's principal aide, he played a central administrative role, but he remained decidedly unhappy about the confusion of channels and the lack of clarity of who was in command. Sturgis soon concluded that "if it is war, we must have virtual dictator to be obeyed by everybody, military, police, civil service, etc. As it is, we are a great, sprawling, hydra-headed monster spending much of its time using one of its heads to abuse ... the others."[17]

Another organizational problem that had long hindered good governance in Ireland, in addition to the widely deplored incompetence of the senior civil service, was the lingering lack of clear delineation between the role of viceroy (or lord lieutenant) and that of the chief secretary. In centuries past, the viceroy, resident in Ireland, had clearly been king of the castle, but in more recent decades, the office had become more analogous to that of a constitutional monarch. The military forces, ostensibly under the command of the viceroy, in fact took their orders direct from the War Office. The viceroy was kept informed of the civil state by courtesy only. Since Arthur Balfour in 1905, civil governance had passed largely into the hands of the chief secretary resident in London. Upon him "fell the full burden of answering questions and defending the Government's Irish policy in the House of Commons ... The unhappy incumbent was of necessity greatly dependent for information and advice on the reports of the Under Secretary in the Castle."[18] In light of questions in Parliament and the recommendation of Warren Fisher that the vice-regal post simply be abolished, the government had reconfirmed that ultimate responsibility rested with the chief secretary, answerable to Parliament.

Lord French, the viceroy, remained in Dublin, rumours that he was to be appointed governor general of Canada having proved to be unfounded. It was more convenient to keep his mistress, Winifred Bennett, in Ireland than in England (his private secretary unkindly described Bennett, the wife of a diplomat, as "the wreck of a Continental Harlot").[19] French, something of a spendthrift, had recognized that if he wished to retain both his mistress and his salary in Ireland, he must accept the inevitable dilution of his authority with the appointment of a new chief secretary, following the departure of Macpherson whom he had been able to dominate.[20] To be sure, in neither French nor Macpherson had the prime minister chosen well but, in their defence, he never set out a clear policy for either to follow.

From the Treasury, the candid Warren Fisher, while declaring that policy proposals were "quite outside" his mandate, soon added a "bold and liberal" policy recommendation to his concurrent administrative reforms. There could be no solution by arms alone, he argued, an understanding soon shared by the newly arrived Macready. Dublin Castle must stop the practice of simply lumping all opposition together as Sinn Fein. Improvements to the decrepit administration would count for little if they were not matched by what Macready also called a "bold

stroke." Writing to Bonar Law, Fisher summarized his early understanding that "anything very much short of Dominion Home Rule is
unlikely to achieve a satisfactory result."[21] In the House of Commons,
Asquith, in his continuing bitter attacks on Lloyd George, was also urging no less.

When John Anderson arrived in Dublin as the new assistant secretary
on 22 May, he reflected the thinking of his mentor, Warren Fisher, by
immediately endorsing Macready's recommendation to the cabinet
committee that "a broad measure of Dominion Home Rule" should
be at once instituted. Anderson shared Macready's conviction that
the limited reforms in the still pending legislation were insufficient.
Fisher and Anderson were convinced that the new bill for the "Better
Government of Ireland" had no friends in southern Ireland, since it in
effect divided the island into two parts, each with its own legislature.[22]
Even at this point, moderates might welcome the model of Canadian
self-government. Such an initiative might yet wean them away from collaboration with radical Sinn Fein and republicanism. In Macready's
words, Fisher and Anderson were at one in their conviction that "coercion has been tried in the past and failed ... give the people the very
fullest measure of self-government within the Empire."[23]

The prime minister, however, restrained by Bonar Law, continued to
put the restoration of law and order before concessions in civil governance. He had declared to his cabinet in late April, "Disorder must be
put down at whatever cost ... Home Rule would be a failure unless and
until order were [first] restored." As the IRA's campaign of intimidation, systematic killings of policemen, and threats to their families
mounted in the latter half of 1919 and into early 1920, RIC resignations
had so increased that new recruitment, already faltering, could not
keep up. Macready told the cabinet that the unarmed "Dublin Metropolitan Police's morale had been destroyed by the murders, and the
R.I.C.'s is threatened."[24] The military were not trained as policemen,
and the army should not be asked to do much in their support. In these
circumstances, the urge to retaliate in kind, to meet murder with murder, was beginning to spread throughout the police.

As early as May 1919, Walter Long had explored with the viceroy
the idea of recruiting unemployed English veterans as reinforcements
for the hitherto all-Irish RIC, a proposal seconded in September by
the general officer commanding in Ireland. The next month, once the
cabinet endorsed the proposal, presented collectively by Churchill,

Macpherson, and Long, the net was widely cast.* As soon as the authority was given in December to recruit volunteers – still during Macpherson's term – newspaper advertisements and posters in England and recruiting offices in London, Birmingham, Glasgow, and Liverpool called for volunteers, candidly warning them that they would "face a rough and dangerous task." Recruiting began on 1 December 1919 and the first English veteran was enrolled in the RIC on 2 January 1920. An initial contingent disembarked in Dublin on 25 March 1920. They soon became known as "Black and Tans" after their unorthodox mixture of khaki uniforms of the army and the black webbing and dark green headgear of the RIC. Ten shillings a day all found proved to be irresistible to many unemployed and restless English veterans, but they were not well trained or suited for what awaited them. They had little or no affinity with the Irish people. And the hit-and-run tactics of the IRA had nothing in common with their experience of the static warfare of massive armies in the trenches of Flanders.

By the end of March 1920, as the first contingent of Black and Tans disembarked, the appointment of the "new men" at Dublin Castle had all but been completed. The most visible appointment was not until 4 April when the Right Honourable Sir Hamar Greenwood, MP, became chief secretary for Ireland. In February and March, Macpherson had pressed for a transfer to another ministerial post, partly in light of his failure to obtain from the prime minister a clear policy on Ireland. The *Toronto Mail and Empire* repeated rumours of his early resignation: "He has been represented in many recent despatches as weary of his irksome post, and remaining only because he felt it was a point of loyalty to stick to the Coalition Government until victory for the new Home Rule bill was assured."[25] A botched attempt by the IRA to murder French in the week before Christmas 1919 had rendered Macpherson even more fearful for his own life, particularly in light of the prime minister's offhand reaction: "They are bad shots."[26] By late March, arrangements had been made for him to take up a more sedentary appointment as minister of pensions (without a seat in cabinet).

Lloyd George may well have been aware of Greenwood's letter to Redmond of four years before, setting forth his credentials to be chief secretary in succession to Birrell, but at least to George Garro Jones,

---

* The Ministry of Labour estimated that there were approximately 167,000 fit veterans receiving unemployment benefits in the United Kingdom.

private secretary to Greenwood, the offer of the prime minister seemed to have come out of the blue. Greenwood was in his constituency of Sunderland with Garro Jones when an urgent message arrived from the chief whip that the prime minister wanted him to go to Wales to speak in a by-election for a coalition candidate against the formidable Asquithian Liberal candidate, Sir John Simon (he of the Amery wedding party). That disagreeable task accomplished, Greenwood was summoned to the prime minister's rooms in the House of Commons. Garro Jones reconstructs what unfolded: "'Hamar, I want you to go to Ireland!' Sir Hamar was surprised and a little baffled by this request, well perceiving that not even the most roseate imagination could view it as an opportunity. Dare he refuse? Dare he go? It was a choice of Hercules with his twelve tasks rolled into one. Sir Hamar had no oracle to aid him in his decision – unless, indeed, full credit is given where it is due, for the role of Pythia was ably filled by his gracious wife. She courageously advised him to go."[27]

More than two years after he offered the chief secretaryship to Greenwood, Lloyd George recalled the situation in Ireland in early 1920:

> We were confronted with a situation in Ireland where ... a formidable body of men... demanded complete separation from the British Empire ... There were bombs. You never knew who was your friend there. I said: "I want a man of courage, a man prepared to face difficulties and a man who would not run away when he was in trouble" and I said, "I know him and his name is Sir Hamar Greenwood." I sent for him. "Well," he said, "I am a family man." I said to him, "It is a dangerous job. It is dangerous physically. I am not going to conceal anything from you. There are plots to massacre every official there." I thought it was right to tell him. So he said, "If you allow me to consult my wife", and they both came along the following morning. They said, "If you think we can render service, we will take it," and they both went there.[28]

Greenwood's own recollections of the circumstances of his appointment were more cryptic than those of either the prime minister or Garro Jones. That both Greenwood and his wife were eager for him to be in the cabinet was never in doubt. Three months before, on 30 December 1919, he had written to Lloyd George immediately following the general election, "In forming your new administration, I hope that you will this time give me a chance to serve you and the state."[29] As the prime minister was fully aware, Greenwood had long had his eye on the home secretaryship, but that was not an early prospect if ever a real one, filled as it was by Edward Shortt, Macpherson's predecessor as chief secretary. The Greenwoods gambled that by his accepting a job that no other minister wanted and, much more problematically, by successfully restoring order in Ireland, he would be rewarded with a more comfortable seat in the cabinet, if not eventually the home secretaryship itself. (Ironically, it was John Anderson who went to the Home Office in 1922 for a decade as permanent under-secretary and, as a peer, home secretary in 1939–40). On 13 July 1920, at a dinner of the Canada Club in Greenwood's honour (attended, among others, by eight visiting bishops of the Anglican Church in Canada), he provided his own recollection of his appointment: "One day ... in the first week of April ... the Prime Minister called him into his room at the House of Commons just after question time, shut the door, put his back to it, and said in his clear, decisive way, 'Hamar, you and Lady Greenwood are going to Ireland.' All political parties were agreed, he said ... that some form of Home Rule should be granted to Ireland ... It will enable the Irish people to settle the Irish problem ...The people are strong in their religious and strong in their political views, but when the Protestants and Roman Catholics do meet together, as they do in many organizations ... they work well together."[30]

If Ireland offered the only route to the cabinet, chief secretary for Ireland Greenwood would be. Daunting although that route was, the Greenwoods recognized that it was his only cabinet prospect at the age of fifty, especially since the number of Liberal places in the Conservative-dominated cabinet were few. In terms of Ireland itself, given the fact that Canada, since the time of Gladstone, had been held up as the model for a Home Rule Ireland – or, later, a Dominion Home Rule Ireland – Lloyd George saw a certain congruity in having a Canadian as chief secretary. At a minimum, Greenwood could not be dismissed as yet another indifferent or hostile Englishman. As Lloyd George himself could recall, he had long been a notably articulate exponent of Irish Home Rule from their first days together on a Liberal platform in Wales in 1895. Even at this late date in the Irish imbroglio, memories of Greenwood's advocacy in both Britain and Canada of Home Rule for Ireland might still be revived. Greenwood had hoped so in 1916, and now he hoped so again. On 2 April 1920, in an interview for the *Daily Mail*, he repeated for the journalist points that he had made to Redmond four years before: "I am a Canadian Home Ruler. I was born in a Home Rule country. My appointment is a sign – and is intended to be a sign – of the British Government's earnest desire to settle the Irish question along Home Rule lines once and for all." To the *Toronto Daily Star*, he described how he was "given the appointment by Mr. Lloyd George because I was a Canadian, along with other reasons, because I knew at first-hand self-government under the flag of the Empire."[31] However, one senior Irish civil servant, Sir Henry Robinson, was quite certain that Greenwood's Canadian background would count for nothing with militant republicans: "He came over [to Dublin] with the evident belief that, as a colonial and naturally as a firm adherent to the principle of self-government, the Irish people would not regard him with the same aversion as the average English Chief Secretary is regarded, but for all the difference his colonial breeding made in the eyes of the [hostile Irish] Republicans, he might just as well have been King of the Cannibal Islands."[32]

The third and most important element in Lloyd George's thinking was simply that Greenwood was a brave man. The prime minister was no exception to the rule that most of us admire in others those virtues that we recognize that we most lack ourselves. He once cryptically told Austen Chamberlain of Greenwood, "I don't like the fellow,"[33] but there was no question that he admired his fortitude – and his wife. It was widely known in the upper reaches of the government that Lloyd George was himself a physical coward. Frances Stevenson is only one of several intimates who attest to the fact. She first noted it during the Zeppelin raids on London during the war, when Field Marshal Haig taunted him behind his back for cowardice, and then saw it again and again, most recently when he learned of Irish plotting to assassinate or to kidnap him. Margo told Leo Amery that "Lloyd George was terrified of being murdered, especially after an occasion in the spring [of 1921] when two [alleged] Sinn Feiners were found lurking in the grounds at Chequers. Next morning when she drove up with him and Miss Stevenson to London, they had a burst tyre and while the car was standing still, Lloyd George was in terror lest he should be shot through the window."[34] The prime minister no doubt saw the courage of the Greenwoods as one more reason to have Greenwood as chief secretary; however, one journalist*

---

* The journalist Amy Charlotte Stuart Menzies (née Bewicke), who knew Margo well, was a noted gossip writer, as reflected in the titles of her other books: *Memories Discrete and*

pondered: "I wonder sometimes that Lady Greenwood with her clear vision and judgement allowed her husband to undertake what could only be a thankless task under such a moral coward as Mr Lloyd George."[35]

Yet another factor recommended itself to the prime minister: Greenwood was expendable, while Law, Balfour, Chamberlain, and Churchill were not. If Greenwood were killed, he could be replaced; they could not. However much Lloyd George admired Greenwood's pluck, he never mentioned any contribution that Greenwood made to Irish policy generally or to the later negotiations with Sinn Fein in particular. Greenwood was just the man Lloyd George wanted. He did not want an eminent colleague who might attempt to pursue his own policies or interfere with whatever he himself had decided. He believed that, despite the multitudinous demands of other postwar issues, he alone would be able to work the wizardry necessary to achieve an Irish settlement. Accordingly, he did not seek policy advice from his new chief secretary. What he did seek was someone of undoubted courage to hold the ring until he himself, who displayed almost unique ingenuity in negotiations, sensed that the moment had finally arrived to drive a near-impossible bargain with Sinn Fein on the one hand and the Conservative-Unionists and Ulster on the other.

Two years later, in response to the comment of one of his own staff that "Hamar Greenwood was not exactly a first class statesman," Lloyd George replied "that a Prime Minister did not want too many first class statesmen about him, but rather good counsellors." A month later he observed, "Hamar Greenwood had shown great courage – or insensibility – as Chief Secretary. The best Ministers would not take it on."[36] (H.A.L. Fisher declined it, and Neville Chamberlain, who might possibly have accepted, was not offered it.) Greenwood himself noted how other ministers "would have promised him anything, they were so anxious he should go."[37]

Lloyd George's personal approach to the question of Ireland and Greenwood's role therein accord with Stevenson's astute observation

---

Indiscrete; Further Indiscretions; Recollections and Reflections; and Life as We Live It. She was also a pronounced Unionist who had no time for Irish republicans and little for Nationalists. Her assessment of the Irish situation is explicit in such statements in *As Others See Us*: "If ever a country needed grim and ruthless government Ireland did" (63), and "It is a pity we have no Cromwell to-day" (70).

about how he always worked diligently and deviously to get what he wanted. As early as 1915 she had been impressed by the "*thoroughness*" with which, once Lloyd George had conceived of an idea, he set about accomplishing it:

> He is indefatigable in his efforts, probing every source from which he may gain information which may be of some use of him, scrutinizing every difficulty which might present itself, and adopting flanking movements ... when a frontal attack is not likely to prove successful, "roping in" persons whose influence is likely to prove helpful or whose opinion counts for something, seeking out those who are "on the fence" and whose opposition would be dangerous, then talking them round, using all the arts of which he is a past master. He seems sometimes to the casual observer to be impulsive and impatient, rushing at things in his desire to "get something done," but no one who has watched him ... can fail to abandon that first impression. His patience in overcoming obstacles, and in returning again and again to their attack with undiminished cheerfulness and confidence, his tirelessness in examining and arranging for details, above all his complete self-effacement ... his absolute disinterestedness which gives him such a clear vision. He knows when he has hit upon the right idea ... And then he will never give in: he never despairs of accomplishing what he has in view. He clings to his object with a tenacity which is almost incredible, and which is only equalled by his confidence and cheerfulness.[38]

All of the above and more was the way in which Stevenson understood how her lover approached Ireland in 1920–22, not acknowledging the occasional admixture of duplicity and mendacity which others identified. Some intimate observers, Churchill, Northcliffe, and Birkenhead among them, regarded him as something of a northern magus, a magician of folklore, "a little Welsh wizard." The iconoclastic Maynard Keynes was less romantic: "Lloyd George is rooted in nothing; he is void and without content; he lives and feeds on his immediate surroundings; he is an instrument and a player at the same time."[39] A.J.P. Taylor was less *ad hominen* in describing the political tightrope that challenged the prime minister following the 1918 election which placed the survival of his coalition government in the hands of the Conservative-Unionists:

Lloyd George was now a renowned world statesman and slipped easily into dictatorial ways. He treated his most distinguished colleagues, except Law, as subordinates, disregarded the cabinet ... [but the Conservative] Unionists had an independent majority and could set up a government of their own if Lloyd George broke with them ... [He] had to rely upon his personal achievements. His own instincts were all for conciliation: of Germany, of Soviet Russia, of Ireland, of the unions. These policies were repugnant to his Unionist supporters, and Lloyd George had to follow devious ways ... on the hunt for success, [he] had to handle every problem for himself: peace abroad, reconstruction at home, Ireland, the Empire. He darted from one problem to another, rarely finding enough time to work one of them through to the end ... In practice, Lloyd George handled every big question himself, using his colleagues as reinforcements in disputed issues.[40]

In time, Margo came to sense the downside of the prime minister's handling of disputed issues, including how he exploited her husband as both player and instrument. He had promoted Greenwood to the cabinet, but he had been less than candid in why he wanted him. In time she recognized that "Hamar is being used as the 'Stick Shaker' ... as the big stick man."[41] She and Greenwood came to understand that his thankless role was largely confined to that of holding the ring in Ireland and attempting to answer in the House of Commons for Lloyd George's personal Irish policy – or non-policy.

Another factor in Lloyd George's opportunistic thinking in making the sudden offer of Ireland to Greenwood was that he wanted to do something for Margo, and he also wanted her in Ireland as a further source of information and policy recommendation. Each of the above accounts of how Greenwood was appointed explicitly include the provision that Margo was to accompany him, the prime minister stating simply, "You and Lady Greenwood are going to Ireland." Garro Jones implies that the prime minister had already ascertained from Margo that her husband would accept or, more cynically, he may have exploited their former relationship to ensure that the ambitious Greenwood *did* accept. That Margo was at least as ambitious politically as her husband was attested by all who knew her. Much later, following Greenwood's death, she told the co-executor of her estate, Major Alexander Greenwood, that she had been Lloyd George's mistress some

years before her husband's appointment as chief secretary. Her executor did not know when Greenwood learned of their affair.[42]

When Greenwood was an undergraduate at the University of Toronto,
he had declared that he would marry the Queen of Sheba if it would
advance his political career. Perhaps he did so in marrying Margery
Spencer. If her affair with Lloyd George had by then already run its
course, she may have told Greenwood of it before their marriage. Or,
less likely, the affair may have begun after their marriage in 1911, in
which case she may have sought his prior agreement. In either case he
may well have been aware of it and possibly even condoned it as a means
for furthering their mutual political ambitions.

A Pussyfoot Chief Secretary, 1920

In May 1920, immediately before the Greenwoods embarked for Dublin, Margo met alone with her past – or present – lover. She and Lloyd George agreed between them how in the time ahead she would send to him her own observations about events, people, and policies in Ireland. The channel was to be Frances Stevenson, to whom she soon reported from Dublin that the "interview I was granted after lunch the day we left ... I'll never forget."[1] That Margo should have found the tête-à-tête unforgettable is hardly surprising, since the prime minister was asking her to go behind the back of her own husband – one of his cabinet ministers – to help keep him informed about the situation in Ireland and to recommend to him what should be done. Stevenson cannot have been too surprised. She had earlier recorded in her diary how Lloyd George in his several ministerial roles was always "probing every source from which he may gain information which may be of some use to him."[2]

Margo's collaborator on the ground in Ireland was Mark Sturgis, the worldly assistant under-secretary in Dublin Castle. From his amusing and articulate diaries and letters, it is apparent that he soon became fully aware of Margo's backdoor role. He was also quite charmed by her and she him. She clearly liked the breezy and optimistic old Etonian and Oxonian who was only two years older than she. Thereafter, he played the covert role of her man in Dublin. He spent more and more time with her whenever she was there or when he was in London, helping her in her private communications to the prime minister via Stevenson. Sturgis was familiar with informal channels to the top from when he had been an assistant private secretary to Asquith, who had maintained for several years an apparently platonic but certainly intimate relationship with Venetia Stanley, the daughter of Lord Derby.

Sturgis was delighted that Margo was a ready channel to Lloyd George: "She's a cute [acute] lady as well as ornamental, and I don't think there's much gets past her."[3] Margo was no less delighted to have her *sympathique* contemporary always close at hand with his ready understanding of the different characters of the two Greenwoods. Sturgis observed, "At first I thought the CS [chief secretary] was a play actor [which he once was as an amateur but] he is much more than that. He is very emphatic in his decisions and takes up a strong position on most things and sometimes has to retreat. He is not so instinctive as she is – she takes a point at once very clearly and is not a bit dependent on others for her ideas and does not hesitate to express a different opinion – and her view is always clever and sensible."[4]

In the letters she wrote to Stevenson to be passed on to Lloyd George, Margo frequently concluded with a brief message of regard and admiration. There is, however, only one letter extant in which she recalls to "My dear Miss Steve" other days with him. On 6 April 1921, having attended a meeting with Lloyd George and her husband about Ireland, she wrote, "As for me I am sad. I know I was good and right, but have I hurt anyone's feelings? Does the P.M. ever mention my name in that quarter? No answering spark there now I'm sure. All quenched."[5] Perhaps not quite quenched, at least not in Margo who was always defensive of her former lover. Stevenson recorded in her diary, "Lady Greenwood is furious with her [his youngest daughter, Megan], especially since M. informed her that she 'considered father was becoming quite impossible; it was time someone taught him a lesson.'"[6] As late as 1923, Lloyd George could still tease Margo, "You are the little devil …"[7]

The Order-in-Council appointing the new chief secretary is dated 4 April 1920, but the Greenwoods did not cross to Dublin until 6 May, a month after Macready.* A member of Parliament, upon being made a cabinet minister, was by tradition required to seek re-election in his constituency. Greenwood, while being briefed in London, concurrently campaigned in Sunderland. The demands of the by-election campaign were not especially onerous; even a newsreel film was readily made. In the event, only a little more than half the all-male eligible voters participated, but the by-election necessarily delayed the Greenwoods' crossing to Dublin. During his short and successful campaign, Greenwood

---

* Macready and Greenwood had met in 1917 at a dinner at Gray's Inn in honour of the Royal Flying Corps and the Royal Naval Air Service, which was also attended by Lloyd George, Smuts, Churchill, F.E. Smith, Lansdowne, and Beaverbrook.

had sought the support of the two New Brunswickers, Bonar Law and Beaverbrook. To the latter he wrote, "Naturally, I want all the publicity I can get and I hope you will give me a good backing in your next *Sunday Express*."[8] Margo shared with the voters her husband's understanding of the formidable challenges that awaited them across the Irish Sea: "Our aim was to bring Ireland into such a state that other peoples' lives would not be in danger."[9]

When Greenwood won his pronounced majority in the Sunderland by-election over his Labour and Asquithian Liberal opponents (presumably his vocal detractor, the Conservative-Unionist Samuel Storey, kept out of it), he proclaimed to the electorate, "I go to Ireland as a friend of Ireland. I will do my best to bring peace." He engaged in some harmless hyperbole when he hailed his by-election victory "as an emphatic vote of confidence in the Government [which] gives Lady Greenwood and myself the greatest encouragement in ... the most important question before the English-speaking world to-day."[10]

By the time that Greenwood was appointed chief secretary, much of the English press, even the *Times*, had become in widely varying degrees critical of the government's handling of the deteriorating situation in Ireland. In England, public meetings and other protests increased in number and size – even the older sister of Lord French, the socialist-pacifist-suffragette Charlotte Despard, was on the platform at a mass protest meeting at Albert Hall. Debates in Parliament became yet more virulent with both Labour and Asquithian Liberals increasingly trenchant in their attacks on the coalition government. The *Times* was not alone among newspapers in its doubts about the government's commitment to an early, imaginative, and peaceful solution. On 3 April 1920, the day before the order-in-council appointing Greenwood, the *Times* faintly praised Macpherson for his fifteen-month term: he had survived "a time of terrible disappointment, mental strain, and physical danger." The prospect of an early improvement depended on Parliament's attitude to the Government of Ireland bill in committee stage and a more intelligent and efficient handling of the campaign against violence. In the longer term, Dominion Home Rule was seen as the panacea for the troubles in Ireland, but no one was certain of precisely what was intended.

The *Times* was hardly more optimistic about Greenwood's appointment. It reported that he had begun his ministerial career only a little over a year before as under-secretary at the Home Office, had been promoted in a few months to parliamentary secretary to the Overseas Trade Department, and after a few more months assigned to "one of the

most responsible and difficult offices in the whole administration ...
[His] chief qualifications for the Chief Secretaryship [for Ireland] are
presumably that he has courage and believes in himself. He can have
little experience of Irish affairs as he was not even a member of the large
Cabinet committee which drafted the Home Rule Bill ... He enters
upon his duties at one of the darkest periods of modern Irish history
and with a commission many think is forlorn."[11]

Greenwood's difficult term as chief secretary was marred by two basic
controversies: first, by his practice of attempting to put the best public
face on the mounting turmoil in Ireland, to the point of being accused
of frequent lying by opponents, and second, by his condoning the
brutality of English volunteers in the RIC, the Black and Tans, and
Auxiliaries, generally expressed in reprisals.

In his unfailingly optimistic public statements, Greenwood followed
the lead of his prime minister in the ultimately hopeless task of attempting to balance conflicting Liberal and Conservative values and priorities. During the fifteen months of his active secretaryship, he was able to
spend only limited time in Ireland. His selection by Lloyd George, after
other ministers had declined, had been in part based upon his undeniable courage, and he displayed it readily on his visits to Dublin. However,
it was more in the House of Commons under relentless daily questioning that he showed a fortitude of a peculiar order. The prime minister
wanted only confident answers to hostile questions, as he himself offered
while attempting to grope his way toward a settlement that would somehow carry the support of both Conservative-Unionists and Liberals.
While he was so engaged, Greenwood was not to give anything away to
Sinn Fein or to the IRA. Statements and replies in the House were to be
uniformly positive – as they had purposefully been even in the darkest
days of the world war itself. If his statements were frequently ambiguous
and sometimes exaggeratedly optimistic, they were what Lloyd George
wanted to help stifle any impression of irresolution.

The journalist Mrs Stuart Menzies offered her own observation of
Greenwood's performance: "I have heard him stating in the House what
I knew was not true. I told him one day that he told his tarradiddles very
badly in the House, and that a child could see that he was not stating
facts. He said in reply, rather apologetically I thought, that he had to say
what was prepared for him to say!"[12] Certainly it appears that on a number of occasions in defending acts of the crown forces, Greenwood was
either highly selective in what he told the House, or "economical with
the truth" or simply ill-informed. He justified to himself, as presumably

the prime minister did to him, that positive statements were the necessary corollary to doing down the gunmen, to catching murder by the throat, with the simultaneous exploration of possibilities of achieving, sooner or later, a peaceful settlement with the more moderate nationalists, based on Dominion Home Rule.

When Greenwood was campaigning in his Sunderland by-election, the cabinet, preoccupied by deepening labour unrest, reaffirmed that any talk of a possible Irish settlement was premature: "Before embarking upon any such step, it was necessary for the Government first to secure the upper hand in their policy of establishing law and order." Lloyd George left no doubt where he stood. Upon his return from a hurried trip to Paris, the prime minister, in keeping a wary eye on his Conservative-Unionist colleagues, had come down firmly on the side of order. "Disorder must be put down at whatever cost. If there were a truce it would be an admission that we were beaten and it might lead to our having to give up Ireland ... Home Rule would be an utter failure unless and until order were restored. There were to be no negotiations and no truce until the police, backed as necessary by the army, had countered the insurgents."[13] Churchill sounded like the prime minister: "No course is open to the Government but to take every possible measure to break the murder campaign and to enforce the authority of the law, while at the same time pressing forward the Home Rule Bill."[14]

An overburdened Lloyd George, dependent for the survival of his government on the continuing support of Conservative-Unionists, had convinced himself that sooner or later he alone could develop the approach that would finally settle the Irish problem. To restore public order, however, he needed more time to bring along at least more moderate Conservative-Unionists. Second, with an Irish police force increasingly demoralized and a public service in urgent need of reform, Greenwood would achieve nothing by appearing pessimistic. Third, given his long-standing ambition to be home secretary, he had to be seen as successful in restoring order as the essential foundation for any settlement. By stating repeatedly that the conflict with the IRA was being won, he strove to keep it on the wrong foot, to whatever degree that was possible, by claiming to be winning the struggle against terrorism. Throughout his short term as chief secretary, he steadily pursued a publicly optimistic stance, especially given the government's flaccid performance in the propaganda contest that accompanied the mayhem. Despite the incredulity, derision, and contempt this position attracted from those strongly opposed to Lloyd George's cautious partisan balancing act, the Greenwoods remained ever hopeful that sooner or later the reward for their loyalty to the prime minister would be another and more congenial cabinet appointment.

Maurice Hankey, the cabinet secretary, shared the doubts of the *Times* about Lloyd George's choice of Greenwood for chief secretary. On 28 April, the prime minister, on a rare appearance in the House of Commons, made a major statement on Ireland, centred on the prior need to deal conclusively with terrorism and restore law and order. Two days later, he held a long meeting with Greenwood and the viceroy. Lord French "made it quite clear that the Sinn Feiners regarded themselves as being in a state of war, and the continual murders merely as acts of war." Hankey thought that Greenwood "talked the most awful tosh about shooting Sinn Feiners at sight, and without evidence, and [about] frightfulness generally. He has not been to Ireland yet, and will no doubt be sobered by responsibility." Certainly there was no doubt where Hankey himself stood: "Terror must be met by greater terror."[15]

With the by-election behind them, Greenwood and his wife crossed the Irish Channel on 6 May in the safety of a Royal Navy destroyer in early May 1920, but returned almost immediately to London. The belief later grew that the chief secretary spent the greater part of his time in Dublin, but the opposite is true. The Greenwoods continued to live mainly in London, crossing to Ireland only as sittings of the House and frequent cabinet and cabinet committee meetings allowed.

From his first days in Dublin, Greenwood wrote to Bonar Law, it had become evident to him that he and Macready were widely agreed, including in their opposition to martial law, unless, in Macready's words, "the Government were prepared to take the country [England] with them."[16] Greenwood was, however, shocked by the "sloppiness in administration and a lack of cohesion in the protective forces that is amazing. The army and police are immobile and therefore glued to the ground. The police in Dublin and many of the RIC are shakey [*sic*]. The civil service is nervous and everybody is more or less scared." With the murder of four constables in one day in May, he added, "The whole situation in the south ... is bad and everyone seems on edge ... I am appealing in every way possible ... for the support of all moderate opinion against murder. I have released certain prisoners and not signed a single deportation order."[17] He immediately saw representatives of the RIC sergeants and constables. As a counter to their depleted morale, he recommended large bonuses. Instead of "talking the most awful tosh about shooting Sinn Feiners at sight," Greenwood in fact opposed Walter Long's idea of "special tribunals" to try suspects, contending that civil courts should be allowed to continue. "Violent Sinn Fein is on the ebb ... moderate men are trying to assert themselves. As we grow stronger these moderates will grow less terrified. The RIC and soldiers are getting on top ... and I'm certain we'll keep on top."[18] In short, he was "desirous of conciliatory rather than of coercive measures."[19] Hunger strikers and other prisoners were released from jail, deportations curtailed, and emergency powers restricted.

However, Greenwood's major challenge was not in Dublin but in London. His private secretary summed it up succinctly:

> Sir Hamar, however, had a better plan ... a plan of concession, bold and sweeping, and it was an earnest of this yet remote solution that a son of the greatest Dominion should be called to the Cabinet Board ... He knew that ... if he coerced, he would be abhorred by the Left [at Westminster]; if he conceded, he would be despised by the Right.
>
> The new Chief Secretary was prepared to go far to appease. He announced his pacific intentions and his earnest hope of saner counsels ... He saw many deputations, probed the minds of all his advisors, and even allowed hints of Dominion Home Rule to go uncontradicted ... The nature of his difficulties from the London end showed unmistakeably in a letter from Mr. Walter Long, then a powerful Coalition Minister, who had set himself up in the Cabinet as a watch-dog against Liberal heresy. Having heard some rumour about concessions he wrote to the Chief Secretary harshly enquiring, 'What's all this blatter [*sic*] about Dominion Home Rule?' The 'blatter' ceased for a year, but when it was heard again the sound of it drowned discord and brought settlement if not peace.[20]

Following Greenwood's first brief sojourn at Dublin Castle, his refusal to embrace the Conservative-Unionist line became especially stark in the face of the continuing killings of police, hunger strikes of prisoners, labour disruptions (especially on the Irish railways), and passive resistance elsewhere, including boycott of the judicial system. The viceroy was no help. When Greenwood was appointed chief secretary, French assured Bonar Law that he had been "in communication with Sir Hamar Greenwood whose selection I am pleased to see." (Greenwood had by chance participated in French's farewell parade in France.) However, according to Edward Saunderson, the secretary to the viceroy and son of an Ulster MP related to Carson, "the little man [French] has practically ceased to take any active part in the government ... [but] has taken up the position that I must see everything ... This is a very difficult position in which to place me and one likely to be resented by our Pussyfoot Canadian and Macready. I am greatly afraid that Greenwood is being carried away by Papist blather and flattery."[21]

A few days after the "Pussyfoot Canadian" arrived back in London in mid-May, he attended cabinet committee meetings on Ireland chaired by Bonar Law (the prime minister was in Paris). There the absence of a coherent Irish policy again became evident. On 24 May, Macready, endorsed by Greenwood and supported by Warren Fisher, recommended at once the offer to Ireland of Dominion Home Rule with the six counties of Ulster excluded, pending plebiscites (as had been advocated by Asquith months before).[22] Somewhat taken aback by this conciliatory policy on the part of a general, the cabinet committee, aside from H.A.L. Fisher, exhibited little enthusiasm. It did, however, endorse Macready's request for more military transport to provide greater mobility to the police and army, and there was ready agreement that the depleted ranks of British intelligence had to be strengthened. (Its few officers, agents, and eager informers were prime targets for IRA gunmen.)

More difficult were discussions in the cabinet committee about how to reinforce the army and especially the RIC. Macready, who had requested eight additional garrison battalions, was asked to accept a delay, given the conflicting demands of Mesopotamia, India, and Egypt. Churchill, the secretary of state for war, preoccupied by the continuing failure of the Allied intervention in the Russian civil war, instead urged again the enlistment of a "special emergency gendarmerie ... of 8,000 old soldiers" so as to be rid once and for all of the Irish nuisance.[23] General Sir Henry Wilson, the acerbic chief of the General Staff, was unimpressed: "The Cabinet are a pack of fools. They have now given up the idea of raising 8 batts. and propose to raise 4,000 R.I.C. I asked Winston why they did not make it 20,000 at *least*. He had no answer."[24]

On 31 May a cabinet meeting heard Greenwood sound like Lloyd George in describing Britain's "great task" as "to crush out murder and arson."[25] However, he immediately added, "When I took over the position [of Chief Secretary], I had just been fighting an election [i.e., by-election] during which I got as much publicity as possible for the Irish question. There is so much publicity now that this country has been roused and also moderate opinion in Ireland on behalf of the Executive [Dublin Castle]. The real difficulty in Ireland is not so much the big issue of putting down crime as the inadequacy and sloppiness of the instruments of Government ... I have tried to lay down two policies, to protect and to remedy. As to protection, we are getting a number of recruits, but also resignations from the R.I.C. at the rate of 200 a week as against 25 before ... The men are resigning because of the terror felt by their families."[26]

Local recruitment for the RIC had been trailing for some time. To raise and train any sizeable separate and distinct gendarmerie would take as much as a year and would accordingly afford no early relief to the hard-pressed constabulary. Three weeks before the cabinet meeting on 31 May, Bonar Law had written to Greenwood about plans for additional English reinforcements for the RIC. Picking up Long's proposal of a year before, Law suggested, "A special body of ex-service men should be enlisted on special terms as a gendarmerie. It would of course cause a great row politically."[27] Similarly, at the cabinet meeting on 31 May, Churchill recalled that the recruitment of "a special force of 8,000 men" had been approved (presumably by the Irish committee) "some days ago," but what the cabinet finally decided was to accelerate and increase recruitment of volunteers from among veterans in England.

When the Greenwoods had first arrived in Dublin, almost 1,500 Black and Tans had already been attested, many soon reinforcing depleted RIC posts across Ireland. More were on their way, in the hopeful words of Lloyd George, "to restore order and protect the innocent" (the king having earlier called upon his government "to protect the lives of unoffending people in Ireland"). Amery reflected the optimism of many Conservative-Unionists at their recruitment: "Hamar was a man of quick clear-cut decision and of unflinching moral and physical courage. He realized at once, on the one hand, the futility of trying to suppress gangster terrorism by the clumsy machinery of military operations and, on the other, the sheer numerical inadequacy of the Royal Ulster Constabulary to cope with a problem which had been allowed to become so formidable ... Dubbed 'Black and Tans,' these new constables soon justified themselves by their efficiency and, on the whole, by their discipline. That they were occasionally driven to measures of reprisal was not to be wondered at, considering the kind of warfare to which they were exposed."[28]

The Black and Tans were not, as some later alleged, the sweepings of the jails of England, but a sizeable minority were a rough lot whose instinct was to meet murder with murder and to match attacks and ambushes with swift reprisals.* Macready's advice to avoid recruiting "scallywags" does not appear to have been always followed. Certainly the young son of one RIC constable was unimpressed with many of the volunteers:

> They had had all sorts of occupations; there were lapsed motor mechanics and cooks and retired professional boxers, over-weight jockeys, ex-commercial travellers, unsuccessful university students, unskilled labourers, tinkers, tailors and candlestick makers; there were confidence men, petty crooks, congenital loafers, card sharpers and gun-happy adventurers. There were decent men and scoundrels, adventurers and frightened youths, domesticated family men and fugitives from deserted wives; there were English and Scottish and Welsh, Jew and Gentile. They came in all sizes and for all sorts of reasons, the most unlikely of which was probably to do a policeman's job ... [They] had neither religion nor morals, they used foul language, they had an old soldier's talent for dodging and scrounging, they spoke in strange accents, called the Irish 'natives', associated with low company, stole from each other, sneered at the customs of the country, drank to excess and put sugar on their porridge.[29]

The Black and Tans had no understanding of policing or even irregular combat and were given no training in how to deal with ambushes and killings by insurgents, who were, in effect, the heirs of the clandestine chouans, carbonari, and klephts of the nineteenth century, not of the vast regimented armies of the First World War. The English volunteers, already well entrenched as a major part of the security forces, were to give the chief secretary almost as much trouble as the Irish insurgents. Greenwood publicly had to support the Black and Tans, having been afforded by the prime minister no other assistance to help meet his requirement that the restoration of law and order must precede any settlement.

Following their arrival in Dublin in April and May, the under-secretary John Anderson, Alfred Cope, and Sturgis, each in his own way, showed a more realistic awareness than the prime minister of the poisonous deadlock that was emerging from his precarious balancing act as he

---

* An estimated seven thousand volunteers in total were recruited for the Black and Tans and the Auxiliaries.

had played for time. Beaverbrook's friend Tim Healy, a leading Irish Nationalist MP and journalist, explained to Sinn Fein what was happening in the coalition government: "You can only get as much as the Conservative Party will give you. The Premier himself [Lloyd George] is in chains to the Conservatives."[30] Cope shared with Warren Fisher in London the conviction of the new arrivals in Dublin Castle that Sinn Fein was incapable of stopping the outrages unless "they can go forward with an open and definite undertaking that Dominion Home Rule will be given."[31] Lloyd George was also caught in a circle. It was impossible for him to offer Dominion Home Rule if IRA violence continued, but support in Ireland for the IRA would only increase if Dominion Home Rule were not offered.

From the summer of 1920, the violence in Ireland grew rapidly, marked by murders and reprisals on both sides. As early as 11 June, French had told Riddell that "he had urged that the country should be placed under martial law, but the Cabinet would not agree. The Prime Minister was not favourable ... if the Irish were met by a proper military force, the whole agitation would be crushed in a few months. Hamar Greenwood and Macready did not agree with French. But they were new to the job. He [French] thought they would alter their views."[32] The cabinet committee on Ireland recommended to cabinet that "the moment has arrived for the Government to actively assume the offensive in its Irish policy, and to come to grips with Sinn Fein," both politically and militarily.[33]

Greenwood, whatever his private understandings, had in the meantime embarked upon his assigned course of public optimism despite mounting public scepticism and ridicule. He seldom moved away from his publicly stated conviction that the IRA "murder gang," numbering a few thousand activists at most, would eventually be put down and the way thereby opened for the orderly introduction of Dominion Home Rule. He was clear about what the offer should be: "We won't stand for independence. We won't have a republic. Short of that, if this campaign of violence and anarchy ceases, the Irish people can have any measure of home rule they can agree on."[34]

Margo Greenwood soon made her own indirect presence felt in Irish policy debates. Cope's description of how she first entered the political scene is cryptic, but it reflects her arrival as a source of information in whom Lloyd George had special confidence. Cope was aware of her peculiar status, discussing with Warren Fisher her recruitment by the prime minister as a trusted observer and even as an informal policy advisor. Cope, who acted as far as possible independently of the chief secretary, seldom telling him much, knew that Margo was also bypassing her husband in the covert role that Lloyd George had asked her to undertake. Cope and Sturgis lunched with the Greenwoods in mid-June. "We pumped in our views. The lady took them in, and I still plump for her."[35] Thereafter, Sturgis worked especially closely with Margo, constantly employing her channel to Lloyd George via Frances Stevenson.

On or about 19 July, when Sturgis was first appointed to Dublin Castle, Margo was back in London, so confident of the validity of her brief initial impressions of Ireland that she shared them immediately with the prime minister. When she met with him alone at No. 10, she pressed him to listen at first hand to senior officials from Dublin Castle. These were duly summoned to London to confer for the first time with the cabinet committee on Ireland: Anderson, Macready, Tudor, W.E. Wylie, and Cope met with Churchill, Balfour, Birkenhead, Long, and Greenwood. Incongruously, one backbench MP was also invited, apparently at Margo's suggestion: her brother-in-law Wilfrid Ashley, a Conservative-Unionist and Irish landowner who in June had opposed any form of Home Rule and called for the immediate imposition of martial law.[36] He was not invited again, but he did continue to call in the House of Commons for the imposition of martial law.

Greenwood emphasized in the discussions that the response could not be force alone: "I have the greatest possible reluctance to apply martial law at present."[37] In fact, Bonar Law soon ruled it out. Macready knew better than anyone that it was in any case impracticable, beyond the limited capacities both in quantity and quality of the soldiers in Ireland. Further, "I do not think for one instant that the British public would stand for martial law ... for a week."[38] Accordingly, the contingent from Dublin Castle was more or less at one in its advice to the cabinet meeting of 23 July that the Government of Ireland bill should be expanded promptly to embrace Dominion Home Rule. Wylie, the able law advisor at Dublin Castle, spoke with especial conviction that, given the breakdown in civil administration including the police and the courts, there remained two stark alternatives: either to impose martial law or to negotiate with Sinn Fein. In Wylie's view, which Greenwood, Anderson, and Macready supported, martial law would merely postpone a permanent settlement; the option of negotiating with Sinn Fein could yet call into being an Ireland reconciled to a place within the British Empire comparable to Canada's, with the six counties of Ulster having the right to remain part of the United Kingdom, as Bonar Law and other Conservative-Unionists had long demanded.

Both Greenwood and Macready were unambiguous that force alone could bring no lasting peace, but they already recognized that "throughout the greater part of Ireland criminal justice can no longer be administered." Special tribunals and courts-martial (with the right to sentence limited to that of civil courts) might need to be substituted. Anderson wrote to Greenwood recommending the immediate offer of a package of reforms that would appeal to moderates, thereby helping to isolate Sinn Fein radicals.[39] Macready agreed: "nothing but what might be called a bold, dramatic, political stroke will solve this matter."[40] Wylie informed the prime minister that "Macready's plan and mine was that the British Parliament should put on the statute book a measure of complete Dominion Home Rule for Ireland patterned on Canada, but not a republic."[41] Lloyd George responded that he was constrained in any such initiative by the Conservative-Unionists in his government. He went to the very core of his dilemma when he stated flatly that he refused to "break up the coalition for Ireland."

Given the increasing threat of Ireland to the unity and longevity of his coalition government, Lloyd George began to engage himself more in the issue, even though postwar problems in both Europe and the Empire still pressed in on him. In his response to the mounting violence in Ireland, he continued to align himself with Conservative-Unionists in placing priority on the restoration of law and order, along with a publicly stated recognition that Ulster must not be coerced. He had made it clear to Tudor where he stood: "LG was very emphatic upon the necessity for strong measures. He said, 'When caught *flagrante delicto*, you must shoot the rebels down. That is the only way.'"[42] C.P. Scott, a former Liberal MP who had become the notable editor of the *Manchester Guardian*, recorded an even starker judgment of his friend from anti-South African War days: "He believes far more in the efficacy of mere force than he did before the [world] war."[43]

The cabinet meeting on 23 July was offered the collective opinion of Dublin Castle that "no amount of coercion can possibly remedy" the increasing violence in either the north or south of Ireland. Macready stood by his statement to Greenwood of the week before that neither coercion nor martial law would provide a solution.[44] After Lord Curzon, the Conservative grandee, stated unexpectedly that the government would sooner or later need to negotiate with Sinn Fein, Churchill again urged a two-track policy: first, "raise the temperature of the conflict to a real issue and shock, and trial of strength ... in the hope that there would then be a chance of settlement on wider lines." Once order had thereby been restored, then "go on much further with concessions than the Government [of Ireland] bill." He was "not afraid of full Dominion Home Rule." By contrast, Balfour supported unenthusiastically the limited Government of Ireland (i.e., Home Rule) bill still making its leisurely way through the House of Commons (and likely to be stalled in the House of Lords) as representing the maximum that Britain should offer to organized assassins. "He was not in favour of ... contemplating a modification of the Bill later in the direction of Dominion Home Rule." Birkenhead went farther in his opposition to any conciliation, calling for yet more militant measures. Greenwood welcomed Churchill's support for Dominion Home Rule, but he was equally aware of Lloyd George's unwillingness to go that far in the face of the conviction of leading Conservative-Unionists (Birkenhead and Long preeminent among them) that only "strong measures" would succeed. In limiting himself to answering technical questions about the administration of the law, Greenwood left the impression that Lloyd George had asked him to limit himself in broad policy debates to allow more time for colleagues to speak. The prime minister would himself take the lead and hear the opinion of the cabinet. The meeting ended inconclusively, the prime minister simply repeating that the enforcement of the law was necessary to bring order to Ireland before negotiation.

Contrary advice was offered the next day by a perturbed T.J. Jones, the trusted assistant cabinet secretary (who conversed privately with Lloyd George in Welsh). He wrote to the prime minister that "repression, however drastic will still leave the Irish problem unsolved ... Before resorting to this final course, [I recommend that] you announce that ... the Government will grant Dominion Home Rule... to the South ... with self-determination for Ulster, provided the [Sinn Fein] leaders ... agree to accept this as a final settlement, and undertake [the enforcement] of order and the suppression of outrage and murder."[45] There was, however, no immediate reaction from Lloyd George, at least none in writing. Later in the same day, amidst a cabinet discussion of the deteriorating situation in Silesia, the prime minister suddenly touched tangentially on Ireland, volunteering that Greenwood was doing well and showing courage. The same day, Lord Riddell, the newspaper proprietor, asked his old friend, "What are you going to do to quiet matters?" Lloyd George replied briefly, "It is very difficult to control an unfriendly population unless very violent measures are resorted to,"[46] echoing C.P. Scott's earlier observation that he had an exaggerated belief in the efficacy of force.

At the cabinet meeting on 23 July, Balfour had repeated his opposition to Dominion Home Rule (a negative stance welcomed by a deputation of diehard Tories who met with the prime minister three days later). On the other hand, Anderson, with Greenwood's support, again contended that an early offer of Dominion Home Rule could prove to be the key to an eventual settlement: "[If] what is commonly described as Dominion Home Rule – with protection for Ulster – could be offered immediately sufficient popular support would be obtained in Ireland to enable the suppression of crime and the re-establishment of law."[47] To no avail: instead, a separate bill for the Restoration of Order in Ireland, unlike the still-pending Government of Ireland bill, was hurried through both houses and received royal assent on 9 August. Bonar Law, now the lord privy seal, explained that the more coercive bill was being adopted first since "the great mass of the Irish people, whatever their views, however strong their desire for independence, would rejoice if this criminal conspiracy of murder could be put an end to."[48]

Lloyd George, in responding to Asquith, who also urged an immediate offer of Dominion Home Rule, kept his eye as always on the Conservative Unionists. He declared, "We cannot accept it [secession]. It would be fatal to the security of the Empire. Until, therefore, Irish opinion accepts the fundamental, indefeasible fact that Britain will never consider those terms, it is futile to attempt to propose alternative schemes ... They decline to accept the autonomy of Ulster. They decline to accept the authority of the Crown. They decline to accept the defence of the realm. These are three fundamental conditions. What is the use, then, of talking about schemes of self-determination and of Dominion Home Rule until, at any rate, some gleam of sanity is introduced into the minds of those who are responsible for directing the majority of Irish opinion?"[49]

In a memorandum to the cabinet, Greenwood joined others in observing that "throughout the greater part of Ireland criminal justice can no longer be administered by the ordinary process of trial by judge and jury." Accordingly, the Restoration of Order in Ireland bill provided, among other things, a range of emergency powers: arrest and imprisonment without trial, courts-martial, and the detention of potential witnesses, all intended to assist in the restoration of law and order before the Government of Ireland bill was implemented. Lloyd George, Bonar Law, Long, and Greenwood had heard such advocacy on 4 August when they met a delegation of businessmen from the south of Ireland, all deeply concerned about the deterioration in the Irish economy as well as in civil society. The delegation sought an offer of Dominion Home Rule. Lloyd George, conscious that he could not yet carry the Conservative-Unionists with him, deflected the suggestion by sounding more like Balfour in asking a series of rhetorical questions: What would be the position of Ulster? Who spoke for the nationalists in the south? Would Ireland pay its share of the massive war debt? etc., etc.[50]

In London on 7 August, Warren Fisher, Anderson, Wylie, and Sturgis lunched with the Greenwoods. According to Sturgis, Greenwood was "bombarded on all sides" about the sterility of the prime minister's policy on Ireland, "but we did not make any obvious impression."[51] However, "the Lady," as Sturgis frequently names Margo in his diary, listened attentively. Three days later she lunched with him, Fisher, and Anderson. In another four days, Sturgis met with her again, the same day that the prime minister made a somewhat more flexible if still vague statement in the House that he was ready to discuss with authentic Irish representatives any proposals on three general conditions: special treatment for Ulster; the essential unity of the United Kingdom under the crown; and the security of the British Isles. A response came immediately from Margo: "Your speech on Ireland has spread consternation in the ranks of Sinn Fein and great joy and encouragement in the ranks of the Black and Tans and other well disposed persons."[52] But Lloyd George had made no reference to Dominion Home Rule as such. Why was he, contrary to the repeated and pressing advice of Greenwood and Anderson and many of their colleagues and senior officials, against an early offer of Dominion Home Rule and instead giving priority to the much more limited Government of Ireland bill and, concurrently, the suppression of violence?

The short answer is that the survival of the government continued to be dependent upon the support of Bonar Law and his increasingly restless Conservative-Unionists. They believed that the crown forces should put down the IRA before the introduction of Home Rule in the south and autonomy for Ulster. The harassed prime minister was convinced that more time had to be allowed for backwoods Tories to recognize that coercion alone would fail, as Dublin Castle itself had long since concluded. He continued to find Ireland a nuisance, endlessly complicating the deepening unease of his relationship with Conservative-Unionists in his fragile coalition and diverting his attention and that of others from more important economic and social problems at home and across the wider world. Even delegating Ireland to Bonar Law and to an Irish situation committee of cabinet had not freed him from such a tiresome distraction. If, however, Greenwood could successfully hold the ring in Ireland until the insurgency could be put down, then time would become available to define a lasting settlement that, with the exclusion of Ulster, could possibly win Conservative-Unionist support.

On 25 August the Greenwoods left London for Switzerland to join Lloyd George, Hankey, and Stevenson for a ten-day "working holiday" at Lucerne. Much of the prime minister's time was taken with the vexed question of relations with Poland and with the new Soviet Union and meetings with the prime minister of Italy; but Ireland was also to the fore, if for no other reason than a total of twenty-four Swiss police as well as the usual complement of British plainclothesmen guarded both the prime minister and the chief secretary against omnipresent IRA threats. A well-publicized hunger strike by Terence MacSwiney, the imprisoned IRA lord mayor of Cork, became a focus for the secondary discussions about Ireland. Lloyd George was against his release, confiding in a letter to Law that in his view it would "completely disintegrate and dishearten the Police Force in Ireland and the Military ... we might as well give up attempting to maintain law and order."[53] Balfour, Edward Shortt, Churchill, and Greenwood differed, arguing that the mayor should not be allowed to die, thereby making himself into a martyr, but Lloyd George publicly overruled their advice. The mayor was left to pursue his prolonged hunger strike to its fatal end.

More Irish matters were injected into the Lucerne sojourn by the arrival of a letter of 29 August from Sturgis to Margo. He again pressed for a clear unity of command in Ireland instead of having Greenwood, Anderson, French, Macready, Tudor, and their various deputies all more or less running their own separate shows. But the main burden of Sturgis's letter was the same as his later journal entry: "The entire population of this God-forsaken island is terrorised by a small band of gun men, Sinn Fein on one end of the stick and Orange[men] on the other. Between them is the *whole* of Ireland pining for a settlement and afraid to do more than to whisper it behind shut doors. We must bring in a Dominion Home Rule bill on most generous lines ... [but] we must not expect one single Irishmen to step up and say, 'This is good' or raise a finger to help us to help themselves."[54] The IRA could not, however, yet know whether the crown forces might in time win the initiative by either superior discipline or by continuing to match brutality with brutality.

At Lucerne, Margo read Sturgis's letter to the prime minister. On her return to London, she told Sturgis that his letter "had a success with the PM." Greenwood added that Lloyd George had "liked it well."[55] On this occasion, Greenwood appears to have had some knowledge of the correspondence between his wife and Sturgis – and the prime minister – but apparently felt that he had quite enough to do at Westminster without attempting to constrain the covert activities of either his wife or his staff. In Sturgis's words, Greenwood "did not want to know any more about it." He had already decided that Anderson in Dublin should feel free to see anyone. The highly competent deputy secretary, who appears to have had limited regard for Greenwood's capacities (although he was too tactful a civil servant to admit it), simply went around his minister as occasion demanded. Their relationship was never easy. Margo candidly told Sturgis that whenever she talked with Anderson, she felt "like a little girl waiting to be rebuked and that he treats Hamar too much like a child!"[56]

Anticipating another discussion with the prime minister when they were all back in London, Margo asked Sturgis "to put on paper again [his ideas] about unity of command, etc." (Lloyd George never sought any such recommendations from Greenwood.) Accordingly, on 20 September, Sturgis again wrote at length to Margo, first reviewing his letter with Wylie, the legal advisor, and sending copies to Warren Fisher, Anderson, and Macready (who was also an occasional correspondent with Stevenson, who duly passed his letters to the prime minister). In response, Margo, acting through Sturgis and not her husband, induced Fisher to cross to Dublin "for a general talk," despite his many burdens at the Treasury. Leading topics would again include whether to let all hunger strikers expire if they persisted in refusing food. Sturgis regretted that he could not spend more time talking about all such matters with Margo alone, she being his direct channel to the prime minister. He did, however, discuss with her his role at Dublin Castle in light of an offer that she had brought to him from London to become secretary to the viceroy in place of the Unionist Saunderson. "She was very kind, and nice, and told me … she spoke to the PM about it who thought I might be too Asquithian, but Lady Greenwood persuaded him!"[57] In the event he did not want the transfer. To his satisfaction, he remained at Dublin Castle where the action – and sometimes Margo – was.

Reprisals and Reprisals, 1920–1921

The first major controversy that marred the course of Greenwood's Irish secretaryship was, as already described, over his endless optimism, to the point of his being accused of mendacity. The second major controversy was reprisals. They fed the rancorous Irish debates at Westminster that took much of the second half of 1920. It was, however, well before Greenwood's appointment that the melancholy, year-long litany of reprisals began. The Greenwoods arrived in Dublin to be confronted with a "degeneration of the conflict into tit-for-tat killings and reprisals."[1] Throughout that summer, violence continued to mount, with both the IRA and the RIC, especially the Black and Tans, engaging in an accelerating scale of mutual reprisals, with one incident capping another in a seemingly endless chain. Greenwood's private secretary recorded the mood in Dublin Castle: "Each crime led to a counter-crime, each counter-crime to a reprisal, each reprisal to a new spirit of revenge … until the whole world was baffled to know which were the murders and which the reprisals."[2]

As early as August 1920, Sturgis had mused, "I've no doubt reprisals do good of a sort. Tudor is sure of it, but it's death to a disciplined force to countenance them, but if they sometimes give a man, caught red handed … a damn good hiding instead of arresting [him] … it's all to the good."[3] Many Englishmen, however, did not agree that other Englishmen in the crown forces should administer "good hidings" on their own volition. Riddell told Lloyd George, whom he rightly regarded as ultimately responsible for reprisals, that he was convinced that although "95 per cent. of the British public were strongly in favour of enforcing the maintenance of the union between Great Britain and Ireland, they would not be prepared to support anything in the nature of terrorism. They would not be prepared to combat outrage with outrage. I had several long talks with Macready, who told me he was strongly adverse to reprisals ... So far as he was concerned, he would rather die than carry out a reprisals policy."[4] Macready issued a statement to the army "explaining the wickedness of reprisals" and threatening punishment for those guilty, but exactly where at any point he stood on reprisals was never quite clear.[5] Sometimes he appeared to be in favour, at other times opposed. In the same week in which Riddell noted Macready's opposition to reprisals, Churchill wrote a long memorandum to Field Marshal Wilson about a press interview by the general in which he appeared to question how the soldiers were "defending themselves from cowardly and treacherous attacks ... [This] seems to me ... to go much too far in that opposite sense ... An official enquiry should be addressed to General Macready."[6] It never was, although later Macready did offer his reflections on the distortions in popular accounts of reprisals:

> The Government began to feel somewhat anxious as to the effect of unauthorized reprisals on public feeling in England, and the Chief Secretary was told to check the activities of the police in that direction. Various minor palliatives to ease the situation were discussed, but the politicians would not face martial law, which I urged as offering the best chance to cope with rebel activities and to enforce discipline among the police.
>
> The failure of the Government to dominate the Sinn Fein propaganda contributed very largely to the difficulties of the situation, the descriptions of the reprisals on the part of the Crown forces which found their way into the press, generally through Sinn Fein sources, being so ludicrously exaggerated as to be hardly recognizable by those who knew the true facts. Equally coloured in a reverse manner were the excuses put forward by the militant Chief Secretary in Parliament when called upon to take up the defence of those acting under his orders. What was required was a cold statement of fact in each case bringing out the cause that led to the outburst, and describing what actually occurred without any attempt to minimize or exaggerate the action of either side. If such information could have obtained the same publicity as the highly coloured effusions emanating from Sinn Fein sources, the reprisals, justly deplored and reprobated, would have assumed in their true perspective a very different aspect.[7]

Given the continuing ambiguities and contradictions between the public and private stance of the prime minister, what Greenwood and Macready were to say publicly about reprisals was never clear.* Privately it became clear that Lloyd George supported reprisals. In the wake of a Black and Tan sacking of the town of Balbriggan and killings in County Clare, Churchill arranged for Tudor to see the prime minister on 23 September. Field Marshal Wilson, who was at the meeting, recorded that Lloyd George had assured Tudor "that he would back him ... through thick and thin."[8] Margo learned (from Stevenson?) that he had told Tudor that "while publicly disavowing reprisals, privately [he] was all for them."[9] The minister of education – and eminent historian – H.A.L. Fisher recorded in his diary that the prime minister had told him, "You cannot in the excited state of Ireland, punish a policeman who shoots a man whom he has every reason to suspect is connected with the police murders. This kind of thing *can* only be met by reprisals."[10] Field Marshal Wilson was convinced that "Lloyd George is under the ridiculous belief that for every one of our people murdered, two Sinn Fein were murdered! And [he] was gloating over this and hugging it to his heart as a remedy for the present disgraceful state of Ireland."[11] With reprisals being "carried out without anyone being responsible," Wilson himself was in no doubt about what should be done. On 29 September he told Lloyd George and Bonar Law, "It was the business of the Government to govern. If these men ought to be murdered, then

---

* In the propaganda competition, something of the same questions of censorship that the British had already addressed in starker terms in the First World War arose again in Ireland. A frustrated Macready joined others in condemning what he regarded as lies and other excesses of several Dublin newspapers, including the long-standing *Freeman's Journal.* In December 1920 its owners and editor were tried by court-martial for misrepresenting alleged acts of the Black and Tans. Two directors and the editor were imprisoned and the newspaper fined, but its managing editor, Henry Newton Moore, was not charged. Moore was the son of a Methodist minister in Montreal (his wife had achieved a certain fame as an ambulance driver during the war; they later moved to the United States where he became editor of the *Philadelphia Inquirer*). Whether Moore was cleared as a result of the intervention of the chief secretary is unrecorded, but Riddell noted in his diary on 2 October 1920 that he had intervened with Greenwood on behalf of three Irish newspapers that were reportedly being threatened by the Black and Tans. "Greenwood promised to do his best to protect them" (Riddell, *Intimate Diary*, 239). Having been regarded as a pro-IRA newspaper by Macready and others (despite its eventual support for Dominion Home Rule), the premises of the *Freeman's Journal* were destroyed not by the British but by Republicans in the Irish civil war that followed hard upon the settlement of December 1921.

the Government ought to murder them. Lloyd George danced at all this
... I still sticking to it ... I got some sense into their heads, and Lloyd
George wired for Hamar Greenwood, Macready, and others to come
over to-morrow night."[12]

Whether Lloyd George listened to Wilson – whom he reportedly liked
– is an open question; he once observed, "I can never get a sane discussion with him."[13] After a meeting with Law, Greenwood, Anderson,
Macready, and Tudor on 1 October, Lloyd George again tacitly condoned reprisals in telling Margo that he was "immensely pleased with
the trend of events."[14] More explicitly, in a conversation with the former
foreign secretary, Lord Grey of Fallodon, he "strongly defended the
murder reprisals." Reprisals "had from time immemorial been resorted
to in difficult times in Ireland; he gave numerous instances where they
had been effective in checking crimes. He quoted two eminent [Irish]
Nationalists who had told him in confidence that the Irish quite understood such reprisals, and that they ought not to be stopped ... The truth
is that these reprisals are more or less winked at by the Government."[15]

That such a practice was seen by Lloyd George as a major way of countering IRA attacks did nothing to ease growing English misgivings that
they were simply not the English way of keeping civil order. H.A.L.
Fisher spoke for many Liberals when he wrote that the only result of
lootings and burnings by crown forces would be "to induce Englishmen
to say that if we can only govern Ireland by such means as these, we had
better not govern Ireland at all."[16] For many Liberals, the prospect of
early Dominion Home Rule for Ireland was not so dire that it was worth
killing people to prevent it. Further, if the Irish wanted so badly to withdraw from the Empire that they could engage in such gross brutality to
each other, as well as to the war-weary English, then good riddance.
Only in the autumn of 1920 did the prime minister finally begin to put
a stern public face on reprisals in an attempt to counter increasing concerns in England. Greenwood issued a statement on 28 September:
"There is no truth in the allegation that the Government connives at or
supports reprisals. The Government condemns reprisals and has issued
orders condemning them and has taken steps to prevent them."[17] Two
days later he cautioned a parade of the RIC in a speech intended for
publication:

> You are a disciplined force, and I confidently count upon you to
> maintain that discipline, no matter what the provocation. Accounts of
> reprisals in certain newspapers are always misleading, and frequently

misrepresent acts of justifiable self-defence as reprisals, but there are cases in which unjustifiable action has undoubtedly been taken. These cases are being carefully investigated. Meanwhile it is necessary to repeat and to emphasise that reprisals will ruin the discipline of the force, and cannot be countenanced by those in authority. The great provocation under which men suffer who see their comrades and friends brutally murdered is fully recognised, and by no one more than myself; but the police are urged to maintain, in spite of this, that self-control that has characterised the force in the past.[18]

"Sir Hamar was no doubt sincere in his detestation of these reprisals," a historian of the Black and Tans, Richard Bennett, has commented, "and quite correct when he told a London paper in an interview, 'the number of reprisals is few and the damage done is exaggerated.'"[19] The reference is to the *Pall Mall Gazette*, which had carried a statement from the chief secretary: "There is no truth in the allegations that the Government connive in or support reprisals. The Government condemn reprisals, have issued orders condemning them, and have taken steps to prevent them … In spite of intolerable provocation the police forces maintain their discipline, are increasing in numbers and efficiency, and command the support of every law-abiding citizen."

One of the few Irish Nationalist members remaining in the House of Commons asked the prime minister on 1 November for a judicial inquiry into reprisals. Lloyd George rejected the idea by asking in reply how one could have an impartial enquiry when the gunmen had so cowed the people that no one would dare cooperate. The judicial system in Ireland was coming to a halt. No witnesses to murder or reprisals would give evidence. No juries would convict. On 3 November, Churchill, again opposing martial law on the grounds that he could not spare sufficient troops to make it workable, presented his colleagues with a paper recommending a "Strictly defined policy of reprisals" that would be "less discreditable and more effective than what is now going on." It was, in any case, simply "Not right to punish the troops who, when goaded in the most brutal manner and having no redress … take action on [their] own account."[20] One week later, Lloyd George chaired a meeting of Law, Churchill, Shortt, and Greenwood to consider Churchill's recommendation of "the substitution of regular, authorised and legalised reprisals for the unauthorised reprisals by the police and soldiers." The prime minister summed up his own ambiguous approach: "I want no reprisals … but the I.R.A. have no right to complain of reprisals."[21]

With no unanimity emerging, a decision was again deferred. Random spontaneous reprisals continued. Pending a final decision from the prime minister, Greenwood rejected Anderson's recommendation that a permanent police review board be appointed. He knew that Tudor would resign if it were.

Popular misgivings in England, frequently expressed in the House of Commons by Liberal and Labour members alike, continued. What a later generation of soldiers would call "rules of engagement" limited the freedom of the police and the army in matching violence with violence. The outcry in war-weary England against the excesses of crown forces also reflected the belief that Irishmen might engage in covert brutalities, but Englishmen – at least in the British Isles – should not. Caught between the prime minister's private support for reprisals and the need to explain them away publicly, Greenwood attempted, without notable success, to describe on an almost daily basis in the House of Commons – from the moment it reconvened in October – why it was natural for there to be police or even army reprisals against the gunmen, while at the same time condemning them as unauthorized. However, Greenwood's stalling tactics in the Commons, pursued at Lloyd George's behest, could not counter that growing unease in popular thinking in England about the retaliatory acts of crown forces in John Bull's other island. In cabinet, emphasis came to be placed on how the police might be further augmented – beyond the Black and Tans – so as to enable them to enforce order without relying on the hard-pressed army to supply additional troops. No less a person than King George V himself pressed on his prime minister the advice that the Black and Tans should be disbanded and the Royal Irish Constabulary made into a quasi-military force under the direct command of Macready, who would then apply military discipline.[22] Tudor recommended the recruitment of a new, separate unit of the RIC that would employ something of the same methods as the IRA. Churchill, for his part, momentarily advanced the remarkable idea of recruiting thirty thousand Ulstermen to uphold the authority of the crown throughout the whole of Ireland.

Tudor's recommendation for an additional unit of English volunteers to be called RIC "Auxiliaries" – but certainly not Churchill's unorthodox proposal of having northern Irish Protestants police southern Irish Roman Catholics – was more or less adopted. In July, in light of continuing IRA terrorism and RIC resignations, there was gradually injected into the depleted RIC a more undisciplined and brutal element than even the Black and Tans: Auxiliaries, of whom a total of 2,214 were recruited (although probably not more than 1,500 actively served).* Their recruitment had been proposed by Tudor and endorsed enthusiastically by Churchill, who had initially urged it in cabinet on 11 May (the end of Greenwood's first full week in office), partly as a means of taking pressure off the War Office to find additional soldiers for Ireland. The new recruits were mainly ex-officers from Kitchener's New Army (which Greenwood and Amery had helped to recruit six years before), not regular career officers but in most cases "Hostilities Only" men who had been accorded wartime field commissions from the ranks. Unemployed in the uncertain postwar economy, they, like the Black and Tans, eagerly volunteered for work that, however grim, offered in their case the then-large sum of a pound per day (double the remuneration of the Black and Tans).

Undisciplined and unsuited for systematic police work and ignorant of Ireland, "Tudor's Toughs" soon proved even more problematic than the Black and Tans. Under Brigadier General Frank Crozier, an eccentric Irishman recently returned from having been inspector-general of the embryonic Lithuanian army, the Auxiliaries by the early autumn of 1920 were adding to the swift reprisals that were already anathema to many English and Irish alike.† For those added excesses, Greenwood

---

* A.D. Harvey in "Who Were the Auxiliaries?," 665–9, analyzes the background and wartime service of the Auxiliaries. He concludes, "the Auxiliary Division of the R.I.C. offered a haven for these psychological casualties: schoolboys who had become killers instead of going to university, working-class men disoriented by wartime promotion to the status of officers and gentlemen, fractured personalities whose childhood maladjustments had found temporary relief in the 1914–18 War and whose outward stability depended on the psychic reassurance of a khaki tunic on their back and a Webley .455 at their hip." Six Auxiliaries had served in Canadian regiments. One anonymous Canadian, "C," allegedly involved in a murder in Cork, was helped to escape Scotland Yard detectives either by George Garro Jones or Beverley Baxter, both of whom contended for that dubious credit (Garro Jones, *Ventures and Visions*, 111–13; Baxter, *Strange Street*, 171–4).

† Frank Crozier, at one time a friend of Tudor, was born in India of Irish parentage. He was a veteran of the South African War and various colonial skirmishes in West Africa. Having become an alcoholic and found guilty of fraud, he was asked to resign his commission in 1909, whereupon he emigrated to Canada. After four years in Manitoba, where in time he became a teetotaller, he returned to Northern Ireland in 1913. He joined the British League for the Defence of Ulster and the Union, commanding the Special Services Section of the West Belfast Regiment of the Ulster Volunteer Force. With the coming of the First World War, the regiment was absorbed into the Royal Irish Rifles. Crozier's memoirs, *A Brass Hat in No Man's Land*, "spell out the beliefs and methods

was required to answer in the House of Commons. Parliament accordingly held him in London during much of the autumn of 1920, attempting to meet the almost daily challenge of explaining away abuses while putting an optimistic face on the trend of events, pending a decision by the prime minister that order had been so restored in Ireland and Conservative-Unionists at Westminster so placated regarding Ulster that the time had finally come to negotiate a settlement. In the meantime, Greenwood would afford the insurgents no comfort by publicly displaying misgivings or by withholding support from the security forces. Greenwood, "who neither originated nor administered coercive policy, became identified with it as its most conspicuous spokesman."[23]

Greenwood's performance in the House over reprisals received decidedly mixed reviews from the beginning. The senior Irish civil servant G.C. Duggan reflected the differing estimates of him: "He had a certain native shrewdness which served him in good stead when cornered, but no one could regard his intellect as brilliant or his conversation as sparkling. His manner in the House of Commons was [however] impressive."[24] Years later, Amery loyally wrote in the *Times* how "old Parliamentary colleagues will best remember the hard-hitting yet impetuous good humour with which [Greenwood] stonewalled against an unceasing bombardment of excited and hostile questioning and his loyal refusal ever to let down his subordinates."[25] Sturgis, on the other hand, recorded candidly that at least two cabinet colleagues did not find Greenwood's comportment in the House "impressive."[26] Edwin Montagu, the decidedly liberal secretary of state for India, who as early as 1918 had recommended Dominion Home Rule for India as well as for Ireland, "read with a glow of hope the Chief Secretary's assurances that things are improving. Am I wrong in thinking this splendid optimism must sometimes be daunted by what appears to be the increasing frequency of murder on the one hand or the other?"[27] Neville Chamberlain was more ad hominen in his criticism. The chief secretary appeared to him to have "little tact in answering questions, but his speeches have made a good impression ... All the same, I don't think he has the stuff in him to go very far."[28]

---

which gained him the reputation of being a martinet. He believed it was necessary to inculcate a spirit of blood-lust to prepare essentially kindly men for the barbarity of combat" (Bond, *Survivors of a Kind*, 115). In one of his rambling books, *The Men I Killed*, Crozier describes how he habitually executed any of his own men whom he suspected of what he deemed cowardice, *pour encourager les autres*, no doubt.

With Greenwood engaged in his apologia at Westminster, Under-Secretary John Anderson presided over Dublin Castle whenever he too was not required in London. Macready viewed this situation as administratively absurd: "The whole burden rested on Anderson, and it was to him that I turned in all matters affecting the civil administration, the visits of the Chief Secretary ... being so few and far between as to make him somewhat of a mythical personage, about whom one read in Hansard, but who was rarely seen in the flesh in the land of his appointment." Macready again recognized that the hollow role of apologist that Lloyd George had handed to the chief secretary had been rendered yet more difficult by the absence of effective British counter-propaganda in Ireland or abroad: "The Chief Secretary himself on occasions did his best to beat the propaganda drum in the House of Commons in defence of the police and soldiers, but unfortunately his superabundant energy so often carried him beyond the boundaries of fact that he soon became as one crying in the wilderness."[29]

By the end of September, Greenwood assured Bonar Law that "the hostiles are growing frightened and ... the mass of Irishmen are losing faith in Sinn Fein as a winning side. The tide has turned."[30] Macready too viewed the situation as improving. According to Jones, Macready, upon his return from a month-long holiday with his mistress on the French Riviera, held "the belief that a few months of resolute government would bring anarchy to an end and enable peace to be made with the moderates. Lloyd George 'thanked God for Sir Hamar Greenwood and General Tudor.'"[31] But the prime minister again rejected Dominion Home Rule as advocated by, inter alia, Lord Grey of Fallodon and Asquith, given his understanding that Sinn Fein and the IRA were now in the grip of the crown forces. He spoke instead in support of "RIC reinforcements" (i.e., more Black and Tans and Auxiliaries).[32]

At Caernarvon in his native Wales on 9 October, Lloyd George continued his hard line, including his opposition to Dominion status for Ireland. The journalist Mrs Stuart Menzies was convinced that she knew who had put him up to it: "It is not generally known, but it is nevertheless a fact that Mr. Lloyd George's finest effort – his Caernarvon speech – was due to Lady Greenwood's influence, even if she did not write it for him ... Lady Greenwood was closely watching events; she is a clever and observing little woman with an acute *flair* of what is 'going to go' in politics, with that quickened perception that comes to those who love their man and see him being ridden into a corner: she quickly discovered what Sir Hamar was up against, and she undoubtedly held Mr. Lloyd

George to the policy of coercion long after his shifty soul felt like renouncing it."[33] One month later at the Guildhall in London, the prime minister famously repeated, "We have murder by the throat ... We struck the terrorists and now the terrorists are complaining of terror."[34] A meeting of ministers the next day took the decision that the moment was not opportune to decide about reprisals.*

In turn, the chief secretary repeated that same month the prime minister's optimism in a speech in Belfast (where he had gone "to receive deputations"), but on this occasion he included what was for him a rare public excursion into policy comment. The government, he stated, was prepared to enlarge its Home Rule bill – something that the prime minister had in fact not offered – "in the most generous way possible and to go farther on the financial side." At the same time and whatever the cost, "the Government would deal unflinchingly with the campaign of murder, arson and intimidation ... the Government was breaking the terror. In many counties, the boycott of the police had ceased." Greenwood confirmed publicly that "a force of Special Constables" – the Auxiliaries – was being recruited, repeating the same optimistic analysis to the cabinet. But at a meeting of ministers on 13 October the prime minister contradicted him by rejecting his recommendation of a new Government of Ireland bill cast in "the most generous way possible." As a self-proclaimed "Gladstone Home Ruler," Lloyd George was convinced that the existing Government of Ireland bill "was a good and generous one, and under it, it would be possible to keep the United Kingdom, which was a small country, together in some sort of unity and enable it to face the future."[35]

In his constituency of Dundee on 16 October, Churchill spoke with optimism greater even than that displayed by the prime minister and Greenwood. "We are going to break up this murder gang. That it will be broken up utterly and absolutely is as sure as that the sun will rise tomorrow morning ... [There will be no] surrender to a miserable gang of cowardly assassins." The British Empire would not be destroyed by "malevolent and subversive force, the rascals and rapscallions of the world." Churchill supported the recommendation of Walter Long and Field Marshal Wilson for the government either to assume

---

* That same week may have been further cheered for Margo by the arrival in Dublin of Eric Geddes, sent as minister of transport to help counter the disruptions of Irish rail workers committed to Sinn Fein. He was, however, accompanied by a female "secretary."

responsibility for future reprisals by crown forces or, failing that, for the imposition of martial law throughout Ireland, now being advocated by Macready. Churchill preferred the former course: "Reprisals under strict limits and under strict control, in certain districts ... should be declared."[36] He later added that "large numbers of people in England ... were sincerely shocked by such undisciplined conduct. However, it will always be very difficult to persuade armed bodies of men to endure with impassive good humour for any long period being hunted down and murdered one by one."[37]

Four days later in the House of Commons, the Labour leader, Arthur Henderson, put a motion: "That this House regrets the present state of lawlessness in Ireland and the lack of discipline in the armed forces of the Crown ... and is of the opinion that an independent investigation should be at once instituted." Henderson had already denounced in Parliament Lloyd George's tacit acceptance of reprisals: "The Government's agents ... had made the forces of the Crown, which existed only to maintain law and order, the instrument of a blind and ruthless vengeance. This was not 'resolute government' but primitive barbarism." Greenwood, leading for the government, replied with some emotion:

I have laid down a code of still more severe discipline for the Royal Irish Constabulary ... I myself had a parade of a large number of the Royal Irish Constabulary. I addressed them. I saw that what I said was published in nearly every paper in Ireland ... I put the matter in as strong words as I could command that their business, and mine, was to prevent crime and to detect criminals, and when there was great provocation they must not give way. But I cannot in my heart of hearts ... it may be right or it may be wrong – I cannot condemn in the same way those policemen who lost their heads as I condemn the assassins who provoked this outrage ... The best and the surest way to stop reprisals is to stop the murder of policemen, soldiers and loyal citizens. I regret these reprisals beyond words. It is a reflection on the discipline of a famous force. It is a reflection on my administration as political head of that force. But if I could bring to the minds and hearts of every member of this House – I do not care on what Benches they sit – the two years of agony, of the intolerable provocation that these policemen, and some cases soldiers, have gone through, the situation would be better understood, and reprisals, whilst condemned, and properly condemned, would also be understood.[38]

Lloyd George was delighted. He told Riddell that "Greenwood had made a first-rate speech on the Irish question – good from every point of view."[39] The vote on Henderson's motion, given the large Conservative-Unionist majority, was handily defeated.

Neville Chamberlain recorded in his diary his satisfaction that the Irish debates had gone well for the government. The chief secretary, "though he shouts too loud and is too emphatic for my taste, yet made a very good speech and created a favourable impression and the House was pleased to hear his statement that the Sinn Feiners were on the run. Nothing succeeds like success."[40] Sturgis was gratified: "I don't think they knocked many spots off him."[41] A week after the vote, the Labour Party sent a small delegation of enquiry to Ireland. Back in Dublin, the Greenwoods invited the "deputation" to "meet the Heads of Departments, Generals, Officers of the Police and others who can speak with knowledge."[42] One of the delegation took the occasion to tell Greenwood (in Margo's presence) "in strong language what he thought of him."[43]

The prime minister repeated from Paris that the IRA was on the run. With regard to reprisals, he rejected the control recommended variously by Long, Wilson, and Churchill. The government would neither assume direct responsibility for reprisals by crown forces nor would it impose martial law under which reprisals would be made official. Upon his return to London, the prime minister instead repeated in the House his conviction that "we are breaking up this conspiracy ... the men who are suffering in Ireland are the men engaged in a murderous conspiracy."[44] The War Office knew better. In a blunt memorandum of 3 November, Churchill candidly admitted that the troops were still "getting out of control, taking law into their own hands, and that besides clumsy and indiscriminate destruction, actual thieving and looting as well as drunkenness and gross disorder are occurring."[45] He again recommended "a policy of reprisals within strict limits and under strict control in certain districts." Jones, the prime minister's principal secretary, "loathed the reprisals, and told Lloyd George what he thought of them."[46] But such advice was futile. The prime minister had not lost "his love of, and exaggerated belief in, the use of force."[47]

Raucous and bitter as the parliamentary debates on Ireland always were, they required that Greenwood and often Anderson be in London when the House was sitting, as Macready deplored. Sturgis for one saw the detaining of the chief secretary at Westminster as part of a Sinn Fein subterfuge to keep him away from Dublin Castle as much as possible while it expanded its own efforts to offer an alternative government: "There is a regular conspiracy to snow us under with Parliamentary Questions, and Private Notice Questions are put daily ... usually culled from the most sensational paragraph they can find in the morning paper ... It is a new form of Irish obstruction in the House and should be dealt with as such."[48] Sturgis was convinced that the debates in the House of Commons were frequently mendacious, lending themselves readily to Sinn Fein propaganda. He wrote to Margo that "all importance ... attaches to the support that these vain fools [the gunmen] read into antics of London MPs ... [whose] efforts merely encourage these vain fanatics who won't realize that most of the support of English MPs is merely a chance stick with which to strike at L.G. [Lloyd George]."[49]

After a debate in the House on 18 November in which the prime minister again proclaimed that things were getting better in Ireland, they suddenly got much worse. On the morning of 21 November – one of several Bloody Sundays that have marred Irish history – Michael Collins had his gunmen kill fourteen British officers, several of whom were, as intelligence officers, among his chief targets. That the killings took place in the centre of Dublin is said to have caused Lloyd George to observe wryly, "Our organisation is in need of improvement," but the revulsion across England was profound. In response, some contended yet more vigorously that the sooner Britain left Ireland – south *and* north – to its own bloody devices, the better. Others argued the opposite: martial law and authorized reprisals should be applied ruthlessly until the murder gangs were exterminated, freeing the mass of Irish people from intimidation.

That same afternoon, 21 November, unauthorized reprisals followed. Black and Tans and Auxiliaries killed twelve people and wounded more at a Dublin football field, Croke Park, where they had reportedly been sent to conduct a routine search for concealed weapons. The Bloody Sunday revulsion in Ireland then paralleled the Bloody Sunday revulsion in England. Paradoxically, the event supplied a sort of respite for Greenwood from the relentless attacks on him in the House of Commons by Labour, Asquithian Liberals, and the few Irish Nationalists still sitting. Warren Fisher knew what the impact of Bloody Sunday on British public opinion would be: "This idiotic ghastly shooting ... is the worst thing the Shinns could have done from their point of view."[50] Greenwood's cabinet colleague H.A.L. Fisher had earlier noted that Greenwood, in some of his over-optimistic and misleading statements to the House, had been skating on thin ice.[51] Sturgis repeated to

Greenwood that he had been a heavy man to be on thin ice, but now the killings had thickened the ice beneath him to two feet.[52]

Earlier, Asquith, disgusted by the cycle of reprisals and always eager to express his animosity against Lloyd George, had put down a motion in the House for 24 November, which now turned out to be four days after the Bloody Sunday killings. Tied to the procedural stake, the former prime minister was not let off by a now largely hostile House. He of course deplored the murder of the officers, but at the same time attacked reprisals and all other real or alleged police and army violence. In his lengthy and stiff response, Greenwood summed up his answer to his old chief by asking bluntly, to the cheers of government supporters, "who is for Ireland and the Empire, and who is for the assassin?"[53] Even the *Times,* never a supporter of Lloyd George's stark law-and-order policy toward Ireland, hailed "the greatest success he [Greenwood] has yet had in the House."[54] Sturgis congratulated him "on wiping the floor with 'em." The chief secretary was "in very good form – said he knew that we'd been through a serious time in Dublin, but that these absurd lunacies ... were all in our favour."[55]

On 30 November in London, at the prime minister's request, Greenwood discussed with Churchill and Field Marshal Wilson what was needed in way of martial law and military reinforcements in the wake of Bloody Sunday. That night the Greenwoods returned to Dublin, he to confer with officials about imposing martial law in Cork and, as Churchill had again recommended, the feasibility of restricting reprisals to military discipline. At the urging of Macready, several Sinn Fein leaders (including Griffith but not de Valera) were arrested.

On 28 November, a week after Bloody Sunday, an IRA ambush had killed seventeen Auxiliaries and mutilated their bodies near Cork. Eleven days later, on 11 December, after further terror and counter-terror, part of the centre of Cork was burned, the arson being immediately ascribed to marauding Black and Tans and Auxiliaries bent upon retaliation for the murder of their fellows. Their lawlessness in Cork provoked in turn almost unanimous condemnation in the British press. To the incredulity of those on the scene and many at Westminster, Greenwood, basing himself on telegrams from Dublin Castle, suggested on 13 December that there was no reliable evidence that crown forces had started the fire (as he had also denied in the case of arson in Tipperary a month before). He speculated that the fire, ignited in two houses, might have spread naturally or even been set by the IRA. Lloyd George added later that "from some of the lower quarters of Cork the population came forth ... and was guilty of looting."[56] The Labour Party, having immediately despatched several of its MPs to Cork, condemned the statements by the chief secretary as "grossly inaccurate."[57] More consequentially, Greenwood approved an order to Major General Sir Edward Strickland, commanding the Sixth Division in southern Ireland, to conduct a court of enquiry that met 16–21 December.

Despite the turmoil at Cork, Margo attempted to take a longer view and continued to send optimistic reports to Lloyd George about other counties. In part she was influenced by Sturgis, who had "no doubt that with improving transport the RIC are getting a bit of their own back and morale is improving. Another excellent thing is that SF funds are said to be getting very low. It is said that the most notorious gun men 'on the run' now get only £3 a week 'subsistence.' Very little money is coming in from America and now that the Presidential Election is over [the Republican Harding was elected],[*] this may stop altogether."[58] In her letters to Lloyd George, Margo as always hoped she was playing his music, but with him not even she could be quite sure. In any case, she wanted to be certain that no one doubted the commitment of her and her husband to whatever Irish policy the prime minister was attempting to pursue at any given time. In the wake of Bloody Sunday and the Auxiliaries' mayhem at Cork, and with the House of Commons soon rising for Christmas, Greenwood again crossed to Dublin from where he reported to Lloyd George that "the various [move]ments for peace are growing in strength. Meantime, we must keep the pressure on to secure the murder gang."[59]

Margo wrote to "My dear Miss Steve," asking her to show her letter to the prime minister:

His children are very happy being back together on this playground [Dublin]. We are hoping we may remain here for a while. Sturgis reports that the troops are in fine fettle and RIC now means 'Radiant Irish Constabulary.' Everywhere one now notices a feeling of dogged confidence and certainty that the recent horrors and assassinations have done nothing to shake. They have only strengthened the determination to go through with it, with absolute certainty to the result, as long as the Government hold firmly to

---

* Sturgis was correct. The flow of money from the United States to Sinn Fein and the IRA was reduced although not eliminated under the Republican President Warren Harding, the Irish vote traditionally going to the Democratic presidential candidate.

present policy which everyone feels they will do. The sort of remark being made all around is "Lloyd George won't let us down." "The Prime Minister is behind us this time and he means business. And thank God he's sent a Chief Secretary who is a man. The first one we've had."

Despite her knowledge of a variety of peace feelers (including that of the retired General Wanless O'Gowan), Margo added, "No one in the executive [Dublin Castle] seems anxious to see peace hurriedly negotiated, as all are convinced that time is in our side and that what approximates to [IRA] surrender will follow peace feelers."[60]

However promising Margo saw the future, immediate threats to both Greenwoods and even to their three small children continued to follow them everywhere. As early as May 1920, six weeks after Greenwood's appointment, the *New York Times* and the *Toronto Globe* had joined the London press in reporting: "Information indicating a serious plan by Sinn Feiners to kidnap the three [Greenwood] children ... reached the Secret Service recently. Sir Hamar is accustomed to receiving threatening epistles, often merely crudely scrawled messages written on scraps of paper, but this threat against his children was not intimated in this way. It was to be a spectacular coup by Sinn Fein extremists ... It was discovered, however, in one or more of the raids in Belfast ... and careful precautions [were] taken to defeat the plot."[61] Later in the year, the director of intelligence at Scotland Yard informed Lloyd George, Law, Churchill, French, and Greenwood that at "a private house in Glasgow last Saturday night it was decided [by the IRA] that the best form of reprisals upon the British Government would be the kidnapping of any of [them],"* £250 having been allocated for the expenses of the six would-be kidnappers.[62]

Greenwood did acknowledge that "my job is a tough one, and a lonely one, but Lady Greenwood and I refuse to be depressed."[63] He admitted to Riddell that "his life was constantly in danger," but Riddell observed that "he seems to be tackling his job with great fearlessness and to be giving the Sinn Feiners some of their own medicine."[64] The Greenwoods

---

* One of the more elaborate threatened reprisals was sent to Greenwood from one J.V. O'Connor, who signed himself "President, Amalgamated Irish Societies of America": "For every man, woman, or child is murdered ... by the cowardly English soldiers and police, three Englishmen in this country will pay the penalty" (Street, *Administration of Ireland*, 371).

were accompanied everywhere by bodyguards. Protection for their three children in London was provided by the Metropolitan Police (which Macready had so recently headed). Margo, like Macready, Tudor, and her husband, carried a small revolver with her everywhere. With some astonishment, Greenwood reported to Lloyd George that his wife had proven to be a better pistol shot than he was himself. Although aware of various IRA plans to kidnap or kill him or her, including at the funeral service at Westminster Abbey for the murdered officers of Bloody Sunday, Greenwood made light of all such threats. Hankey noted that while Greenwood "was 'quite unshaken by his recent nerve-[w]racking experience as Chief Secretary,' Lloyd George went in terror for his life"; and on returning from Lucerne he constantly moved about between various houses."[65] Garro Jones, Greenwood's private secretary, who had been an infantry subaltern in Flanders, recorded the state of alert in the Greenwood residence:

I slept with four Mills bombs [a type of hand grenade] and a loaded automatic at my side … I and the butler and the footman would have been the last line of defence … but we should have constituted, perhaps, a formidable trio, for the butler and footmen were … trained to arms! Indeed, they were more skilled in their latent than in their apparent qualifications, and frequently I watched a pained expression on Lady Greenwood's face as they moved among her dinner guests, untroubled by the need for silence, or for precision and judgment of distance in placing plates upon the table, or by any of the deft touches which stamp the gentleman's gentleman! They were, in fact, tough guys, men who would have fought, and been as glad of the chance as any Irishman.[66]

Greenwood continued to belittle the constant anonymous threats. To cabinet colleagues thinking of visiting Dublin (unsurprisingly, none did, except Eric Geddes), he joked, "All my household are armed, my valet, my butler, and my cook. So if you have any complaints about the soup you may know what to expect."[67] In response to such anecdotes, Lloyd George sent a message to the Greenwoods in Dublin: "I trust you and Lady G. are enjoying your Irish rest cure!"[68]

12

Peace Feelers, 1920–1921

Despite continuing tensions and accusations in both London and Dublin over reprisals, informal contacts between Sinn Fein and Whitehall proliferated as aspirations and contradictions multiplied and led to even greater untidiness and anomalies in policy. John Wheeler-Bennett, in his biography of John Anderson, has summed up how it proceeded in Dublin from the British side:

> Both John Anderson and his two Assistant Secretaries [Sturgis and Cope] were involved in varying degrees in these activities, but Anderson preferred, on the whole, to leave such matters in the hands of his [two] subordinates, perhaps wisely. In him [Anderson] the Sinn Fein leaders recognized – and respected – a man of authority and integrity but without that flexibility of mind which they counted upon for negotiation ... But Andy Cope was in his element; bursting with energy and living on his nerves, now riding the crest of the wave, now wallowing in the Slough of Despond; deeply sincere in his desire to bring about peace; fiercely denunciatory of the influences in Dublin and in Westminster which opposed him, yet revelling withal in the whole crepuscular nature of his work. He laboured untiringly and fearlessly for a settlement and to his eternal credit, succeeded not only in winning the confidence of the Sinn Fein moderates but also in retaining that of his own colleagues and his superiors. No move was made by him without Anderson's knowledge and, though he had personal and direct access to No. 10 Downing Street, in using it he never abused the trust which Anderson reposed in him.[1]

In his candid assessment Wheeler-Bennett makes no mention of Greenwood as standing between Cope and the prime minister nor of Greenwood being kept informed by Anderson and Cope. For example, in contacts with Arthur Griffith, the Sinn Fein founder and vice-president, Anderson led the way. He had attempted, with Greenwood's approval, to meet Griffith in Dublin on 26 September. In fact the conversation did not take place, but even the rumour that it had was of symbolic value, as was a meeting in November in London between Lloyd George and two self-appointed and well-intentioned Irish exponents of Dominion House Rule – the first such meeting in which the prime minister had directly involved himself.

In early November two Sinn Fein members from the self-proclaimed Irish Parliament, the Dáil Éireann, saw Lloyd George, Bonar Law, and Greenwood, who received from them the surprising assurance that a large portion of their fellows would accept the current Government of Ireland bill (although it offered decidedly less than Dominion Home Rule), the exclusion of Ulster, a share of the imperial war debt, and the indefinite guarantee of facilities for the Royal Navy in several small ports on the Atlantic coast of Ireland. They raised, but did not press for, the full fiscal autonomy that Canada and other Dominions enjoyed. Greenwood wrote to the prime minister in their support, "I have always advocated putting this problem [of Ulster] ... on the Irish themselves ... I am told and believe that Sinn Fein will go a long way to meet Ulster."[2] Upon their return to Dublin, however, the two members of the Dáil did not seek to take a lead in further contacts. For his part, Lloyd George came away from the meeting convinced – at least publicly – that there was no need to go beyond his current bill. At about this time he described how Europe "had glided, or rather staggered and stumbled" into the Great War; he was not about to stagger or stumble into any premature, ill-conceived and politically awkward initiative – as he saw it – in Ireland.

Asquith joined in the attacks on his successor in the House of Commons. His former secretary, Mark Sturgis, was not impressed: "It's a bad moment to campaign on the side of the poor Irish. He blames us for not making peace and we must presume that he does not know that *they* know perfectly well that they could have to-day as full a peace from Lloyd George as Asquith or anybody else would dare to give them and of course the vast majority of Irishmen would not only accept but welcome it – but the gunmen are obviously out of hand and their own leaders seem scared to death of them."[3] The prime minister was, however, becoming more willing to explore various peace feelers, including those of several leading Irish businessmen. Greenwood for his part reported that he was "watching every man and movement that makes for peace and will keep you informed."[4] In the first week of December, Art O'Brien, the Sinn Fein representative in London, reported to Griffith that "a Mr. Proctor of Finchley, a personal friend of Hamar Greenwood," had contacted him to express "anxiety to get in touch with Leaders of the movement here [London]. He says that a majority of the Cabinet are anxious for peace, but Long and Churchill are obstructing."[5] Mr Proctor of Finchley was not heard of again (he may in fact have been a prospective British Intelligence plant), but the prime minister did meet with several Irish labour leaders before seeing Patrick Clune, the visiting Roman Catholic archbishop of Western Australia. He was "a nice old boy," in Lloyd George's estimate, "an excellent fellow" in Anderson's; Sturgis thought him "a good fellow and most cheery to talk to." The prime minister had expressed confidence in Clune's "absolute loyalty to the British Empire" when the archbishop volunteered to act as an interlocutor with Sinn Fein leaders, guided in part by Cope and in contact with Greenwood.

O'Brien told Griffith that the archbishop would put the question to him: "If Lloyd George gave a guarantee to stop 'reprisals', could a guarantee be sured [secured?] from Sinn Fein leaders that the killing of crown forces in Ireland would cease?"[6] What in fact subsequently passed between Clune and Griffith (whom he saw in jail) is now unknown, but the prime minister informed the House of Commons that the archbishop, who had spent a total of several weeks crossing between Dublin and London, had been "very anxious before he returned to Australia to try and restore peace to his native country ... I certainly had a good many discussions with him and I believe he had discussions with the leaders of Sinn Fein ... He was anxious to negotiate a truce."

Michael Collins, who was to dismiss Clune as "Lloyd George's envoy, not ours," had drafted for him a list of possible Sinn Fein conditions for a truce, but Lloyd George, after "consulting those who are responsible for order in Ireland," decided to accept "no truce except on the express condition that arms should be surrendered" so as to prevent the IRA in its "shattered condition" from regaining any initiative. Yet the cabinet knew from Dublin Castle that the surrender of arms was an unacceptable condition for Sinn Fein.[7] De Valera, in hiding in Dublin upon his return on Christmas Day from his native United States, gave to the Dáil Éireann in January his version of what had happened with regard to Clune. The Sinn Fein cabinet, he said, "intimated its willingness to observe a truce for a month during which there would be no arrests, pursuits, raids, burnings or courts martial; and the other side undertook to use all possible means to stop acts of violence."[8] Although Dublin Castle was opposed to the condition requiring the surrender of arms, the prime minister was resolved that it could not be waived. The archbishop was informed on 31 December that the cabinet had "disposed of the prospect of the negotiations."[9]

Also in early December in London the prime minister saw Father Michael O'Flanagan, a vice-president of Sinn Fein, and Sir James O'Connor, lord justice of appeal of Ireland, who from early 1920 had been expounding Dominion Home Rule. O'Flanagan, who years before had been a leading advocate of land reform and an occasional lecturer in Canada and the United States on the Gaelic Revival, as well as a leader in Sinn Fein, differed from most of his colleagues in proclaiming the heresy that "the island of Ireland and the national unit of Ireland do not coincide." In other words, he could contemplate – heresy of heresies – a division between the Protestant north and the Roman Catholic south.

O'Flanagan had sent the prime minister a telegram from Dublin on 13 December about a possible truce before Christmas in "the spirit of the founder of our civilization." No one, however, was certain for whom he spoke nor what response the prime minister might best give. Even Hankey, the cabinet secretary and "man of secrets," had noted in his diary on 9 December that he was "not completely in the P.M.'s confidence about Ireland ... Neither is any member of the Cabinet except Bonar Law."[10] For his part, Sturgis saw the contacts with Clune and O'Flanagan as part of "the PM's policy ... [of] cracking the whip with one hand and holding out the carrot in the other. He intends to show clearly that the war on the gunmen is *à la outrance* and at the same time to encourage the peacemakers."[11] On 10 December, Greenwood offered a truce, but only if the rebels laid down their arms. The cracking of the whip was to be heard again when the prime minister confirmed his intention to proceed with the Government of Ireland bill and to proclaim martial law in four southern counties.

On Christmas Eve, before yet another inconclusive cabinet meeting, both Greenwoods lunched with the prime minister to discuss his two-pronged approach. Sturgis and his wife (she had remained for the most part in England) spent Boxing Day with the Greenwoods. Sturgis recalled, "The talk was intimate and general and no opportunity for the talk which I should like to have with the Lady. I'm sure she could tell me many things that I don't understand on the old subject of just what we're driving at ... I *did* say that I was awfully disappointed that the Truce talk had come to nothing and she said, 'So were we!' but O'Flanagan couldn't deliver the goods ..." Sturgis: "Oh, I wasn't thinking of O'F[lanagan], but of Clune, who seemed much nearer reality; Clune felt that you [the Greenwoods] had jumped a fence and were talking peace terms whereas he was talking of truce terms."[12] Clune, however, had returned to Australia. It was instead O'Flanagan who was to try again in the new year. The House of Commons had risen on 23 December, not to sit again until mid-February, the Government of Ireland Act having finally become law that day, in a classic case of much too little much too late.

At a cabinet meeting on 29 December, the prime minister accepted the conclusion of the Strickland enquiry that a company of ill-disciplined Auxiliaries and several RIC were at least partly responsible for the arson at Cork on 12 December. He decided, however, that publication of the findings "would be disastrous to the Government's whole policy in Ireland." He emphasized "the importance of preventing such incidents ... and asked that General Tudor ... deal strongly with any case of indiscipline" in the RIC.[13] At a further cabinet meeting on New Year's Eve, attended by the soldiers three, Macready, Tudor, and Strickland, as well as Anderson, Sturgis recorded that "not much was decided, I'm told, but much [was] discussed."[14] The cabinet was well aware that in 1920 a total of 176 RIC and 54 soldiers had been killed. Against that background it debated a truce of either one month or two, to be arranged by the indefatigable Cope.[*] Winston Churchill, Austen Chamberlain, and, not surprisingly, H.A.L. Fisher supported the proposal. On the opposite side was Macready, who argued that, given the recent progress by crown forces, it was only a matter of time before the IRA was reduced to little more than a public nuisance. He contended that only then would Sinn Fein begin to negotiate seriously, finally abandoning any demands for a republic.

Even though the idea of a truce with a limited term had been raised by the prime minister himself, the cabinet, dominated by Conservative-Unionists, rejected it. Macready's request for martial law in four more counties from 4 January 1921 (additional to the four placed under martial law on 27 December) was instead approved. That same week in

---

[*] Sturgis had protested against the condition of surrendering arms as required by Lloyd George. He spoke for Dublin Castle when he said to Greenwood "that to give up all arms was a surrender, not a truce" (Sturgis, *Last Days*, 26 December 1920, 100).

London, Greenwood spoke to the annual dinner of the Pilgrims, with Sir Campbell Stuart of Montreal, the managing director of the *Times*, in the chair. Greenwood introduced himself to the partly American audience – it was a combined meeting with the Bath Club, a US group – as the only man in Ireland who was enjoying perfect health, no anxiety, and great optimism. Of the latter he gave his audience an example: "The Irish question ... was coming to an amicable settlement ... in six months from now two parliaments would be working in Ireland with powers greater than those enjoyed by any two American [state] legislatures. That would be the opening of the happiest chapter in the history of Ireland and of the English-speaking world. It was a source of legitimate pride to him as a Canadian that he had been a factor in bringing that about, for what he had in accent and physique he owed to his Yankee ancestry" (a reference to the United Empire Loyalist ancestors of his mother).[15]

Margo had kept a diary since their marriage in 1910, but it was destroyed in the London bombings of the Second World War. Only the few entries for the nine days between 2 and 10 January 1921 were found later in their seaside house in Brighton.[16] As she records, following Greenwood's speech to the Pilgrims, the couple spent New Year's 1921 with Lloyd George and Frances Stevenson at Philip Sassoon's house at Lympne.

Sunday, 2nd Jan. 1921
Hamar sent for to see Bonar [Law], Cope having come over from Ireland with more "peace" talk. Father O'Flannigan [*sic*] now willing to come over [to England] and talk, but preferably not in Downing Street. Hamar gave his opinion that the meeting, if held, must be there. Heads of British Government cannot run off round corners to meet Sinn Fein leaders ...

Hamar returned to lunch with news that the P.M. wished him and me to motor down to join him at Lympne. Lord Riddell, Winston [Churchill], Miss Stevenson ... also there ... After dinner, music, laughter and song. Hamar and I contributing a dance or two and he the famous *Solomon Levi* turn. Winston repeated by heart verse after verse of Churgwin's the White-Eyed Kaffir's Music Hall Songs.

Monday, 3rd Jan. 1921
... Peace with Ireland discussed as we all ate [breakfast], Winston punctuating the conversation with shrewd comments ... All inclined

for peace, if Sinn Fein comes far enough. Lord Riddell and Winston
and certainly the P.M., but it must be a good one. Hamar thinks
O'Flannigan will come with "impossible terms." The P.M. said,
"I hope he does." I think he means so that we can show them *we*
are not giving in and that we are now on top and victorious. They
must sue and not attempt to dictate ...

The P.M. says he is having a trying time over the taking over of
Chequers [the gift of Lord and Lady Lee to the nation as a country
residence for the prime minister. The Lees] are inviting the P.M.'s
intimate friends next weekend there, including Hamar and me for
the house warming.

Although the prime minister's mind was chiefly on the dire economic
challenges in the year ahead (the *Economist* was to describe 1921 as "one
of the worst years of depression since the Industrial Revolution"),
he shared with his fellow guests at Lympne "that the Home Rule [the
Government of Ireland] Act was the most important measure the Government had passed, and that he thought de Valera recognized this.
He had returned to Ireland [from New York], first, because he felt that
the militant Sinn Feiners had been beaten, and second, because he was
anxious to capture the Irish Parliament [established by the Government
of Ireland Act] and be in a position to say, 'Look what we have compelled them to give you!'"[17]

The following weekend the Greenwoods joined Lloyd George in
Buckinghamshire on the occasion of Lord and Lady Lee presenting
Chequers to the nation.

Saturday, 8th January, 1921
[Lord Riddell, Reading and Milner and Sir Robert Horne and the
United States ambassador – Lady Lee was an American – were at
Chequers] ... After tea talk became brilliant and amusing [with most
of the men claiming to be self-made]. Hamar asked how many had
taught school ... They all had – or lectured. "How many had taught
Sunday School?" "How many had sung in their village choirs?" And
Lee brought the house down by adding, "I suppose, Hamar, these
are the questions you put to your Black and Tans when they want to
join for service in Ireland" ... Lord and Lady Lee signed the last
deed whereby they relinquished Chequers. Finally Hamar (whose
office had not been included in the deed as it was to disappear
under Home Rule) and Mr. Davis, the American Ambassador, added
their names as witnesses.

Greenwood, supported by Tudor, had recommended that Strickland's report, pointing to the culpability of K Company of the Auxiliaries in the Cork arson, be released at the end of December. At Chequers the prime minister repeated that it would not be, despite his earlier public commitment to do so.

> Monday, 10th Jan. 1921
> Hamar and I motored back to town together. The P.M. apparently not coming up yet, so the Strickland report will have to wait till the Cabinet does meet to consider it. Hamar thinks it should be published and the consequences faced. It would show the impartiality of such inquiries.

Undeterred by Lloyd George's procrastination, four days later Greenwood read the entire Strickland report to the cabinet. He had already condemned the prime minister's decision not to publish it as "a blunder of the first order." Macready agreed that it was "a mistaken policy since it gave greater scope to the rebel propaganda ... The proper course ... would have been to mete out exemplary punishments to the responsible officers, and to any men who could be identified."[18] The cabinet decided to appoint a joint civil and military tribunal to undertake a yet more exhaustive review. If he did not already know it from Margo or others, the prime minister probably sensed Greenwood's mounting unease at the delay in establishing exactly what had happened. At Chequers he had redoubled his efforts to assure Greenwood that a shining political career stretched before him, although Greenwood knew perfectly well that to win another cabinet appointment required him to persevere in his present assignment. The one certain vehicle for the prime minister to send him his encouraging message was Margo. Before returning to London on 10 January, she recorded in her diary:

> Sunday, 9th Jan. 1921
> The P.M. said he hoped I looked forward to the time when Hamar would be Prime Minister and I should reign at Chequers. I said truthfully that Hamar and I were very contented serving as at present ... We talked then of ambition and I admitted that Hamar had ambition, but it was not the kind that looked at the Premiership and strove for it at all costs. (I do not honestly think he really wants it.). He would like to make a name "and succeed in whatever job he has got." He [the P.M.] said: "Yes, that is where he differs from Winston.

Winston's is the other kind of ambition, and he must have a stunt, he is not content to do the ordinary work that goes with his post.

[The P.M.] then got back to Ireland and the delay even under Martial Law in Kerry in getting sentences carried out … It was good to hear him say: "Oh, Hamar has done very well there – splendidly – you've every reason to feel proud." He discussed the Home Office as a possibility for Hamar … I replied that H. might be thought a bit of a "showman" but he was no "flunkey."

Monday, 10th Jan. 1921

… The P.M. said to Hamar: "You above all others have earned promotion and I should like you to go to the Home Office, but if you went now it would look as if there was some disagreement on Irish policy." Hamar concurred, saying he wanted in any case to stay on in Ireland till after the elections [under the 1920 Act]. The P.M. agreed this was the right thing …

Greenwood, increasingly uneasy about unauthorized reprisals, regarded the prime minister's decision at the end of December not to release the Strickland report as a part of his continuing ambiguities, public and private, towards Ireland. But when Lloyd George would not administer justice in what Greenwood regarded as an even-handed manner, rumours of the resignation of the chief secretary began to spread. The prime minister, concerned that Britain was losing the propaganda contest both at home and abroad, had now convinced himself that opinion in England – at least Conservative opinion – had to be coaxed to a final recognition that there was no longer any alternative but a truce and then negotiation. Such recognition would be more readily given if it were seen as a step freely taken by Westminster and not forced. Accordingly, he continued to pursue his dual policy of carrot and stick. His chief secretary, in Margo's words, was to be "the big stick man" while the prime minister devised the carrot. Such a role was so onerous that Greenwood at least twice considered resignation, but a vulnerable prime minister continued to dangle before him various rewards. Lloyd George was fully aware that, amidst the mounting political controversies, the resignation of his chief secretary would "look as if there was some disagreement on Irish policy," and this could bring down his already fragile government. Hence, he flattered Margo with the hyperbole that her husband was doing so remarkably well that he could in time become prime minister, following his promised term as home secretary. For their part, the Greenwoods knew that Ireland was the only route to the coveted Home Office. Greenwood did not resign, having at least in principle achieved a more authoritative review of the Cork rampage. He chose to remain for the time being in his difficult role of attempting to put the best public face on the situation in Ireland while at the same time acting to restore a greater degree of discipline in crown forces.

Indirect and covert contacts between Dublin Castle and Sinn Fein resumed in the new year. On 6 January, Anderson, building towards his longer-term goal of a meeting at No. 10 Downing Street between Lloyd George and de Valera, had first brought together in London the prime minister and the chief secretary with O'Flanagan and O'Connor. Sturgis, who was temporarily using his old office at No. 10, recorded after the meeting that O'Flanagan "gave us to understand, but without any pledge, that if he got a promise of the [Government of Ireland] Act plus fiscal autonomy, most of the Dáil Éireann members elected on a republican ticket would resign or stand aside and give the Act a fair chance. Both [O'Flanagan and O'Connor] said that the PM had not been encouraging, had spent most of the time praising the Act … and had finally hinted that further fiscal concessions would be a good boy's reward after they had started to work the Act satisfactorily, which, said O'Flanagan, gave him nothing new upon which to make a move."[19] This encounter was the basis of the revelation on 8 January in the *Daily Mail* (with whom Margo was in contact, thanks to Riddell) that the prime minister was meeting secretly with Irish Republicans.

On the same day, both Greenwood and Margo lunched with Carson and raised again the possibility of a meeting between him and de Valera. She explained to Sturgis that "the PM's great difficulty is to add anything to the Home Rule Act now that it *is* an Act and that the Shinns should have made their proposals before it passed into law. That Lloyd George wants peace sincerely, but would risk losing much [Conservative] coalition support if he sought at this eleventh hour to amend an *Act*."[20] The following day, 12 January, Lloyd George himself confirmed to O'Connor, "If the Southern Counties decline to work the Act to the point of refusing to use its machinery to secure extensions [i.e., additional powers more akin to Dominion Home Rule], I am afraid they must put up with the existing Government from Dublin Castle. I deeply regret their decision, but it is theirs and not mine so they must abide by it until Ireland reaches a saner temper of mind."[21]

O'Connor replied on 17 January. He acknowledged that he was not authorized by Sinn Fein to negotiate, but he asked whether "authorised negotiators" would be received in London to begin discussions of a possible settlement based on the act and no coercion of Ulster. In light of the exchanges with O'Flanagan and O'Connor, Sturgis again recommended to Margo that the prime minister take the initiative of offering "a positive step" (at a minimum the Government of Ireland Act coupled with fiscal autonomy and the separation of Ulster). She duly set out Sturgis's latest thinking in a letter to the prime minister via Stevenson with information "lately gleaned from de Valera's friend with whom they are in pretty close touch ... O'Flanagan was unable to state definitively that he spoke for Sinn Fein ... de Valera is now stated to be willing to go over himself [to England in secrecy] if he can be given reason to believe that he will not merely be told, 'We've got you beat, you must surrender, and you will get no concession of any kind.' He must be given something as a face saver before he can turn around and recommend the working of the Act and the forsaking of the republic ideal." Margo ended her letter with the affectionate "Be good sweet maid, although you can't help being clever."[22]

Margo's letter achieved a certain prominence in a cabinet meeting when the prime minister misplaced the letter from de Valera in which he had confirmed that he was ready to meet him secretly. Although Lloyd George was continuing to stall over such a meeting before the crown forces had gained the upper hand, he wanted to show de Valera's letter to Bonar Law and other cabinet members, but neither he nor Stevenson could now find it. Instead, to a presumably astonished cabinet, Stevenson "produced a letter from Lady Greenwood* ... in which it was quite plain that while protesting her neutrality she was keen that the P.M. should see De Valera. She said that what De Valera wanted was a 'face-saver', that he was willing to drop the republic and even fiscal autonomy if that could be done."[23] Margo's enthusiastic letter to Stevenson notwithstanding, Bonar Law remained unconvinced that de Valera would ever forego his goal of a republic. Accordingly, he told Jones that "coercion was the only policy: that in the past it had been followed by periods of quiet for about ten years: that that was the most we could hope for from the present repressions, and that he had come to the simple conclusion 'that the Irish were an inferior race.'"[24] From this basic conviction, he never really moved.

For their part, Anderson, Sturgis, Cope, and Margo all concentrated on their longer-term goal of bringing together Lloyd George and de

---

* Sturgis characterized the anonymous Margo as an "intimate and trusted friend" of Lloyd George.

Valera. In a lengthy conversation, Sturgis again suggested to Margo, as he had earlier to Anderson, that the prime minister should offer Sinn Fein "'the Bill + X' ... let them refuse and the PM is in the position of having for the sake of peace made an offer over and above his Act and of having had it rejected."[25] On 20 January Margo laid out for Sturgis in yet more detail what Lloyd George had told her. In response to Sturgis's repeated suggestion that the possibility of a Lloyd George–de Valera meeting would be enhanced if the prime minister conveyed in advance that he was prepared to go beyond his Government of Ireland Act, Lloyd George had told Margo that if he met with de Valera, he would not "risk a failure. [He was] willing to talk with de V. if he came prepared to do business ... What he would *not* do was reopen a question which was now settled by the Act without almost a certainty that Peace would result: that the H. of C. [the Conservative-dominated House of Commons] which had passed his [Government of Ireland] Bill for him would not stand any further negotiations or 'treating with the enemy' except at the price of success."[26] Here was the log jam: de Valera would not move unless assured in advance of major changes, but Lloyd George, given the coalition nature of his government, would undertake no such changes to the act without a guarantee in advance from de Valera that they would ensure peace.

Tudor had told Sturgis that he had seen the prime minister in London, who had assured him that "he is all for fighting."[27] In turn, Sturgis urged Margo to forward to Lloyd George her own analysis and recommendations "so that this business may not have as its only starting point O'C[onnor]'s letter [of 17 January]."[28] When she did so, the prime minister responded by telling her in confidence that Carson was willing to meet de Valera, the first direct contact between the two Irish leaders. Before undertaking to make arrangements for such a unique meeting, Sturgis informed Anderson of the prime minister's letter to Margo, but asked him not to reveal to her that he knew of it: "It might be an embarrassment to her to know that the Under Secretary knew what the Chief Secretary [her own husband] didn't."[29] Margo again wanted no doubt left in Lloyd George's mind of her husband's and her commitment to see the job through. She wrote to Stevenson on 23 January, "Don't let the PM bring Hamar back to London ... or he will be a greater 'brute' than he is always calling someone else."[30]

That same day Greenwood called for improved discipline in the RIC. The previous day, following the return of Macready from his prolonged holiday on the French Riviera, the chief secretary had arranged to lecture the Auxiliaries as well. With his wife and Sturgis accompanying him to the parade ground at Beggar's Bush Barracks in Dublin, Greenwood had attempted to strike a balance between support and reprimand: "In carrying out your stern and oftentimes dangerous duties, you can count on His Majesty's Government to champion you in the House of Commons and to reinforce and back you up." But he immediately added, "It is your duty and mine to rescue Ireland from the assassin ... I have supported and will support the gallant forces of the Crown in Ireland, but I have asked for, and will insist upon, a discipline worthy of the great and honourable cause for which you and I are fighting. You are here to maintain the United Kingdom intact, and to break up that conspiracy which has for its object the smashing of the British Empire."[31]

In Macready's opinion, Greenwood had at that point concluded that "the time had not arrived for a settlement. He was pushing on with the arrangements for the two Irish parliaments. He hoped that when the elections were held, Ireland would be in such a state that the electors would be able to record their votes without fear or favour. He also hoped that independent candidates would come forward in the South and that a representative Parliament would be elected ... If we effect a premature settlement we may lose the benefit of all we have done. Ireland has been terrorised. We must free her from the terror. There are already signs that the Irish people are breathing more freely."[32] Macready was doubtful. He deplored to Stevenson "the Chief Secretary's optimistic frame of mind for which none of us living in Ireland could see any grounds."[33] In a letter of 11 February to Lloyd George (via Stevenson), Macready protested against Greenwood's continuing optimism which created "an infinity of harm" and, contrary to discouraging the IRA, encouraged them to step up their activities to show that "Hamar was talking nonsense."[34]

The Greenwoods spent the weekend of 12–13 February with Lloyd George, who commissioned Margo (not her husband) to attempt to make the final arrangements for a Carson–de Valera meeting. Accordingly, Cope and Sturgis resumed contact with O'Connor and O'Flanagan. Sturgis read O'Flanagan extracts from Margo's letters confirming that Lloyd George had sanctioned a meeting between Carson and de Valera before he himself met with them. Sturgis "gave no hint [to O'Flanagan] of the identity of the writer about whom I only said he [sic: Margo] was not a Member of Parliament and not a Civil Servant, but a friend of mine and an intimate and trusted friend of the PM's ... [I] said no more about plans and places than if de Valera wanted to go and see Carson

I was in a position to make the arrangements and guarantee secrecy and safety. I said that it seemed that the meeting ought to lead to settlement, but I was careful not to give any chance of an impression that either Carson or the PM were tumbling over themselves with anxiety to meet de Valera." Cope and O'Flanagan then considered together the possible peace terms that both Lloyd George and Sinn Fein might accept, Sturgis repeatedly bringing them back instead to the question of what they would first discuss with Carson, "the question of the moment." O'Flanagan replied that "Dominion status would settle the thing." As an aside, Sturgis noted that his colleague Cope was "a queer sensitive old thing. He was up to his neck in all this from the start and he is I think jealous of the Lady's hand in the game."[35]

On 29 January, O'Connor, always a somewhat verbose interlocutor, conveyed to Dublin Castle that he had seen Carson in London, who stated again that he was willing to meet de Valera. Sturgis, in passing this message to Margo, asked her to confirm with Carson that he was in fact ready to do so. The next day she replied that he was. She was dining with Lloyd George that same evening and would seek his specific authority to facilitate an early meeting between the two Irishmen. Margo cannot have had high expectations upon going into dinner, the prime minister having presumably already shared with her the statement of Bonar Law of that afternoon that the only answer to the Irish troubles remained coercion. Nevertheless, a week later Lloyd George wrote to Margo confirming that "Carson was willing to meet de Valera and that he had great hopes of results from such a meeting,"[36] to which she replied that at Carson's request the meeting must be in England, not Dublin. The prime minister continued in his opinion that the best way forward would be for de Valera and Carson to agree between them as much as they could before he saw them both in England.

Sturgis sent to Margo his diary entry for 6 February, describing the meeting that Cope and he had had that day with O'Flanagan and O'Connor and asking her to read it to the prime minister. She reported back the following day that Lloyd George had "nodded and grunted approval." She added for Sinn Fein ears, "I do wish they would realize that the sooner they come the more they'll get – and if they keep nibbling and then *not* coming, impatience with them at this end [the prime minister's] grows."[37] To what extent Greenwood was aware of all this coming and going, much by his own wife, is unclear. There is no evidence that Sturgis kept him briefed, as was his responsibility as undersecretary. Perhaps in such a complex role, ignorance was for Greenwood bliss. In any event, he was in good humour at private dinner parties in Dublin on 2 and 3 February when he again performed "Solomon Levi" to enthusiastic applause, a performance that he seems to have repeated ten days later at another weekend with the prime minister at Chequers, at which Greenwood gave other guests "a glowing account of the improvement in the Irish situation."[38]

On 15 February, the first day back for the House of Commons and the day after the cabinet decided not to publish the Strickland report, the prime minister acknowledged that "there had been acts of indiscipline on the part of some of the Auxiliary forces ... we have taken the sternest action with regard to offences committed by members of these forces." However, he continued to dodge and weave in rejecting repeated calls for the immediate publication of the report, denying that he had ever undertaken to do so. He indulged himself with a syllogism: "If we publish the report of one inquiry, there is no reason why we should not publish every report." Having satisfied himself with that non sequitur, he wandered off into a sort of apologia for his handling of reprisals. With Tudor present in the gallery of the House of Commons, he proclaimed, "There are armed men who are going about the country ambuscading soldiers, firing from houses, one moment parading the streets and the roads like harmless civilians, the next moment hiding with arms in their hands to fire at the very police who allowed them to pass with impunity a few minutes before ... When you have a life-and-death struggle between those responsible for establishing order in Ireland and those who are resorting to methods that are not countenanced by any civilised people in the world, you must consider what is the best thing in the interests of re-establishing the authority of the law of the country."[39] Accordingly, the best thing was to follow precedent and not to publish the Strickland report.

Although acknowledging acts of indiscipline by crown forces, the government House leader contented himself with stating simply, "I promise the question of publication will be considered by the Chief Secretary." Greenwood, who had strongly urged publication, was left to explain that the government simply could not be expected to publish such confidential reports, discretion had to be applied, etc., etc. No one but die-hard Unionists were convinced. The eccentric if not unbalanced Brigadier General F.P. Crozier, commanding the Auxiliaries, summed up: "Mr. Lloyd George had promised Parliament, in advance, to publish the report, but when he saw it he did not dare to do so, as it was a truly alarming document calculated [sic] to drive any cabinet from office."[40]

Despite Greenwood's repeated pleas to Lloyd George for the report to be published as evidence of the even-handed character of British justice, it never was. That Greenwood was increasingly unhappy over the decision not to publish it and, more generally, over his unease at his role as apologist, was reflected in the fresh rumours of his resignation that began to circulate. He had long recognized that he was being held responsible for the reprisals and other excesses of indiscipline of the RIC, the Black and Tans, and Auxiliaries while such excesses were being "winked at" by the prime minister.

On the day following the cabinet's decision not to publish the Strickland report, Anderson lunched with Jones, who said that Bonar Law "was one of the most persistent opponents of conciliation and had greatly influenced the P.M. throughout. Anderson agreed that [Law] was worse than Carson, but the P.M. was really the person responsible for the policy of reprisals. Anderson had the feeling that whenever Tudor came over to see the P.M. he returned very much strengthened – that even if not in words yet by atmosphere and suggestion the P.M. conveyed his encouragement to Tudor."[41]

During the first months of 1921, the policy emphasis continued mainly on the use of force to restore law and order. Lord Chancellor Birkenhead, speaking for the government, stated flatly, "Without vigorous assertion of force, you cannot cure the mischiefs of Ireland to-day." On the day before the House of Commons resumed, Lloyd George had moved Churchill from secretary of state for war to secretary of state for the colonies, as part of a minor cabinet shuffle that, as anticipated, did not include Greenwood going to the Home Office. That same day Churchill wrote to his wife regretting the current "bad" relations with the United States: "Any improvements, however, must wait for the growth of better feeling which will certainly come when the Irish question ceases to be in its present terrible condition. If anything, it has been getting more grave in the last few weeks, and the confident assertions of Hamar Greenwood and the military do not seem to be borne out by events. I am feeling my way for a plan for submitting the cases both of Ireland and Egypt to the Imperial Cabinet, which meets in June and where all the [Dominion] Prime Ministers will be assembled."[42] Clementine Churchill, who considered Lloyd George "the direct descendant of Judas Iscariot,"[43] replied promptly from a hotel in Beaulieu-sur-Mer in France:[44] "You say that the confident assertions of Hamar do not seem to be borne out by events. It makes one blush to think that men of the calibre of yourself and the P.M. should have listened to a man of the stamp of Hamar who is nothing but a blaspheming, hearty, vulgar, brave knock-about Colonial. I think he has done his executive part pluckily and efficiently [but] ... it always makes me unhappy and disappointed when I see you *inclined to take for granted* that the rough, iron-fisted 'hunnish' way will prevail."*

It was at this same time that Greenwood capped his series of aggressive statements to the House with his most extravagant claim:

> For years past and now Sinn Fein extremists and their Soviet colleagues in Ireland – there [is] Sovietism [*sic*] in a marked degree in Ireland – have conspired to smash the Empire.† A policy of brutal arson and murder, with all its ghastly consequences, remains uncondemned by Mr. De Valera and the Sinn Fein leaders. The authors of that policy hope to terrorise into submission the British people and the British Government. It is the policy of the assassin we are fighting, and it is watched by sinister eyes in Great Britain, in Egypt, in India, and throughout the world. Its success would mean the break up of the Empire and of our civilisation.[45]

Despite such fulminations from Greenwood, Northcliffe and his newspapers were as convinced as Clementine Churchill that "hunnish"

---

* Clementine Churchill added, "I have made the acquaintance of your formidable [Canadian] foe, Lt. Col. J.B. Maclean" of the fortnightly *Maclean's* magazine and a growing variety of other successful periodicals. She ascertained to her satisfaction that the root cause of the paradoxical dislike of the strongly imperialist militia officer Maclean for the strongly imperialist Churchill was simply that Churchill was a friend of Birkenhead, whose outrageous behaviour on a 1917 visit to Canada and the United States he excoriated. It would have come as no surprise to her to learn that Smith had been drunk at every public dinner and offended the women present by his conduct toward them."I then encouraged [Maclean] to talk about Canada and himself which he did, at enormous length. He is naïf, vain, touchy, kind-hearted, horribly energetic and vital."

† Greenwood's reference to Soviet Russia is illuminated by Richard Bennett in the *Black and Tans*: De Valera "had conducted negotiations with the Soviet Russian delegation, which was also seeking recognition at Washington. After some discussion, preliminary heads of agreement for an Irish-Soviet treaty had been drafted; a copy of this document was later discovered in a raid in Dublin and published in a White Paper, to confirm the darkest suspicions at Westminster. But no Russian gold flowed into the Irish Republican coffers. The traffic was the other way, and the sum of 20,000 dollars was secretly loaned from the Treasury of the Irish Republican Mission to the Soviet Mission in the United States, who gave some pieces of smuggled jewellery as security. The Irish Government still possesses part of the Russian Crown Jewels as a memorial to the negotiations for what might have been a most interesting political alliance" (132).

ways would never prevail either in the propaganda contest or in the conflict itself. In March Northcliffe suggested to Greenwood that "hanging six young men at intervals of two hours on the same day was hardly good propaganda in view of our difficulty with the United States." Greenwood explained that "he could get only one executioner, an Englishman, who could not come very often, so that the six executions had to be hurried forward in order to suit the hangman's convenience. Thus we are governed."[46]

Some weeks after the arson in Cork, Crozier dismissed twenty-one of the Auxiliaries and held five for trial, following drunken excesses including looting of a shop at Trim. However, Tudor had for some time been contemplating dismissing Cozier (with whom he had served in the First World War); the brigadier general's summary conduct in bypassing normal military channels of enquiry was only the latest of several incidents. Tudor altered the sentences of dismissal of the Auxiliaries to suspension, pending, he stated, the conclusions of a full military court of enquiry. Crozier, who had always been an unlikely choice to command the Auxiliaries under Tudor, resigned on 19 February before he could be dismissed. He had joined the Ulster Volunteer Force in Belfast in 1913 to help train it in the use of German arms against British troops sent to support the inclusion of Ulster in a Home Rule Ireland (at the same time that Macready was in Ulster attempting to prevent any such insurrection). By 1921, however, Crozier appears to have reversed himself on Home Rule and, although still proclaiming himself a loyal Ulsterman, deplored the employment of the Auxiliaries whose command he had earlier sought.[*]

Upon Crozier's resignation, Tudor assumed direct command of the Auxiliaries as well as continuing in overall command of the police throughout Ireland. Crozier thereupon made public statements and fed material to London newspapers that reflected his erratic evolution from a pre-war instructor of Orange fanatics to a postwar opponent of

---

[*] Something of the erratic and unpredictable nature of Crozier was adapted by George Bernard Shaw in his play *On the Rocks* (1933) as the partial model for Sir Broadfoot Basham, commissioner of the Metropolitan Police. With regard to the widespread social unrest in Britain, Sir Broadfoot is urged to use "'volunteers, special constables, auxiliary forces.' Basham (flinching violently) 'Auxiliary forces! I was in command of them in Ireland when you tried that game on the Irish, who were only a little handful of peasants in their cabbage patch. I have seen these things. I have done them. I know all about it … It means extermination, and when it comes to the point, you can't go through with it. I couldn't. I resigned.'"

unauthorized reprisals. Macready wrote to Stevenson – for the eyes of the prime minister – that Crozier had been "quite unsuitable for the work here."[47] On at least this occasion Macready would have agreed with Mrs Stuart Menzies, who speculated that "if General Tudor had had time to make more enquiries, General Crozier would not have been employed ... this gentleman did not set a very good example in the matter of discipline, and as to the reprisals, he said he would have nothing to do with [them although] he was the man who taught them to his men."[48] Certainly Sturgis was not fooled about Crozier: "This beauty ... is ... more truly responsible for indiscipline in the Auxiliaries whom he commanded than anybody else ... [He] has seized a golden opportunity to resign posing as the upholder of order who was not supported from above; a glorious martyr! ... There is no doubt he is a perfectly worthless fellow."[49] In return, in his later memoirs, *Impressions and Recollections*, Crozier contended that "Sir Nevil [Macready]'s administration had failed hopelessly," that his two-volume autobiography, *Annals of an Active Life*, was full of inaccuracies, and that Dublin Castle was "chiefly remarkable for the venomous language used against me by Sir Hamar Greenwood, a Canadian."[50]

Crozier's sudden resignation complicated the public clamour about reprisals in both England and Ireland. In response to the resignation, newspapers called – briefly – for the resignation of the chief secretary. The *Manchester Guardian* was in the vanguard of Liberal and Labour critics, but the *Times* was hardly less condemnatory: "We have long known that the Auxiliary Division was designed for a purpose which we have regarded as foolish and immoral and that the very nature of its employment renders discipline in its ranks almost impossible."[51] In the House of Commons, the attacks on reprisals if anything mounted, Greenwood being left to explain away what Lord Irwin (the future Lord Halifax, viceroy of India and foreign secretary), in speaking against coercion, had called "happenings by a section of the Crown's officers of which every Englishman must be ashamed. Instead of deluding public opinion with a notion that a sufficient application of force will supply a remedy, a wiser course would be to set about taking such steps as may be the means of recovering that consent without which society in Ireland cannot exist."[52] Within the higher reaches of Parliament, however, there was a certain hypocrisy in the widespread condemnations by ministers, including by the prime minister. Balfour, the lord president of the council (and a former coercive chief secretary for Ireland) began to have doubts about the Black and Tans and Auxiliaries. Lord Curzon, who had earlier justified reprisals against the IRA, joined in the condemnation of "methods which would disgrace a Hottentot in the bush."[*] Arthur Henderson, the Labour leader, had been a member of Asquith's government that in 1916 had endorsed retroactively the execution of those most prominently involved in the Easter Rising and had deported many others to jails in England.

The prime minister again sought to appear publicly to be countering excesses of crown forces in order to placate Liberals and Labour in particular.[†] He wrote to Greenwood on 25 February about his dissatisfaction "with the state of discipline of the Royal Irish Constabulary and its Auxiliary force ... Accounts reach me from too many and too authoritative quarters to leave any doubt in my mind that the charges of drunkenness, looting and other acts of indiscipline are in too many cases substantially true ... the violence and the indiscipline which undoubtedly characterise certain units in the RIC should be terminated in the most prompt and drastic manner."[53]

On 23 February, Sturgis met with Margo at the Irish Office in London, following a call on his old chief, Asquith. The former prime minister, who never forgave Lloyd George for usurping his office and persisted in his animosity toward him, had denounced his handling of "the most scandalous chapter ever in the annals of Irish Government." Lloyd George may have thought Sturgis too Asquithian, but it was Sturgis who took the initiative to remonstrate directly with the former prime minister. On 23 February "without saying a word to anybody I ... spent an hour with my late Chief ... As one much mixed up in 'Peace plotting', I could assure him that the vain Shins took the greatest comfort to themselves from the utterances of the Opposition in Parliament and mistook attacks on the Government for support for their cause. Mr. Asquith said quite clearly that I could not ask for silence from him and his whatever the effect on the enemy until we had the police in line."[54]

Immediately following his interview with Asquith, Sturgis lunched with Margo, Warren Fisher, and Stevenson, to report on his conversation and to carry forward their "peace plotting." In his diary he recorded

---

[*] Lord Curzon's metaphor was employed in the opposite context by Macready when he spoke of "acts of provocation [by the IRA] such as would not be indulged in by the wildest savages of Central Africa."

[†] In the first three months of 1921, 208 Black and Tans and fifty-nine Auxiliaries were dismissed; an additional twenty-eight RIC and fifteen Auxiliaries were discharged as a result of prosecutions; and twenty-four RIC and Auxiliaries were court-martialled, bringing the total of removals to 334 in the first quarter of 1921.

that Margo had told him "the whole scene was set last week. Carson ready and the P.M. pleased and ready himself to join the other two actors [de Valera and Lloyd George] on the ring of the telephone ... After getting from her the answer 'No, nothing definite from Ireland', [Lloyd George] has drifted off to European affairs ... After lunch, the Lady drove me into the Park and we went for a walk in Kensington Gardens. I talked *sans cesse* – surprising! – and I hope cheered her up. It mostly came to this anyway – for goodness sake let's get Peace! She gave me a hint that Hamar – or she for him – has thought of resignation." The response of Sturgis to Margo's revelation was a more robust "Rubbish, so like England to begin to get the wind up about reprisals just when we are really getting the Black and Tans in line."[55] Why resign when prospects were improving?

That Greenwood was still considering resignation during the worst of the troubles suggests that he simply disagreed with the convoluted and self-serving policy of the prime minister. It certainly would not have been from fear of assassination, Lloyd George and others being accurate in their high estimate of his physical courage. What pressures against his resignation the prime minister or others deployed is unknown, but in any event Greenwood knew that if he once resigned, any prospect for a further cabinet appointment would be at an end, especially the coveted Home Secretaryship. He did not resign, but Lloyd George was fully aware of his continuing deep unease and did consider offering him the Duchy of Lancaster.* However, since it was a nominal office without a portfolio, he assumed that Greenwood would reject it "with contempt."[56]

Meanwhile, more remained to be done to bring greater order to the RIC, the Black and Tans, and the Auxiliaries. Greenwood informed the prime minister on 3 April, "Macready also agrees that there is a great improvement in the discipline of the police. This is undoubtedly true. I've told Tudor that discipline must be maintained or he and certain subordinates must go. He's a gallant man and it's hard to be blunt with him, but he appreciates the situation."[57] Three days later, Margo wrote

---

* The chancellor of the Duchy of Lancaster was generally a cabinet appointment without portfolio, although occasionally a portfolio or special assignment was coupled with it. It was a convenient place to park cabinet ministers briefly on their way up or down. For example, Churchill, upon resigning as first lord of the admiralty in May 1915, for a short period became chancellor, and Beaverbrook was chancellor in February 1918 as well as minister of information (a non-war cabinet post). Oswald Mosley was chancellor in Ramsay MacDonald's government of 1929.

to Stevenson asking her to assure Lloyd George that her husband was acting "swiftly and thoroughly" in countermanding violations by the Black and Tans and Auxiliaries. To that end, Greenwood conferred repeatedly with Macready and Anderson. He "had Tudor ... up about the burnings at Westport. He gave [him] ... a very stern warning ... He had a meeting of all Divisional Commissioners from all parts of Ireland and gave them an equally straight talk on discipline, obedience of [sic] his orders and the Government attitude."[58] The prime minister repeated to Greenwood on 21 April, "Nothing is more important than that strict discipline should be established and maintained,"[59] but Lloyd George's newfound unease about reprisals hardly squares with the statements of Hankey and Margo that he "was all for them." For his part, King George remained deeply uneasy. In early May his private secretary asked Greenwood, "If this policy of reprisals is to be continued ... where will it lead Ireland and us all? It seems to His Majesty that in punishing the guilty we are inflicting punishment no less severe upon the innocent."[60] The king, having become convinced that his government was in fact covertly following a policy of reprisals, would have better addressed his reservations directly to his prime minister, who was still supporting them. Macready concurred, later observing that "certain persons in high places in London [Lloyd George and Bonar Law] were convinced that terrorism of any description was the best method with which to oppose the gunmen."[61]

The way to a settlement was marginally eased by the disappearance of Bonar Law from the Irish scene. Seriously ill, he resigned from the coalition on 17 March 1921 to recuperate in France. Until he resumed the leadership seven months later, in mid-October, he was succeeded as Conservative leader and lord privy seal by the more flexible if wooden Austen Chamberlain – who was in the insidious position of being neither trusted nor feared by his fellow Conservatives.

Lloyd George's further admonitions to Greenwood about discipline were in part an attempt to placate the still growing numbers of his Liberal and Labour critics and to shift to the Irish secretary the blame for the failure to eliminate all reprisals by crown forces. Or, given the prime minister's mercurial, opportunistic character, the demands of his one-man show, and his desire to keep his options open for as long as possible, he juggled with contradictory attitudes in his attempts to satisfy both Liberals and Conservative-Unionists. Greenwood, with resignation always in mind if not in practice, told Riddell frankly that "he had not been responsible for the reprisals in Ireland. On many occasions, instructions had been given behind his back, and of course he had had to bear the blame ... he did not agree with reprisals."[62] Lord Northcliffe wrote about the same time that "the unfortunate Greenwood is what the Americans call the 'goat' of the piece – no authority and all the blame." The adverse impact that the conflicting demands of the prime minister were having on him were becoming visible: he "has become an ancient man in the last three or four months."[63]

In short, Greenwood knew perfectly well that Lloyd George had left him to carry the can on reprisals while at the same time winking at them. Sturgis and others became aware at the end of April that Greenwood was again moving toward resignation. Even more aware was Lloyd George, who continued in his conviction that the resignation of the chief secretary would be a disaster for his precarious balancing act. Not surprisingly, in a speech to the House of Commons he made "no reference ... to the persistent rumours of Hamar's immediate resignation."[64] Fully aware of his yet greater discontents amidst the continuing reprisals controversy, the prime minister again hastened to repeat to Greenwood – or at least to Margo – that if he would only hang in a little longer, the Home Office would be his. That same week in April, Margo confided in Sturgis that the prime minister had again assured her – as he had done in January – that "Hamar is going to be Home Secretary."[65] The London newspapers and the press in the United States and Canada duly reported that it was only a matter of weeks before this indeed happened.

13

Final Manoeuvrings, 1921

After a month of effort, the persistent attempts of Lady Greenwood and Sturgis to effect a meeting between Carson and de Valera finally came to naught. The last stage of their long manoeuvres is presumably described in two letters from Margo to Sturgis of 17 and 26 February 1921 in which she signs herself anonymously as "Statesman."* "Using the code names of Violet for de Valera, Carrie for Carson, and Bishop for Lloyd George, Lady Greenwood and Sturgis strove unsuccessfully to bring de Valera and Carson together in London."[1] Instead a meeting was substituted with James Craig, who had assumed the leadership of Ulster, Carson having made way for him in anticipation of his own early appointment to the bench. It was not until 20 March that Sturgis in London received indirectly a reply from de Valera in Dublin that he was "prepared to meet Craig or any other *Irishman* to discuss the welfare of Ireland but that the real quarrel is between the English and Irish nations and that internal Irish squabbles [i.e., north-south] will be easy of adjustment when the main fight is won: he will be no party to any attempt to make more palatable the Partition Act of a foreign Government." Sturgis continued, "I have talked to Lady Greenwood and urged that Hamar should speak to Craig with a view to a suitable reply from him."[2] Anderson and Cope did see Craig, partly at Margo's urging, but de Valera did not respond to their initiative, adamant that any such meeting would be tantamount to recognition that Ireland had been divided in two.

* These letters are presumably in a Lady Greenwood file among the papers in the possession of Sturgis's grandson. They are unavailable, although Hopkinson in editing Sturgis's *Last Days* evidently had sight of them (256n106).

To the extent that Greenwood was aware of his wife's covert manoeuvrings, he was unhappy about it. Sturgis recorded that he "thinks we are peace plotting behind his back and says the PM does not like it ... We don't tell him about them all, not to deceive him, but because we think as Chief Secretary it would embarrass him." Sturgis told Margo that he'd "heard we lads had been a bit too independent and had incurred the wrath of the powers that be, but she scoffed at the suggestion, so that's all right."[3]

When Sturgis was soon thereafter discussing his thinking about Ireland with Frances Stevenson, Lloyd George promptly invited him to luncheon. The Greenwoods were also present. The conversation was mainly about the possible imposition of martial law throughout Ireland, which Greenwood had reluctantly come to accept. After the luncheon, Sturgis told both Greenwood and Stevenson that in his view martial law would fail unless it were matched with a clear, take-it-or-leave-it peace offer (including fiscal autonomy), an approach supported by Irish labour leaders who sought a meeting with Lloyd George in London. Sturgis added to Stevenson, "I would suggest that the PM should see them without the CS [Chief Secretary] whom it is their bad taste at the moment to hate like the very devil."[4] The prime minister did see the labour leaders, but it soon became evident that their initiative was not endorsed by Sinn Fein, who strove to keep exclusive control of any negotiations.

Lord Northcliffe summarized the months of covert contact with Sinn Fein: "Many private negotiations with Sinn Fein take place, but all have synchronised [i.e., coincided] with unfortunate incidents which have abruptly stopped the *pourparlers*."[5] The cabinet had itself seldom touched upon Ireland between February and April 1921, so serious was the economic depression and the industrial strife spreading across Britain through the spring. For his part, Churchill, who as secretary of state for war had taken a lead in suggesting how crown forces could best restore order in Ireland, was now as secretary of state for the colonies primarily occupied with the uncertain postwar scene in the Middle East, especially the turmoil created by nationalists in Egypt, the several uncertainties in the newly created Iraq, and the Balfour Declaration placing a Jewish homeland in Palestine. He was absent in the Middle East from 1 March to mid-April 1921.

On turning his mind to Ireland, Lloyd George told Riddell on 2 April that he was convinced that moderate Irish Nationalists "dare not stand for the new Irish Parliament or they would be shot ... there is a reign of terror in Ireland which is being carried on by a comparatively small number of desperate men." The terrorists were being put down – "we struck the terrorists and the terrorists are complaining of the terror" – but he concluded realistically that "shrewd observers say that it will take twelve months. The question is whether the people of this country are prepared to go on for twelve months."[6] Greenwood, with his advisors including the generals now telling him that progress could not be more rapid, described himself as no longer as optimistic as he had been six months before, gloomily adding that pacification would come in years, not months. Preoccupied though the prime minister was by a national coal dispute and strikes by rail and other transport workers, Margo did send him a summary by Sturgis of the various ceasefire contacts. For the moment, however, such contacts would not be actively pursued. In return she passed to Sturgis part of a letter from Stevenson stating "flatly that the Prime Minister would not himself see 'unofficial' negotiators, but 'properly credited representatives are welcome at any time.'" Margo added to Sturgis, "There is another line, and a more important one, working."[7]

This anonymous more important "other line" was the influential Conservative grandee Lord Derby, Greenwood's mentor at the War Office seven years before and his close colleague in the Pilgrims. Derby arrived in Dublin on 22 April in the transparent disguise of "Mr. Edwards." The impetus for his brave initiative appears to have come in part from Edward Saunderson, who had the year before dismissed Greenwood as a "pussy-cat" influenced by papist "blather." Saunderson had written to Derby a month before his visit in disguise to Dublin, "Welsh juggling will never solve the Irish question" – and, quoting Balfour –" the Irish will trust no one except a gentleman."[8] Whatever else Derby was, he was certainly a gentleman. The prime minister may have been doubtful about the efficacy of Derby's disguise as Mr Edwards, but he was gratified to have such an eminent Conservative undertake "peace feelers." On 22 April, Derby saw "some influential s f s," including de Valera who, according to Sturgis, gave him "a clear assurance … that they will accept less than a Republic if Lloyd George will make them an offer, but that they will not say this openly or put it in writing until they have the P M nailed."[9] Not so, according to the contrary recollections of de Valera of thirty years later: "[Whatever] some influential Sinn Fein had said, I made our position clear: that the republic had been declared and that it would have to be accepted as a basic fact," a condition that he of course knew full well was unacceptable to Downing Street.[10]

On 26 and 27 April, cabinet discussion about the elections in the north and south provided for in the Government of Ireland Act surged back and forth, the prime minister finally deciding to proceed with the elections on 24 May, mainly as a way of demonstrating commitment to the act. More indirectly, Lloyd George's intent was to underline to Conservative diehards that Sinn Fein was winning substantial popular support and that Britain was losing the propaganda contest, including in the United States and the Dominions. The prime minister also noted his dissatisfaction with Cope's tendency to make too many offers of a truce to Sinn Fein, leaving the impression that the crown forces were on the run. Greenwood in reply assured the cabinet that he was putting his foot down on Cope.[11]

In standing by the Government of Ireland Act, the unbending Lloyd George and Balfour repeated their scepticism about Dominion Home Rule. As for an immediate offer of a truce, the majority of the cabinet were against it on the grounds that the crown forces were gradually gaining the ascendency and a cessation of hostilities would allow the IRA to regroup and re-equip. The cabinet meeting concluded with a vote of five in favour of an early truce and nine (including the prime minister) against it.

Although Margo continued to cooperate fully with the prime minister behind her husband's back, she was increasingly uneasy about the lightning-rod role to which he remained relegated and which had prompted his thoughts of resignation. She shared with Sturgis her misgivings that "Hamar is being used as the 'Stick Shaker' to the last – that he had a lot of pacific stuff in his [28 April] speech [to the House of Commons] which the PM made him cut out, keeping the 'offer' stuff for himself."[12] Accordingly, in the House on 28 April, Greenwood made no reference to "the pacific stuff," leaving it to the prime minister to follow with a statement of his unconditional readiness to see any representative Irishmen, but "no reference was made to the persistent rumours of Hamar's immediate resignation nor was a word said about Lord Derby's visit."[13] Lloyd George was increasingly eager to appear himself to be wielding a carrot as well as a stick, but in the debate he listed in detail the continuing IRA targeting of Irish policemen. Asquith in turn declared flatly that his successor's Irish policy was a failure, as unrest among Coalition Liberal MPs became more evident. The vote supporting the government was 176 to 65, but the chief whip had reported to the prime minister that from an earlier meeting of MPs "and from other sources ... it is *only sheer loyalty* that restrains a large number of Coalition Liberals from openly opposing certain aspects of the Irish Policy."[14]

Contrary to a comment by Anderson to Sturgis the week before that the former Irish secretary, Edward Shortt, would remain at the Home Office, Sturgis said that Margo still maintained that "Hamar is going to be Home Secretary or 'something', but that L.G. hasn't said whether they are to go now, in a week, or a fortnight, or two months. She said quite spontaneously, without any drawing, that she quite saw that the PM having used Hamar as the big stick man might now want to withdraw him as an awkward fence in the peace course."[15] Shortly after, she wrote to Stevenson, for the eyes of the prime minister, asking him to let them remain in Dublin, thereby herself refuting any rumours of imminent resignation: "We *are* hoping so much that we may stay here a bit unless urgently wanted back in London. Also I'm hoping that if the latest and most promising [peace] move becomes an accomplished fact, that Hamar [does not resign and] may still be Chief Secretary when it matures. He has had to go through so much, although willingly. Naturally as a fond wife I would like to see his administration end well. But we have always both felt that what the P.M. wishes must be our law and always shall [be]. Much love to you."[16]

Greenwood had already written to Lloyd George along the same lines as Margo, asking him not to "call us back to England until it is really necessary."[17] Presumably having become as aware as Anderson that his appointment as home secretary was not an early prospect, he again pressed the prime minister to leave them in Dublin and not require them to spend so much time in London – and hence in the House: "Please leave us here as long as possible ... I can keep my hand on things so much better." And Margo's presence was a major asset: "There's only one Margo!"* Two days later he added, "Please leave us here over Whitsuntide. It is so much better to be on the spot."[18]

Greenwood now confirmed his renewed optimism on an almost daily basis. With his own early escape from the Irish quagmire in mind, on 3 May he assured the prime minister that "the military and the police are hitting hard and sure. Attacks on forces are rarely successful now,

---

* Greenwood's cabinet colleague, Eric Geddes, would have agreed that there was only one Margo, having become one of her many admirers, but "a lady of the stage" was also distracting him at the time. To the satisfaction of Stevenson, Lloyd George would not dine with them. She recorded complacently, "the great Eric will be furious, but I love doing him in as he is such a hypocrite over affairs of the heart – thinks nothing of having violent affairs" (Stevenson diary, 1 May 1921, PA, FLS/4/7).

and the enemy finds it safer to attack civilians."[19] The "inside news," he reported, "is that the murder gang are getting worried and they want a way out … We're winning in fighting and in politics."[20] He wrote to the prime minister about the "failure of their [IRA] campaign to intimidate you and your government … we're pressing on after the IRA. I know we're defeating them, though we're bound to lose brave men. Reprisals outside the martial law area were very few, and declining to nil."[21]

On 5 May, James Craig visited Dublin overnight, ostensibly to pay his regards to French's successor, Lord FitzAlan, a son of the Duke of Norfolk and, as of 3 May, the first Roman Catholic viceroy. Greenwood hailed this appointment as "a master stroke" (Lloyd George's earlier musings about appointing the Dublin-born press baron Northcliffe were dismissed as one of his jokes). Arrangements having been made through Cope and O'Flanagan and endorsed by the Dáil Éireann, Craig was taken to a secret rendezvous with de Valera in north Dublin in the care of "three of the worst looking toughs I have ever seen."[22] Nothing tangible, however, came of the meeting, de Valera repeating that the *whole* of Ireland had been proclaimed a republic at Easter 1916, and Craig equally insistent that Ulster must remain part of the United Kingdom. The one thing that they did agree upon was to meet again after the now-imminent elections.

The following day, Greenwood again wrote to the prime minister along the lines of what he wanted to hear: "Some of my advisors think … that now is the time for a cessation of hostilities. That's not my view. The opportune time may come soon, but it is not to-day," with a second meeting pending between Craig and de Valera.[23] The "some of my advisors" with whom Greenwood disagreed on the question of the timing of a truce (although not on the idea itself) were Anderson and Cope. Sturgis observed that on 6 May, the first anniversary of the initial crossing of the Greenwoods to Dublin, "Hamar is against doing it at once. He says Wait."[24]

Without waiting for the proposed second Craig–de Valera meeting, however, Greenwood authorized Anderson to make preparations to issue a positive statement about a truce "in case of need."[25] He told Anderson – and Margo told Sturgis – that although the gunmen were now on the defensive, they "would take immediate advantage of a lull [i.e., a truce] to recoup and reorganise. This has always been the obvious argument against a Truce. A Truce means a big risk and we must take risks to accomplish anything." The question between Greenwood and Anderson was one of timing, not whether a settlement should be sought but when it should be, Cope acknowledging that Greenwood "is really most keen and anxious for the success of this step [i.e., a truce] towards settlement."[26] As for a truce to accompany the elections, the prime minister had told Riddell on 4 May that "from information he had received [from Margo], Sinn Fein was being got under ... There had been a proposal for a truce, but he was against it ... Everyone present spoke in high terms of Hamar Greenwood's courage. He, too, is against a truce. Horne [chancellor of the exchequer] remarked that he would not have Greenwood's job for money or distinction."[27]

With the elections in both the north and south of Ireland imminent, the cabinet on 11 and 12 May reviewed the continuing lack of real progress against the IRA and the circumstances in which an early truce might be agreed. With Greenwood in Dublin, the prime minister

> read the memoranda received from Hamar Greenwood, General Macready, Sir John Anderson, and General Winter and then half apologetically [read] a summary of the case against the truce ... from Lady Hamar Greenwood. All were against a "truce" in the fullest sense of the word, but Anderson was favourable to a cessation of hostilities while the others were for "going straight on" ... P.M.: Hamar is obviously against it. "Go straight on he says." It is a very serious thing to overrule your C.-in-Chief [Macready] who on the whole has been pro-Irish. [Austen] Chamberlain: He has a good civilian mind. Shortt: He's a Home Ruler' ... [Austen Chamberlain noted that Anderson] gives striking testimony to the success of Crown forces. That impressed me much more than if it came from Hamar Greenwood. He says: 'The position of the Crown forces is stronger and improving every day." To a large extent the offer of the so-called truce would be a confession of failure.[28]

The deciding vote was of course the prime minister's. He opposed an immediate offer of a truce: "We've been generous in the Home Rule Act. Anything beyond that would contain germs of trouble ... I'd support the Chief Secretary. These people will come around sooner or later." Only five ministers, Churchill included, supported the proposal for an early truce; nine, including the prime minister and all eight Conservative-Unionists, were opposed. The idea, for the moment, went nowhere, the cabinet concluding that "it would be a mistake to take the initiative in any suspension of military activities ... the present policy ... should be pursued."[29]

A variety of contacts continued over the possibility of an early truce, some rising, some falling. In the first week of May, Margo had told Sturgis that the Irish labour leaders who had reappeared and others who had recently crossed to London had found the prime minister more forthcoming than they had expected, especially in offering what they understood to be an unconditional meeting with de Valera (e.g., no longer requiring a surrender of arms in advance of a truce). Talk of "an informal truce" continued.

The Greenwoods lunched with King George in the first week of May. He acknowledged progress in the repression of violence, but spent more time berating Lloyd George's policy as expressed by Dublin Castle. In particular, "he hated the idea of the Black and Tans."[30] On 8 May Greenwood wrote, "I'm certain these Irishmen [north and south] will come together ... The enemy is losing by capture great amounts of arms and ammunition." The next day he added, "Sinn Fein ... is growing smaller, losing heavily, and certain to be defeated."[31] After a weekend with the prime minster at Chequers at the end of May, Margo told Sturgis that he had concluded that Sinn Fein "must make peace now or expect a drubbing."[32]

As the cabinet had finally decided in early March, the Government of Ireland Act had come into force on 3 May with its provision for elections to the two new parliaments. "After the elections," Greenwood contended with his customary optimism, "there will be a new set of facts, and all the more favourable to peace or cessation [of fighting]." Anderson had sent him "an excellent short memorandum" in support of a cessation of hostilities over the election period. He recommended it to London "in favour of a 'cease-fire' order initiated by the Government ... as a recognition of the obvious desire for peace as pointed out by the Craig-de Valera meeting," but once a truce was agreed on, it would be difficult if not impossible later to resume the fighting. Greenwood added, "The idea of a truce or a cessation *for* or *because* of the elections is not a serious proposition ... A cessation now may mean its recovery ... When de Valera is ready to advocate cessation – and he will be soon – then I am for dealing handsomely with him, as we did with Botha" in consolidating the Empire. The prime minister should await a more favourable moment for a ceasefire *after* the elections, Dublin Castle being convinced that the Black and Tans had finally become a more disciplined and hence a more effective counter-insurgency force. "The position of the crown forces is stronger than it has ever been. It is improving every day."[33]

As widely expected, upon the closing of nominations for the elections, on 13 May, Sinn Fein was unopposed in all but the four Trinity College seats, a result that gave additional legitimacy to its claim to be the real government of Ireland. Cope reported that all the Sinn Fein candidates elected unopposed on 24 May would not sit in the new parliament in Dublin but in what was proclaimed the second Dáil Éireann. Greenwood wrote to Lloyd George on 15 May that "the IRA was the only barrier to the peace" wanted by everyone; "only the crown forces can end the terrorism." This statement reflected his basic credo throughout his term as chief secretary: the IRA were terrorists who did not represent the great majority of Irish people, many of whom who were simply cowed by them. The only power capable of freeing the people from terrorism and opening the way to Dominion Home Rule was the forces of the crown.

On election day, 24 May, 124 Sinn Fein members were, as foreseen, returned unopposed in the south. The Dublin Parliament met only once – on 28 June – in the presence of the four Unionist members for Trinity College. Lacking a quorum, it then adjourned, never to meet again. In the north, Unionists won forty seats and Sinn Fein and Irish Nationalists the other twelve of the fifty-two seats in the new legislature in Belfast. The elections had in fact solved nothing, although perhaps the Sinn Fein showing even in the north gave Lloyd George a little more leverage against the diehard Conservative-Unionists. Upon receiving the results in the north, Craig resigned his junior ministerial post at Westminster (financial secretary to the admiralty) to become on 7 June the first prime minister of Northern Ireland. With that, Carson withdrew from active politics to become a lord of appeal.

Following the elections, the violence, if anything, mounted. On 25 May the IRA burned the Dublin Customs House, an outstanding example of Irish Georgian architecture. The response to the arsonists by the Auxiliaries was prompt and deadly, although they could not prevent the conflagration itself. In the House of Commons, Greenwood continued in the role assigned to him by Lloyd George: he was still the big stick man who pledged that the government would "go on with patience and courage until the last revolver is plucked out of the hand of the last assassin in Ireland." In the House of Commons on 1 June, Greenwood again encountered a barrage of criticism in the face of continuing if diminished evidence of bloody reprisal for bloody deed, leaving him with little more to say than to offer a promise of yet another review. Tim Healy, MP, the future governor general of the Irish Free

State, wrote to Beaverbrook (who acknowledged that Healy "had a great influence on the political judgments I have formed") roundly condemning the chief secretary: "Out of Bedlam no such councillor of the King as Greenwood could have been selected. His lies alone would set the hearts of the people ablaze. They make no account of the loss, deaths and wounds he has inflicted on them and they will take a vengeance more fearful than any he can decree."[34]

In light of the widespread criticism of reprisals and the continuing terrorism, the cabinet on 2 June discussed a recommendation of its Irish committee to impose martial law on the whole of Ireland. Macready again reversed himself by advocating both martial law throughout Ireland and all-out coercion. Greenwood again disagreed, at the same time opposing a total economic blockade that would, echoing the king, "afflict the innocent far more than the gunmen." The cabinet finally decided to proceed with martial law from 14 July.

On the same day as their martial law decree, 2 June, Lloyd George repeated to the House of Commons his pledge to restore law and order before any negotiations with Sinn Fein. Churchill understood the course that the prime minister was pursuing: "Up till the summer of 1921 no one was more resolute or ready to be more ruthless ... than Mr. Lloyd George. He had constantly to measure the British political situation [i.e., chiefly the attitude of the Conservative-Unionists]. This required, as a prelude to any form of Home Rule, first the security of Ulster and secondly a clear victory over the gunmen."[35] To be sure, the prime minister was again stalling for time until he was certain that he could carry the Conservative-Unionists with him, but Anderson's advice remained pressing. Anderson wrote to Greenwood on 18 June, "If the Government decides to go in for Martial Law on Macready's lines it is essential that they should first announce the extreme limit of concession to which they are prepared to go in the direction of Dominion Home Rule. With this – and it will have to be given in the end – there is some hope of the policy succeeding; without it, I am convinced there is none."[36]

About this time fissures began to appear in the façade of the Conservative-Unionists hostile to a negotiated settlement. With ten other like-minded Conservative members, Sir Samuel Hoare, in despairing of a solution by force, parted company with diehard colleagues. In his promotion of negotiations, he requested a meeting with the prime minister, Chamberlain, and Greenwood to present a memorandum that, among other things, deplored the inadequate British Intelligence: "Having run our Secret Service in Russia and Italy for four years, I knew enough of Intelligence methods to convince the Prime Minister that his [Intelligence] show in Ireland was rotten from top to bottom. Greenwood tried to bluff, but the case against our Intelligence is overwhelming ... Lloyd George showed great momentary interest ... but nothing seems to have happened except that the rotten regime has become more rotten."[37] Using the word "rotten" in the same way that Macready had earlier employed it about the RIC and Dublin Metropolitan Police, Hoare was a little dated in his adverse evaluation, and his work in Russia and Italy was not much regarded. In fact, British Intelligence, employing informers, was finally regaining much lost ground.

Jan Christian Smuts, now prime minister of South Africa, in London in June for the 1921 Imperial Conference, had long interested himself in the Irish question. In July 1919, for example, he had proclaimed that it was poisoning public life in Britain and threatening the British Empire. He told Scott that he had become convinced that Lloyd George "believes far too much in force ... there is a curious element of brutality in [him]."[38] A month before, Jones had received a paper for the prime minister by some Oxford dons suggesting the designation of "the Dominion Premiers as arbiters of the sort of Dominion status which might be conceded to Ireland." And Wickham Steed, the editor of the *Times*, reportedly urged on King George's secretary that the king propose a truce for the whole of Ireland. At this point the plot decidedly thickens.

Keith Middlemas, a meticulous British historian, in editing the three volumes of Whitehall diaries of T.J. Jones, deputy secretary to the cabinet, says that it was de Valera who first put the idea to Smuts, who in turn proposed to the king that he make a conciliatory speech. According to Middlemas, "De Valera approached Smuts, who lunched with the King, pressed him to use the occasion of his speech to the Belfast Parliament to make a grand gesture of reconciliation."[39] Middlemas gives no authority for his editorial statement that the original idea came from de Valera. He notes only that Cope kept the channels of communication open between Sinn Fein leaders and Lloyd George and that de Valera's initiative was "through the mediation of Art O'Brien."[40]

In any case, what is clear is that Smuts proposed to the king over luncheon a conciliatory speech at the opening of the new Northern Ireland parliament nine days hence. (The basic idea was not novel: Asquith had pondered whether the king could play a role between north and south before the Irish conference of 1914 at Buckingham Palace.) Smuts wrote to Lloyd George that his recommendation to

King George reflected his conviction that his own liberal-imperialist approach would be endorsed by all the Dominions. The worldwide British Empire was a system of governance that rested on certain principles and ideals of freedom and cooperation "which must find their application in Ireland no less than in other parts ... I need not enlarge to you on the importance of the Irish question for the Empire as a whole. The present situation is an unmeasured calamity; it is a negation of all the principles of Government which we have professed as the basis of Empire, and it must more and more tend to poison both our Empire relations and our foreign relations. Besides, the present methods are frightfully expensive in a financial sense no less than in a moral sense; and what is worse they have failed."[41] Frances Stevenson was not impressed with Smuts's condemnation, noting in her diary that he "is inclined to be tiresome over Ireland, and suggests we should give them Dominion Home Rule. D's [Lloyd George's] reply was: The British Isles are a federation [sic]: you do not contemplate giving Dominion Home Rule to Natal, or the Orange States. Why then do you suggest it for us? But Smuts is always a little slim, and is probably running with Asquith and Co. in case this Government falls."[42]

Slim or not, Smuts found the prime minister in fact receptive – and perhaps a little slim himself. Although he did not share with Smuts exactly how he envisaged exploiting any opening offered by the king's speech, he declared to the cabinet on 17 June that the royal visit to Belfast was "an occasion for a big question." A new draft of the king's speech (to replace one prepared in the Irish Office) was circulated by Edward Grigg in the prime minister's office on 14 June to Greenwood and Balfour, among others.[43] However, on 21 June, Birkenhead, without waiting to hear (he probably already knew) what the king would say the following day, stated in the Lords that the government would never bow to force. In the words of the *Times*, he "ruthlessly dashed all hopes that their hearts might have changed and decreed intensified warfare in Ireland to the bitter end."[44] Lloyd George did not mind: "In dealing with the Irish you must shew that you mean to go on."[45]

On 22 June, the king opened the Northern Ireland Parliament with a well-crafted and even emotional plea for reconciliation.* He made no

---

* King George V had only visited Ireland on two occasions, first as the Duke of York in August 1897 and then immediately after his coronation in July 1911. He was so pleased with what he regarded as his enthusiastic welcome and the bond of affection between the Irish people and the monarchy that he retained deep regard for Ireland – which did not, however, extend to Dominion Home Rule.

mention of the prior need to restore law and order and no reference to martial law or reprisals. He eloquently addressed the whole of Ireland: "I speak from a full heart when I pray that my coming to Ireland to-day may prove to be the first step towards an end of strife amongst her people, whatever their race or creed ... I appeal to all Irishmen to pause, to stretch out the hand of forbearance and conciliation, to forgive and to forget, and to join in making for the land they love a new era of peace, contentment, and goodwill ... North and South, under one Parliament or two."[46] His plea was immediately hailed by the *Daily Mail*, the *Manchester Guardian*, and the *Times*, among many other newspapers. It offered Lloyd George a rare opportunity – as he himself had no doubt already recognized and possibly even helped to contrive – to break out of the policy sterility of the past year, escaping from the endless challenge of attempting to reconcile the conflicting demands of Liberals and Conservative-Unionists in his coalition government.

14

Truce, 1921

Only one day after the king's speech, the prime minister suddenly confirmed to Greenwood, newly arrived in London with Macready and Anderson from the parliamentary ceremonies in Belfast, that he had decided to embark upon an attempt to negotiate a settlement. The following day, 24 June, Cope too was summoned from Dublin to a cabinet meeting to endorse the offer of negotiation. (Anderson was in London with Greenwood for much of the six months between the king's speech and the end of the year, leaving Sturgis next in line as Anderson's surrogate at Dublin Castle.) Cope, at the epicentre of the direct contacts between the prime minister and Sinn Fein, had sought to be included in the London meeting. Greenwood, who six weeks before had described him as "my excellent Cope," now began to declare that he was never certain of what Cope was doing and was uneasy at his influence on policy.[1] Sturgis observed that "Greenwood … had no intention of taking him [Cope] to the Cabinet. He got there thanks to the Lady." Margo, again disagreeing with her husband, had arranged through Stevenson for Cope to be included. With great nervous energy, Cope "harangued His Majesty's Ministers … He talked failure without an offer and Greenwood told him [in front of the cabinet] 'to curb his Sinn Fein tendencies'. However, they heard him out … [Anderson] gave support."[2]

In stating his conviction that an offer of negotiation must now be made, Lloyd George did not refer to the king's speech directly (Conservative-Unionists needed no reminding of any speech by the monarch) but instead offered to the cabinet the explanation that in "the last three days we have received indications [via Cope] that De Valera is in a frame of mind to discuss a settlement on the basis other than of independence."[3] Cope immediately took a personal invitation

from Lloyd George to de Valera in Dublin. It was worded "in most dignified statesman-like terms sincerely asking him and any of his colleagues
to meet him [Lloyd George] and the representatives of Ulster in
London to support the King's wishes as announced at Belfast and see if
it isn't possible to give this distracted country peace."[4] The invitation
was matched by a readiness to declare jointly a truce effective 11 July,
three days before martial law would otherwise be extended to the whole
of Ireland. Additionally, the cabinet decided to ask Smuts, now the
South African prime minister, to cross over to Dublin to discuss the invitation with de Valera and Griffith.

De Valera replied that he wanted to consult with a range of Irish opinion before committing to a meeting in London, adding again his two
conditions that Britain had to recognize the unity of Ireland and her
right of self-determination. From Belfast, James Craig, now premier of
Northern Ireland, while accepting Lloyd George's invitation in principle, declined to participate in the consultation with de Valera since he
had already accepted an invitation to meet the prime minister alone at
Downing Street. Against this background on the weekend of 3–4 July,
Chamberlain, Balfour, Carson, Smuts, and Hamar and Margo Greenwood
gathered at Chequers. Cope was among the few officials present. He
stated that de Valera was ready to cross to London in a matter of days,
although Frances Stevenson believed that he was still hesitating. "Smuts
has gone over again to see De Valera. They say he waited to see whether
D.V. was likely to come, and now will take the credit for having persuaded
him to come."[5] The next day, Smuts "returned from Ireland, but not having accomplished much. De Valera would not discuss anything with him,
but simply said that their demands were for a Republic." De Valera had
in fact rejected Smut's advice: "I cannot advise you too strongly against a
republic. Ask what you want, but *not* a republic."[6]

To sum up: if the historian Keith Middlemas is correct, the progression in the months of June and July is striking: the cabinet decision of 2
June to impose martial law on the whole of Ireland in July; the king's
conciliatory speech of 22 June; Lloyd George's sudden statement to
Greenwood the next day, 23 June, that he had decided to seek negotiations with Sinn Fein; de Valera's acceptance on 8 July of a truce beginning on 11 July and of the invitation to a "conference" in London on
14 July, the same day that martial law was to be imposed on the whole of
Ireland and the stillborn parliament in Dublin was to sit. The events are
either a series of remarkable coincidences or de Valera was at least privy
in advance – via Cope? – to the conciliatory nature of the king's speech

and the date of the decision to impose martial law on the whole of Ireland. Was the progression to some greater or less degree mutually and covertly contrived, or was it merely a coincidence?

In any event, in England both the truce and the invitation to Sinn Fein to negotiate were unacceptable to many Conservative-Unionists, who strongly opposed suspending the fight when the crown forces reportedly had the gunmen on the run. Greenwood repeated his refrain to the prime minister: "We're pressing on after the IRA. I know we're defeating them." Sir Henry Robinson, the vice-president of the Local Government Board wrote, "General Tudor ... a most intrepid and resourceful soldier, seemed to be rapidly gaining the upper hand." Amery spoke for the diehards when he later declared, "What was sheer weakness and folly was the Government's yielding to de Valera's insistence that the negotiations must be accompanied by a truce. This enabled de Valera and his *Dàil* to figure openly as a government in being, and hopelessly weakened such authority as the Government still exercised in the country. For Hamar this was a bitter blow, for he had no doubt but that he was winning the day."[7]

By early July it had become evident that a truce was increasingly likely, but Frances Stevenson noted that "De V. keeps repeating that if he comes to London, D. [Lloyd George] will have him in a trap. D's retort is: 'If he *doesn't* come he will certainly be in a trap.'"[8] The weekend of 8–10 July, Stevenson as usual was with Lloyd George at Chequers.* "While he was changing in my room, the telephone rang ... D. then spoke to Macready himself, and learnt that events had been happening very quickly in Dublin. De Valera had agreed to come over this week, was going to issue orders for a truce, and had sent for Macready. The whole atmosphere was changed and Macready [pistol at the ready in his tunic pocket] had been given a wonderful reception by the Dublin crowd."[9] With the truce of the next day, 11 July, Greenwood wrote to Lloyd George, "May I congratulate you on the success of a straight, strong policy in Ireland. You are the only Prime Minister who has ever succeeded in Ireland ... I am sincerely proud to know that my brave wife and I have not failed you in the long, hard, stern fifteen months that has led to your victory."[10] Greenwood added that all

---

* Later that weekend the premiers of the Dominions, Canadian Prime Minister Arthur Meighen included, arrived at Chequers where, among other things, Lloyd George (without the assistance of his chief secretary for Ireland) gave them a briefing on what he regarded as the rapidly evolving and promising developments in Ireland.

Ireland, including the Sinn Fein leadership, wanted peace, prompting Sturgis to rank Greenwood as "an ardent pacifist."[11]

At noon on 11 July a truce was mutually implemented. All British troops returned to their barracks, and the IRA put up its arms. Sturgis in London recorded in his journal that "those who matter here know now just as well as Dublin does that Andy [Cope] takes first prize. Lady Greenwood asked me this morning in mockery, 'Who *has* made the truce, Smuts or the ViceRoy?' 'Neither,' says I, 'but one Cope' ... Everybody who counts knows he is the author of the whole thing and Macready himself would be amongst the first to admit it."[12] In fact, Macready had called for the removal of Cope in April, but in his later memoirs, he reversed himself and conceded that "no other man could have carried the matter through."[13] On the other hand, Mrs Stuart Menzies spoke for many diehards when she described Greenwood as being "caught up in the great deluge of surrender which ... Cope had invoked to his everlasting shame." Sir Henry Wilson, the chief of the imperial general staff, dismissed Cope as "a hopeless ass."[14]

As expected, no Sinn Fein representative elected to the new Irish legislature appeared on 14 July, the day of its formal inauguration. Sinn Fein's refusal to take the oath to the king totally negated Lloyd George's Government of Ireland Act. That same day the first of four meetings of de Valera with Lloyd George at No. 10 Downing Street was held in the same cabinet room in which the Dominion premiers had just gathered. In the event it was Margo, not her husband, who had a role. Upon checking the arrangements, she recommended to the prime minister that a large world map be hung, displaying in red the remarkable postwar extent of the British Empire. Indicating the great map, Lloyd George described to de Valera the recent gathering of the leaders of "the British Empire [as] a sisterhood of nations – the greatest in the world. Look at this table: There sits [South] Africa – English and Boer; there sits Canada – French, Scotch and English; there sits Australia, representing many races ... there sits India; here sit the representatives of England, Scotland, and Wales; all we ask you to do is to take your place in this sisterhood of free nations."[15]

Margo's ability to concentrate on such arrangements for the initial meeting was impressive. At a Chequers weekend ten days before, the irrepressible Eric Geddes had declared himself to her. Stevenson had recorded in her journal that he was "the most aggressive and pushful personality I know ... He is in love with Margot [*sic*] Greenwood who is keeping him at a distance at present, though rather liking him and flattered by his attentions."[16] By using the phrase "at present," Stevenson clearly expected something more to come.*

Margo and her husband, however, on 14 July were together in an anteroom at No. 10 – as close as they got to the discussions with de Valera. "The P.M.'s first idea had been to have with him Balfour, Chamberlain [both Conservative-Unionists] and Hamar Greenwood, but luckily de Valera did not want any [of his] colleagues with him, so the P.M. was able to drop his." Despite being excluded from the talks, Greenwood was "in great spirits." In the anteroom he bet H.A.L. Fisher "a good top hat we shall get a satisfactory settlement."[17]

After a week of cabinet and committee discussion, the prime minister, with the support of Birkenhead and Austen Chamberlain, wrote on 20 July to de Valera, finally offering Dominion Home Rule on the pattern of Canada ("one of the most generous acts in our history") – but without the six counties of Ulster. Smuts followed up with a letter of 4 August, strongly urging de Valera to adopt, as South Africa had done, a gradualist approach, recognizing that Dominion Home Rule would in fact give just about all that he could possibly want. Bonar Law, writing to Jones on 30 July from his convalescence in the south of France about the offer of Dominion status, sounded a little more moderate. "If anyone can carry it is the P.M. ... Personally, now that the Unionists in the South are all for agreement with Sinn Fein, I would give the South anything or almost anything, but I would not attempt to force anything on Ulster."[18]

On 10 August, de Valera rejected the British offer: "*Dail Eireann* could not ... accept the proposals of your Government."[19] He added about proposed Dominion status, "Everyone who understands the conditions knows them to be illusory. The freedom which British Dominions enjoy is not so much the result of ... treaties as of the immense distances which separate them from Britain and have made interference by her impracticable."[20] Ireland, he maintained, was too proximate to England to enjoy any real autonomy. De Valera did, however, leave a vague impression that "free association with the British Commonwealth"

---

* In 1923, almost two years later, when Margo's fourth child and second son was born, he was named Eric after his godfather, Eric Geddes (his other godfather was Lord Riddell). Following the death of his father in 1948, Eric, an active homosexual from his days at Eton, changed his name to Michael, for some reason disliking his name Eric. Given the amorous activities of Margo, Major Greenwood speculated to the author that Eric was the natural son of his godfather, though acknowledging that there can be no proof in the pre-DNA era.

might possibly be acceptable, but only if Ulster were to be included. Otherwise, a southern Ireland divorced from the North must simply be a republic. He proposed instead some form of "external association" with the British Commonwealth without allegiance to the monarch.[21]

Lloyd George and de Valera continued to exchange letters dealing with the scope of the negotiations: what Dominion Home Rule would mean – allegiance to the crown or to a republic – and how Ulster could pursue its own Protestant destiny as part of the United Kingdom. (The Conservative-Unionists took the view that Ulster "had just as much right to shape her own destiny against the south as Ireland could possibly have as against Great Britain.") Greenwood and Lord FitzAlan joined in drafting the various letters from Lloyd George, the prime minister being kept informed the whole time by Cope about Sinn Fein's real thinking, whatever its letters said. Even the conciliatory Liberal H.A.L. Fisher found de Valera's letter of early September puzzling, with its "insolent, defiant opening, a rude, abrupt and apparently irrevocable rejection of the Government offer, followed by a passage which appears to indicate a readiness to enter into direct negotiations."[22] De Valera sought another meeting with James Craig, but the premier of Northern Ireland now declined, rejecting any invitation that might call into question the legality of the Ulster parliament. Southern Ireland must get what it could from direct negotiation with the United Kingdom.

In London in mid-August, the cabinet continued to monitor and assess what de Valera was saying and what should be said to him. At the unusual venue of Inverness in Scotland (near where Lloyd George was to go on a fishing holiday), Lloyd George had invited his wife, Stevenson, the Greenwoods, Macready and his secretary J.T. Davies to pass judgment on an initial draft letter of invitation; it had carried by one vote. When the cabinet met in Inverness on 7 September, it discussed, amidst a range of pressing economic subjects including mounting unemployment and German reparations, the terms of an invitation to Sinn Fein leaders to participate in negotiations to agree – in the words of the ninth and final draft – "how the association of Ireland with the community of Nations known as the British Empire can be best reconciled with Irish National aspirations."[23] Even as the king was urging his government to send nothing in the way of an ultimatum nor of a character likely to precipitate a renewal of hostilities, the prime minister assured de Valera that if the current dialogue were to be broken off, the British armed response "will be much more thorough than anything we have had yet and [would entail] a complete smash up of the revolutionists."[24]

The cabinet discussion focused in part on whether any prior conditions should be attached to the invitation sent to de Valera. Birkenhead, Churchill, Geddes, and Greenwood supported the inclusion of several conditions, but the majority of the cabinet would have only one: Ireland must continue in some form or other to be aligned with the British Empire.

Cope, who had been "very effective in removing passages [from each of the nine drafts] likely to be objectionable to the Sinn Feiners,"[25] continued to be inexhaustible in his covert role as go-between. Supported by Anderson, he urged patience on the cabinet while providing it with constant exegeses of what de Valera's inflexible and windy replies really intended. But neither Lloyd George's invitation to negotiate nor de Valera's replies settled anything. Further exchanges of correspondence over the next month reached no conclusion about how best to proceed. Finally, Greenwood and several other ministers, meeting with Lloyd George on his fishing holiday at Gairloch, agreed on a last invitation to Sinn Fein to talks in London. Writing to the prime minister, Greenwood later praised the ultimate invitation, "the Vital Document," as ensuring that "Ireland, like Canada, will be a 'free nation' in the British Commonwealth and like Canada swear allegiance to the same King."[26]

In the face of widespread popular support in Ireland for the cease-fire and for the proposed negotiations, on 30 September de Valera finally accepted the invitation to an initial meeting in London on 11 October. Lloyd George asked Chamberlain, Birkenhead, Churchill, Hewart, Worthington-Evans, and Greenwood to join him. Griffith, Collins, Robert Barton, and Gavan Duffy, without a clear mandate, represented Ireland. De Valera himself declined to participate. By remaining in Dublin, he retained a free hand to pursue his ultimate goal of a republic. John Wheeler-Bennett's later conversation with de Valera is also germane: "I asked him why he did not come himself ... 'What, and leave all my cabinet behind me? I shouldn't have lasted five minutes' was his reply. But he went on to denounce Lloyd George and Winston Churchill for their guile and subtlety in seducing Arthur Griffith and Michael Collins from their loyalty to the principle of a republican government in Ireland to accepting the compromise of 'Dominion status'. This [action] Dev never forgave."[27]

The first meeting at No. 10 on 11 October was as expected awkward and stiff, a formality rather than a real exchange. For the ministers involved, much of October was taken with the preparation of a detailed statement in reply to various points made by the Irish during the

seemingly endless sessions that followed the initial meeting. The indefatigable T.J. Jones, acting as the British secretary, sought from
Greenwood, "the only Colonial in the Cabinet," his comment on a
draft comprehensive response. "His attitude ... is very much more
instinctively sympathetic [to the Irish] than that of several of his colleagues. When he came to the words 'free partners' he exclaimed
'That's Canada', and so right through he took a very favourable view of
the document."[28]

C.P. Scott noted in his journal on 28 October that Lloyd George in
the House of Commons had "opened up at once on the rather critical
nature of the situation. Tories restive, Sinn Feiners very difficult. Had
gone down to the House on the previous day [27 October] when Hamar
Greenwood was to be bombarded by the Tory cave[men], in order to
judge the feeling of the House. [Conservative-Unionist] attitude towards
Hamar Greenwood very bad. Towards himself [Lloyd George] better,
when he also was questioned, but still bad. [He] decided at once to challenge opponents."[29] On 31 October the prime minister defeated a resolution in the House of Commons with which suspicious diehards
attempted to block what they regarded as a sell-out in Ireland. In the
face of appeals by leading Conservatives, Chamberlain and Birkenhead
prominent among them, to trust the coalition government, the resolution had little support. The vote in the House was 439 to 43 against it.
The prime minister could now proceed to negotiate with more confidence. The final draft of his statement elicited a slightly more forthcoming reply from Griffith on 2 November, but parallel contacts with Craig
made clear Ulster's continuing refusal to consider any single, all-Ireland
settlement.

At the talks themselves, Greenwood's participation was excluded by
Lloyd George as part of the price that he paid to win from Birkenhead
the surprising commitment to participate in the negotiations. This
manoeuvre was of a piece with what Stevenson had written of Lloyd
George seven years before: he was highly skilled at "'roping in' persons
whose influence is likely to prove helpful or whose opinion counts for
something, seeking out those who are 'on the fence' and whose opposition would be dangerous, and then talking them around, using all
the arts of which he is a past master."[30] Beaverbrook, a generally well-
informed if somewhat erratic observer of the Irish discussions, offered
in his 1963 *The Decline and Fall of Lloyd George* a recollection of what had
happened forty-one years before: "Bonar Law was ... against the whole
Irish negotiations ... Churchill was prepared to carry out a policy of

repression. Birkenhead was of the same view." Nevertheless, on 26 October, Lloyd George made his move on Birkenhead:

> The Prime Minister had sought him out and asked him to join in exploring all possible projects for an Irish settlement. Birkenhead was reluctant. He was asked to put his whole future with the Tory Party to the hazard, and in partnership with a man who had shown him little trust or confidence. He was only willing to undertake such a task if Churchill was admitted to the negotiations. He demanded that Sir Robert Horne, Sir Eric Geddes and Sir Hamar Greenwood, who had become close associates of the Prime Minister ... should be expelled from his intimate political circle. Birkenhead and Churchill, supporting the Prime Minister, would make up a triumvirate, thus forming what is usually termed the Inner Cabinet ... Birkenhead argued that all three – Horne, Geddes and Greenwood – knew nothing of nor understood the Tory temperament of the House of Commons, and that they were persistently misleading the Prime Minister through their ignorance of Conservative opinion.
>
> Lloyd George consented to Birkenhead's requests. Henceforth all estrangement between Lloyd George, Churchill, and Birkenhead would be a thing of the past; they pledged that they would see this [Irish] task through, and together ...
>
> A few days later Miss Stevenson was to write in her diary: "He [Lloyd George] has successfully wrangled Churchill and Birkenhead so that they are all out for it" ...
>
> The Ministers driven from paradise to outer darkness by the Lloyd George-Birkenhead concordat – Horne, Geddes and Greenwood – were no longer called to supper or to sing. It was as though a venetian blind had been pulled down. They could peek through the slats, but from without.[31]

What Churchill later said about the proposed agreement could apply equally to his own decision and especially to that of Birkenhead to reverse themselves: "No British Government in modern times has ever appeared to make so complete and sudden a reversal of policy."[32] Churchill's reversal may have arisen from little more than boredom with Ireland, a feeling that it had become a tiresome distraction from far more important imperial ventures. Certainly he shared Macready's later observation that "people in Great Britain were tired to death of Ireland and its affairs."[33]Additionally, Churchill was a Liberal. His newfound enthusiasm to conclude an early settlement sat well with many hitherto uneasy fellow Liberals. Before Lloyd George induced Birkenhead to participate in the negotiations, he had frankly acknowledged the failure of the policy of force. Separately, Churchill's past friendship and collaboration with Birkenhead contributed to the lord chancellor's readiness to work with him and the prime minister to attempt to persuade at least the more moderate in the Conservative-Unionist ranks of the merits of negotiation.

Why Birkenhead felt compelled to accept Lloyd George's politically hazardous proposition to be a principal negotiator remains unclear. Churchill in his *Aftermath* sounds surprised at the capitulation of his friend. Birkenhead "was prominently connected ... with resistance to Home Rule. He had been in comradeship with Sir Edward Carson; he had used to the full those threats of civil war which had played their part in the 1914 phase of the Irish conflict. There was no man who would have gained greater personal advantage by opposing the Irish Settlement; and none who would suffer more reproach by sustaining it."[34] Birkenhead, having been the prosecutor of Roger Casement and later the committed advocate of the Black and Tans and Auxiliaries, told Riddell three months after the event that "while the Conservative Party were unable actively to oppose the settlement, they had been displeased with it and thought that he and Chamberlain had sold the pass."[35] Both within the Lords and without there were those who ever thereafter regarded Birkenhead as "an unspeakable turncoat who for personal ambition ... had ratted on his old allegiances."[36] Certainly Clementine Churchill never had any regard for him: "she suspected ... F.E. Smith [Birkenhead] of leading Winston astray, encouraging him to drink and gamble and keep louche company."[37]

Admiring biographers of Birkenhead have postulated a high-minded conversion to an early negotiated peace, once the separation of Ulster had been secured. However, it was Mrs Stuart Menzies who put the question that remained in the minds of many: "Gifted man as he is, he has made a mess of his life, ruined his own career ... through his infirmities, lack of principle and his bitter tongue... Lord Birkenhead told us that Ireland should be ruled ... with a firm hand ... he said he would be no party to giving Ireland, through Sinn Fein threats, violence and murder what could not be gained through reason. Then without apology, excuse, or camouflage he suddenly turned around and ate his words, and he joined his Chief [Lloyd George] and [Austen] Chamberlain in wholesale surrender to crime, threats and violence. I have wondered what made him do this."[38]

The contrast with Birkenhead's past commitment to Ulster and to coercion and his hostility toward Dominion Home Rule makes the high road not entirely convincing. As for the low road, it is likely that the prime minister and undoubtedly Beaverbrook had means of moral suasion. Both were aware that the lord chancellor had long been seen as engaged in financial improprieties with brewers, publicans, and shipping interests in his Liverpool constituency (although nothing on the grand scale of impropriety that Lloyd George himself was pursuing in his wholesale of honours for personal as well as political gain). Birkenhead, "always in debt and frequently drunk," had been prompt to defend in the House of Lords the prime minister's financial waywardness, perhaps in return for acquiescence in his own manoeuvres.[39] Birkenhead has been described as "a close friend of Maundy Gregory," the prime minister's highly unsavoury agent in his blatant sale of honours "by whom it was rumoured he was being blackmailed."[40] Earlier, confronting Birkenhead with evidence of his alleged plotting with Churchill to force the prime minister out of office, Lloyd George had described him as a man who "does not care what lies he tells."

Additionally, among the many to whom Birkenhead owed money, he was "in Beaverbrook's hands." [41] Beaverbrook, perhaps at the prompting of his friend Tim Healy, exploited that leverage to encourage Birkenhead to perform his extraordinary political somersault. Whatever the understanding that Beaverbrook struck, he saw Birkenhead and Churchill almost every night. He increased his backing of them in the *Express,* so "that their signatures on a settlement might [not] spell their ruin."[42] Certainly Beaverbrook, whom Lloyd George regarded as an "unreliable, poisonous little man," never hesitated to manipulate those who owed him money or otherwise had left themselves open to his pressures; but there is another hold that Beaverbrook (and behind him Lloyd George) may have used on Birkenhead. The lord chancellor, chief law officer of the crown, had had in 1919 what English courts of the day would have called "criminal conversation" with a female minor. In Paris, on the fringes of the Peace Conference, Birkenhead at age forty-seven had seduced Mona Dunn, the seventeen-year-old daughter of Sir James Dunn, a Canadian industrialist and fellow New Brunswicker of Beaverbrook and Bonar Law. Birkenhead's daughter viewed with intense disapproval her father's affair with her school chum. If Lloyd George and Beaverbrook (who played Pandarus by lending Birkenhead his house in Fulham for assignations) needed any more leverage on Birkenhead, *l'affaire Mona* could have supplied it.[*]

Michael Collins was pleased at the presence of Birkenhead in the British negotiating triumvirate, believing he could still play a part in inducing other Conservative-Unionists to accept, however reluctantly, whatever agreement might be eventually reached. Collins remained, however, wary and mistrustful of Churchill. He was also gratified that amongst those who had been eased out was Greenwood, "a man who earns my personal detestation."[43] There now began a series of smaller and more informal encounters between Lloyd George, Birkenhead, and Churchill on the one hand and Griffith and Collins on the other (with time off for the prime minister to take the Greenwoods to the theatre on 28 October and 16 November, public displays of his approbation). During those final weeks of negotiation, Greenwood wrote to the prime minister, with the success always in mind of the Canadian federation in creating peaceful co-existence for French and English, Protestant and Roman Catholic, "The really decisive factor now left is as to how a parliament for all Ireland can be set up while at the same time an Ulster Parliament can carry on. To me, as a Canadian. It is a simple problem and simply must be settled now."[44]

Concurrent debates in the House saw the diehards attacking the pussycat Greenwood for surrendering to the gunmen. On the other hand, among Liberals and certainly in Ireland he continued to be portrayed as the opposite: the bombastic, prevaricating, pompous minister responsible for the brutal Black and Tans and Auxiliaries and their deadly reprisals. With the truce, however, the abuse of Greenwood from both sides of the House had trailed off. On 10 November, almost a month before the conclusion of the negotiations, Parliament prorogued, removing that particular burden from Greenwood. Bonar Law, home from his convalescence in France, resumed his role as the guardian of the interests and of the bigotry of Ulster. C.P. Scott found Law "reasonable and moderate up to a point … At heart [however] he was an Orangeman and the Orange fanaticism was there, he had brought it with him from Canada."[45]

---

[*] James Dunn was one of Lloyd George's many customers for an honour. He purchased his knighthood in 1918, although Beaverbrook attempted to convince his boyhood friend that it was he who had induced the prime minister to recommend it. Mona Dunn died in December 1928 at age twenty-six from peritonitis, possibly complicated by narcotics. Birkenhead, according to Stevenson, was rumoured to be "doping."

The meetings throughout October and November between Lloyd George, Birkenhead, and Churchill on the one side and Griffith and Collins on the other have been described and debated amply elsewhere. They ranged widely over a mixture of questions large and small, such the control of several small but important naval ports, fiscal provisions, allegiance to the monarchy, and, above all, the terms of the relationship between a Dominion of Ireland and the United Kingdom and the future of Ulster. On the question of allegiance to the crown, Lloyd George put it squarely to Griffith and Collins: "We are taking great political risks. The life of the Government is put in issue by our proposals ... Can you under no condition accept the sovereignty of the King in the sense that Canada and Australia accept it?"[46] The two Irishmen knew well the negative answer that de Valera would give, but they eventually accepted a watery formulation that got them around that point, fundamental to the continuation of Lloyd George's coalition government. Even on the division of Ireland, anathema to de Valera and his republican followers, Lloyd George found a way to convince at least Griffith and Collins – who were possibly seeking to be convinced – that any separation would only be temporary, with economic pressures in time inexorably driving the two parts of Ireland back together again. Into the first week of December, the frequently discursive and convoluted exchanges, marked by threats and persuasion, continued, with de Valera in Dublin dissenting. The British press, including the *Times*, was largely unanimous in calling for compromise on both sides. The Conservative Beaverbrook supported the negotiations in his newspapers, as did the Liberal Riddell at the *News of the World* and the Liberal Scott at the *Manchester Guardian*.

As his diary reflects, T.J. Jones on the British side was tireless in his search for words and ideas to foster a final agreement. On 6 December he was finally able to write to cabinet secretary Maurice Hankey, "I have had much the most frantic time of the last five years during the last five weeks: endless meetings and secret interviews by day and by midnight. However the climax was reached at 2:10 this morning when the P.M., Chamberlain, Birkenhead, Churchill on our behalf and Griffith, Collins and Barton on behalf of Sinn Fein, signed the 'Articles of Agreement' ... It was left open to Ulster to come in to an All-Ireland Parliament or to stand out."[47] Dominion Home Rule was accorded to southern Ireland, with the six counties of Ulster to be defined more exactly by an eventual border commission. The new Dominion would have full responsibility for administration, including the police, army and fiscal policy – a status, in short, "comparable in almost all respects to that of Canada and the other Dominions"[48] (which were promptly informed by telegram of the birth of their new sister Dominion). C.P. Scott knew very well what both Griffith and Collins had early recognized, but what de Valera did not want to see or would not believe: "The Dominions were virtually independent states and could secede [from the Empire] at any time if they chose."[49] De Valera, wanting an instant republic, denounced the agreement the next day.

On 6 December, the day of its signature, Scott was in London, lunching with the prime minister and, among others, the Greenwoods. He was not much pleased by the company, except for Margo, whom he considered much too good for her husband, who was "a dreadful person, vulgar and soapy like the worse type of Methodist preacher, only less sincere."[50] The next day the chief secretary added his signature to the agreement, but it was to Margo and not to him that the prime minister presented the pen with which he had himself signed it. The Irish civil servant G.C. Duggan was not surprised: "Though his signature appears on the treaty, [Greenwood] was but a puppet in more powerful hands." [51] It was later alleged that Griffith and Collins would not sign in Greenwood's presence. On the other hand, if Margo's later recollection is accurate, "When it was all over, Hamar asked Michael Collins if he had any complaint to make of the behaviour of the Black and Tans. He replied: 'I have no complaints. We are not going to be as gentle as you were with those who are opposing us." He was referring to anti-treaty republicans in the subsequent vicious Irish civil war, in which he himself would be ambushed and killed.[52]

15

A Resolution of Sorts, 1921–1922

With the signature of the agreement, Greenwood continued to be available in the House of Commons where his primary task now was to counter the bitter attacks of diehards on the agreement as a sell-out.* Here again, G.C. Duggan, the witty Irish civil servant, was amused to see how with "an air of great earnestness and appearance of sincerity, [Greenwood had previously] scouted all suggestions that the Black and Tans were other than *chevaliers sans peur et sans reproche*, so now everything that the Sinn Fein did was held up in the British House of Commons as either a model of moderation or the exuberance of a country intoxicated with the draught of freedom."[1]

Until the truce, both Greenwoods had repeatedly joined the prime minister in portraying the IRA as a small number of fanatical gunmen who had successfully intimidated moderate, reasonable Irish nationalists. If the merciless gunmen could be repressed, the way would be opened to negotiate with the nationalists about the future of a Dominion of Ireland within the British Commonwealth of Nations. In fact, by mid-1921 the more disciplined Black and Tans and Auxiliaries had, as Michael Collins himself allegedly conceded, begun to make headway in curbing the IRA. W.E. Wylie, the highly able and conciliatory law advisor to Dublin Castle (whom the Irish Free State was to appoint a judge of its High Court in 1924), had told Sturgis in June, a month before the truce, "of the vast improvement in the manner and discipline of the

---

* After the conclusion of the agreement, one or two of the more mischievous members of Parliament with long memories could not resist asking Greenwood, now that he was chief secretary, to justify the continuing embargo on cattle from Canada, an embargo so beloved of Irish farmers and so opposed by Canadian.

'Black and Tans', now a first-class force which everybody can respect. He said that if they had behaved all through as they behave now the result would ... be very different and the enormous bulk of public opinion would now be on their side versus the gunmen."[2] Greenwood was frequently ridiculed for what was seen by friend and foe alike as his endless, unwarranted optimism that the gunmen were being done down. To be sure, throughout much of the conflict, General Macready and he continued to believe that crown forces, adequately disciplined and supported, would open the way to Dominion Home Rule. That the crown forces were so doing in the early summer of 1921 was attested by Collins, if Margo's recollection of 1951 is accurate: "You had us dead beat and we could not have lasted another three weeks," she recalled Collins saying. "When the offer of a truce came we were so surprised we thought at once the Government was mad."[3]

The British historian Correlli Barnett, in *The Collapse of British Power*, was in no doubt about what had happened in the first half of 1921. War-weary and impoverished Britain had lost the stomach for the continued employment of force as the sole route to an Irish settlement:

> The English were in fact defeated – not in Ireland, but in England, for Liberal consciences flinched at the violence and human misery incidental to the maintenance of imperial power, especially when so near home. The public platform rang with reproaches; the letter columns of the newspapers were filled with lamentations. Sir John Simon, later Chairman of the Indian Statutory Commission, and later still a Foreign Secretary, was horrified. So was Edward Wood, later, as Lord Irwin, Viceroy of India, later still, as Lord Halifax, another Foreign Secretary. So was Lionel Curtis, who wrote in *The Round Table* in June 1921 "If the British Commonwealth can only be preserved by such means, it would become a negation of the principle for which it has stood."[4]

Whether additional repression of the IRA during the second half of 1921 (from the truce in July to the signature of the agreement in December) would have led to a different settlement can only remain a matter for speculation. Macready evidently thought so, although it was never an easy to know where exactly he stood at any given time. To Field Marshal Wilson he put his finger on why he thought that Britain had agreed to negotiate a settlement when it did: it was the result of "having to run in harness with a lot of double distilled blithering idiots like Hamar."[5] Wilson, long an Ulster fanatic who had himself dismissed his minister, Winston Churchill, as "an idiot statesman," would no doubt have agreed.

In finally getting Dominion Home Rule for Ireland, Lloyd George exhibited those characteristics that Stevenson had identified five years before: "his patience in overcoming obstacles, and in returning again to their attack, his tirelessness in examining and arranging for details ... He knows when he has hit on the right idea ... and then he will never give in; he never despairs of accomplishing what he had in view."[6] To be sure, there was never any question that the prime minister would "break up [his] coalition [government] for Ireland," but once King George had spoken in Belfast, providing the public impetus for a truce, and once Birkenhead had been landed, Lloyd George acted. Macready for one was not convinced: "Whether Mr. Lloyd George in ... dealing with the South may have hit upon a solution of the problem which for so many centuries had baffled his predecessors in office, time alone will show."[7] The satisfaction of both British and Irish exponents of the settlement – as must have been realized by some – was to a degree self-delusory. As Max Beloff has observed, "What for the British seemed an honourable settlement with concessions on both sides seemed to the Irish as to the Afrikaners before them, a mere halt on the road to total independence in external as well as internal relationships. The fact was disguised for a time by the struggle against the treaty waged by the more extreme faction in the Irish civil war of 1922 ... The Irish treaty was the final achievement of, and in its fate the final commentary on, the ideal of a liberal empire."[8]

To Greenwood's own great satisfaction, the first article of the agreement stated simply, "Ireland shall have the same constitutional status in the community of nations known as the British Empire as the Dominion of Canada." In all constitutional questions, including the relationship to the crown, the position of Ireland would be that of Canada, an equal in a global league of equals, a comity of democracies not dominated by Britain. Ireland would have its own military and civil administration with complete autonomy in finance (including taxation), justice, health, and education. The *Toronto Daily Star* of 10 December gave Greenwood full marks for his role in the Irish settlement: "As a Canadian, Sir Hamar knew all along what Dominion status is, and how far it was possible to go with Ireland, so long as the essential ties of allegiance to the King and inclusion in the Empire were preserved ... with his Canadian point of view, the Chief Secretary has been well out in advance of his colleagues in advocating those concessions to Ireland which at last have been granted in full quantity, after all efforts at withholding and subtracting from them have been of no avail."* In the House of Lords Birkenhead rejected utterly the contention of his old friend and ally Edward Carson – now the Viscount Carson of Duncaire – that the settlement revealed that Britain, having failed in nearby Ireland, could hardly hope to uphold British rule throughout the Empire. Suddenly sounding uncannily like Greenwood, Birkenhead called upon the Lords to support the settlement by foreseeing "an Ireland which, sitting when the Dominions meet … to decide, according to evolutionary organisation of the British Empire, the supreme issues of policy which affect that Empire, the Prime Minister of Ireland, an equal by the side of equals, will lift up his voice to support and give expression to the historic destinies and rightful influence of that country."9 As was to be expected from Birkenhead's former colleague in pre-war Ulster intransigence, Carson bitterly denounced the agreement not as a Liberal failure but as sure evidence that Britain no longer had the will to pursue an imperial destiny: "If you tell your Empire in India, in Egypt and all over the world that you have not got the men, the money, the pluck, the inclination and the backing to restore order in a country within twenty miles of your own shore, you may as well begin to abandon the attempt to make British rule prevail through the Empire at all."10

Not surprisingly, Greenwood presented the Irish agreement as another manifestation of liberal imperialism and the precedent-making role of Canada therein. Still chief secretary in name at least, he told a Canada Club dinner in London on 13 December, one week after the signature of the agreement, "I may say of myself with modesty and pride, that a Canadian has borne some part … in the treaty which has just been signed. The great contribution that Canadians have made to the common stock of the Empire lies principally in the fact that long, long ago they solved the problem of how different races can live together in friendship and live within the single boundaries of the British Commonwealth. That was a contribution … initiated in Canada, which

* The two leading Irish newspapers in Canada, the *Catholic Register* and the *Catholic Record*, also welcomed the settlement. They had been anti–Sinn Fein until April 1916. They had supported Redmond's constitutional nationalists, opposed conscription and denounced the "British Prussianism" of the Black and Tans, but never abandoned their support for an autonomous Ireland within the British Empire (i.e., Dominion Home Rule). They subsequently denounced the republican-inspired civil war.

has made possible the marvellous progress of the British Empire and its future strength possible."[11] Greenwood's conviction that Canada was a motor of the emerging Commonwealth had been reinforced by the Irish settlement. One month later, speaking to the 1920 Club at the House of Commons, he again attempted to refute the diehards (both his brothers-in-law remaining prominent among them) and any others who were still attacking Lloyd George and himself for the agreement. According to Amery, Greenwood maintained that "the Government had at least brought an Irish settlement to a reality. Others had failed, and it was no good now saying, 'We could have done better'. He did not believe that it could have been done one day before it was done, and that was the opinion ... of over ninety per cent of the Irish people."[12]

For Greenwood personally, the long Irish imbroglio had ended not in a celebratory bang but in a recessional whimper. As the prime minister had applied himself ever more diligently to winning agreement on Dominion Home Rule, Greenwood's presence was less required in the House. As he faded into the penumbra of the always uncertain Irish scene, he spent much of his time overseeing the establishment of a separate civil service and the Royal Ulster Constabulary in the now self-governing Northern Ireland. It was left to Macready to investigate alleged IRA violations of the truce. In accordance with the prime minister's wish, Greenwood had never played a leading role in the formulation of policy. With the truce and Lloyd George's task of convincing the Conservative-Unionists and Ulster on one hand and de Valera and Sinn Fein on the other that a negotiated settlement was possible, his thankless task of holding the ring had ended – and he knew it. Writing some years later, his private secretary resented the fact that Greenwood "has received from the nation no plaudits for his decision to accept the task, or for the courageous work which followed it ... for some years [afterward] he was execrated by the unappeasable fanatics in Ireland, and hardly a voice was raised, in the country which he had served, to defend him."[13]

A few voices in Ireland were prompt to praise him. The moderate Unionist Sir John Ross, the judge who, contrary to the wishes of Lord Chancellor Birkenhead, had been appointed by Greenwood lord chancellor of Ireland, wrote to him, "If we had not had the good fortune to have got a man of dauntless courage to stand in the gap, all would have been lost and thrown away. You had savage enemies before you, treacherous people behind you, and weak-kneed folk all around you, but you stood your ground ... I congratulate Lady Greenwood on having a real hero for a husband."[14] Churchill was not far behind in his praise for his sometime parliamentary private secretary: "He had borne the brunt during the most terrible period, showing the utmost courage as a man and never losing hope of a statesman-like solution."[15]

Following the signature of the agreement, Lloyd George on 21 December assigned to Churchill the chairmanship of a cabinet committee made up of Greenwood, Edwin Montagu, Alfred Mond, John Anderson, Lord FitzAlan, and C.T. Davies to deal with all questions arising from the establishment in the South of the new provisional government. Soon Greenwood could assure Lloyd George that "Winston gave such a momentum to his Committee that it is working continuously and most efficiently."[16] Greenwood's own ministry, the Irish Office, continued to exist in a caretaker role, especially with regard to Ulster, but to have the chief secretary conduct business with the new government in Dublin was seen as a contradiction of its newly achieved Dominion status. Further, the Irish Office remained less than happy with Churchill's ad hoc committee. It was constantly frustrated by Churchill's Colonial Office simply taking whatever it wanted. In the new year 1922, as Lloyd George, accompanied by Churchill, departed for meetings with the French prime minister at Cannes, he was done – as far as he was concerned – with both Ireland and his controversial chief secretary. Thereafter he again absented himself as much as possible from the Irish scene, his mind even more centred on the survival of his coalition government amidst the challenges of postwar reconstruction across Europe, continuing labour strife, and personal vilification.

Soon after the prompt repudiation of the Irish settlement by the republican de Valera on 8 December, an acrimonious debate began in the Dáil. In Ulster, James Craig proved suspicious and obdurate about a proposed commission to delineate the boundary between North and South (which, after many delays, Sir Robert Borden, the former Canadian prime minister, declined to chair in light of the refusal of Craig's government to participate[17]).* As the Dáil debated ratification, Greenwood reported from Dublin on 29 December, "I am glad to report

---

* Robert Borden wrote to Beaverbrook: "I was prepared (although with great reluctance) to accept the Chairmanship of the Irish Boundary Commission if Northern Ireland would appoint a representative and if both the Irish Governments would express their desire that I should undertake the task." Lloyd George would not have forgotten Borden's experience of border delineation. Early in 1919 at the Paris peace conference, he had sounded out Borden on becoming the leader of a British Empire delegation at a proposed conference with the Russian Bolsheviks. When that did not materialize, he asked Borden to be Empire delegate on a committee to define the boundaries between Greece and Albania.

that Ireland is quiet ... Winston has no doubt told you of the great progress [made] ... to transfer the Government of Southern Ireland to the Provisional Government."[18] He was even more gratified to add nine days later, on 7 January 1922, that the Dáil had approved the agreement, despite all de Valera's arguments against it, by a vote of sixty-four to fifty-seven. A provisional government headed by Arthur Griffith, with Michael Collins as his principal lieutenant, was elected by the Dáil, with de Valera and his republicans opposing. Dublin Castle was thereupon transferred to the provisional government on 16 January. That same evening, after twenty months in Ireland, Under-Secretary John Anderson embarked for England, never to return.

From that promising high point in what was to become known as the Irish Free State, Ireland descended into a complex and destructive civil war that claimed more lives than the crown forces had done during the two years of "the troubles." De Valera's denunciation of the agreement triggered a civil war and a resumption of the now-familiar reprisals, arson, executions, hostage-taking, fatal hunger strikes, and other excesses, but this time Irishmen visited the outrages exclusively on their fellow Irishmen in both the South and North. Killings also increased along the provisional border with Ulster and in Belfast itself between republicans and loyalists, Protestants and Roman Catholics, evoking from C.P. Scott the comment, "Who could have believed that, having got rid of us, the Irish would start a terror of their own?"[19]

All of this was bad news for supporters of the settlement and the Irish Free State. Jones observed in his diary, "Greenwood reminded the Cabinet that Ireland [both North and South] was ten times more armed now than in his day and the situation was therefore incomparably worse for us than when we concluded the truce."[20] Greenwood had no direct part in Churchill's decision to supply Collins and the provisional government of the new Irish Free State with more arms, including artillery, against those republicans who would overthrow it. He did, however, work with Churchill as an occasional apologist for the agreement and as an additional channel in keeping the cabinet informed about the uneven progress by both Britain and Ireland in implementing the agreement's details. With Dominion Home Rule proclaimed, major units of the British army were rapidly withdrawn, and the battered and undermined Royal Irish Constabulary was formally disbanded. The son of one RIC constable watched their departure, observing, "The Black and Tans were the first to go. Seeing them in civilian clothes, carrying their shabby luggage to the station, one was struck by their very ordinariness. The name Black and Tan had aroused fear and hatred throughout the country, but stripped of their uniforms and fearsome trappings, they seemed insignificant little men on their way back to their working-class homes in the industrial towns and cities of Britain ... I had never seen so many drunk men. They got a boisterous, good-humoured send-off."[21]

The civil administration having been turned over to the provisional government, Greenwood was left with – among other residual duties – the immediate discharge of the remaining Black and Tans and Auxiliaries. Margo believed that he "would have resigned there and then but the King who knew how staunchly he had stood up for the [Royal Irish] Constabulary was very anxious that he should stay on in order to protect the Constabulary, their pension rights, etc."[22] Additionally, Greenwood was trying to get the Dominions to take veterans of the now disbanded RIC, including Black and Tans: "I gather that Ontario is most inclined to help." Certainly the premier of Ontario (and future high commissioner in London), Howard Ferguson, had readily agreed, being an out-and-out imperialist.[*] It was Churchill who, conscious of the heavy costs of the Palestine mandate, had proposed to Tudor as early as September 1921 the recruitment of volunteers from among the Black and Tans and Auxiliaries for the Palestine Police and for the Royal Air Force armoured car companies in Iraq. Tudor was himself appointed head of the police and air officer commanding in Iraq and Palestine in May 1922, with the dual rank of major general and air vice marshal. He wrote to Churchill, "Your idea of using the 'Black and Tans' [in the Palestine Police] ... has been a great success. They have had a great influence already in keeping things quiet [between Arab and Jew]."[23]

After the ratification by the Dáil, the institution of Dominion Home Rule, and the assignment to Churchill as colonial secretary of the conduct of relations with the new Dominion, the prime minister could at any time have abolished the office of chief secretary for Ireland. Presumably he did not wish to deprive Greenwood of his ministerial salary. (The *Pall Mall Gazette* of 30 June 1922 noted sourly that he was being "magnificently remunerated for doing nothing at all, in spite of

---

[*] Certainly Greenwood continued to attempt to participate in Anglo-Canadian relations. On 17 October 1922, for example, he dined with the Canadian high commissioner, Peter Larkin (the financial benefactor of Laurier, Lapointe, and Mackenzie King and a staunch supporter of Ulster) and the visiting Canadian ministers Lapointe and Fielding to discuss yet again that perennial irritant, the British embargo on the import of cattle from Canada (which he had attacked in his maiden speech in the House of Commons twelve years before.)

the outcry for economy.") More problematically, not seeing how he could open the Home Office or another senior cabinet post to Greenwood, Lloyd George would have been regarded as demoting or even repudiating him if he had swiftly removed him. Worse, he would have cast doubt on his own handling of the Irish problem if he offered Greenwood some markedly lesser appointment. More to the point, Lloyd George, always considerate of former mistresses like Margo who had played the game, allowed her husband to linger on as chief secretary to the next election (although Alfred Mond, the minister of health, briefly and vainly revived the idea of appointing Greenwood chief whip).

Greenwood now had ample time and reason to refurbish his Canadian contacts. In March he had written to congratulate Mackenzie King on getting "well started in your first Parliament. You can understand the keen interest I take in Canadian politics, especially having regard to the fact that you and Arthur Meighen are the leaders of the two old parties in the Dominion ... It is really a great romance to find you Prime Minister of Canada and myself Irish Secretary in the Imperial Cabinet and Meighen Leader of your Opposition. I think we all had commendable ambitions at the University, but who could have prophesied our positions at the present time?"[24] In London in April 1922 Greenwood presided over a dinner of the Canada Club to welcome the new Canadian high commissioner – the tea merchant Peter Larkin, Mackenzie King's financial benefactor. In the presence of the Duke of York (the future King George VI), Greenwood extolled Larkin as "a great citizen of a great city, Toronto." In reply, the new high commissioner dutifully echoed his prime minister in describing how "Canadian relations with Great Britain on the one hand as the motherland of a large portion of her people [Larkin was himself of uncertain Ulster descent], and the United States, a friendly neighbour on the other, with a 3,000 mile invisible frontier line, placed her in a position of peculiar influence and responsibility to link them together in a brotherhood, for the peace and prosperity of the world."[25]

The civil war in Ireland between the Irish Free State and the republicans had by May reached such a pitch that Churchill gave "a very distressing report" to the cabinet. Lord Crawford, the minister of transport, a former Conservative-Unionist whip but nevertheless a Lloyd George loyalist, was pessimistic: "The moral degeneration of Ireland proceeds apace. Ireland has acquired her freedom after a struggle lasting for a century and now can only use her liberty for the purpose of assassinations, blackmail, burglary, arson. What a god-forsaken race! The whole Liberal tradition that Ireland is capable of self-government has been dispelled during the first few months of trial."[26] While the bloody civil war continued, an additional complication arose over the final drafting of the constitution for the Irish Free State. It had been agreed that it would embody the settlement of December 1921, but the draft that came back from Dublin pointed in the direction of the early establishment of a republic. Crawford's diary entry of 30 May 1922 reflects the discomfort of Griffith and especially of Collins, caught between their commitments to Lloyd George of December and de Valera's readiness to refute those commitments by force. Having just returned from the funeral in Herefordshire of his reclusive father-in-law, Greenwood took little part in what Crawford described as a "V important cabinet":

> The new Irish constitution was to embody the terms of the Treaty – to embody the whole agreement. The document, prepared for the Free State government ... is a real negation in spirit and in form of the Treaty, and in effect establishes a Republican constitution. Lord Harcourt has been examining this document on our behalf and has pointed out its diametrical conflict with the pledged word of the signatories. Lloyd George saw Griffith and Collins, and pointed all this out with direct and uncompromising earnestness. The latter made a lot of vague and unsatisfactory excuses but did not venture to deny the implication that the draft repudiates their pledged and solemn word. It is a very grave situation. Lloyd George failed to persuade them to acknowledge that the whole thing must be redrafted from the beginning. Collins seemed to be in a half-hysterical condition and several times said "We will give you Ireland as a present" – that was pretty paradoxical, but he even went so far as to suggest that our troops should reoccupy the South under martial law! The P.M. said he could not help laughing at this proposal and rallied Collins upon such a *volte face* – no, said Collins, the people like the soldiers and would behave better if they were back at Cork and Limerick. Whereupon A.J.B. [Balfour] said, 'But didn't Collins see the ridiculous side of this idea – has he no sense of humour?' ... It was decided to send a formal letter to force the Free State ministers to define their position, otherwise we shall have to take drastic action, which will entail terrible consequences.[27]

On 22 June two IRA gunmen murdered Field Marshal Wilson (who upon his recent retirement from the army had become an Ulster MP) on his London doorstep, an act that almost drove enraged diehard Conservative-Unionists MPs into open revolt against the settlement and rendered Northern Ireland even more alienated from the South. As the less than heroic civil war mounted, additional deaths soon followed. The overtaxed Griffith died of cerebral haemorrhage in August, and Collins was assassinated by anti-treaty Irish republicans ten days later. It was evident that the agreement, like many agreements, wholly satisfied no one, except possibly Lloyd George, at least to the degree that he had finally succeeded in bestowing Dominion Home Rule on both Northern and Southern Ireland without immediately undermining his government. Yet even for him the treaty was soon to prove troublesome. It became what he had from the beginning feared: one more reason why the Conservatives would withdraw their support from his coalition government.

With mounting desperation, he concentrated even more upon ensuring his political survival. Infatuated with conference diplomacy rather than bilateral diplomacy, he concluded that a foreign policy initiative might distract attention from the widespread domestic turmoil. A successful international conference dealing with war reparations and the place of the new Soviet Union in the comity of nations might possibly help to remedy his declining electoral fortunes. First at the conference at Cannes in January 1922, then at Genoa in April, he hoped to settle several contentious questions, including a reduction in German reparations and in trade barriers, as the way to European economic recovery. He was on the right track, but without participation of the United States and with the unyielding conviction of the French that Germany must pay in full, neither initiative nor a reparations conference that he convened in London in August was successful.

Churchill understood the indirect consequences of the failures for the coalition. Cannes and Genoa had not provided any distraction from the popular unease at the concurrent state of affairs in Ireland. "The event was fatal to the Prime Minister. Within a year he had been driven from power. Many other causes ... contributed to his fall; but the Irish Treaty and its circumstances were unforgiveable by the most tenacious elements in the Conservative Party."[28] Churchill himself later abandoned Lloyd George over the Irish settlement, even though he himself had done so much to bring it about. In 1925 Beaverbrook wrote to Rothermere that Churchill "criticises [Lloyd] George very freely for the wicked Irish Treaty and declares that the Coalition Government ought to have continued to prosecute the war against Sinn Fein for another winter. I tried to shame him into acknowledgement of his leading part in making the Treaty. It is not easy to succeed."[29]

Adding to Lloyd George's mounting problems was the taint of malodorous sleaze that was gathering around him, culminating in a confrontation in the House of Commons in mid-1922 over his blatant sale of honours (the Marconi scandal of a decade before – in which Churchill had defended Lloyd George – had not been forgotten). Both Greenwood and Birkenhead told Riddell that the prime minister "had been very perturbed about the [sale of] honours, and that he had never seen him so much worried about anything."[30] One result was that more Conservatives became convinced when the House rose on 4 August that it was past time to withdraw from the coalition and reassert their own party identity and integrity.

Another major nail in the coffin of Lloyd George's hopes for re-election of his coalition government was confusion over Allied policy in Turkey. Personally committed to supporting Greece against Turkey since 1912, he had been a consistent and sometimes irrational partisan at the peace treaty negotiations at Paris and Sevres of the expansionist Greeks over the Ottoman Turks. In September 1922, resurgent Turkish units under Mustapha Kemal defeated a Greek force, reoccupied Smyrna, turned toward the Dardanelles, and advanced on the town of Chanak, held by a small Allied garrison. Lloyd George, enamoured (as Riddell had noted) of the use of force, joined in the eagerness of Churchill and Birkenhead to confound Turkish ambitions to recover full sovereignty over the Straits. In their bellicose confrontation with Turkey, the triumvirate alienated many in war-weary Britain, Australia, and Canada. Mackenzie King, prime minister from the year before, refused to respond to a sudden query about military assistance, maintaining that it was up to Parliament to decide. He continued in his pre-war conviction that Canada retained a relationship with Britain that somehow prevented him from simply replying with a flat "no" (as Borden had done in the case of Churchill's requests for continued Canadian participation in the Allied intervention in the Russian civil war). King, as often in the past, was particularly alienated by what he saw as the bellicosity of his fellow Liberal, Churchill: "It is a serious business having matters in [the] hands of a man like Churchill." A month later he concluded, "It would be a good thing for England if she could get rid of Churchill."[31]

Stanley Baldwin, president of the Board of Trade, was convinced that Lloyd George was attempting to exploit the possibility of conflict with Turkey as a means of winning support for the coalition government in the election that could probably not be much delayed. It was an explanation that Mackenzie King for one found wholly convincing. What had happened in the understanding of Greenwood, who attended the cabinet meetings, was yet another example of the deleterious effect of mixing alcohol with public policy. More than twenty years later, King recorded his recollections of his teetotaller friend: "Churchill, Lord Birkenhead and Lloyd George had all been out dining pretty well ... and the decision to fight the Turks and to send out the appeal to the Dominions to aid in preventing the advance of the Turks was made under those conditions. Greenwood [ever the temperance advocate] ... was deploring the effect that alcohol had on men who have to deal with national affairs and how whole nations may be brought into the peril of their lives through this painful influence."[32]

Anti-French feelings had mounted in the United Kingdom since the end of the war; the mutual agony and sacrifice of the conflict had not resulted in a trusting Anglo-French partnership. French demands in the peace negotiations and in German reparations discussions appeared to the British government to be excessive and vindictive. France, suspicious of any policy that smacked of conciliation and preoccupied with its border security, advocated policies that many British, including Lloyd George, regarded as having the potential to alienate further rather than in any way conciliate the common defeated enemy. And events in the Levant, long a source of Anglo-French discord, convinced British intelligence – and the prime minister – that France was engaged there in anti-British "dirty work," including suspicions that France was behind the resurgent Turks as a means of reducing the paramountcy of British influence in the former Ottoman Empire. Certainly Greenwood was in no doubt about *la France perfide*. According to Crawford,[33] at a cabinet meeting "Hamar Greenwood in his stentorian voice asked, 'When are we going to base our policy on the incontestable fact that France has ceased to be our friend? So far as Eastern policy is concerned, France has clearly become an avowed enemy – supplying Kemal [Ataturk] with munitions after she made a separate peace behind our backs, intriguing against us incessantly ...' Greenwood's question received no answer, but it was good to hear the remark."[*]

* Lord Crawford added inconsequentially, "A few months ago [spring of 1922], Asquith told me that Greenwood was a Jew. I have often looked at him since, but find it hard to

Greenwood was, however, no supporter of Lloyd George's aggressive stance at Chanak. He told his electorate in Sunderland that he would support the government – of which he was still a member – only if it dealt faithfully with the Turk. Bonar Law, now back as Conservative leader, abruptly terminated the ill-considered Chanak adventure with a negative statement of 6 October. Stanley Baldwin was equally condemnatory: "We should never have got into such a mess."[34] On 11 October, the Turks agreed to respect the neutral zone until final dispositions were elaborated in a still-pending renegotiated peace treaty.

Within a month of Chanak, a meeting of Conservative parliamentarians at the Carlton Club, called by Austen Chamberlain on 19 October to bring Conservative backbenchers together behind the coalition government, had the direct opposite result. Inspired partly by Baldwin and urged on by the "revolt of the Under-Secretaries" – Amery prominent among them – the vote in favour of the withdrawal of the Conservatives from the coalition, opposed by the loyalist Austen Chamberlain but supported "reluctantly" by Bonar Law, was 187 to 87. Lloyd George's government had no option but to resign the same day. Encouraged as always by Beaverbrook, Law resumed the next week the leadership of the party, his health seemingly restored. For his part, Lloyd George put his best face on his defeat, declaring blandly that he had no desire to remain as prime minister and that he was willing in the future to support any government that was "neither revolutionary nor reactionary." Frances Stevenson noted that he had told Greenwood privately that the "whole thing [was] a preconceived intrigue against him and [he is] determined to fight for all he is worth."[35] Despite various efforts, however, Lloyd George never held office again.

---

believe. Yet the name has a Semitic sound ..." This tale had a certain longevity. For example, the *Irish Times* of 23 February 1939 carried the text of a manifesto of the "Irish-Ireland Research Society" in which a fanatical anti-Semitic Roman Catholic priest referred to Greenwood as the "Jewish commander-in-chief of the Black and Tans."

16

Postwar Alarms and Excursions, 1922–1924

Beaverbrook had the political situation in 1922 about right when he observed trenchantly that Lloyd George had been a strong man but was now a weak one. As a weak man, Lloyd George never rewarded Greenwood for his role in helping to create the circumstances to make it possible to get out of Ireland without immediately splitting his coalition government. Despite persistent rumours from as early as March 1920 that the prime minister would make Greenwood either home secretary or, less likely, secretary of state for India, he did neither. Some interpreted that omission as simply arising from a desire in the uncertain political times to avoid the by-election required when a minister moved to another cabinet post. Others saw the prime minister as having concluded that there was nothing to be gained by honouring a man whom many Liberals and Labourites regarded as his willing accomplice in a coercive regime in Ireland. Greenwood got nothing. There was to be no reward for having pursued what Warren Fisher once sourly described "as a pure PM-pleasing policy."[1] For diehard Conservatives, on the other hand, he was looked upon as Lloyd George's pussycat for giving Ireland away to the gunmen. To be sure, Bonar Law as prime minister differed from the diehards in moving from his pre-war confrontations with Greenwood over Home Rule and Ulster to a sort of backhanded admiration, but the chief secretary for Ireland was still held in repugnance by many Conservatives. Mrs Stuart Menzies had her own explanation of what had happened to Greenwood in the wake of the Irish settlement:

Like all Canadians, Sir Hamar Greenwood is a Home Rulite [*sic*], and probably that was one reason why Mr. Lloyd George chose him as Chief Secretary for Ireland, meaning to use him as an end to his schemes; and if any man has been badly let down by his friend that man is Sir Hamar Greenwood ... Perhaps, not being a rich man, it was a case of needs must when the devil drives; also he may have considered it his duty to do the dirty work of an unscrupulous Coalition Government, rather than follow the dictates of his own heart ... Sir Hamar did the disagreeable work he was asked to do to the best of his ability, and I know that all sorts of promises were made to him and to Lady Greenwood of good things in store for them in return for their assistance; all sorts of rewards, yet when the list came out of those whose services should be acknowledged, his name did not appear ... Mr. Lloyd George did not hesitate to throw unpleasant work upon Greenwood in following his shifty and unholy policy, and then left his friend in the lurch without as much as a mention.[2]

Loyalty was not a notable Lloyd George characteristic. As the British historian A.J.P. Taylor once observed, "Lloyd George had no friends and he did not deserve any."[3]

At the time, Riddell spoke with Greenwood at a dinner in London given by the high commissioner in honour of the visiting Canadian Bar Association. Greenwood was "very bitter at the way in which he has been treated. He says that when he went to Ireland, the cabinet would have promised him anything, they were so anxious he should go. When parting with him, Bonar Law was in tears and said he feared he would never see him again. As it is, he [now] finds himself without a position."[4] Yet Greenwood did not waste much time in frustration and bitterness. His comment to Riddell suggests that he had long sensed that his doing "the dirty work of an unscrupulous Coalition Government" would in the end go unrewarded. The prime minister could at least reward his former mistress both for her overt and covert roles in London and Dublin without incurring any political penalties. Two years before, he had made his own long-suffering wife a dame commander, Order of the British Empire, an honour that he had described to her as "the greatest and highest of all." In the New Year's honours list of 1922, he also made Margo a dame commander, Order of the British Empire for, *tout court*, her "services in Ireland."*

* In 1920 Margo had received the Companion of the Order of the British Empire (CBE) for her wartime charitable work, having been the first treasurer of the Consultative Committee of Women's Organisations and first head of the Women's Section of the Comrades of the Great War, later the British Legion.

With the resignation of Lloyd George's coalition government in October 1922 and the formation of a Conservative government by the ailing Bonar Law, re-election prospects were decidedly unpromising for Greenwood. The *Toronto Daily Star* reported, "Sir Hamar has become somewhat unpopular ... [not over Ireland but] because ... electors think that he has neglected the constituency."[5] Whether valid or not, this personal criticism masked a more fundamental problem. In the wake of the world war, the Liberal Party, divided in two, was going nowhere but down, with the Labour Party going up. As the campaign of November 1922 began, Dame Margo, now aged thirty-five and three months pregnant with her fourth child, was depressed at the unpromising prospects facing her husband in his constituency. Still hoping that Lloyd George would form the next government, Greenwood invited him to speak on his behalf in Sunderland. Margo followed with a plea to Stevenson on 31 October: although her husband was "making a desperate effort and working like a Trojan, our fate depends on Lloyd George coming." Greenwood felt betrayed by the Conservatives: "The seat has suddenly become insecure for us owing to the action of a few diehard Tories [words illegible] wishing to run a second Tory candidate."[6] The implacable Samuel Storey, the Conservative-Unionist agent, and other Conservatives in Sunderland, who had made it clear to Bonar Law the little that they thought of Greenwood, reaffirmed their dislike by nominating two Conservatives for the two-seat constituency, leaving no agreed opening for a coalition Liberal.

While Margo was promoting her husband among the newly enfranchised women of Sunderland, Lloyd George did arrive to speak on his behalf. In a major speech on 7 November, a week before the election, he extolled Greenwood's parliamentary record and his personal fortitude as "a man of courage, a man prepared to face the difficulties and a man who would not run away when he was in trouble." He concluded with the flat statement: "If it had not been for the resolute fight put up by Sir Hamar Greenwood you would never have had that Treaty with Ireland to-day."[7] Separately, in response to the plea from the Greenwoods, Winston Churchill went farther than Lloyd George. In a telegram of 9 November intended for publication, he assured Greenwood:

> You have been treated very unjustly and unchivalrously by various
> sections of the public. When you went to Ireland there were no
> other candidates for your job. Anyone could see quite apart from
> the risks which you and your wife faced so courageously that you

were bound to incur political reproaches and vendettas of a serious and lasting kind. You went only from impulse of duty and you did your duty and you did your best and never lost heart under circumstances most cruel and trying. But I should like to testify that at the same time that you were endeavouring to quell the Irish rebellion you were always hoping that the day would dawn when a reconciliation could be effected between the two islands. No one welcomed that day more than you, and no man more proudly wrote his name across the great Treaty which in the mercy of God may yet draw a curtain of blessed oblivion across the long and sombre past.

. Since I took over the management of Irish affairs you have helped me in every way, never thinking at all about yourself or your own position. Now I understand you are being attacked by the local Tory caucus. I am sure you will make a splendid fight, and I believe the working class electors of Sunderland will give you fair play and not allow Mr. Lloyd George's representative and friend to be knifed and trampled down amid the prevailing confusion.[8]

In the event, not even the combined efforts of Lloyd George, Churchill, Greenwood, and Margo could prevail against the alienated Conservatives in Sunderland. On election day, 15 November 1922, the leading Conservative candidate polled 28,000 votes and the second 24,600. In the two-seat constituency, Greenwood was third with 19,000 votes. Asquith wrote, "The thing that gives me the most satisfaction [about the election] is to gloat over the corpses left on the battlefield, Winston, Hamar Greenwood ... Montagu ... all of them renegades."[9] The final results were a disaster for the deeply divided Liberal Party: Conservatives 344; Labour 138 (the official opposition since the December 1918 election); Liberals (Asquithian) 60; and National Liberals (Lloyd George) 57. The Conservatives had a clear majority over all other parties, bringing Bonar Law to office as prime minister (and making Amery first lord of the admiralty). But Law lasted in office only 209 days, having again to resign, this time fatally ill with cancer, in May 1923. Before that, however, in the brief parliamentary session before the year's end, "Law had the task of ratifying the Irish Treaty in the Irish Free State Bill, a task that gave him neither enthusiasm nor satisfaction. He had to placate the extreme elements in his own Party and avoid accusations of betrayal."[10] Both Houses of Parliament would adopt without any notable satisfaction the Irish legislation in March 1923. Two months later, on 20 May, Law resigned and was succeeded by his chancellor of the exchequer, Stanley Baldwin, who had inherited from the coalition an economy plagued by the decline of iron and steel and other traditional heavy industries, high unemployment, and widespread labour unrest.

In a real sense, although of course it was not then recognized – including by himself – Lloyd George's prospects of ever again achieving high office had ended with the election. Enoch Powell, in writing of Joseph Chamberlain, rightly observed that "all political lives, unless they are cut off in midstream at a happy juncture, end in failure."[11] That was so in the case of Lloyd George. For more than two decades he lingered on in the House of Commons, but he and his remnants of the deeply divided Liberal Party never again had any real chance of regaining office. And with the defeat of the coalition government in November 1922 – one month before the departure of the last British troops from Ireland – any hopes that Greenwood at age fifty-two still had to be in a future Liberal cabinet ended.* Beverley Baxter, the Canadian editor of Beaverbrook's *Sunday Express* (and later himself a Conservative MP), wrote a finale of sorts to Greenwood's years in the House of Commons: "Sir Hamar Greenwood had succeeded in his policy of violence [in Ireland], and the Sinn Feiners were coming to London to ask for terms. It is the end of Greenwood's political career. This learned, affable, temperance-lecturing and quite fearless Canadian had been given a dirty job to do and has done it. He has not even propitiated the gods of criticism by saying that he had done it out of love for the Irish people. There is no further office for such a one. Not for the first time in England's rough Island story, a man has been broken on the wheel of policy for a success that has proved embarrassing."[12] Beaverbrook, Baxter's boss, later echoed him: Greenwood's "administration, although denounced by all Ireland and by many of his Liberal Party Colleagues, was a most impressive success. And his courage and devotion to duty in the face of threats of assassination won him credit and high praise."[13] So much for the condign strictures of his friend Tim Healy.

---

* Greenwood was on 7 February 1922 able to take time off from his now reduced responsibilities to give away his youngest sister, Gladys (known as Sadie) in marriage to a twenty-six-year-old stockbroker, the Hon. Simon Rodney (1895–1966). Rodney was the third son of the Lord Rodney, upon whom, for some reason, Greenwood had called with his father during their visit to Wales in 1885. Alexander Greenwood described Sadie as a "successful social climber without equal." Before the wedding, she gave her age as twenty-seven, whereas she was in fact thirty-five, nine years older than her husband-to-be.

While the confused political manoeuvrings and the economic decline of the early 1920s in both Britain and Ireland played out, Greenwood, like many Liberals, vacillated between traditional liberal free trade and protectionism, between a Lloyd George revival and a Stanley Baldwin safeguard against socialism. Greenwood did assist Lloyd George in arranging his visit to the United States and Canada in the summer of 1923 (his second visit to Canada after three decades). The former prime minister's progress across North America as the "man who won the war" was everywhere a triumph – not least in Toronto. But his arrival back in Britain was decidedly not. The question of "tariff reform" and an imperial tariff preference, launched by Joseph Chamberlain two decades before, had gained new life amidst postwar economic uncertainties. Bonar Law had rejected any idea of tariff protection, promising in the 1922 election campaign "no fundamental change in the fiscal system." However, his successor, Stanley Baldwin, faced with yet more unemployment and contemplating an early election to endorse – or reject – his new government, feared that Lloyd George on his return from North America might advocate a general tariff, opening the way to an imperial tariff preference. Baldwin acted. "The Goat was in America. He was on the water when I made the speech [contemplating a general tariff], and the Liberals did not know what to say. I had information that he was going protectionist and I had to get in quick. Dished the Goat."[14] Although the Goat had himself toyed with the idea of a general tariff, on returning to London he immediately denounced Baldwin's trial balloon as "unutterable folly" and as "an insult to an intelligent but starving people."[15] Greenwood, with his old friend Alfred Mond, attempted to restore links with the Conservatives by hastening to Churt, Lloyd George's new house in Surrey (paid for by Riddell), to plead with him to support Baldwin in his newfound tariff enthusiasms. Convinced that, among other things, he would on his own merits be again prime minister, Lloyd George rejected any idea of collaboration with Baldwin.

Before the 1923 election campaign, Baldwin had an imperial conference to chair. With Margo and Peter Larkin, the high commissioner, Greenwood waited on the platform at Euston Station on 30 September 1923 to greet Mackenzie King, arriving from Canada for the six-week imperial conference, accompanied by Ernest Lapointe and Vincent Massey and, from outside the government, the arch-isolationist O.D. Skelton of Queen's University (in Kingston, Ontario) and John Dafoe, editor of the *Manitoba Free Press*. Although King had been in office for almost two years, he still had little confidence in his ability to counter at the conference the concept of a coordinated Empire foreign policy endorsed at earlier conferences by Robert Borden and Arthur Meighen.* "I am far from prepared ... I am filled with terror," King had written to Amery. "I dread somewhat my own lack of experience in gatherings of the kind."[16] He sailed from Quebec City convinced that "the whole purpose of the Conference is a centralizing imperial policy first re foreign policy to be made in London and next for control [of the] Navy and distribution of cost of upkeep among outlying Dominions," all anathema especially to Liberals in Quebec.[17]

The presence on the Euston platform of Angela Greenwood, aged eleven, his goddaughter whom he was meeting for the first time and in whom "I have a special interest," may have momentarily distracted King from his myriad anxieties about the devious plots of Whitehall centralists. He was still preoccupied with restoring the unity of the Canadian Liberal Party and holding onto Quebec in the wake of the deeply divisive conscription crisis of six years before. In any case, he was careful in his conversations with his old classmate, who was both the controversial former chief secretary for Ireland and a colleague of Churchill. Greenwood and Churchill were, in their own ways, advocates of a collaborative, coordinated Empire, a concept that, with his eye constantly on Liberal fortunes in Quebec, King opposed. Imperial centralists, real or more often imaginary, were long his bogeymen. But by the end of the 1923 imperial conference he congratulated himself that he was successfully disengaging Canada from supposed imperial obligations which he was convinced were cherished by Canadian as well as British diehard Conservatives. In fact, neither the Conservatives Borden nor Meighen, with their concept of the Empire as a family of equals, recognized any such unilateral obligations. As one student of the inter-war years of the Empire has written, they held the constructive view that "they should [not] separate from the Empire, but that they could assert a positive influence in a new, reshaped Empire."[18]

At the conference, Mackenzie King cautiously and briefly welcomed the recent settlement in Ireland but continued to resist any suggestion of an imperial foreign or (by extension) defence policy, asserting

* As the *Ottawa Journal* had speculated on 9 May 1923, the prime minister must have had some doubts about what on a personal level awaited him in London. To embrace the Asquithian Liberals would be ill-advised, given the confusions amongst Liberals. Equally, however, to "give precedence to an old friend like Sir Hamar Greenwood, who is a valiant Lloyd Georgian, he will also find himself in trouble ... It is a pity that our Premier should be confronted with so grave a social problem."

post-Chanak the absolute right of Canada to make its own foreign policy and rejecting Australia's – and Borden's – earlier endorsement of periodic imperial consultations and a voice in imperial policy-making. The Foreign Office was clear, in any case, that such a voice would be limited unless it was matched by an acceptance of obligations. Lloyd George's private office in the midst of the war had been convinced that "directly the Dominions begin to have strong feelings about general foreign policy we are up against the fundamental issue because no [British] government which is responsible for foreign affairs can possibly undertake to subordinate its views to those of other people unless those are willing to share the responsibility for and the consequences of policy."[19] Borden and Meighen had been prepared to share foreign policy responsibility, but "on the understanding always that imperial and international commitments needed parliamentary sanction, [they] had sought for Canada a status within the Empire of equality with Britain, and had established through the League of Nations the beginnings of an international Canadian personality."[20]

For his part, the isolationist Mackenzie King continued to fight straw men, ignoring Balfour's accurate observation of two decades before about "self-governing Colonies of the Empire over which no office in this country has any control at all."[21] On 18 October, in the midst of the imperial conference, Larkin chaired a Canada Club dinner to honour King. In attendance, among others, were Neville Chamberlain, Churchill, Greenwood, and the US ambassador. King took the occasion to elaborate his pious conviction that "in the old continent of Europe there remained an amount of suspicion, hatred and revenge which the newer countries would like to see removed … He could think of no finer ideal for the British Empire than that which the King [George V] recently gave to the school children – that it should be a community of free nations."[22] However, he did tell Baldwin before his departure that if "a great and clear call of duty" came, Canada would be at Britain's side, as it had not been at Chanak. On a quite different plane, before his arrival in London, King had recorded in his diary that Edward Beatty, president of the CPR and his and Greenwood's former classmate, "spoke highly of [Edward] Peacock [a master at Upper Canada College from 1895 to 1902 who had become a leading London financier] and well of Greenwood, [but said] the Prince of Wales was drinking a good deal and a great deal after women."[23]

Following the imperial conference, Baldwin called an ill-judged and unwanted general election in December 1923. The central plank in his platform was tariffs: "the unemployment problem is the most critical ... the only way of fighting [it] ... is by protecting the home market."[24] Tariff protection, he gambled, could help to revive British industry. It could also open the way to an imperial preference, if his government were later so minded. Amery for his part was elated: here was a Conservative leader finally advocating the controversial policy of Joseph Chamberlain of thirty years before which could lead to an imperial tariff preference. He worried, however, that Baldwin's unexpected tariff initiative was premature. Mackenzie King had taken no public position on tariffs at the 1923 imperial conference. Tariffs were for him a matter for the United Kingdom and each Dominion alone to decide (as reflected, for example, in Baldwin's earlier introduction, as Lloyd George's president of the Board of Trade, of selected tariffs in the Safeguarding of Industries Act).

In the election, Greenwood remained, in the words of the *Ottawa Journal*, "a valiant Lloyd Georgian." In what was to be his final bid for re-election in Sunderland, he set himself against Baldwin's free-trade heresy. He continued to support the Liberal free trade manifesto endorsed, in a rare show of unity, by both Lloyd George and Asquith. Beaverbrook recalled that in the campaign Greenwood "was an orator with fixed political views, and noted for his platform repartee. His accent gave the impression that he was speaking through his nose. When an opponent at a public meeting, who supported tariffs against foreigners, cried out, 'You speak through your nose', Greenwood answered, 'If you get tariffs, you will pay through your nose.'"[25]

For a second time in twelve months, Greenwood was defeated in Sunderland by the two sitting Conservative members. He had, however, fought a tight contest; this time only 1,500 votes (rather than 9,000) separated him from the leading Conservative. Nationally, the Conservatives were reduced to 257 seats, less than Labour and Liberals combined (350 seats). Baldwin did not promptly resign but soon after the House met he was defeated in a confidence vote. Accordingly, on 22 January 1924, Britain's first Labour government came into office under Ramsay MacDonald. Greenwood presumably speculated to himself that he would henceforth need to make his own way through the increasingly unstable political scene (with three national elections in as many years). On 9 December, immediately after his defeat in Sunderland, Greenwood – with Margo present – had spent the day with Alfred Mond, his fellow advocate of imperial economic collaboration, discussing with an uncertain and erratic Lloyd George their common political fortunes.

Greenwood urged him again, in light of Labour's surge in the polls, to support Baldwin as a way of restoring his own waning political capital through a gesture of generosity. "Lloyd George's answer was that 'Baldwin knifed me and I am going to knife Baldwin.'"[26] As for himself, unlike some of his erstwhile Liberal colleagues, Greenwood, in giving up on the fractured Liberal Party, shunned Labour. Along with Churchill, he moved toward the only other non-socialist option, the Conservatives.

In the spring of 1924, having been absent from Canada for eight years, Greenwood began to think of making a visit. He hinted to Larkin that he would appreciate a free pass on the government-owned Canadian National Railway to supplement transatlantic steamship arrangements that he had made with Edward Beatty. Reciprocating Greenwood's earlier words of praise, the high commissioner duly recommended – at least in a backhand way – the request to Mackenzie King: "Whatever faults he may have had in the opinions of many, he has always been a good Canadian. He did everything possible to help me in regard to the removal of the cattle embargo [and in the complex purchase of Canada House] and proved a very good adviser.* I am sure that if Sir Hamar were able to go through the country Canada would be repaid a hundred times the cost in publicity."[27] A CNR pass was duly added to the CPR one.

Before embarking for Quebec City in August, Greenwood was present in July at the opening by King George V of the ambitious British Empire Exhibition at Wembley Stadium in London. Twenty-seven million visitors – equal to half the population of Britain – joined in admiring imperial displays including an equestrian statue of the Prince of Wales made entirely of Canadian butter. The exhibition also had a serious purpose: it and the parallel establishment of the Empire Marketing Board were part of what Amery and other imperial enthusiasts saw as ways of setting the stage for an effective imperial tariff preference. Greenwood also presided over a Canada Club dinner, this time for J.H. Thomas, the bumptious union leader in the 1919 rail strike and the first Labour secretary of state for the Dominions. Peter Larkin took the occasion

---

* Greenwood had given Larkin continuing advice as he attempted to pick his way through the peculiarities of London real-estate practices and the conflicting guidance that he received from King in Ottawa. The difficulties eventually resolved themselves into Larkin's purchase in 1923 of the Union Club premises on Trafalgar Square as the new chancery for the Canadian High Commission, to be known as Canada House.

in his speech to salute Churchill, an earlier secretary of state for the colonies, who, following the departure of the Irish MPs from Westminster, "was responsible for the removal of the embargo on the import of Canadian cattle, which had lasted for twenty-eight years."[28] Greenwood in turn praised Larkin, praise he knew would be welcome to Mackenzie King.

In writing to King of the dinner, Greenwood indicated the political route that he was pursuing before the next election, foreseen within a year: "The old Liberal Party as we knew it in England is in my opinion breaking up and will be absorbed in the main by the Conservatives who have become Liberal Conservatives or by Labour who are Radicals with a Socialist left wing."[29] In replying to Greenwood's speech, King included a convoluted apologia for his independent stance in imperial relations: "The determination to maintain Canada's position with some degree of appreciation of what is owing to the Dominion in inter-imperial relations and negotiations, which … I have exhibited at times, is not as pleasing to officialdom in the Old Land as the ready experience which in former times too often characterized Canada's attitude toward whatever was done or left undone by the British authorities."[30] Implicitly he was attacking Robert Borden and those who, like Greenwood, had advocated a consultative and collaborative Empire.

In late August 1924 the Greenwoods disembarked in Quebec City from the CPR liner *Empress of France*. After three days in Quebec, where Greenwood called upon the provincial government, they spent several days in Toronto as guests of the chief justice of Ontario and chancellor of the University of Toronto, Sir William Mulock. At Oshawa they were the guests of Sam McLaughlin, the president of General Motors Canada. In neighbouring Whitby, Margo presented a silver cup to the winner of a contest to select "the Empire's bonniest baby," an event that attracted widespread newspaper coverage. From Toronto the Greenwoods, accompanied by the Ontario minister of agriculture, travelled in a private rail car as the guests of J.P. Bickell, the affluent owner of Porcupine Mines, to "view the prospects at first hand" in Sudbury and other mining towns of northern Ontario. In Ottawa, King welcomed them to his country house at Kingsmere, enquiring closely both about the British political scene and about his god-daughter, Angela. Throughout their travels, the Greenwoods were accompanied by a Scotland Yard detective with whom the RCMP closely collaborated, Irish malcontents still issuing threats on their lives.[31]

In his many speeches and newspaper interviews during his visit, Greenwood, ever the imperialist liberal, defined himself, somewhat torturously, as being "on the right politically, because I do not believe that the ... [Asquithian] Liberals and Labour have as strong a conception of Empire as the imperialist Liberals or Conservatives have."[32] In a speech in September to the Canadian Club in Ottawa, he associated himself with "the most articulate protagonists of the Dominion Idea ... [who] insisted that the Empire offered a capacious mould into which the special identities of the Dominions could be poured."[33] But to Mackenzie King, Greenwood must have sounded more like Robert Borden. Describing the Empire as "an equal partnership," Greenwood rejected by implication the isolationist negativism of O.D. Skelton, now Canada's under-secretary of state for external affairs (King doubled as prime minister and secretary of state for external affairs), who "smelt the [foul] odour of imperial federation in every proposal for co-operation."[34]

Instead of embracing the King/Skelton idea that Canada should confront any imperial centralists while pursuing a straight line to what they regarded as full autonomy, Greenwood, following Laurier and Borden, proclaimed that Britain and the Dominions "must come together sooner or later and thrash out a policy which, while preserving the sovereignty with the Constitution you now enjoy will do something toward equalizing the burdens ... not only Canada, but the other Dominions, must find a common policy for the common burdens of the Empire."[35] Mackenzie King – and Skelton– could not have disagreed more. King wrote in his diary, "Greenwood gave a characteristic address. Sees himself always as *dramatis persona* no.1. This time it was as the only living Canadian who had been a member of an imperial cabinet. After his address [and before tea together at Laurier House and dinner at the Country Club] I told him there had never been such an institution. That there was a self-constituted imperial council, but not a cabinet with imperial policy responsible to a people who had elected them."[36]

Several years later Greenwood was still speaking along liberal-imperialist lines to the Royal Colonial Institute in London, taking the Dominion of Ireland as the starting point for elaborating again his life-long commitment to a cooperative and collaborative Empire (or later the British Commonwealth of Nations or, later still, the Commonwealth): "Ireland must now be regarded as our partner in our great Commonwealth of Nations, and everyone must do his and her best to help the latest Dominion carry on." Then Greenwood endorsed the position that Borden had argued at the end of the First World War and that had been so unwelcome both to King on the one hand and the Foreign Office on the other: "Up to the World War, the Foreign Office had acted for the whole Empire. Because of the War [however] the Dominions wanted to take their fair share in our Commonwealth conferences on foreign affairs. [They] should be adequately represented in London [i.e., by cabinet ministers] and in the closest possible touch with the [British] cabinet. The Dominions would be ready to bear their part of the responsibility and burden which must come from any foreign policy thereby arrived at."[37]

By his return to Britain in the early autumn of 1924, Greenwood, along with Churchill, had finally given up on what were in effect two Liberal Parties. He declined a proffered Liberal Nationalist (Lloyd George) nomination in Cardiff Centre in the pending election. Although his Welsh ancestry might have stood him well, he was certain that the addition of a Liberal Nationalist candidate to those of the Conservative and Asquithian Liberal candidates, already nominated, would simply open the way for Labour to win the Cardiff Centre seat. There should have been instead a single agreed Liberal candidate to embrace, in Greenwood's words, "a policy for opposing all attacks on our constitution and economic liberty and for maintaining the strength and developing the resources of the British Commonwealth."[38] He arranged instead to be endorsed by the Conservative Party as the "Constitutional and Anti-Socialist candidate" for East Walthamstow, a lower-income constituency in northeast London (as Churchill did in nearby Epping).

In an election speech at the end of October, Greenwood deplored, among other things, the divisions "of the old political parties ... on minor issues," opening the door again for Labour, who in its first government had failed to deliver on promises of jobs and improved pensions. Instead, it had lent millions of pounds to Bolshevik Russia, an undemocratic, communist, and anti-Christian government that covertly carried on a revolutionary movement against the British Empire. Greenwood also offered a defence of his earlier role as "Minister responsible with my Cabinet Colleagues for the administration of Ireland in 1920 and 1921." He rejected the allegations of his opponents that "British soldiers, and the Royal Irish Constabulary, the majority of which fine force was composed of devout, Roman Catholic Irishmen, treated women and children brutally and misconducted themselves personally during the rebellion in Ireland." He continued, "Of course this suggestion is untrue, and all the more cruel because hundreds of these brave Englishmen and Irishmen were murdered, while carrying out their duties to keep Ireland within the Empire." He quoted from Lloyd George's supportive campaign statements in Sunderland in November 1922 (cited above): "'I tell you that Treaty would never have been signed ... had it not been for the unpleasant, the disagreeable, the dangerous operations which Sir Hamar Greenwood had to conduct, not with a view to crushing Ireland, but with a view to inducing Ireland to come into conference with us and end for ever this quarrel. I met those two great Irishmen, two of them dead, Mr. Arthur Griffith and Michael Collins ... I never heard a word of complaint from them of the action taken by Sir Hamar Greenwood – never, neither from them nor any of their associates.'"[39]

Greenwood won the East Walthamstow seat. "It was a very tough fight," he wrote to Mackenzie King," but "as usual Lady Greenwood, who is an excellent speaker, was my strong right arm."[40] On 29 October 1924 he polled 11,312 votes, well ahead of Labour at 8,246 and the Asquithian Liberals at 3,745. Nationally, the election was a disaster for Ramsay MacDonald's Labour government. It was out after only ten months, the Conservatives having swept back into office with 419 seats to Labour's 151. Back in office, Baldwin said nothing more about trade protectionism, interpreting his defeat the year before as a popular rejection of the idea. Both Churchill and Greenwood had been supported by the local Conservative Party apparatus on the understanding that if elected, they would take the Conservative whip. When the House sat, both duly proclaimed their new allegiance. Baldwin unexpectedly made Churchill his chancellor of the exchequer, and Leo Amery received what he had long wanted: the Colonial Office (to which later was added the newly created Dominions Office). Greenwood's other brother-in-law, Wilfrid Ashley, became minister of transport. But there was to be no ministerial appointment for Greenwood, the controversial former Liberal Irish secretary – not even a junior one.

For almost five years until the next election in 1929, Greenwood sat on the Conservative backbenches. He intervened only occasionally in debates on various economic questions, the pressing need to protect the British steel industry from imports, "safeguards" on immigration to counter employment, the tardy administration of justice, and the generally deplorable state of the courts. It soon became evident that, despite his convincing electoral victory in East Walthamstow, it would be his last term in Parliament. Although Amery later explained that for health reasons his brother-in-law would not stand again, the reality was that both Margo and Hamar recognized that he had no ministerial prospects. Like many Conservative MPs, he instead began, at fifty-two, to concentrate upon building profitable commercial ties. Additionally, as he wrote to Mackenzie King, "I have settled down to my Bar work and the prospects are good."[41] He was gratified by a visit to his constituency of the Duke and Duchess of York (the future King George VI and Queen Elizabeth), saying, "Their Royal Highnesses ... have [even] commanded the respect ... of certain extremists who have hitherto worked against some of England's cherished ideals."[42]

17

Egypt and Palestine, 1925

The time of Leo Amery, the new colonial secretary, was much taken by a myriad of Middle East questions, but among the most pressing of them was the rise of nationalism in Egypt. In the hope that a firm hand there, as in Ireland, would maintain law and order, Lloyd George had in early 1919 appointed Field Marshal the Viscount Allenby as high commissioner to Egypt, which Britain had regarded as a protectorate since the construction of the Suez Canal more than fifty years before. Lord Allenby's appointment reflected his renown as the determined general who had served with distinction first on the Western Front and later in command of the victorious Egyptian Expeditionary Force over the Turks in Palestine in 1917–18. When he arrived in Cairo in March 1919, Egypt was in turmoil, British forces and Egyptian police together having just suppressed a popular revolt.

The leading nationalist, Saad Zaghlul, and his Wafd Party – which Churchill compared to Sinn Fein – vainly petitioned the great powers at the Paris peace conference for recognition of Egypt's independence and for its representation at the conference. Balfour, the foreign secretary, responded curtly that "the stage has not yet been reached at which self-government is possible." Zaghlul was exiled to Malta shortly before Allenby's arrival, resulting in riots across Egypt. British police, soldiers, and officials were murdered, with martial law bringing only gradual and uncertain pacification. All this was a highly unwelcome distraction to Lloyd George, preoccupied as he was with the concurrent and convoluted peace proceedings in Paris.

During the August 1919 weekend at Trouville with the Greenwoods, Lloyd George, still believing in the wholesale use of force, had given Allenby the broad mandate "to take all measures necessary and expedient to restore law and order" and to preserve British suzerainty over the Canal Zone. However, Allenby, from his wartime experience, was convinced that Egypt could not be ruled by force alone, although General Bulfin had succeeded in doing so temporarily before his arrival. The first step to restoring stability would be the summoning of an assembly of leading Egyptians. Allenby subsequently concurred in the assembly's recommendation that Zaghlul be allowed to return from exile. Thereafter, the high commissioner came to be regarded by English diehards as a dangerously lenient and pro-Egyptian pussycat. In their view, Britain should either govern or clear out. Lloyd George, however, continued to hope that the undeniable personal courage of "the Bull" – Allenby – might enable him to buy enough time for London to turn from the seemingly endless conundrums left by the war to a successful longer-term policy for an Egypt astride the imperial route to the East.

To recommend that longer-term policy, Lloyd George sent a commission of enquiry, headed by Lord Milner, the colonial secretary, to Cairo in May 1920, a year after Allenby's arrival. The Milner commission was to propose ways to promote prosperity and self-government under an Egyptian monarch. It was, however, boycotted by leading nationalists and greeted by demonstrations and riots. From Baghdad the eminent Arabist Gertrude Bell, echoing Lord Curzon and others in London, saw Egypt turning "into a second Ireland largely by our own stupidity."[1] Following the return of the commission to London, Allenby forfeited the confidence of Churchill, the colonial secretary, who regarded coercion as the best way of maintaining certain reserved powers embodied in a treaty with a quasi-independent Egypt. Those same imperial demands were one reason that Zaghlul and his followers promptly rejected Milner's recommendations, proclaiming that not a single British soldier must remain on Egyptian soil; if negotiations failed, Egypt would fight like Ireland. The insurgency continuing and exchanges between London and Cairo leading nowhere, at the end of 1921 Allenby sent Zaghlul back into exile, this time to the Seychelles.

In London in early 1922, Allenby forced Lloyd George, at the threat of his own resignation, to grant unilaterally a form of independence to Egypt. On the last day of February 1922, with the coronation of King Fuad, London proclaimed that the "British protectorate over Egypt is terminated and Egypt is declared to be an independent sovereign state"[2] – but not as sovereign as most independent states. Britain again reserved certain major powers, reflecting what were regarded as essential imperial interests. The reservations included the security of the Suez Canal

and of Egypt itself, the protection of foreign financial and other interests, the safeguard of minorities, and control over the Sudan and the
headwaters of the Nile.

Lloyd George, beset by a multitude of postwar problems including
Ireland, did not follow Churchill's advice to put down ruthlessly the
continuing demonstrations and riots in a now supposedly sovereign
state. He recognized that the overstretched British army alone could
not bring about a resolution. He had to accept Allenby's more conciliatory approach but, as he observed to King George V, "I know why he
[Allenby] is called the Bull; he has gotten into our Eastern china shop
and is breaking everything up." On the other hand, Lord Carnarvon, on
a visit to the archaeological sites of his protégé Howard Carter, criticized
Allenby as having "been very weak, is badly advised, and I am sorry to say
drinks ... he is very straight, but slow and rather stupid."[3]

The Egyptian insurgency mounted as the Irish insurgency moved
toward a negotiated settlement. As attacks on British soldiers and
Egyptian police multiplied, British diehards continued to denounce
Allenby for his leniency. Zaghlul, now back from exile in the Seychelles,
became prime minister in the election of early 1924. Violence, however, continued unabated, culminating in the assassination in Cairo in
November 1924 of Allenby's friend, Major General Sir Lee Stack, the
commander of the Egyptian army and concurrently governor general
of the Sudan. Following the summary demands of a now enraged
Allenby, Zaghlul resigned and was succeeded as prime minister by a
moderate nationalist.

Six weeks after Stack's assassination, on New Year's Day of 1925, the
Greenwoods crossed the Alps by train to Trieste, en route to Egypt and
Palestine, having left their now four young children in London in the
care of nannies. Greenwood had been the member for East Walthamstow
– and Baldwin prime minister – for only a few weeks.* In the Levant,
given the continuing threats from Ireland, a British bodyguard accompanied the couple everywhere. An Egyptian policeman was added
in Cairo, surely not a service that would likely have been provided if

---

* In Baldwin's newly formed cabinet, Amery was colonial secretary, Churchill was a
rather surprising chancellor of the exchequer (his long-term free-trade credentials
affirming that Baldwin would not resort to protectionism), and William "Jix" Joynson-
Hicks, Greenwood's Conservative opponent in the election of December 1910, was
home secretary.

the Greenwoods had elected to travel privately and entirely upon their own initiative.

What were the Greenwoods doing in Egypt? Did Amery ask his brother-in-law to report on the deteriorating situation and particularly Allenby's current thinking – and his health? Throughout their six-week visit, Margo cryptically refers in her Egyptian journal – which happily survived the Blitz – to her husband having various meetings with Egyptian ministers and senior officials as well as with British officials about "the business," in quotation marks. Her journal offers no clue whatever of what "the business" was, concentrating instead upon the political and social turmoil and nationalist agitation with which Allenby was trying to cope. Possibly Greenwood was attempting to develop commercial interests in Egypt arising from his 1919 involvement with Iraqi petroleum. Or possibly his friend Alfred Mond – "Alfred the Great," in Margo's diary – or someone in London may have suggested that he should take the occasion of a winter visit to Egypt to share with Allenby et al. his experiences in Ireland. Visitors to Cairo at the same time included Mond; Lord Stanley (the heir to Lord Derby); Lord Inchap, the shipping magnate; Sir Herbert Samuel, the former home secretary and until very recently high commissioner in Palestine; and Samuel Samuel (the Conservative MP whom Greenwood had defeated in the election of December 1910, and, like Mond, an active Zionist). All were pursuing business or other interests in Egypt or Palestine. Possibly their presence in Cairo at the same time as the Greenwoods was coincidental.

Margo's nightly diary entries recorded the conversations that she and her husband had with Allenby.[*] Since their lively days together at Trouville six years before, she found him remarkably changed. "The Bull ... seems shaken. He stops in the middle of a sentence and can't remember what he is saying. He also repeats himself at close intervals ... He speaks jerkily and loudly." He did remain, however, enthusiastic in recalling Lloyd George's house party near Trouville, praising how "Geddes had sung and Hamar had danced 'Solomon Levi' which he hoped he would repeat in Cairo."

Allenby described for the Greenwoods how he had attempted, from his arrival in early 1919 six years before, to follow London's uncertain and uneven policies as best he understood them. He recalled how, in

---

[*] The direct quotations that follow in this chapter, unless otherwise indicated, are from the diary of Margo Greenwood in the possession of the late Major Alexander Greenwood.

mid-1920, the visiting Milner commission, although boycotted by nationalists, had spent some weeks in attempting to determine the seriousness of the independence movement, but its enquiries had simply encouraged the nationalists. Allenby said he had told Lloyd George "that damn'd fellow Milner had been the curse of the thing and if Egypt went to ruin, it was his fault." He shared with the Greenwoods his conviction that part of the problem was that on his arrival Milner had declared himself an envoy plenipotentiary, with full powers to commit the British government to whatever he proposed. With his vague commitment to independence, Milner "promised the Egyptians all sorts of things which he should not have promised them … [Allenby, who] did not agree with Milner on his policies … wired London, 'You have made promises to the Egyptians and you must keep them … You can't chop and change, and if you don't keep your word, I go.'" As early as the summer of 1921, as the uncertain stalemate continued, he had predicted that with Lloyd George and his coalition cabinet "all much stiffer than I am … we shall have an absolute rupture, with another Ireland in Egypt." He had urged Lloyd George, however distracted by postwar problems, to recognize that no early agreement with Zahglul about a treaty to replace the protectorate was possible. Instead, a unilateral declaration should be made abolishing the British protectorate and recognizing Egypt's independence, while maintaining several of the "reserved subjects" of the past. Allenby recalled to the Greenwoods that Lloyd George, with his eye on his Conservative-Unionist cabinet colleagues already uneasy over his stance in Ireland, had accused him of asking the government "to abandon our entire position in Egypt without guarantee." Allenby described how he has been prepared to resign when Lloyd George suddenly capitulated, accepting all of his terms. The prime minister, if not his full cabinet, recognized that coercion was no longer practicable and that a unilateral declaration could open the way to a decidedly greater degree of independence for Egypt. Allenby outlined to the Greenwoods the challenges he had encountered in attempting to contain the growing and increasingly violent demand in Egypt for full independence and to win in the interim a minimal acceptance of something less. Zaghlul, as prime minister, hoped that the new government of the Labourite Ramsay MacDonald would prove more forthcoming and flexible than those of Lloyd George, Bonar Law, and Baldwin. When it did not, Zaghlul's popularity declined, and radical nationalists resumed their violence.

Allenby told the Greenwoods how, two months before their arrival, he had responded to Stack's assassination. Without waiting for authorization from London, he had immediately presented Zaghlul with a longer list of demands than London had in mind. Margo wrote, "He felt he had taken a risk ... issuing his ultimatum before he had time to get full authority [from London]. He did so because he heard Zaghlul was going [to resign] so he went straight to him at once with the ultimatum ... He said that [the visiting] Asquith was lunching with him that day ... and saw Stack brought in there and put wounding and bleeding on a sofa. It shook up Asquith and brought things home to him, which Allenby thought was 'a good thing.'" He was not surprised, and the ambitious King Fuad was gratified, when in the face of his unilateral demands for retribution and compensation, Baldwin's government endorsed the high commissioner's stance. Amery's later comment on Allenby's action was accurate: "For all his dramatic action on the occasion of Stack's murder," he "was in general sympathetic towards Egyptian national aspirations and inclined to concessions."[4]

Zaghlul nevertheless resigned, and the Egyptian parliament was dissolved, with elections to be held in March 1925. A few weeks before the Greenwoods' arrival, Zaghlul was succeeded as prime minister *ad interim* by the elderly, genial, and more pliant Ziwar Pasha (who reminded Margo of Campbell-Bannerman). Although Allenby remained in Cairo, still attempting to keep the lid on, his wife told Greenwood that above all things he would like to succeed Lord Byng as governor general of Canada.[5]

What the Greenwoods did in Egypt thereafter remains unclear, even in Margo's private diary. At Allenby's request, Howard Carter escorted them on a visit to the tomb of Tutankamen; but they had not come to Egypt, as many British did, for winter tourism. Throughout their six-week visit, Margo refers repeatedly to her husband calling on the king, the prime minister, several ministers, and British as well as Egyptian officials about "the business." Was "the business" an assumed commercial cover for Greenwood's real purpose? Was he there to share with British officials his experience as chief secretary for Ireland? When the Greenwoods arrived in Cairo, Baldwin had been in office only a matter of weeks. It seems unlikely that he would have promptly despatched to Egypt a former Liberal cabinet minister, especially one who had just become a Conservative MP. Even less likely, did Allenby himself, recalling their weekend at Trouville, decide to seek the Greenwoods' first-hand advice? More likely, did a senior British official in the Foreign

Office or Intelligence recommend the visit? It would not have been the first time that the Foreign Office had sent someone covertly to Cairo represented as a tourist, to report on Allenby's performance as high commissioner. It was perhaps no coincidence that the first Egyptian minister whom Greenwood met in Cairo was Ismael Sidky, the minister of the interior, responsible for, among other things, the police. Margo never records any purpose for their visit except "the business," but she would hardly have mentioned any clandestine role even in the privacy of her journal. She does, however, make several explicit comparisons between the turbulent Egypt of early 1925 and the turbulent Ireland of three years before. And she notes that on the first day of their visit, Archibald Clerk Kerr, the first secretary at the high commission, had told them that "he badly wanted a talk with us as we had much the same problem in Ireland as they are up against here ... He seemed very uneasy about the situation."

During their six weeks in Egypt, Greenwood called upon Ziwar, the new prime minister, several times, as he did on the more astute and devious minister of the interior, Ismail Sidky. Margo found him "urbane, imperturbable, slow in speech, quick in mind, full of self-confidence" – clearly a future prime minister. He was fluent in French (which he had employed to full effect during the futile mission of Egyptian nationalists to the Paris Peace Conference, where his "activities in the night-life ... were reported as establishing various records").[6] In most of Greenwood's meetings, Margo acted as interpreter so that no third person needed to be privy to them. She records little in her diary of these interviews, except to note that the king, prime minister, and minister of the interior were all well informed about events in Ireland. As a digression she added that there was one advantage in the way that self-government had been accorded Egypt in the 1923 constitution: "What is done is done is in the name of the Egyptian Government, and not, as when we were in Ireland, by the 'foreign oppressors.'" On the other hand, it was even more difficult to place British "light-skinned informers" among Egyptian ministers and officials than it had been among the Sinn Fein and the IRA.

Ireland was never far from the Greenwoods' thoughts in Egypt, especially during a brief rail journey that they and their bodyguards made through light snow flurries to Palestine in the fourth week of January. Upon their arrival in Jerusalem, Colonels McNeil and Foley and other officers and men of the Black and Tans were on the station platform to greet Greenwood. "Hamar immensely pleased by the compliment and very happy to see some of the old 'Black and Tans' again," Margo wrote. Later, at nearby Mount Scopus, "All those men in the British Gendarmerie who had served under Hamar in Ireland as Black and Tans were drawn up. He inspected them and made a speech." They appeared happy in their new police work, Margo thought. Sports facilities were abundant, and they could even listen to "Stompin' at the Savoy" on their short-wave wireless. Happily, "all seems peaceful and orderly after the first two fights shortly after they arrived ... Fortunately, one was with the Arabs and one was with the Jews so the 'impartiality' of the force was clearly demonstrated and had 'no trouble since.'" One officer from Ireland not on hand to greet the Greenwoods was Hugh Tudor who, after serving almost two years as air officer commanding in Iraq and the effective head of the Palestine Police, had retired to Newfoundland twelve months before.*

A dinner given by King Fuad concluded the Greenwoods' visit before their departure for London via Constantinople in mid-February 1925, when Margo's diary ends. They left an Egypt still restless, but after Zaghul's death in August 1927, Sidky, now prime minister, saw it in his short-term interests to cooperate with the king. For whatever reasons, commercial or otherwise, Greenwood retained ties with Egypt. In December 1939 he would become chairman of the Anglo-Egyptian Chamber of Commerce in London and the recipient of the Cordon of the Order of Ismail from King Farouk.

* Shortly before his departure from Palestine in May 1924, Tudor was knighted. Soon thereafter he went to live in St John's, Newfoundland, where he spent the next forty years before his death in 1965 at age ninety-five. His wife and three children remained in Britain, never crossing to see him. Possibly he had been advised to seek refuge overseas from IRA gunmen, on whose hit list he ranked high, but Newfoundland was for a number of reasons an unlikely place, given that an estimated one-third of the total population is of Irish descent. Further, his local address consistently appeared in St John's directories; there was no apparent attempt to disguise his presence in the city. Additionally, it was well known that he worked in the fishing industry, first as managing director of Templeman Ltd in Bonavista and later as a partner with a fisheries agent, George Barr, in St John's. It may be that he had retained some link with Newfoundland from seven years before when the Royal Newfoundland Regiment had been made part of his 9th Scottish Division on the western front. In any event, as late as the 1950s the IRA organized a plot to kill him, but the two Irish gunmen sent to do so did not in light of the advice of a local Roman Catholic priest of Irish descent. The priest apparently did not speak against their proposed murder of Tudor, blind and in a wheelchair, but rather cautioned them that their planned escape route from the island would likely fail. Tudor died in the St Johns' General Hospital on 25 September 1965 (Coogan, *Wherever Green Is Worn*, 417; *St John's Standard*, 26 September 1965).

Three months after the Greenwoods left Cairo, Amery, as secretary of state for the colonies, arrived. Greenwood had presumably described to him beforehand what he and Margo had seen and heard in both Egypt and Palestine. En route from London to Cairo, Amery spent a fortnight in Iraq, including a visit to the oil fields of Mosul. Stopping in Geneva on his return trip to London, he carried to a conclusion the British case at the League of Nations for continuing suzerainty over Iraq, especially its oil. Turkey had asserted at the League a claim on the fields, which would have set aside the agreement that Greenwood had negotiated with Berenger in Paris six years before. Following the visit of a commission to Baghdad, the League in July 1925 confirmed the British mandate over Iraq, including control of the Mosul oil fields.

18

Last Days in the House of Commons, 1925–1930

On his return with Margo from Egypt and Palestine in February 1925, Greenwood resumed his various activities at Westminster, in his London constituency, at Gray's Inn, and in the City. Against a background of continuing labour unrest (including a short-lived general strike in May 1926 and a much longer coal strike), Greenwood in a low-key way – and with continuing police protection – consolidated his hold on Walthamstow East. In November 1925, Laming Worthington-Evans, his former cabinet colleague and now secretary of state for war, joined him as a speaker at a local Conservative rally. The same month, Dame Margo, in her role as the first head of the Women's Section of the Comrades of the Great War (later the British Legion), unveiled the local memorial with its long lists of war dead.

In parallel, Canada remained Greenwood's avocation. He presided over a dinner of the Canada Club in October 1926 for Lord Byng following his term as governor general, which had been marred by a constitutional controversy with Mackenzie King. The Prince of Wales, Churchill, Amery, Mond, and Allenby (who, home from Egypt, had not realized his ambition to succeed Byng) were among the guests. Surprisingly, given his recent dispute with Byng, so was Mackenzie King, in London for the 1926 imperial conference. King stated to the dinner that "there was no one for whom he had greater personal regard and personal affection than Lord Byng."[1] To his diary he confided, "Greenwood made a first-rate speech and Lord Byng's was distinctly good ... Amery's was a little over-studied. Churchill's was a great effort."[2]

As secretary of state for dominion affairs, Amery may well have appeared to King to be lacking spontaneity. Three months before, Amery had written personally to Byng, "It was no less wise than

courageous of you to refuse flatly Mackenzie King's preposterous suggestion that you should cable me for advice ... He of all people should
have been the last to try to invoke, in his personal interest, that depen-
dence of Canada upon an outside authority which he has always so
strenuously denounced in public. He has cut a contemptible figure in
the whole business. His letter to you, with its threat of an Empire-wide
agitation, was scandalous."[3] At the dinner King may have ventured his
laudatory – and, as he stressed, *personal* – statement about Byng against
the background of Balfour's recent report regarding Britain and the
Dominions as "autonomous communities within the British Empire,
equal in status, and in no way subordinate to one another in any aspect
of their domestic or external affairs." King and Greenwood regarded
the Balfour report as reflecting what each, in quite differing ways, had
sought, one as an isolationist and the other as a liberal imperialist.

Economic uncertainties and discontents in Britain continued, culminating in a brief but deeply troubling general strike in May 1928. While
he was the member for the heavy industry constituency of Sunderland,
Greenwood had begun to advocate "safeguarding measures" (i.e., tariff
protection) for the failing steel industry, beset by subsidized imports.
Additionally, sometime prior to July 1928, he paid a visit to Warsaw,
prompting him to put a question in the House about inexpensive Polish
coal undercutting and replacing domestic supply. He had become convinced that with tariff protection and with the assistance of the new
Industrial Transference Board, the obsolete steel industry could be
reformed to play its essential role in combating unemployment, in promoting economic recovery, and in the rearmament of the United
Kingdom. In an undated publication *Prominent British Steelmakers* the
once free-trader Greenwood was saluted for having taken a lead in
Parliament "in advocating protection for the iron and steel industry."[4] A
more tangible reward would in time be the chairmanship of one of
Britain's largest steel companies.

In the House of Commons, Greenwood, as a barrister dissatisfied with
the functioning of the courts, also pressed questions about the administration of justice. In June 1928 in a debate on a justice bill, he elaborated his earlier recommendation that members of the judicial
committee of the Privy Council – still the supreme court of the Empire
– should be drawn from the total Empire and not pre-eminently from
the United Kingdom. Empire-wide confidence in judgments would
thereby be enhanced and imperial collaboration fostered. Two decades
before, Greenwood had appeared before the judicial committee on

behalf of the governments of British Columbia and Quebec. Fully aware of the discomfort in Canada with the distant Judicial Committee of the Privy Council as the final court of appeal, he called for a truly Commonwealth court by urging its reform. No such reform was forthcoming, however, and no call came; only in 1949 – the year after Greenwood's death – was the right of appeal to the Judicial Committee finally abolished in Canada.

As chairman of the long-standing Canada Club, Greenwood invited Beaverbrook to a dinner on 11 July 1928 for the visiting – and imperially minded – premier of Ontario, Howard Ferguson. (Two years later, R.B. Bennett would appoint Ferguson high commissioner in London.) After extolling the Prince of Wales as "the idol of the Canadian people," Ferguson called for Canada "to play an ever greater part ... in the constructive progress and development of our common Empire,"[5] to loud cheers and applause in which no doubt Greenwood and Beaverbrook joined. But Greenwood's mind for the moment at least was chiefly on acquiring corporate directorships. His first came from a fellow Canadian and friend of Beaverbrook, Sir James Dunn. In 1926 Greenwood had become a director of Dunn's Société internationale d'énergie hydro-électrique, a Belgium-registered company that controlled electricity generation and distribution in Barcelona. The next year he had joined the boards of two related electrical companies, Edison Swan Cables and Altrincham Electrical Supply.

Greenwood made the decision not to stand in the May 1929 election. In the event, the Conservatives were reduced to 261 seats; Labour increased theirs to 287. With the tacit support of the Lloyd George Liberals, Ramsay MacDonald formed his second Labour government. Amery, who had been re-elected but was no longer secretary of state for the Dominions and colonies, travelled to Canada to scale an 11,000 foot peak in the Rockies named for him by the Canadian government (as the South African government had also done in the Drakensberg Mountains).*

The next month, Greenwood, as a life-long temperance advocate, was invited to become chairman of the board and a shareholder in the Aerated Bread Company – the ABC, as it was popularly known. Its temperance founders had seen tea shops as an alternative to the public

---

* Despite the continuing threats against his brother-in-law, Amery also visited Dublin in 1929 as the guest of Tim Healy, the governor general. He wanted to show that, although a diehard Unionist, he had no hard feelings toward the new Dominion.

houses that they so deplored. From ABC's first shop in the Strand in 1801, it had grown into a chain of more than one hundred across greater London, later in vigorous competition with Lyons Corner Houses. Although Greenwood was paid a handsome fee as chairman, offered large share options, and provided with a Rolls Royce and driver, his debut in the corporate world was not entirely auspicious. After only a few months as chairman, he summoned the managing director, Arthur Pierce, and "referred to the decrease in the profits for the year 1928 and said … 'This is a very serious state of affairs. We must call on you to resign.'" When Pierce refused to do so, Greenwood said the alternative was dismissal. Pierce later sued the ABC board and its chairman for wrongful dismissal, convinced that he "had not been dismissed by the board in good faith, but through the personal malice of Lord Greenwood."[6]

Corporate directorships were not often readily bestowed upon former members of Parliament; peers were another matter, some enterprises taking especial satisfaction in having a title or two on their masthead. Both Greenwoods recognized that his successful transition to the corporate world would be easier if he were first made a peer. According to a Canadian Press story,[7] Dame Margo had declined an offer to succeed her husband as the Conservative candidate in East Walthamstow in the May 1929 election. Instead, she deployed her abundant energies and wily organizational skills in an ultimately successful campaign to see her husband transferred seamlessly from the Commons to the Lords. Convinced that the Lords would be a promising springboard into the world of lucrative directorships and business associations, she recognized well before the election that there was no time to lose. As they had planned, Margo portrayed her husband as being simply too proud to seek for himself a peerage. She, as a Dame of the British Empire (and, to a few intimates, as a former mistress of Lloyd George), was seen as the supportive wife.

Leo Amery, well primed in advance, undertook the solicitation among his Conservative colleagues of support for his brother-in-law's elevation. On 11 June 1929, he sent carefully crafted letters to Baldwin, the prime minister; Austen Chamberlain, the foreign secretary; Churchill, the chancellor of the exchequer; and Balfour, the president of the council. "Whether the policy which he [Greenwood] pursued in Ireland was the right one or not, nobody can say … We may hope it may prove a success. Indeed, many believed with him [Amery himself being one] that he had almost won through when the change came … Lloyd George I know promised him a peerage at the time."[8] Balfour responded promptly, "Whatever view we took about the policy that was suddenly adopted by Lloyd George toward Ireland, I think we all agree that Hamar showed great ability, energy and courage in fighting the old policy. His own view always was that he was just winning through and the rebellion was almost suppressed when Lloyd George started negotiating." Churchill, who in Amery's personal recollection, always "had a good opinion of him,"[9] supported the nomination of his PPS of almost thirty years earlier. Separately, Beaverbrook, in writing to regret that Greenwood had decided not to seek re-election in East Walthamstow, added the hope that before long he would "join our mausoleum [the House of Lords]."[10]

It was soon evident that Margo had not acted in vain. Ten days after sending his letters, Amery confirmed to her that Baldwin had recommended Greenwood for a barony. She replied with gratitude, "It was all that he [Hamar] had wished ... I've seen him go through so much and seen him let down so badly after it all that I ... feel deeply grateful."[11] She was pleased, but it was still not all that *she* wished. She continued to believe that her husband should have been made not merely a baron, the lowest rank in the peerage, but a viscount, as former cabinet ministers frequently were. In time she would launch a successful second campaign to that end.

Greenwood, after spending a total of more than twenty years in the Commons, was formally introduced into the Lords on 6 November 1929 as Baron Greenwood of Llanbister in the County of Radnor. In the next four years, as he pursued his outside interests, he spoke in the Lords less than a dozen times. On the few occasions that he did so, the unity of the Empire was his theme, amidst the political and economic uncertainties of postwar Europe. On several occasions he emphasized such practicable steps for unifying the Empire as regular economic conferences and improvements in cable and wireless communications. He acknowledged that the First World War had converted him from free trade to "tariff reform" (i.e., protectionism).[*] If the Dominions had tariffs, he asked, why not Britain? As for the unemployed, why not absorb them into protected industries by erecting barriers both to imports and to immigrants? On 25 November 1930, he chaired a Canada Club dinner in honour of Churchill, following his recent visit to

---

[*] The free trade tradition of the Liberal Party was first breached in 1915 by the introduction of duties against the wartime importation of luxury goods (with a tariff preference one-third for such imports from the Empire).

Canada. To the chairman's gratification, Churchill proclaimed that "Canada knew that all parts of the Empire had equal status, and that there was no question of any overlording. The ties which bound us together were so flexible and so easy of comprehension that there was no possibility of friction. The Empire system was based on freedom and good-will, each unit seeking to do its best for the whole combination."[12] Greenwood would have cried amen to that.

Directly after becoming a peer, on 1 January 1930 Greenwood was made treasurer of Gray's Inn, its highest honorific post, bestowed by the benchers annually. It was a notable distinction in the world of the law, assisting him indirectly in his transition to both the Lords and the corporate world. He was aware of the irony that in becoming treasurer he was succeeding Tim Healy, the new governor general of Ireland (who in 1921 had denounced him as a privy councillor "out of Bedlam").[13] With Greenwood's elevation to the peerage and his distinction at Gray's Inn, Beaverbrook continued to keep his eye on his Canadian colleague (and even more so on Margo). During his five years as the member for East Walthamstow, Greenwood for his part had kept furbished his contacts with Beaverbrook, seeing him, however undependable and meretricious, as a potential helper in acquiring more corporate directorships. The two had been acquaintances in the Commons before the First World War but not close friends. They had differed over Ireland, the Conservative Beaverbrook (influenced by Healy) surprisingly urging in his *Daily Express* that the Black and Tans must be reined in, a settlement promptly reached, and Greenwood retired as chief secretary. Now, however, with Ireland behind them, Greenwood had become a Conservative and his wife Beaverbrook continued to find appealing.

Following the Irish settlement, Greenwood and Healy patched up their differences, and Beaverbrook began to see Greenwood as an ally in his enthusiasms for greater imperial unity. It would not have escaped Beaverbrook that at a dinner of the Canada Club to which Greenwood as chairman had invited him, there were three hundred or so British and Canadian guests and "two or three princes and a good fraction of the cabinet" to honour Baldwin upon his return from a visit to Canada. In the wake of the Conservative reversal in the election of 1929, Beaverbrook became convinced that imperial free trade was the only certain route to the restoration of the Empire – or the British Commonwealth – to anything like its prewar pre-eminence in the world. At his own expense Beaverbrook launched in July 1929 his highly controversial "Empire Crusade," a campaign to change the course of the Conservative Party, including the replacement of Baldwin as its leader. Regarded by some as just one more of his stunts, his "crusade" was simple enough in outline. Joseph Chamberlain, twenty-five years or more before, had called for an imperial customs union in which Britain would impose duties on imports, partly so that it could then offer a tariff preference to the Dominions. Now Beaverbrook modified Chamberlain's proposal by calling for complete free trade within a self-help Empire: that is, the abolition of all tariffs among all members (with each maintaining whatever tariffs it chose against extra-imperial imports). Imperial free trade would engender economic self-sufficiency and open the way to greater political union. There were, however, fundamental flaws in Beaverbrook's enthusiasms, including a reluctance throughout much of the British Commonwealth to eliminate all tariffs on imports of British manufactured products, which were feared as undercutting higher-cost domestic production.

A motley lot ranging from Bruce Lockhart to Arthur Conan Doyle and several unemployed peers and a few industrialists, Tory backbenchers, and of course Beaverbrook's editor, Beverley Baxter, joined Beaverbrook as imperial crusaders, as did eventually Lord Rothermere, another strongly anti-Baldwin press baron. Beaverbrook looked upon Greenwood as a valued potential recruit for his newly established United Empire Party.[*] Greenwood and Amery were both attracted by "Lord Bunty's" bumptious and beguiling crusade, but put loyalty to the Conservative Party first. Baldwin had burned his fingers in raising the tariff question in the election of 1923 and was not about to divide his party further by doing so again in 1929.

Greenwood chaired a Canada Club dinner for Amery in September 1929 in the midst of Beaverbrook's plotting and enticements, but as Peter Larkin, the high commissioner, told Mackenzie King, Amery as speaker carefully avoided any reference to Beaverbrook's Empire

* Four days before the armistice, Greenwood spoke in the House of Commons on the vote of funds for Beaverbrook's Ministry of Information. During its brief and uneven course, the minister had encountered frequent criticism, not least from the press itself, but Greenwood was direct in his praise of his fellow Canadian: "His career at the Ministry of Information has been one of the most successful of any Minister in this Coalition Government ... It has brought together the remotest parts of the Empire. It has strengthened the feeling which is not always as keen as some people try to make out, between different parts of this Empire ... and the Mother Country" (Parliamentary Debates, House of Commons, Fifth Series, vol. 110, 7 November 1918, cols. 2379–81). In return, Beaverbrook invited Greenwood as a special guest to a dinner he gave on 6 August 1919 for the staff of the Canadian War Records Office.

campaign. Limiting himself to Iraq and Palestine, he "sketched the manner in which these countries had come under the domination of Great Britain and what had been effected. He was most interesting and had a very appreciative audience because I think [he is] highly intelligent.* [However] I do wish that he would stop his sing-song intonation. He invariably makes my eyelids feel as heavy as lead."[14]

In December 1929, as newspaper accounts of the Empire Crusade began to appear, Greenwood sent Beaverbrook what most would regard as a polite rejection of his overtures to take a lead. Beaverbrook did not, however, give up easily. He invited the Greenwoods for two overnight visits to Cherkley, his house in Surrey. He may have been misled in thinking that Greenwood was in fact susceptible after receiving a New Year's telegram from him in Italy on 2 January 1930, wishing him "God speed [in] your great crusade." On 26 January the Greenwoods spent a second weekend at Cherkley; Beaverbrook, according to Lockhart, "wants him very much to become chairman of his campaign committee." Four days later, Amery recognized that Greenwood was "anxious to go on with the chairmanship of Beaverbrook's campaign but would be put in a great difficulty from a point of view of personal loyalty if B[eaverbrook] were violently attacking s B [Stanley Baldwin]." A month later, as Beaverbrook transformed his Empire Crusade into the United Empire Party, Greenwood responded to an invitation from Beaverbrook to nominate three leading businessmen for "our committee." He appealed to Beaverbrook to work only within the Conservative Party. As part of the pressure put on Greenwood, Rothermere through his *Daily Mail* affirmed on the basis of a speech by Greenwood to the British Industries Fair that he was about to assume a leading role.[15] Greenwood did cable Beaverbrook "heartiest congratulations on your splendid campaign in Fulham [by-election] for Empire and Empire trade," but still stood fast with the Conservative Party.

Beaverbrook "tried to convert Winston to Empire Free Trade," as Lockhart reported, but Churchill was "drunk but unconvinced."[16] Even though he, like Beaverbrook and Rothermere, held Baldwin in low esteem and the offer was lucrative, Churchill continued his life-long opposition to any tariff on imported food, whatever its source. Walter Elliot, Neville Chamberlain, and Robert Horne also declined.

---

* In the same letter Larkin noted a contemporary wag's witticism that if Amery's speeches had been half an hour shorter and he had been half a head taller, he could have been prime minister.

Beaverbrook "wooed Amery, who, though in sympathy with his ends, remained wary of his headstrong means ... None of these approaches succeeded."[17] In any case, Lockhart for one did not see Amery as a leader: he "was a clever little man with an encyclopaedic knowledge, but he has no personality and lacks all charm."[18] Broadly, Amery and Greenwood shared Beaverbrook's conviction that somehow the Empire, by the Dominions working together, could escape from the economic depression and chronic unemployment. They knew, however, that Empire free trade was at best a long-term project, given differing attitudes both within Britain and among the Dominions, and could only be achieved by patience and caution – not notably Beaverbrook characteristics.

Greenwood had recommended in vain to Lloyd George as early as the election of 1923 that he cooperate with rather than oppose Baldwin. Now that he had himself become a Conservative, Greenwood was no more inclined to turn his back on the party than was his ever-ambitious brother-in-law. Especially in light of the rise of Labour, both were convinced that crusades and splinter parties had no future. Beaverbrook's siren song was appealing, but both placed loyalty to the Conservative Party ahead of other considerations. Beaverbrook's political manoeuvrings had, however, some brief success. Two by-elections in which United Empire candidates did very well, financed in part by James Dunn, left Baldwin badly shaken. But the nineteen-month crusade petered out after a by-election victory in March 1931 by the loyal Conservative candidate Duff Cooper. Baldwin was thereafter secure, Neville Chamberlain even patching up a sort of reconciliation between him and Beaverbrook. For their part, Amery, the diehard Conservative, and Greenwood, the former Liberal, had unquestionably displayed their loyalty to the Conservative Party, although Amery never revealed any enthusiasm for either Baldwin or his successor, Neville Chamberlain.

In the election of 1929, Baldwin's Conservatives had been defeated by Ramsay MacDonald's Labourites, but in August 1931 a major split in the Labour Party resulted in the formation of a "National" government under Prime Minister Ramsay MacDonald supported by the Conservatives led by Baldwin. Another election in October, following a financial crisis in August, brought into office a second National government, again headed by MacDonald, with a "doctor's mandate" to do whatever appeared necessary to revive the economy. The results of the October 1931 election reflected stronger Conservative support, but Baldwin chose the experiment of a second National Government, with Conservatives having eleven of the twenty cabinet places. Baldwin, as lord president of the council, and Neville Chamberlain, as chancellor of the exchequer, moved toward limited tariff protection combined with reduced or even nil tariff rates for imports from the Commonwealth.

Amery, to his chagrin, was not among the Conservative ministers in the new National government. The early 1930s marked the low point in his political career. (Economically, life had been eased for the Amerys by a bequest to Bryddie of an annuity of £400 from Peter Larkin on his death in February 1930.) Unlike his brother-in-law, Amery was determined to return to the front bench, but his immediate prospects were not promising. Across Europe, Germany was giving rise to mounting if still largely inchoate concerns; Amery shared with Mackenzie King and many others doubts about the ability of the League of Nations and its economic sanctions to keep the peace. Even more worrisome, the world seemed locked in economic depression. At home, the National government was uncertain of how best to respond to Beaverbrook's Empire Crusade, which had not won over the Conservative Party but had had an unsettling impact. The National government, not knowing what else to do, embraced a 1929 proposal of the Canadian Prime Minister R.B. Bennett for an imperial economic conference, the first to be held in a Dominion. With the Conservative election victory of October 1931, the conference was finally convened for Ottawa in mid-1932 under the uncertain chairmanship of Bennett, to design a system of imperial economic collaboration to help alleviate the effects of the depression and to identify what more precisely could be expected over the longer term from lower imperial tariffs and closer economic cooperation. The stage was partly set by the National government adopting in early February 1932 the Abnormal Importation Act of Neville Chamberlain, chancellor of the exchequer, which placed a tariff of 10 per cent on most imports except food, raw materials, and other Commonwealth products. In his role as lord president of the council, Baldwin explained that the import duties would provide "a breathing space" for inefficient and undercapitalized British industry, adding, to Greenwood's gratification, especially for the obsolete iron and steel industry: "Those industries can benefit themselves and the country under the shelter of a tariff, can carry out schemes of reorganisation that can attract capital, and can lay down new plants."[19]

As a personal contribution to furthering British preparations for the Ottawa imperial economic conference, on which great hopes but unfortunately limited preparations were centred, Greenwood, on 29 February 1932, invited the high commissioner, Howard Ferguson, to dine with Baldwin, the lord president (who unfortunately had to leave early); J.H. "Jem" Thomas, the Dominions secretary; Austen Chamberlain, the former Conservative leader and former foreign secretary; and brother-in-law Amery, a former colonial secretary. The dinner was ostensibly in honour of Sir John Anderson upon his appointment as governor of the Presidency of Bengal, but it proved to be something quite different and anything but a success. Both Thomas and Ferguson (like Birkenhead before them) were drunkards. Even at the teetotaller Greenwood's table, "Jem was pretty skin full and he got across with Ferguson [on Canadian tariffs] and he said exceedingly rude things about Canada and at last Ferguson said he would report him to his Government. Austen then apparently did the heavy father, told Jem to remember he was a Minister of the Crown and reminded Ferguson that such unofficial talks are never repeated. But it was all very unfortunate and bodes none too well for [the] Ottawa [conference]."[20] Amery added that Ferguson's statements "let loose Thomas on a perfectly incredible display of his essentially vulgar and rancorous attitude toward the Dominions ... It is perfectly appalling that a man of Thomas's outlook and vulgarity* should be allowed to represent this country at the most critical [imperial] conference there has ever been."[21] Ferguson in turn reported to Bennett, "I did not hesitate to tell him [Thomas] that his attitude would ruin the possibility of achieving anything at the Conference. I added that if this Conference fails, disintegration of the Empire would begin, and his would be the responsibility."[22]

After Thomas's drunken outburst, Greenwood withdrew from any further attempts to help speed preparations for Ottawa to which the large British delegation (headed by Baldwin and including Neville Chamberlain, the chancellor of the exchequer) sailed in disarray, the National Government having failed to get clear in its mind what the United Kingdom was or was not prepared to do to create a viable imperial economic system. Baldwin had welcomed the idea of the Ottawa conference as "one more attempt to keep the sane forces of the world together," but the MacDonald government was "as confused and divided as Baldwin's and Lloyd George's." The frequently ill-tempered and convoluted discussions at the conference made limited progress toward the

---

* Thomas's erratic political career ended abruptly in 1936 when he was found to have leaked details of Neville Chamberlain's budget.

stimulus of any sort of imperial *Zollverein* or even significant imperial tariff preferences (several of which, such as they were, were in any event reduced or eliminated by the Anglo-American trade agreement of six years later). For their part, the Dominions offered little to the United Kingdom other than raising their own tariffs against foreign imports and concluding modest bilateral agreements providing for a degree of reciprocal preferential access with the United Kingdom, the Irish Free State, Southern Rhodesia, and South Africa. One British minister dismissed the confused thinking and bad feeling as springing mainly from "the shallow and restless mind" of the devious and aggressive Bennett, who had proven to be a rigidly inflexible chairman. The Ottawa conference was later described as the ultimate failure of the Empire, although it did bring benefit to Canada. Over the next three years Canadian exports to the United Kingdom increased substantially, but British exports to Canada rose hardly at all.

During the 1930s, both brothers-in-law, neither yet affluent, continued to seek corporate directorships. Greenwood's chairmanship of ABC resurfaced in the press when the former managing director's action against him and the board for wrongful dismissal was finally heard by the slow-moving courts in January 1932. Greenwood and his fellow directors had remarkably little to offer as justification for their termination of Arthur Pierce. At the end of the second day, they reached an out-of-court agreement to pay him the then sizable sum of £15,000 in damages (five times his annual salary) and his costs. In return, Pierce agreed to withdraw his comment about the "personal malice of Lord Greenwood."* The ABC imbroglio does not seem to have set back Greenwood's corporate ambitions. In addition to ABC, he became chairman of Redpath Brown and Co. Ltd, a major construction company in Glasgow owned by Bolckow Vaughan. In late 1929 it had been pushed by the banks into becoming part of a much larger Teeside steel company, Dorman Long, founded in 1889. In October 1934 Greenwood was elected its chairman, retaining the position until his death in 1948.

Members of Parliament for any of the constituencies in the County of Durham – Greenwood's included – were acutely aware of the many

---

* Crozier in his *Ireland For Ever* errs in stating that the amount of the agreed settlement was £25,000 (189). The control of ABC was sold in 1955 to the Allied Bakeries of the Canadian Garfield Weston, who had sat as a Conservative MP at Westminster from November 1939 to June 1945. By then it had grown to 165 self-service tea shops and outlets for baked goods in London.

postwar problems afflicting the coal, iron, and steel industries and thereby the construction, shipbuilding, and armaments industries. The demands of the First World War had undermined the efficiency of heavy industry, leaving it uncompetitive with overseas suppliers in the postwar years. Investment in rationalization and consolidation and in new plant and technology were obviously long overdue. But such investment would only be forthcoming if at least temporary relief from foreign competition was provided by protectionist tariffs – or what were more blandly termed "safeguards." During his twelve years as the member for Sunderland, Greenwood had seen the steel industry, beset by obsolescence, over-capacity spawned by the war, and cheaper imports, move from free trade advocacy to supplication for tariff protection. And he had moved with the industry. Although a free trader, he had begun in 1924 to explore with management and labour representatives what government assistance – preferably temporary – could be most effective. Prior to the election that autumn with its Conservative sweep, he began to indicate cautiously that the postwar circumstances confronting Britain, especially unemployment, had convinced him of the need for "safeguards."

Baldwin, supported by Churchill, rejected any general tariff (and hence any imperial tariff preference, as consistently pressed by Amery). He did, however, attempt a balancing act between protectionists and free traders, putting a review process in place while at the same time pledging that he did not regard possible temporary safeguards as a wedge to ease the way into full tariff protection. His cautious approach was reflected in the appointment in January 1925 of a cabinet committee to consider the rules by which the Board of Trade would grant an enquiry into any application for protection in the face of excessive or unfair foreign competition and whether the applicant was an "efficient industry" of national importance and whether unemployment resulted from the imports. A few "safeguarding" tariffs were instituted, and some rationalization and consolidation did take place, but it was really only after the disappointing 1932 Ottawa imperial economic conference that the British government moved to establish an Iron and Steel Board to monitor further reforms of the industry and "supervise prices in the national interest." To that end, it invited the steel federation to propose plans for a more internationally competitive industry.

Dorman Long for one needed renovation. When Greenwood became its chairman, it was near bankruptcy and in pressing need of reorganization. His election to the chairmanship was fortuitous. Early in the same year, 1934, a Defence Requirements Committee had reported to the cabinet. Although not all the committee's rearmament recommendations were fully implemented in light of economic and political restraints, the rejuvenation of the steel industry was an undeniable priority (steel production had dropped from 9.6 million tons in 1929 to a low of 5.2 million tons in 1931). Within a year, Greenwood could share with Mackenzie King his satisfaction at the pace of the economic recovery of the United Kingdom, citing as an example Dorman Long and its several subsidiaries where the total number of employees had been increased by ten thousand to a total of thirty thousand.[23]

Over the decade of the 1930s, Greenwood's corporate directorships grew to seventeen (for half of which he was chairman), including Lewis Berger and Sons Ltd, Montagu Burton ("the Fifty Shilling Tailor"), the Law Debenture Corporation, and, incongruously, the Agricultural Mortgage Company of Palestine. All of these appointments added to whatever income he had from the bar, necessary to meet the considerable expenses of a baron and a dame seeking to live well at 52 Grosvenor Gardens. To further augment their income, Margo took up again an earlier interest in painting. Through a Brighton dealer she successfully sold her still lifes under the Dutch-sounding, gender-neutral name of "Van Margo."

Leo Amery's directorships also multiplied. In his fifties he joined the boards of Cammell Laird, Southern Railways, Goodyear Tyre and Rubber Company, Marks and Spencer, the Trust and Loan Company of Canada, several small mining companies active in Africa, and even the fledgling air service from Palestine to Cyprus. Unfortunately his financial circumstances, difficult at the best of times, were soured by the escalating misdemeanours of his elder son, John (Jack). After having been a constant problem at Harrow, Jack dropped out of school at the age of sixteen. At twenty, still a minor, he informed his parents that he was about to marry a twenty-two-year-old Piccadilly whore, Una Eveline Wing. The news reached Amery in late August 1932 at the Imperial Economic Conference in Ottawa, which he was attending as a self-appointed observer and a nuisance to ministers (neither he nor Beaverbrook had been invited). Bryddie, hitherto the indulgent mother, finally moved toward something approaching a decisive response. As her husband abandoned the Ottawa conference to hurry back to London, she appealed to her brother, a barrister and former Home Office minister, to prevent his nephew, still a minor, from marrying a woman well known to the London police as "a common prostitute who frequented the West End." When Greenwood successfully prevailed upon the Chelsea registry office to reject the application of a minor for a marriage licence, Jack and Una crossed to France. At Greenwood's request, the British Embassy in Paris instructed its consulates to ensure that Jack did not misrepresent his age in attempting to get a local marriage licence. Continuing their progress across Europe, Jack and Una were wed in Athens, the Greek Orthodox Church being ready to marry any adherents who had reached the age of sixteen.

Once back in France, Jack was arrested for theft from a diamond merchant in Athens. The Amerys continued to send money and to pay his legal expenses in Paris where two Greenwood sisters, his mother and his aunt Sadie Rodney, arrived to visit him in prison. Amery secured his son's release, but only after he had retained a leading Paris advocate and arranged through the embassy in Athens an expensive settlement with the aggrieved jeweller. The Amerys, the Greenwoods, and the Rodneys were appalled at Jack's behaviour, although not quite so much as they would have been if they had known that, clutching his inseparable teddy bear, he was earning occasional income as a male prostitute. Una, whose judgment in such matters can be relied upon, now defined her husband as a "sexual pervert" whose diversions included being beaten by other prostitutes (female) or having sex with another strumpet in front of her, or by Una in turn doing her bit with a compliant (male) customer in front of her husband and then servicing him. Greenwood, in attempting to help in the herculean task of placing his wayward nephew on the straight and narrow, prompted a rare offer of employment from Reuters, which Jack predictably declined. Greenwood then arranged for him to be employed in the Paris subsidiary of Berger Paints (of which Greenwood was then chairman).[24] That pedestrian activity lasted not two months before Jack and Una, with the teddy bear and a loaded revolver, resumed their wanderings across Europe, engaging in petty crimes and repeatedly begging from his parents money that they could ill afford.

19

House of Lords and the World
of Business, 1930–1948

As the introduction to this quest for the Greenwoods noted – and regretted – there is a dearth of material about their public and private lives during the 1930s and 1940s. Most of their papers were destroyed in the London Blitz, and Lady Greenwood destroyed other papers shortly before her death. As a result, a range of questions are left unanswered. For example, how often during those two decades did Viscount Greenwood attend the House of Lords? Early in the war, he and Lady Greenwood appear to have removed themselves from the London scene by spending long periods in the rather dreary Brighton. It is clear from the Lords Hansard that he seldom spoke, reflecting his vocal absence from the great debates of the day, but he did use the Lords for his own ends. He remained a liberal imperialist until his sudden death in 1948, but he did not speak in the Lords about the evolving Empire. There is no evidence that in his later years he corresponded with Churchill or Mackenzie King – or anyone else, for that matter – about Canada in the Empire, or, during the war, about the Canadian forces in Britain or, later, in Italy or Normandy or in northwestern Europe, or even about the general course of the war. He must have given substantial time to his several directorships, chiefly to the steel industry; but how close were his wartime relations with his brother-in-law Leo Amery, or with Beaverbrook, both of them in Churchill's cabinet, or with Vincent Massey, the Canadian high commissioner, who broadly shared Greenwood's life-long liberal imperial commitments?

Equally, what work, charitable or otherwise, did Margo Greenwood undertake before and during the war, building on her experiences during the First World War and its aftermath? She too does not appear to have had any contact with the large Canadian forces in the United

Kingdom, and there is, for example, no indication that she had any role in Alice Massey's Beaver Club (known irreverently by the troops as "Mother Massey's Hash House"). And there is no indication of how the widow Margo, distanced from three of her four children as well as from Canada, spent in London the twenty years between her husband's death and her own. Accordingly, what follows is necessarily a skeletal account of the Greenwoods' lives during the 1930s and 1940s, and in Margo's case, to 1968, based on the very limited papers remaining.

The economic environment of the 1930s in which both Greenwood and Amery sought increased income from corporate directorships remained difficult. Europe recovered only slowly from the worst of the Depression, and the political scene deteriorated. As Greenwood wrote to Mackenzie King in 1933, soon after Hitler became chancellor, "On the Continent hates and fears, and therefore, the shadow of war have made the outlook gloomy. I know Germany, Poland, Czecho-Slovakia, Austria, Hungary, and so forth, and we of the New World cannot understand the incredible hatreds that exist. Whatever the future may be, at this moment Hitler is a very god in Germany." Given his life-long commitment to a cooperative Empire, he added more optimistically, "One permanent effect of the Continental trouble is to more and more turn the eyes and interests of the people of this Island to our own Empire."[1]

In the 1920s and 1930s the successive National governments led by Ramsay MacDonald and the Conservative led by Stanley Baldwin struggled not only with forebodings about the ascent of Hitler and continuing economic problems including lagging British productivity, but also with what response should be made to mounting nationalism in India. As early as 1917, Edwin Montagu, the Asquithian Liberal secretary of state for India whom Lloyd George was courting, had publicly promised "responsible government" in India. The next year the controversial Montagu-Chelmsford report had duly envisaged "the progressive realization of responsible government in British India as an integral part of our Empire ... to the end that British India may attain its due place among our Dominions." India joined the Imperial conference, the British Empire delegation at Versailles, and, with the Dominions, the League of Nations.

During the 1920s the question of Dominion Home Rule for India was given new impetus by the increasing agitation among Indian nationalists, led pre-eminently by Gandhi and his non-cooperation campaign. In 1927 an Indian Statutory Commission was appointed by the Baldwin government, chaired by the Asquithian Liberal Sir John Simon (who had recently appeared for Newfoundland before the judicial committee of the Privy Council to win its case for its boundaries with Quebec). The royal commission included both Lord Strathcona's grandson and Clement Attlee, the future Labour prime minister. Without waiting for its report after its visit to India, the viceroy, Baldwin's close friend Lord Irwin (later Lord Halifax), outflanked it by declaring in October 1929 that "the natural issue of India's constitutional progress ... [is] the attainment of Dominion status." Following the report of the Simon royal commission in June 1930, a first Round-Table Conference of Indian and British representatives (but not Gandhi and the Congress Party) was convened in November 1930. So far so good, but Sir Samuel Hoare (the secretary of state for India from 1931) recognized that "the Conservative Party is obviously very worried about India and is terrified of a repetition of the Irish negotiations."[2] Baldwin succeeded with difficulty in winning his party's support for the promise of Dominion status for India, but it was not unanimous. Birkenhead, only weeks before his death in 1930, joined Churchill – and Baldwin's cousin, Rudyard Kipling – in condemning any idea of Dominion Home Rule, as he had done earlier in the case of Ireland. Of a like mind, Churchill at the end of January 1931 withdrew from the opposition front bench with the paradoxical result that "the Die-hards are [now] led by Winston Churchill, who gave Home Rule to Ireland."[3] Having famously ridiculed Gandhi as a "half-naked fakir," Churchill, supported by the "Indian Defence League" and the newspapers of Lord Rothemere (but not of Lord Beaverbrook), pressed on with his increasingly controversial opposition, rejecting as folly all ideas of responsible government, including Dominion Home Rule, while "India is a prey to fierce racial and religious dissensions and when the withdrawal of British protection would mean the immediate resumption of medieval wars."

Greenwood, however, joined other like-minded peers in supporting the government's white paper on India of 1931, based on the Simon commission and a second Round Table Conference (this time attended by Gandhi). In the face of Churchill's eloquent wrong-headedness, the Labourite MacDonald and the Conservative Baldwin cooperated throughout en route toward Dominion Home Rule for India, but only "when the [Indian] provinces, which should receive the widest autonomy as soon as possible, came together voluntarily to create a new federation – as had happened in Canada and Australia – should British control of India be gradually relinquished."[4] In addition to hearing vocal pro and con advocacy groups, a joint select committee, again under Simon, was struck "with the object of finding a suitable basis for the conversion of the present system of Government in India into a responsibly governed Federation of States and Provinces."[5] The idea was that full responsible government at the provincial level, with the cooperation of the princely states, would lead to an all-India federation with full Dominion status able to play a leading role in the British Commonwealth. Upon the return of the joint select committee from India, a third and final Round Table Conference was convened. J.C.C. Davidson, an influential MP on the committee, a former chairman of the Conservative Party, and Baldwin's faithful henchman,[*] recorded his impressions of his colleagues at the Round Table Conference: "I thought ... one of the ablest of all was the Aga Khan ... Among the British delegates those who stand out in my memory were Hamar Greenwood and Sam Hoare."[6]

As the constitutional debate about India continued with a joint select committee recommending in November 1934 greatly expanded responsible government for the provinces, Churchill was to denounce the proposed Dominion status as a "crime" with all the vigour and invective that only he could muster. In the end, his futile opposition over Indian reform added to his already entrenched reputation for irresponsibility and erratic exaggeration. However, his opposition did not make any easier the efforts of MacDonald and Baldwin – Indian constitutional reform had become that rare thing, a bipartisan policy – to define in detail what their governments through the 1930s had meant by Dominion status for India. To reassure the sceptical, progress toward responsible government in New Delhi would be only "by insensible degrees ... the way by which responsible government grew up in Canada."[7] If any one parliamentary passage can be seen as reflecting the alienation of Churchill and Greenwood, it is the five years or more of often bitter debate over India in which Greenwood, at Baldwin's request, played a valued supportive role among his fellow peers. Any lingering intimacy post-Ireland that Greenwood still had with Churchill had ended.

---

* Following public service as a colleague of John Anderson and later as private secretary to Bonar Law and Baldwin, Davidson became a member of Parliament and eventually chancellor of the Duchy of Lancaster. As a former chairman of the Conservative Party (1927–30) he promoted the appointment of Greenwood as treasurer in 1933. Greenwood in turn invited Davidson to join the board of Dorman Long. (Given Davidson's major land holdings and other interests in Argentina, the company found useful his frequent visits to Buenos Aires.)

Paradoxically, Amery in the House of Commons moved from having been an intransigent opponent of Dominion Home Rule for Ireland to proceeding in step with his brother-in-law as a protagonist of Dominion Home Rule for India. Beaverbrook, deeply engaged in his Empire Crusade, was more muted, but he did use his newspapers to support Indian constitutional initiatives, joining Greenwood and Amery in their conviction that Dominion status for India was the most promising way to hold the kingpin of the Empire in place.

In the midst of the prolonged India debate, Greenwood's commitment to the Conservative Party was further confirmed by his acceptance in 1933 of its treasurership, an unpaid job that few or no one wanted. Drawing upon his locus in the House of Lords, his corporate directorships, and his fundraising success for Gray's Inn, he remained treasurer for five years.*

Meanwhile, as a result of the work of the joint select committee and the three Round Table Conferences, a Government of India bill slowly made its way through Parliament. In its final form, the bill offered much less than originally foreseen by Montagu, Chelmsford, Irwin, MacDonald, and Baldwin, but far more than Churchill and his few score diehards could accept. As Robert Rhodes James has observed, it had "evoked more discussion than any measure since the Irish Home Rule bills ... Churchill stood in the forefront of the opposition to the bill, inside and outside parliament. As a sustained performance of skill and eloquence, it was one of his most remarkable efforts, but rarely can so much resource and ability have been squandered by a major personality for a cause that was so sadly ill-favoured by the facts of the case and the pace of events."[8] The internecine differences in the Conservative Party had also become more pronounced, leaving the coming younger members – Harold Macmillan, Alfred Duff Cooper, and Anthony Eden among them – yet more wary of Churchill, convinced as they were, in Macmillan's words, that "the majority of the Party regarded his attitude as reactionary and unrealistic."[9] Despite continuing uncertainties about what was really intended, the Government of India bill received

---

* Despite his various corporate responsibilities and his role as treasurer of the Conservative Party, Greenwood never forgot his early commitment to the radical MP John Burns. In sending eightieth birthday greetings in October 1938, he saluted his old parliamentary mentor: "Your great career is one of our fixed national assets" (Greenwood to Burns, 3 October 1938, British Library, 46304, f280).

third reading in June 1935 (before the Conservative electoral victory of that year), setting India, it was hoped, on the road to a federation of self-governing provinces. But as John Darwin has observed, "the real question was whether the 1935 Act would create the political conditions in which India would move towards voluntary participation in a Britannic community of self-governing states."[10]

Two months later, after royal assent to the Government of India Act, the Greenwoods spent a weekend with a grateful Baldwin at Chequers (from where Greenwood took care to write to Mackenzie King on Chequers letterhead). The legislation eventually proved to be too little and too late: as in the case of the Government of Ireland Act in 1914, world war in 1939 stopped its full implementation. Margo, however, exploited her husband's active role in the debates leading up to it to win for him an elevation in the peerage from baron to viscount. Her several letters to Baldwin in 1936 had their desired effect. Announced in the prime minister's list of 1 February 1937, Greenwood was reintroduced to the House of Lords as the Viscount Greenwood of Holbourne in the County of London (where stands Gray's Inn), sponsored by Lord Halifax, the former viceroy in India, and Lord FitzAlan, the final viceroy in Ireland (somewhat surprisingly, since FitzAlan had pursued a decidedly reactionary attitude to Indian constitutional reform).

Mackenzie King was prompt in his telegraphic congratulations (he made no mention of the Indian debates). In 1936, when King visited Geneva, Paris, and London in a cautious, covert, but, he believed, divinely inspired foray into foreign affairs, Greenwood took him to a dinner with Churchill, MacDonald, Simon, and the US ambassador, among others. Soon thereafter, the abdication of King Edward VIII and his announced intention to marry the twice-divorced Mrs Wallace Simpson, sensational events both, evoked a longer correspondence between King and Greenwood. In a letter to King of 23 January 1937, Greenwood condemned "this conspiracy (for conspiracy it certainly was)" of Churchill and a few others to form a "King's Party ... to try to down the Government." There is, however, no firm evidence that the infatuated Edward VIII condoned any such conspiratorial proceedings, although they certainly reduced further Churchill's waning reputation, Edward reassuring Baldwin, "I will never act on advice from anyone else." Greenwood was careful to add to Mackenzie King, "You will be gratified to know that your name came up early when the first issue was raised in re the morganatic marriage and S.B. [Baldwin] was greatly strengthened by your fine support."[11] The Church of England could not countenance the monarch's marriage to a divorcee;* accordingly, Edward VIII's younger brother, the Duke of York, was duly crowned King George VI in 1937.

In his reply of 7 March 1937 from a holiday in Virginia, Mackenzie King was more nuanced in his renewed felicitations about Greenwood's enhanced peerage. "You and Viscountess Greenwood would know ... how pleased I was to see you receive further recognition which raised you to a higher rank in the Peerage." But he could not resist adding, "Personally ... I should be happy to see the whole institution done away with altogether ... What pleases me most in the recognition you have been accorded is the fact that you have gained it wholly on your own, and having regard to what privilege in an Old World means against the greatest possible odds."[12] The bulk of Mackenzie King's letter from Virginia was, however, not on things regal or imperial but things American. He described to Greenwood how a few days before, he had "accepted the President's invitation to spend another night with him at the White House ... I had an exceptionally interesting and intimate talk with the President. We had tea pretty much by ourselves, dined and spent the evening together alone, and on the next morning I had a further talk with him while he was having his breakfast in bed. The whole visit was as informal as a day in the country with an old college friend might have been. The hours were profitable to us both and I am not without hope may be of service in a much larger way. I shall tell you of my talk when we meet."

Over the course of the 1930s, Greenwood sent Mackenzie King gifts of books, plum puddings, and a cabinet minister's scarlet despatch box, which, in thanking him, King described as "next to my Irish terrier, Pat, the most faithful sort of companion."[13] King also sent thanks for Greenwood's accounts of recent dinners of the Canada Club (even one for King's *bête noir*, the newly arrived high commissioner, Vincent Massey), but it was the threat of a second world war that was in the minds of both correspondents. During his dinner in London in October 1936 with Greenwood, Ramsay MacDonald, and Churchill, among others, much of the talk was about the increasingly aggressive and violent German Chancellor Adolf Hitler.

---

* The Statute of Westminster of 1931 required the assent of the parliaments of all the Dominions as well as of the United Kingdom "to any alteration in the law touching the Succession to the Throne." The Irish Free State took the occasion simply to remove the crown from its constitution.

With the coronation of King George VI, both Baldwin and MacDonald retired from active political life. Neville Chamberlain, who had been Baldwin's chancellor of the exchequer, became prime minister late in May 1937. During the imperial conference of May-June (the first since the Ottawa debacle of 1932) that accompanied the coronation, Greenwood arranged a dinner of the Canada Club for Mackenzie King and Lapointe and with Massey and Malcolm MacDonald, the secretary of state for the Dominions (and from 1940, the British high commissioner in Ottawa). The dinner was in King's view "a very fine one," Greenwood being "exceedingly generous and friendly in his introduction ... As he said, there was cause for one's feelings being tinged with emotion as we recall our association in university days [and] the position that we have each attained since that time."[14] However, at the imperial conference itself, King, beset as always by feelings of insecurity, in his own estimate failed to make his sought-for "unforgettable impression" with his ramblings about the Empire. With his eye on isolationist Quebec, he rejected any active involvement either in League of Nations sanctions or coordinated Commonwealth military preparations as well as advanced commitments of any sort. He enthusiastically applauded the policy of Chamberlain in attempting to appease Hitler's ambitions by concession. However, he did add that, *pace* the isolationist O.D. Skelton, the under-secretary of state for external affairs, if Britain's very survival became threatened by another war with Germany, the Parliament of Canada would undoubtedly endorse the country's participation.

One month later in early July 1937, Greenwood speculated that King "must have had a most interesting time ... in your visit to Hitler [the previous month]. I am sure the Prime Minister here [Neville Chamberlain] would be very glad if you would send him your impressions."[15] King did send his first impressions, but it was after months of reflection that he recorded complacently in his diary that Hitler was a spiritualist, as he was himself: "He has a vision to which he is being true – his devotion to his mother – that Mother's spirit is I am certain his guide and no one who does not understand this relationship, the worship of the highest purity in a mother, can understand the power to be derived therefrom or the guidance. I believe the world will yet come to see a very great man ... [He] will rank some day with Joan of Arc among the deliverers of his people."[16] King's fulsome praise for Hitler echoed the obsequious comments of Lloyd George after his visit to the German chancellor the year before: "I only wish we had a man of his supreme quality at the head of affairs in our country to-day."[17] King, having satisfied himself that Hitler was both a mystic and the heroic deliverer of his people, redoubled his admiration for Neville Chamberlain. Baldwin had not taken up a recommendation of King, a great believer in personal diplomacy, that he too visit Hitler in Germany; but Chamberlain appeared far more receptive. King marvelled "at the splendid manner in which [Chamberlain] measures up to the exceptional obligations of his high office. He has my best wishes and most sympathetic understanding in all that he has undertaken. When you [Greenwood] are again talking with him, tell him, at all costs, to keep the Empire out of war ... If the British Empire can be kept out of war, it will be able to take care of itself whatever the situations are ..."[18]

As the threat of war mounted, a restless and frustrated Amery remained on the backbenches of the House of Commons, but Sir John Anderson, home from the governorship Bengal and having declined the office of high commissioner in Palestine, made an unusual transition from senior public servant to cabinet minister via the House of Lords as Viscount Waverley, first as lord privy seal (being among other things responsible for organizing the protection of civilians from widely feared air raids, the conviction being that, as Baldwin told the House of Commons, "the bomber will always get through").

As appeasement faltered and rearmament accelerated, and as Greenwood was making his way satisfactorily in the corporate world, the endless antics of his nephew, Jack Amery, again intruded. In a habitual alcoholic haze, Jack and Una continued their wanderings about Europe largely at the expense of Jack's parents (and hence indirectly at that of the late Peter Larkin). Greenwood, again at the urging of his sister Bryddie, offered Jack employment with yet another of the firms of which he was a director, but Jack remained uninterested in any regular employment.[19] Instead, from France, as a now ardent, self-proclaimed anti-communist, he told anyone who would listen that at the root of all Europe's troubles were the Jews (despite being himself, in the later definition of Lord Haw-Haw, a "quarter Yid"). The three-year Spanish Civil War was then deeply dividing Europe. Those to the left of centre supported the republicans, as did Stalin; those to the right supported Franco, as did Hitler and Mussolini. It was with Franco, eventually on the winning side in Spain, that Jack lined up – and profited from running arms to his forces. His increasingly suspicious activities, personal as well as political, more and more undermined his mother's spirits. At the time, Barbara Pym, a popular novelist and friend of Jack's brother

Julian, modelled a gentle and reticent lead character in *Crampton Hodnet* (written in 1939) on Bryddie, "a charming [but] rather pathetic woman, lost, as if her life were without purpose." Greenwood and Sadie provided their sister with what solace they could.

Chamberlain's government is remembered today chiefly for its forlorn efforts to appease the unappeasable Hitler, the League of Nations having become ineffectual without the active support of Britain and France, the lack of collective response to the aggressions of Japan in China and Italy in Abyssinia, and the continuing absence of the United States. In the face of German rearmament, Chamberlain did, however, belatedly accelerate the rearmament hesitantly introduced by Baldwin in 1935. The crucial steel industry was accordingly further if belatedly expanded in accordance with government planning, including a provision for it to pass under direct government control in the event of war. One of the minor acts of Chamberlain's government was to accept, along with the Dominions, a republican constitution for Ireland, devised by de Valera, that led to its exit from the Commonwealth, and to de Valera's remarkable decision to remain neutral in the war against Hitler, that arch-enemy of self-determination for small nations so long advocated by de Valera.

In 1938, Hitler's expansionist ambitions and racial madness joined with the convolutions of Stalin, Mussolini, and Franco to split Britain and Parliament between appeasers and rearmers. Some saw Hitler as the looming threat to Europe, but others who saw him as understandably determined to undo the excesses and injustices of the Treaty of Versailles welcomed him as the bulwark against the spread of communism from the Soviet Union. Greenwood, with responsibilities for the revival of the iron and steel industry, was supporting rearmament. He was, however, cautious in expressing public scepticism of appeasement. "World peace is our only hope, world war our certain destruction."[20] In 1935, two years after Hitler became chancellor, he vaguely supported appeasement in a speech to the Society of British Advertisers (Amery was president of the society, fecund ground in which to seek additional corporate directorships).

With mounting misgivings about Hitler and the growing possibility of war as the League of Nations faded away, the demands on Greenwood at the renewed Dorman Long, and at the Iron and Steel Federation of which he was elected chairman, became such that he resigned as Conservative Party treasurer in February 1938, less than a year after

Neville Chamberlain had succeeded Baldwin as prime minister.* In his letter of resignation at the end of his five years as treasurer, Greenwood assured Chamberlain, "You know you can always count on me to do everything in my power to support you and your Government and our Party."²¹ Brendan Bracken, the Irish Roman Catholic who was long Churchill's confidant and his wartime minister of information, gave Mackenzie King a different account of Greenwood's departure from the Conservative treasurership. According to King, Bracken recalled, "Greenwood had been very brave in the administration of affairs in Ireland … he had been made Treasurer of the Conservative Party, but … they had to change that because he was a prohibitionist. They found that as soon as he came to collect funds they all fell off from the liquor interests. They had, therefore, to make way for someone else."²²

Neville Chamberlain replied in gratitude to Greenwood. But his mind was naturally on his desperate efforts, with widespread support in Britain and of the Dominions, to avoid the horrors of another world war. Amery, however, with the bitter India controversy now set aside, joined Churchill and the troublesome young men in the House of Commons as an outspoken critic of appeasement and an advocate of accelerated rearmament. Anthony Eden having resigned as foreign secretary, Mackenzie King rejoiced in the apparent success of Chamberlain's final effort at Munich in September 1938 to appease Hitler. The reassurance that perhaps all might still be well in Europe was short lived. Austria was seized, Czechoslovakia dismembered, Poland threatened, and unexpectedly a German-Soviet non-aggression pact concluded.

In late February 1938, the Greenwoods escaped the London winter by embarking for Jamaica where they had met twenty-eight years before (and thereby happily avoiding a Pilgrims' dinner for the new and defeatist US ambassador Joseph Kennedy). One year before, Lloyd George

---

* The demands made upon Greenwood as chairman of the Iron and Steel Federation during two terms were many and various as the industry responded to rearmament. Happily, they did not include participation in the Anglo-German trade initiatives of his brother-in-law Wilfrid Ashley. As early as October 1926, almost seven years before Hitler became chancellor, Ashley and two other Conservative MPS organized an Anglo-German economic conference at Broadlands in Kent, the home of Ashley's first wife, Maudie Cassel. In 1934 Greenwood was not yet chairman of the Iron and Steel Federation when it sought cooperative arrangements with the expanding German steel industry as part of "economic appeasement." As late as March 1939 Greenwood declined a visit to Germany with a British business delegation, the president of the federation instead attending.

and Dame Margaret – with Frances Stevenson in the background – had also stayed at the Constant Spring Hotel near Kingston, but whether by plan or coincidence neither the Greenwoods nor Stevenson record. Six months later, in September, the Greenwoods paid what would be their last visit together to Canada. They sailed with their two younger children, Deborah and Eric, on the new and largest CPR liner, the *Empress of Britain,* to Quebec City. From there they travelled by train to Banff to spend a holiday with Greenwood's youngest sister, Margery ("Ulla"), and her Devonshire-born husband, Major Frederick Cross of Lethbridge, an irrigation engineer with the CPR and, like Margo, a gifted amateur painter.

Three years before, at the prompting of the long-serving vice-chancellor and now chancellor, Sir William Mulock, the Senate had offered an honorary doctorate to the former student agitator, acknowledging implicitly that all was now forgiven and forgotten.* Greenwood was, however, unable to accept the invitation until 1938. Mackenzie King, plagued with sciatica, sent his regrets, to be read at the special convocation on 2 September: "We are great personal friends ...Viscount Greenwood and I were of the same year at the University. We were friends as undergraduates. In the years which have since elapsed, our lives have touched each other at many points and in many places alike in the Old Country and in our own ... it is a recognition well merited by his fine career and the high place which he holds in the public life of our day."[23] Conferring the honorary doctorate, the president of the university proclaimed of Greenwood, "His love for Canada is unabated. He is always a potent spokesman for Canada in Britain. He believes in her splendid destiny within the Empire's orbit. He believes in the Empire itself as one of the greatest agencies for good will and peace throughout the world. He and we alike are sure that, whatever may have been or may be the errors made by Britain, the world's best hope rests on her."[24]

In his reply, Greenwood reflected the growing unease of many in the United Kingdom at the possibility, even the inevitability, of a second devastating world war. The greater unity of the British Empire could be the only certain response to the threat of the German and Italian dictators. He did, however, nod in the direction of Mackenzie King when he

---

* William Mulock served for a record term of twenty years as chancellor of the University of Toronto. It was in his then capacity of vice-chancellor (held concurrently with the postmaster-generalship in Laurier's government) that in 1895 he had bestowed a bachelor of arts degree on Greenwood.

added, "whether the Dominions will help and the extent to which they will help is for them to decide."[25] Separately, in a speech to the Canadian Manufacturers' Association in Toronto, Greenwood reviewed Chamberlain's efforts to appease a fanatical racist and militarist dictator, but some in the audience believed that they detected "just a suggestion of hesitation"[26] in his praise for Chamberlain's futile strivings. Clearer was his repeated call for the unity of the Empire in the face of Hitler's ambitions. In Whitby, Greenwood added the rare comment that "Ireland will find a happy way out of her difficulties just as you have done here many times, but ... the way out must be found by Irishmen."[27]

To Kingsmere near Ottawa the four Greenwoods came to visit an ailing Mackenzie King, who recorded in his diary on 6 September, "I was rather deeply touched by the way he [Greenwood] spoke ... I know they value my friendship." Then King echoed his classmate: "Greenwood feels a great pride in the fact that each of us has played quite remarkable roles in the affairs of the Empire since we left University; perhaps no two men of any class in the Toronto University have been as prominent in the political affairs affecting Canada ..." King, who was convinced that he was fulfilling a divinely ordained role in influencing both Hitler and Chamberlain for peace, added, "We had been talking about my visit to Hitler and what I had said to him about ... not to be tempted to acts of destruction, but to carry on with his works for the people ... He [Greenwood] said that he knew my visit to Germany had done great good. I told him to tell Chamberlain by all means to keep on keeping the nations out of war; that he was adopting the Christian attitude of non-resistance in the face of great provocation. That that was appealing strongly to the people and that if action were precipitated the Empire might be torn into shreds."[28]

Six days later Mackenzie King received a letter from Greenwood in Quebec just before embarking, thanking "My dear Rex" for his kindnesses during the visit. "We've kept in step and in stride for forty-five years," but he added gloomily, "We're on the edge of cursed war, forced on us and the world by the modern Goth ... Thank God, the issue is vividly clear and the faith and the hopes are with us and with us alone."[29] (Presumably Greenwood had already written off France.) His letter arrived as King was listening on his Kingsmere neighbour's shortwave radio (he did not have one himself) to a speech by Hitler. "As I opened it [Greenwood's letter], my eyes fell on the words 'Thank God, the issue is vividly clear and the faith and the hopes are with us and with us alone.' I felt that was true but believed that it would be worked out in God's way, possibly by the avoidance even yet of a world war. The sentence which had preceded was the statement that we were on the edge of war, forced upon us by the modern 'Goth' – the ruthless pagan 'Goth.'" Greenwood's letter is one of deep affection and pride in our years of friendship. I was glad to be able to send a direct word to Chamberlain."[30] The following month Greenwood would have been gratified by a diary entry of King's that may reflect their conversations in Ottawa. "There was more real freedom in the British Commonwealth of Nations and a richer inheritance. This I truly believe. We have all the freedom we want and are strengthened by being part of a greater whole, with kindred aims, ideals and institutions."[31] Greenwood could not have said it better.

In the new year, 1939, Greenwood chaired a Canada Club dinner in London in honour of the former Canadian Prime Minister R.B. Bennett, now British domiciled. He also informed Mackenzie King that Stanley Baldwin, upon the urging of the Canadian high commissioner, Vincent Massey, and himself, would shortly visit Canada – his third visit in twelve years – to lecture at the University of Toronto and to receive an honorary doctorate from McGill University. Despite the contempt for Baldwin of Churchill and Amery (among others), Greenwood added, "Our friend is not a rich man and I hope there will not be any expenses for himself or party that he will be expected to pay ... it would be a real hardship to a very great man and a very good friend of Canada to ask him to bear one penny of expense ... Massey is approaching Beatty on the question ... a man of distinction of Baldwin ought to have the best private [rail] car in Canada and every attention from the moment he leaves England until he returns."[32] Baldwin's speeches in Canada did something to reassure Mackenzie King that Armageddon might yet somehow be avoided, although he concluded them with a declaration that Britain was ready, if necessary, to fight Nazism.

In parallel, Mackenzie King recognized that the visit during May and June of King George VI and Queen Elizabeth, the first of a reigning monarch, was part of a larger effort to foster imperial unity in the face of the Nazi threat. Greenwood, in the first transatlantic airmail, extolled the visit as "simply wonderful." He hailed Mackenzie King's welcome to the monarch as helping "to plant a new milestone in the historical development of our Empire." King George recalled for the Canadian Parliament his father's definition of the Commonwealth as a "free association of nations enjoying common principles of government, a common attachment to ideals of peace and freedom, and bound together by a common allegiance to the Crown."[33] In describing the royal visit,

Mackenzie King modestly assured Greenwood that "No event in our history has left a finer impression ... the final word on the position Canada has attained of equality of status not less with the United Kingdom than other nations of the British Commonwealth." Only three weeks before the declaration of war on 3 September 1939, he hoped that the "Our Royal Visit may not be without its permanent effect for good in the international, not less than the national arena."[34] Two weeks later, he sent a message asking Chamberlain "to strongly urge" the kng to appeal directly to Hitler to give more time for further negotiation. A fortnight later, after a parliamentary vote, Canada was also at war and three months later the First Canadian Division, however untrained and ill-equipped, disembarked in Britain.

In December 1939, three months into the war, Greenwood became chairman (having again visited Egypt with Margo in February 1939) of the Anglo-Egyptian Chamber of Commerce, formed partly in recognition of the need to promote exports to Egypt to help pay for British imports. Ever the optimist, he told the founding meeting, "It is probable that never at any previous time were political relations between Great Britain and Egypt more friendly, nor was there a closer spirit of co-operation than at present."[35] His optimism was again to the fore when he reported to the fiftieth annual general meeting of Dorman Long in 1939 that it had flourished since the reorganization begun in 1934, the year he had become chairman. Its 40,000 employees, he told its 28,000 shareholders, were working flat out in Britain, Argentina, and South Africa (as Wade and Dorman). With the industry under the overall direction of the government-appointed Steel Controllers, Dorman Long was making an enormous – if belated – contribution to Britain's rearmament, although as chairman of the Iron and Steel Federation, Greenwood told one of Chamberlain's ministers of his concern at the continuing errors and confusions of the government. As an example, "if the Government had come direct to the big steelmakers, including Dorman Long, the aircraft factories might have been finished three months earlier."[36] In his speech to the Dorman Long annual meeting, Greenwood dwelt not upon the now-confidential levels of steel production but, entirely in keeping with his life-long convictions, spoke instead about the potentials of the Empire: "I fervently hope that the great economic unity of the British Empire, reinforced by the concentration of all its spiritual and material forces to win the war, will be held together for all time as a great constructive instrument for good in world affairs."[37] His report to shareholders for 1939 was the last wartime speech that he made to a Dorman Long annual meeting. Details of production being confidential, his wartime reports were limited to such pedestrian matters as the amount of the company's contribution to the employees' pension fund, although later in the war it became known that its production of steel had reached a record 1.5 million tons annually.[*]

With the end of the "phoney war" in May 1940 following the invasion of Norway and Denmark and the collapse of France and the Low Countries, Amery reflected the darkening mood of the House of Commons by dramatically challenging Chamberlain, "Depart, I say, and let us have done with you. In the name of God, go!" Amidst the dramatic parliamentary debates and Churchill's inspiring pledge as prime minister as of 10 May 1940 to prosecute the war to a victorious conclusion, Greenwood wrote to "My dear Jimmy" (Sir James Dunn), "Max [Beaverbrook] is working with a good will and unanimity that is a tribute to his personal way of doing things and his fine drive in organisation. Winston, of course, is the civilised world's great hope and sure shield. He enjoys the greatest confidence of all parties and persons throughout the Empire, and I think the English-speaking world [i.e., the United States]. We are united here as never before and the tide of resistance and the will to victory is growing every day. In the production of men and materiel we have passed all estimates and in the air and on the sea we can more than hold our own whatever happens. Believe me, everybody is heartened beyond words in this old country at the response of Canada and the other Dominions ... You and I, my dear Jimmy, have marched together for over thirty years and I hope will keep marching on through the war and after. I can't write to many men as I write to you." He added a yet more personal note: "if anything happens to either of us I know I can count on you to keep a friendly eye on my children."[38] Greenwood sent a parallel letter to Mackenzie King, which King in turn noted to Dunn: "I am not surprised that the thought of the future of his young and splendid family should be much in the thoughts of both Greenwood and Lady Greenwood at a time of peril."[39] Deborah was presumably not included in Greenwood's immediate paternal solicitude: she had joined the Women's Auxiliary Air Force (WAAF) in 1940s as – in her father's words – "an efficient young officer." That same year she married a future

---

[*] Decoy flares were placed across the nearby Cleveland moors, successfully diverting German bombers from Dorman Long steel mills, although frequent air raid warnings did disrupt the even flow of steel production.

RAF group captain, Patrick de László, the fourth of five sons of the fashionable Anglo-Hungarian portrait painter Philip de László. David, the
intellectually disabled elder Greenwood son, had been banished to
rural England in the care of a farm family. How Angela (married since
November 1937 to Edward Dudley Delevingne) spent the war is not
known, but Eric/Michael had a brief if inglorious flutter in the Royal
Corps of Signals (the Army at that time was not tolerant of flamboyant
homosexuals).

As Churchill was forming his wartime government, Greenwood
wrote him a fulsome letter of congratulations. In his acting capacity
as president of the Iron and Steel Federation, he recommended to
Churchill to keep the steel industry veteran Sir Andrew Duncan as
president of the Board of Trade (where he had been appointed in
January 1940 by Chamberlain); to move Sir John Reith from the BBC
to the Air Ministry; his fellow Canadians Beaverbrook or Beverley
Baxter to the Ministry of Information; Ernest Bevin to the Ministry
of Supply; "and to keep Amery in mind."[40] Churchill did appoint
Beaverbrook to his war cabinet as minister of aircraft production, and
Amery, the diehard over Ireland but the liberal over India, as, paradoxically, secretary of state for India. But if Greenwood in his recommendations to Churchill was in fact trailing his own coattails from the
House of Lords, he was unsuccessful. Churchill found nothing in his
new government for him. The deep differences between Churchill
and Greenwood aroused by the India debates of the 1930s persisted.
In chairing a Pilgrims' farewell dinner for Lord Halifax, the former
viceroy and foreign secretary and the new ambassador to Washington,
Greenwood sounded like his brother-in-law Amery in advocating the
early implementation of British reform in India.

Greenwood worked with Vincent Massey (who with his wife had in
the immediate pre-war years been especially hospitable to Deborah
Greenwood), in helping to arrange for the safety of other, less privileged children. Through the National Council of Women in Toronto
and later the Children's Overseas Reception Board in London, a total of
five thousand children were evacuated to the safety of Canada. (The
program was later terminated in face of the expanding threat of U-boat
attack.) As president of the British Iron and Steel Federation for a second time and chairman of its emergency committee in 1940, Greenwood
announced the donation by the industry of eighty thousand steel air-
raid shelters, each with a capacity of five persons. The shelters were to

be distributed to local authorities under the guidance of the Home Secretary John Anderson working with Warren Fisher who was "Special Commissioner for Organizing Services and Clearance." Soon there were 1.5 million such "Anderson shelters."

As for the tireless Beaverbrook, there appears to have been little contact between him and Greenwood (any more than between Beaverbrook and his lonely near neighbour, R.B. Bennett). Beaverbrook, first minister of aircraft production and later of supply, had little time for anything but his ministerial responsibilities and for his later campaign for more aid to the Soviet Union. At the end of the war, however, he did single out Dorman Long as the "firm responsible for supervising and co-ordinating all the building operations connected with the Mulberries," the two artificial harbours on the Normandy coast that had required two million tons of steel and concrete to ensure the crucial supply of food, ammunition, and other stores to the Allied armies fighting their way inland from the beaches in June and July 1944. With the growing popularity of the Labour Party, Beaverbrook could not resist adding that whereas the socialists had pointed to the Mulberries as a triumph of public enterprise, anyone could see that they were clearly a triumph of private enterprise, thanks to Dorman Long.

Amidst his wartime iron and steel responsibilities in the north of England, Greenwood did not meet with Mackenzie King on his first wartime visit to London in August 1941 (a fortnight after Viscount Greenwood had sponsored Viscount Bennett in his introduction to the House of Lords). Amidst the official secrecy of King's visit, the Greenwoods did not know that he was in London, but he left for them a framed, autographed photograph. Once King was back in Ottawa, Greenwood sent him a telegram saluting his visit as "a bracing factor in Empire war effort."[41]

Greenwood and Mackenzie King saw much more of each other during King's second wartime visit to London in late April 1944, in the aftermath of the decisive Soviet victories and on the eve of the Normandy landings. Greenwood called upon King the first morning of his visit, knowing exactly what would please his old classmate to hear upon arrival. A much gratified King recorded in his diary that Greenwood had reported that "Churchill had been immensely impressed at the intimacy of the friendship between the President [Roosevelt] and myself. [Churchill] Questioned him [Greenwood] as to how we had become such friends. Said it had made a profound impression on him ... [Greenwood] Said that Churchill ... and one or two others he named were all strong boosters of mine and all converts, but that [Viscount] Bennett was not … Greenwood said that it was quite apparent that [Bennett] having been Prime Minister once, he could never forgive [me] for having beaten him. I said: Of course, I have spoiled his career, and Meighen's career, and they cannot get over that."[42] The account by the teetotaller Greenwood of the alcoholic haze surrounding the Chanak imbroglio[43] would have accorded in King's mind with his further comment that Churchill still "does not understand the Dominions as separate nations" (echoing Amery's observation of 1942, "He has no sort of sympathy with the Dominion point of view").[44] Greenwood hailed King's speech in the long gallery at Westminster following the "splendid introduction Winston gave you" and conveyed to him Smuts's comment that it was "really first class."[45] In turn, King characterized Greenwood's introduction of him at a Canada Club dinner on 28 May as "exceedingly clever."

Greenwood's wartime encounters with Lloyd George were few. In the New Year's Honours List of 1945, Lloyd George finally accepted Churchill's nomination to the House of Lords as Earl Lloyd-George of Dwyer and Viscount Gwynedd. Upon Lloyd George's death three months later, Greenwood spoke in the Lords for the first time since his elevation to a viscountcy ten years before. On 28 March 1945 he praised his former leader – and his wife's former lover. He had little reason to be grateful to Lloyd George, given the way that he had used him, but he did recall, "I knew him well since 1895, when I spoke on a platform [in Wales] to unify the Empire … and scores of times on platforms in different parts of the realm." Perhaps with himself in mind, Greenwood added hyperbolically that the resignation of Lloyd George in 1922 was "one of the most unfortunate things that ever happened … it is one of the profoundest regrets and disasters in the history of the country and Empire that the rigidity of Party politics and other reasons prevented that great asset from ever becoming an instrument for good in this country, in the Empire and in the world."[46]

In the course of the war, Greenwood's life and especially that of his brother-in-law became even more adversely affected by Jack Amery's ever more reckless behaviour in occupied Europe. He drifted on to final disaster, driving his mother into near madness and imposing upon Greenwood and his sister Sadie Rodney (at whose wedding in 1922 Jack had been ring bearer) emotional demands that they had difficulty in sustaining. In 1940 Una abandoned her husband in Vichy, France, and managed to return to England. Continuing his pronounced predilection, Jack then went through a sort of marriage ceremony with a French harlot, Jeanine Barde, undeterred by the fact that in doing so he became a polygamist (when she later died, he married a third strumpet, Michelle Thomas). He remained in Vichy, where he worked with the ardent fascist and anti-Semite Jacques Doriot. The German authorities, under the general direction of Foreign Minister Joachim von Ribbentrop, began to take a pronounced interest in Jack as the pro-Hitler son of a half-Jewish British cabinet minister. Those who had earlier controlled P.G. Wodehouse – whom Jack knew well – now turned their attentions to him. Following the examples of the Anglo-Irish traitor William Joyce ("Lord Haw-Haw") and one or two others, Jack began a series of broadcasts to Britain on 19 November 1942 identifying Hitler as the one sure bulwark against both the spread of communism and the Jewish conspiracy to rule the world. The Amerys, Greenwoods, and Rodneys were all deeply disconcerted and profoundly apprehensive, the distraught Bryddie refusing to believe that the venomous voice on the wireless was that of her beloved elder son.

The next day, Beaverbrook and Robert Bruce Lockhart, then chairman of the Political Warfare Executive, discussed "young John Amery, Leo Amery's son, who is now broadcasting for the Germans and doing 'Haw-Haw' stuff for them, anti-Semitism, etc. He is a young man of no moral backbone whatsoever who has been in many scrapes. Everyone sorry for the father who in this case may have to pay politically for the sins of the son." The following day they listened to Jack again do "a pro-Nazi broadcast from Berlin, the theme being that we were being deceived by the Jews."[47] Rebecca West, who subsequently covered Jack's postwar trial for the *New Yorker*, summed up his treason: "In 1942, where it was becoming obvious that the Allies had at least a chance of winning, he [paradoxically] began to broadcast from Berlin. In 1943, when the Allies' position was improving daily, he went into a camp of British internees at St. Denis, near Paris, and attempted [in vain to raise among them] an anti-Bolshevik Free Corps to fight with the Germans against the Russians. This is the classic type of treachery ... Sir Roger Casement committed it [in Ireland] during the 1914–1918 war and was hanged for it. In 1944, when it was practically certain that the Axis was defeated, the poor young idiot travelled all over Europe, visiting Norway, France, Yugoslavia, and Belgium."[48] Amidst Jack's wanderings, local MI6 agents reported regularly to London on his treason. Near the end of the war, MI5 followed him as he made his way from Germany into northern Italy.

There in some obscure way Mussolini hoped to make use of him in his efforts to escape from the ring of partisans rapidly closing around him.

On the shores of Lake Como, partisans handed Jack over to MI5 agents and British military police, who flew him to London to stand trial for treason. The family hoped that he might claim Spanish citizenship (from his gun-running days for Franco) or plead insanity, but neither idea succeeded. Throughout the autumn, the increasingly frantic Bryddie, comforted by her sister and brother as best they could, wrote to the home secretary, pleading for mercy, as well as going to the court and later to the prison to see her son. By then Greenwood and even Amery no longer shared her desperate conviction that Jack might yet be saved from the gallows, but Greenwood did undertake at her urging a direct appeal to the prime minister. (It was a chilling echo of the vain plea made by the French mother at Trouville in 1919.) On 30 November, at the rather unlikely venue of a dinner of the Pilgrims, Greenwood, acting as chairman in the absence of Lord Derby, had the prime minister on his right. He raised the possibility of a prison term for his nephew instead of the death sentence, asking Attlee whether it was not "time to leave off killing people for what are crimes of opinion and not of action."[49] At Amery's request, his old friend Smuts also appealed to Attlee for clemency. But it was to no avail. On 18 December, Alfred Duff Cooper, who as a Conservative member of Parliament had been with Amery one of the most outspoken opponents of pre-war appeasement and was now ambassador to France, noted sorrowfully in his diary, "I ran into poor little Leo Amery who was looking distraught with misery. He muttered something to me about his misfortunes and I, like a fool, could think of nothing to say but that I had just been to the wedding of Bobbety's [Lord Cranborne's] son – and *his* son to be hanged tomorrow!"[50] Jack, having pleaded guilty to all charges, was hanged, a few weeks before the even more notorious "Lord Haw-Haw." Four months later, the Amerys travelled to Greece seeking in vain for some diversion from their grief. The British ambassador noted that Bryddie "was a very nice person [but] obviously completely broken by the awful tragedy of her son of whom she talks a lot." Amery in a different way never recovered.* Churchill had stood by him throughout his long

---

* Leo Amery later attempted in a pamphlet his own apologia for his son's treason: "John Amery: An Explanation." Amidst the virulent anti-communism of the Cold War, Beverley Baxter passed over Amery's treason and wrote in *Maclean's* magazine of 1 October 1955,

personal ordeal, but in the Labour sweep of 1945, Amery was defeated, leaving office with few resources. He declined a peerage, thereby keeping the House of Commons open for his war veteran son Julian's political ambitions. Amery never returned to Parliament before his death ten years later. (Bryddie lingered on to age ninety-five, dying in 1975.)

Greenwood continued in his directorships during the war, adding the Phoenix Assurance Company and, with Amery, the Trust and Loan Company of Canada. In 1942, Brazilian Traction, Light and Power, the complex Canadian corporation, had deemed it useful to have another director resident in London, especially one who could, among other things, help keep an eye on its investments in fascist but neutral Spain. Before the First World War, James Dunn had been active in the financing of the Toronto-based Brazilian Traction's projects on three continents. With its support, he merged his Société internationale d'énergie hydro-électrique and several smaller companies into one of its many subsidiaries, the Barcelona Traction, Light and Power Company. Thirty years later, in 1946, Greenwood and a fellow director and former president of Barcelona Traction, Sir Edward Peacock (the eminent Canadian financier who was a director of Barings, the CPR, Hudson's Bay, and Sun Life as well as the Bank of England), joined in seeking the help of the Canadian prime minister to fend off friends of Franco who cast themselves as altruistic Spanish nationalists in attempting to force the liquidation of various long-standing British investments and the Canadian-controlled Barcelona Traction. Greenwood was clear in his appeal to Mackenzie King: "Franco and his plutocratic backers, [including] Juan Marsh, are planning to seize by forced liquidation in Spanish courts." Greenwood argued passionately that "this magnificent company, founded by Canadians" must be kept Canadian.[51] Barcelona Traction was not. After prolonged legal battles, it eventually paid its homage to Catalonia.[*]

"The realist or the cynic – often the same person – might say that John Amery was merely ahead of his times."

[*] The fate of Barcelona Traction was not in fact finally decided until 1970. Peacock's presidency had "by no means straightened the twisted affairs of the troubled corporation and although its power-generating system was eventually placed in operation, European and North American courtrooms were to echo to the sounds of squabbling Barcelona Traction investors until 1970 when the International Court in the Hague finally delivered control of the company into Spanish hands" (McDowall, *The Light*, 212). Brazilian Traction later became Brascan and later still Brookfield Asset Management.

As a director of Montague Burton, the Tailor of Taste, Greenwood attempted in the summer of 1946 to assist from London its highly successful founder in his first postwar visit to North America "for the purpose of investigating the progress made in the [clothing] industry since his last visit in 1938." Tip Top Tailors in Toronto was an especial destination, Burton describing its "magnificent tailoring temple on the [Lake Shore] Boulevard." But if Burton had ambitions of investing in the industry in North America, the British Treasury put an end to them; in the immediate postwar years, it was not prepared to release scarce hard currency on a large scale.[52]

As a vice-president of the Pilgrims, Greenwood became the chairman in early 1946 of its Roosevelt memorial committee. The treasurer was Sir Campbell Stuart of Montreal, the managing director of the *Times*. The secretary was Thomas Jones, the confidant of Lloyd George and later Baldwin, and an enthusiastic pre-war appeaser. At a Pilgrim's dinner honouring Eleanor Roosevelt in London on 4 February 1946, Greenwood read a letter from Lord Derby, the society's president, proposing a memorial to Roosevelt (who had died nine months before) to be erected in Grosvenor Square near the US embassy chancery.[*] The third anniversary of Roosevelt's death was set as the date for its unveiling. Further impetus was given to the Pilgrims' proposal at a dinner on 18 May in honour of Lord Halifax and Averill Harriman to which Greenwood took the visiting Mackenzie King (a week later Greenwood was on King's right at a dinner offered by Attlee). The necessary £40,000 was raised within a week, even though no single contribution could exceed five shillings, a restriction intended to underline the popular nature of the appeal. At another dinner, King recorded with satisfaction that "Greenwood made an excellent speech, full of humour, and with many kind references [to myself]."[53]

His earlier fears of wartime travel behind him, King was back in London within two months. Greenwood, as a former treasurer of Gray's Inn, arranged an honour for him (in addition to the welcome Order of Merit recently bestowed upon him by King George VI). He was invited to join earlier honorary Benchers of the Inn, notably Churchill and

---

* Paul Martin, the ever-ambitious secretary of state of Canada, was at the dinner, later informing Mackenzie King, "Greenwood in introducing Mrs. Roosevelt coupled in a most enthusiastic and fitting way your name with that of Mr. Churchill and Mr. Roosevelt as three of the outstanding public figures during the war. So thrilled was I at the more than passing references to my Prime Minister that I spoke to the Chairman [Greenwood] afterwards" (Telegram, Martin to King, 5 February 1946, LAC, MG 26 J1, vol. 412).

Roosevelt. His biography describes it as "the great event of the Prime Minister's brief stay in London." Certainly King was highly pleased, since he was disgruntled at the general lack of recognition of him as a prominent wartime leader. He telephoned Greenwood immediately to thank him: "The thought of becoming a member of the Bench of Gray's Inn was to me something exceptional and deeply moving in what it signified in my life."[54]

Despite victory in the war, the immediate postwar years were dreary for Britain. Economic recovery was distant, and the prospects for exports to war-impoverished markets were minimal. In June 1946, a year after the Labour victory that had swept Churchill from office, Greenwood was still chairman of Dorman Long and well aware of the clause in the 1918 Labour Party constitution calling for "the common ownership of the means of production." Churchill in opposition fulminated against nationalization, but Greenwood in his one speech on the subject was more muted, warning against additional disruptions to exports that nationalization of the steel industry could involve. Nationalization "would militate against the good will which British steel enjoyed abroad ... The steel industry never failed the Government during the war. We shall have a hard fight to recover our position."[55] The nationalization of the steel industry – the only manufacturing industry to be nationalized – was on and off for several years. Attlee's government left it to the end of its ambitious nationalization agenda, following the Bank of England, coal, electricity, gas, and civil aviation. Dorman Long and the other steel companies were finally nationalized in 1951, five years after Greenwood's speech and three years after his death.

In postwar Britain, rationing and austerity were everywhere felt. Greenwood wrote to the rector of All Saints in Whitby, Ontario, "Some of us are having a rough time in the Old Country, but we are determined to keep going and to maintain our position despite many difficulties."[56] On a personal level, "Van Margo" redoubled her efforts to sell her still life paintings. Much of the cold, bleak winter of 1947 the Greenwoods spent in South Africa, in the sterling area where dollars were not required and where Dorman Long had substantial assets.

Two years after the idea had first been mooted, Eleanor Roosevelt, in the presence of the king and queen, unveiled on 12 April 1948 the completed memorial to her husband at an elaborate ceremony in Grosvenor Square. Greenwood, as president-designate of the Pilgrims, took a leading part (the governor general, Field Marshal Lord Alexander, represented Canada). The following evening Greenwood presided over a dinner attended by Princess Elizabeth and the Duke of Edinburgh, the high commissioners of the Commonwealth, and the heads of the armed services, past and present. Five weeks later at their annual meeting, the Pilgrims formally elected Greenwood as their president in succession to the late Lord Derby. At the same time, the *Times* reported that he had "undergone a [unidentified] minor operation ... and his condition is very satisfactory."

In fact, it was not. In June a now-ailing Greenwood managed to attend a memorial service for R.B. Bennett, who had died at his home in Surrey. Two months later, on 10 September 1948, he himself died suddenly, at home in London, age seventy-eight, of an unspecified illness.

The next day in the *Times*, the laudatory obituary – although modestly sub-headed "President of the Pilgrims" – placed Greenwood squarely in his Canadian background: "The experiences of his native Canada in securing self-government were often in his mind during his days in Ireland and in his speeches he made frequent references to precedents chosen from the history and experience of Canada." Amery, writing in the *Times* following the funeral service on 14 September, defined his brother-in-law – as he might have described himself – as being "above all things a convinced imperialist." Amery wrote well of his brother-in-law, but the obituaries in both Britain and Canada and in the *New York Times* were muted, citing in some cases the Roosevelt memorial as his major achievement. A memorial service was held on 21 September at St Margaret's, Westminster, where Greenwood and Margo had married thirty-six years before. She and their two sons and two daughters led the mourners, who included representatives of the prime minister, the king of Egypt, the secretary of state for foreign affairs, and the archbishop of Canterbury. Also present were the Brazilian ambassador (in recognition of Greenwood's directorship in Brazilian Traction); the wife of the United States ambassador and the US chargé d'affaires (in recognition of Greenwood's presidency of the Pilgrims); the acting high commissioner for Canada; the agent general for Saskatchewan; and the widow of Neville Chamberlain. Lord Halifax sent regrets. Churchill, Beaverbrook, and Mackenzie King were unable to attend, the latter simply noting in his diary that Greenwood "has been a good friend and one of the few old friends left."[57]

At the memorial service Greenwood's life-long commitment to the Empire and Commonwealth was reflected in the prayers, which included, "Almighty God, Father of all men, under whose providence we are become members of a great Commonwealth of Nations, and have in our keeping the government and protection of many peoples, give us such a spirit of wisdom and understanding, of justice and truth, that all nations and peoples of the Empire may ever abide in one bond of fellowship and service." Greenwood died less than a year before the Republic of Ireland left the Commonwealth and a little more than a year before the Republic of India elected to remain in it.

Greenwood was buried in the churchyard at Codicote, Herefordshire, Margo's childhood home. He left an estate of £44,800, having possibly, like Beaverbrook, quietly transferred assets from the United Kingdom to Canada to avoid tax.[*]

Campbell Stuart, who had known Greenwood from the First World War, wrote of him in his memoirs in 1952, four years after Greenwood's death, "Greenwood's most responsible days were as Chief Secretary for Ireland in Lloyd George's government. There are differing views as to his conduct of this most difficult office, but it called for high personal courage on the part of himself and his wife, and in this respect they never faltered ... He was a close friend of Lloyd George, Baldwin, and Churchill, and was one of the best public speakers of his time. He had a great capacity for friendship, and few men were better liked."[58]

Twenty years later, on 24 April 1968, Dame Margo, the Viscountess Greenwood, DBE, died at age eighty-one in her London flat adjoining that of her beloved second son, Michael. She had specified that her death notice in the *Times* make no mention of her two daughters, noting only that she was the "Deeply loved mother of David and Michael." She also made no provision whatsoever for her two daughters in her will, her estate of £76, 937 (almost twice that of her husband) being divided chiefly between her two sons. Nor did Angela and Deborah attend her private funeral service, their mother having left instructions to her co-executors that "I do not wish my funeral attended by anybody or any relative who did not bother about me in my life. I would prefer men only."[59]

---

[*] Margo paid a final visit to Canada with her sister Sadie and her nephew Julian Amery in the summer of 1949. King in retirement wrote to Margo regretting that he had been unable to see her in Ottawa (King to Lady Greenwood, 25 August 1949, LAC, MG 26 J1, vol. 444).

Conclusion

Greenwood's life ended, mourned by few, excoriated by Irish Republicans and patronized, if not despised, by those who had cynically manipulated him. Beset by the waywardness of his ambitious wife, the alienation of his erratic children, and the treason of his nephew, his later personal life offered him no more solace than his official life. To be sure, by his death in 1948 he had become something of an anachronism. The British Empire, an icon throughout his life, was evolving peacefully into a Commonwealth but was incapable of playing the vigorous liberal imperial role that Greenwood cherished from his boyhood in Ontario.

A key to understanding Greenwood and his *douleurs,* official and personal, is that he was a liberal imperialist, committed to the dynamic evolution of the Empire, not its sterile conservation. Like many Canadians of his generation, he found Dominion status fulfilling. It is, however, difficult to be certain at any time what precisely he thought the Empire should be. His 1911 book, *Canada as an Imperial Factor,* offers little evidence that he had pondered what exactly he himself or for that matter anyone else meant by liberal imperialism. Such thinking was never subjected to the close analysis that his brother-in-law Leo Amery attempted to offer throughout his years in Parliament. For Greenwood, the Empire was always what a later imperial historian has described as "unfinished, untidy, a mass of contradictions, aspirations and anomalies."[1]

At a minimum, Greenwood throughout his life was in favour of the British Empire as most people are opposed to sin. In broad terms, he saw the Empire as an incubator of democracy, the rule of law, equality of the partners, and other good liberal values, providing a global setting for national self-expression and economic development and implanting parliamentary institutions. The federation of British North America in

1867 had drawn upon the conviction of United Empire Loyalists on the one hand and the rebels of 1837 on the other – Greenwood remained proud of being a descendant of both – that the Empire should bestow all the rights upon the British overseas that their British brethren enjoyed in Britain. Having achieved complete internal self-government at home, liberal imperialists in Canada looked for additional self-expression within a constructive Empire.

Laurier in 1897 was similarly both vague and positive about the Empire. Greenwood quoted him with approval: "As thoughts of separation [from the Empire] disappear, thoughts of a union, of a closer union, take their place ... What will be the future of the British Empire? The time may come – the time is coming probably – when the present citizenship of the Colonies, satisfied as they are with it at present, may become inadequate; when the sentiments and aspirations in favour of a closer union will have to be met and acknowledged and satisfied. In my estimation, the solution may be found in the old British principle of representation."[2] By representation Laurier appears to have had in mind some form of Dominion representation in an imperial parliament and cabinet, having himself earlier proclaimed that "it would be the proudest moment of my life if I could see a Canadian of French descent affirming the principles of freedom in the Parliament of Great Britain."[3]

Greenwood fully agreed, convinced as he was that a British Empire of equals was a good thing and the Dominion of Canada's constitution was a model for others. Although never a racist, he had primarily the white or settlement colonies as first in line in the progression to self-government. After the massive upheaval of the First World War, he saw Dominion Home Rule as not only the solution for Ireland but also for India, each fully capable of representing itself in an imperial federation of equals. More specifically, as a lifelong advocate of Home Rule for Ireland, he was convinced that the mass of the Irish people would welcome Dominion status. A small number of gunmen prevented the realization of the benefits of Dominion Home Rule which he vainly advocated to a procrastinating Lloyd George far more preoccupied with the doubtful survival of his shaky coalition government than with any early reforms which could have been, *pace* de Valera, a panacea for Ireland's woes. Of course on a personal level Greenwood wanted to be seen as doing well in carrying out the prime minister's wishes as the route to realizing his own political ambitions – what office holder does not? – but his error was to continue to accept Lloyd George's Conservative-friendly conviction that an armed response to Irish gunmen had to precede rather than accompany any offer of Dominion Home Rule. To say that to be true to himself he should have resigned as chief secretary for Ireland – as he repeatedly threatened to do – in the face of the prime minister's partisan-inspired political intransigence is incontrovertible, but possibly is a little too demanding of flawed human nature in search of personal advancement.

In the Ireland debates of the 1920s and even in the India debates of the 1930s, Greenwood pointed to the dynamic Canadian model: full internal self-government and participation in an imperial federation where broad foreign policy directions would be the result of continuing consultation among its members. The fact that the British government itself – along with Canada, South Africa, and Ireland – had consistently rejected a collective foreign policy did not deter him. The British had to be brought around to recognize what was in their basic interests as well as in those of the Dominions. He himself had worked for several decades to hasten Home Rule for Ireland against the forces of Conservative diehards who remained blind to the potential of a global, liberal Commonwealth. A few hundred fanatical gunmen in Ireland or a few thousand inflamed activists in India could not be allowed to deprive the masses, whatever their ethnic origins, of the benefits of participation in an imperial federation – as he saw it – of democracy, justice, and liberalism.

Reflected in this and much else, Greenwood and his undergraduate classmate Mackenzie King had been at one when they had joined vocally in defence of freedom of speech at the University of Toronto. Greenwood had also been an active militia officer, and even King, that most unmilitary of persons, was deeply moved during a visit to London in 1899 when he watched the Guards marching off to war in South Africa. Thereafter, however, especially during and following the naval debates of 1911–14, in policy terms they sometimes parted ways, although always retaining mutual regard and personal affection. It has been written that Mackenzie King "had a colonial ragbag of emotions toward Britain and the British: pride, loyalty and even awe, but also suspicion, resentment and more than a hint of inferiority."[4] In way of contrast, neither in Canada nor in Britain did Greenwood ever show any sense of inferiority – as King did – to those British who lived in the British Isles. He was direct in his commitment not to Britain but to the British Empire and what it could offer and what it could yet become. It was the British themselves who did not see clearly its potential. In his *Canada as an Imperial Factor* he wrote of British cabinets as "composed of men who, by training and environment, are by no means always sympathetic with the vigorous overseas Dominions."[5] To his dismay, some Englishmen and many Irishmen – in different ways – did not share his understanding that a diminished Empire would hinder those who lived beyond the British Isles from achieving sound growth to full nationhood within a commonwealth.

Greenwood sounded like Robert Borden in foreseeing an active Canada in a consensual Empire of equals. Mackenzie King, on the other hand, having one eye always fixed on Liberal fortunes in Quebec, argued for maximum autonomy in all matters related to Britain. He certainly never shared Laurier's ideas about imperial representation. He convinced himself that, paradoxically, only by maximum autonomy for the Dominions could the Empire be "saved." He continued to display horror, real or assumed, at centralist bogeymen who followed him to every imperial conference through the 1920s and 1930s. He persisted in his decades-old conviction that to maintain Dominion freedoms required him to be continually vigilant in his dealings with the British – especially Tory – establishment which he was convinced to his death in 1950 would never give up its commitment to a centralized Empire. He was, to the surprise of his colleagues and advisors, certain that even the Second World War had not subdued the dreaded centralists. At least one British historian has described King as an isolationist who did more than any other Dominion prime minister to prevent the Empire from realizing the full opportunities codified by the Statute of Westminster of 1931. "King's broad objective in imperial relations did not differ from Sir Robert Borden's; both wanted Canada to be a completely independent state, especially in foreign affairs. However, whereas Borden [and Greenwood] wished to use this independent position in order to influence an imperial foreign policy that, once agreed, would be supported by Britain and all the Dominions, King wanted the freedom in order to have a *separate* Canadian foreign policy ... even if this freedom really meant, in view of Canadian isolationism, freedom to have no foreign policy ... Domestic political pressures and personal prejudices alike, therefore, impelled King to set out to break up the 'white' empire as an effective alliance; not directly and deliberately, but as the by-product of achieving complete freedom of action for Canada."[6]

The basic difference between Greenwood and Mackenzie King was that Greenwood related comfortably to the Empire whereas King related uncomfortably to Britain alone, seeing the Empire – and even the Commonwealth – as little more than a questionable appendage of the United Kingdom. Greenwood, in contrast, understood Anglo-Canadian relations chiefly in the larger context of a consensual Empire and later a Commonwealth secured by voluntary cooperation. King from boyhood continued to regard the relationship as essentially bilateral: Ottawa-London rather than Canada-Empire. To the forefront of whatever thinking King did about the Empire and Commonwealth and the "League of Notions" were domestic partisan convictions: his exaggerations, fantasies, and suspicions seemed to serve well Liberal fortunes in much of Quebec. Accordingly, unlike Borden and Greenwood, he saw his continuing role as that of resisting and exposing imperial centralists in Whitehall and Westminster intent upon dominating and exploiting hapless Canadians and inveigling them into overseas entanglements. To the essentially suspicious if not antagonistic King, with Quebec votes always very much in mind, the manoeuvrings of British politicians required him to stand on guard for Canada. By contrast, Greenwood and Borden embraced the Empire, secure in their conviction that they were themselves constructive and far-seeing in their understanding of the benefits as well as the responsibilities that it could bring. In Greenwood's view, it was the Dominions who recognized that the imperial framework could best provide for the propagation of parliamentary democracy, justice, and prosperity. In his thinking, home rule and empire were in every way compatible. Had he not himself come from rural Ontario to the traditional centre of the Empire, working for its continued liberal evolution in Ireland, India, and Canada as well as in Britain itself?

All the above is a part answer to the question of what Greenwood believed that he was doing when chief secretary for Ireland. The answer is centred on his lifetime conviction that a constructive Empire was a good thing for all those who found themselves within it. For him such an Empire could only function and even survive if its members across the globe enjoyed domestic responsible government and participation in Empire-wide decisions. He frequently observed that not all Englishmen recognized the potential of a liberal approach to Empire, but they could in time be brought by the Dominions and India to realize the error of their conservative ways. The narrowness of Little Englanders and their self-defeating insularity was an anathema to Greenwood, closing off, as he saw it, the route to imperial consultation, collaboration, and coordination. What one Canadian historian has written applies well to Greenwood:

The imperialists ... were assured that Canadian history exhibited an extraordinarily rapid material growth and the slow and gradual acquisition by colonials of the political rights of British subjects. They were anxious to secure the substance of these rights, to secure for Canadians the same voice upon imperial matters that citizens of Great Britain already possessed. This, they were certain, could only be accomplished within some form of imperial association and, equally, it could only come when Canadians were not only ready to assume responsibilities but also when their material development enabled them to do so. This drive toward full national rights was taken by imperialists to mean the culmination, not the subversion, of the principle of responsible government.[7]

By the time of his death in 1948, shortly after the imperial *nunc dimittis* of the Second World War, Greenwood must have recognized that he had spent his energies working for what had ultimately proven to be a lost cause. Perhaps he took whatever consolation he could from a conviction that it had not been a wholly ignoble quest for continuing imperial reform. In some indirect way it had contributed to the declaration of a Canadian prime minister – like Laurier, a French Canadian Liberal – fifty years later that the Commonwealth had so evolved that "it offered links in a world where there were not too many ... it may well prove to be the most important of all international bodies simply because it has no role and because it emphasizes nothing but the importance of the human relationship."[8]

Biographical Notes

Offices held are British, unless otherwise specified.

Allenby, Edmund (1861–1939). Commissioned in the army, 1882; various
senior appointments on the Western Front in the First World War and
commander-in-chief, Egyptian Expeditionary Force, 1917–19; field
marshal, 1919; high commissioner for Egypt and the Sudan, 1919–25.
Also known as "The Bull."

Amery, Leopold (1873–1955). Editorial staff of the *Times*, 1899–1909;
Conservative MP, 1911–45; assistant secretary, war cabinet, 1917–18; parliamentary under-secretary, Colonial Office, 1919–21; first lord of the admiralty, 1922–24; colonial secretary, 1924–29; secretary of state for India and
Burma, 1940–45.

Anderson, John (1882–1958). Colonial Office, 1905; secretary to insurance
commissioners, 1913; secretary, minister of shipping, 1917–19; chairman,
Board of Inland Revenue, 1919; joint under-secretary of state, Ireland,
1920–22; permanent under-secretary of state, Home Office, 1922–32;
governor of Bengal, 1932–37; Conservative MP for the Scottish Universities, 1938–50; lord privy seal, 1938–39; home secretary, 1939–40;
lord president of the council, 1940–43; chancellor of the exchequer,
1943–45.

Asquith, Herbert Henry (1852–1928). Liberal MP, 1886–1918; 1920–24;
home secretary, 1892–1895; chancellor of the exchequer, 1905–08; prime
minister, 1908; displaced by Lloyd George, 1916.

Baldwin, Stanley (1867–1947). Conservative MP, 1908–37; financial secretary
to the treasury, 1917–21; president of the Board of Trade, 1921–22; chancellor of the exchequer, 1922–23; prime minister, 1923–24, 1924–29, and
1935–37; lord president of the council, 1931–35.

Balfour, Arthur (1848–1930). Conservative MP, 1874–1922; president of
Local Government Board, 1885; secretary of state for Scotland, 1886; chief
secretary for Ireland, 1887–91; Conservative leader in the House of
Commons, 1891–92 and 1895–1902; prime minister, 1902–05; first lord
of the admiralty, 1915–16; foreign secretary, 1916–19; lord president of the
council, 1919–22, 1925–29.

Beaverbrook, Lord (1879–1964). Born Maxwell Aitken in Ontario, raised in
New Brunswick; Conservative MP, 1910–16; Canadian representative at
the front, 1915–16; owner of *Daily Express* from 1916; chancellor of the
Duchy of Lancaster and minister of information, 1918; minister of aircraft
production, 1940–41; minister of supply, 1941–42; lord privy seal,
1943–45.

Bennett, R.B. (1870–1947). Canadian Conservative MP, 1911–17, 1925–39,
Canadian minister of justice, 1921; Canadian minister of finance, 1926;
Canadian prime minister, 1930–35, viscount, 1941.

Birkenhead, Lord (1872–1930). Born Frederick Edwin Smith; Conservative
MP, 1906–18; solicitor general and attorney general, 1915–19; lord chancellor, 1919–22; secretary of state for India, 1924–28.

Borden, Robert (1854–1937). Canadian Conservative MP, 1896–1920;
defeated Wilfrid Laurier in the "reciprocity election" of 1911 and became
Canadian prime minister; resigned in 1920; succeeded as Conservative
leader by Greenwood's University of Toronto contemporary Arthur
Meighen.

Burns, John (1858–1943). Independent Labour MP, 1892; Liberal MP, 1910;
president of Local Government Board, 1905; resigned in opposition to
declaration of war in 1914.

Campbell-Bannerman, Henry (1836–1908). Liberal MP, 1868–1908; leader
in the House of Commons, 1899; prime minister, 1905–08.

Carson, Edward Henry (1854–1935). Conservative MP, 1892–1921; solicitor
general, 1900–05; leader of the Ulster Unionists in Parliament, 1910–21;
attorney general, 1915–16; first lord of the admiralty, December 1916–17;
in Lloyd George's War Cabinet as minister without portfolio, July 1917–
January 18. Leadership of Ulster Unionists passed to James Craig (q.v.)
in 1921.

Chamberlain, Austen (1863–1937). Son of Joseph (q.v.) and elder half-
brother of Neville (q.v.) Conservative MP, 1892–1937; financial secretary to
the treasury, 1900–02; postmaster general, 1902–03; chancellor of the
exchequer, 1903–06, 1919–21; secretary of state for India, 1915–17;
lord privy seal and leader of the Conservative Party, 1921–22; foreign
secretary, 1924–29; first lord of the admiralty, 1931; contended with Walter

Long (q.v.) for the Conservative leadership in 1911 before conceding
to Bonar Law (q.v.).

Chamberlain, Joseph (1836–1914). Liberal MP, 1885–86; Conservative MP,
1886–1903; colonial secretary, 1895; leading advocate of imperial tariff
preference.

Chamberlain, Neville (1869–1940). Son of Joseph Chamberlain (q.v.);
Conservative MP, 1918–40; postmaster general, 1922–23; paymaster general, 1923; minister of health, 1923 and 1931; chancellor of the exchequer,
1923–24, 1931–37; prime minister, 1937–40; lord president of the council,
1940.

Collins, Michael (1890–1922). Born in Ireland; post office and bank
employee in London, 1906–16; participated Easter Rising, 1916; adjutant
general of the IRA, 1917–18; minister of home affairs and minister of
finance in Sinn Féin government, 1919–21; negotiator of Irish Treaty.
Commanded Free State forces against anti-treaty republicans who killed
him in 1922.

Cope, Alfred (1883–1954). Second secretary, minister of pensions, 1919–
20; assistant under-secretary for Ireland, 1920–22; general secretary,
National Liberal Organization, 1922–24; managing director, Amalgamated Anthracite Collieries, 1925–35.

Craig, James (1871–1940). Born Belfast, served in the South African War,
1899–1902, and in South West Africa, 1914. Conservative Unionist MP,
1906–21; with Carson a leading opponent of Irish Home Rule. Fought
against the Germans in South-West Africa, 1914–15; parliamentary secretary, pensions, 1919–20; financial secretary, admiralty, 1920–21; prime
minister of Northern Ireland, 1921–40.

De Valera, Eamon (1882–1973). Born in New York City; took part in Easter
Rising, 1916; president of Sinn Fein, 1917–26. Rejected Irish Treaty and
fought against the Free State, 1922–23; leader of opposition, 1927–32;
head of government, 1937–48, 1951–54, and 1957–1959; president,
1959–73.

Dunn, James (1874–1956). Born in New Brunswick; lawyer and investment
banker; moved from Montreal to London in 1905, where he invested
British capital in Canadian industries. In 1935 gained control of Algoma
Steel Corporation in Sault Ste Marie, Ontario.

French, John (1852–1925). Transferred from Royal Navy to army, 1874;
lieutenant general in South Africa, 1899–1902; chief of Imperial General
Staff, 1912–14; field marshal, 1913; commanded British Expeditionary
Force in France, 1914–15, and Home Forces, 1915–18; viceroy, Ireland,
1918–22.

Geddes, Eric (1875–1937). Engineer; deputy director general of munitions supply, 1915–16; inspector general of transportation, 1916–17; Conservative MP, 1917–22; first lord of the admiralty, 1917–18; minister of transport, 1919–21.

Greenwood, Charlotte (1868–1936). Teacher of art at Ontario Ladies' College, Whitby, Ontario. Married Henry Moore of Toronto; died in Trenton, Ontario. No children.

Greenwood, Florence "Bryddie" (1879–1975). Married Leopold Amery in London, 1910, died in London twenty-seven years after her brother Hamar; mother of the traitor Jack Amery and of Julian Amery, minister in the government of his father-in-law, Harold Macmillan.

Greenwood, Gladys "Sadie" (1886–1966). Married the Hon. Charles Christian Simon Rodney; resided in England throughout her adult life. No children.

Greenwood, Margery "Ulla" (1883–1947). Married Major Frederick Cross of Brookes, Alberta. No children.

Greenwood, Mary (1866–1953). Eldest sister of Hamar, trained as nurse in the United States; nursing superintendant of the Jewish Hospital in Cincinnati, Ohio. Becoming blind, she was later a counsellor to veterans blinded in the First World War; died unmarried, five years after her brother Hamar.

Greenwood, William (1872–1923). Journalist and editor of *London Free Press* and *Toronto World*; resigned as managing director of the *World* in 1911 to manage British investments; during First World War, director of publicity for the Canada Food Board. Following the war, promoted British and Canadian investment in Newfoundland.

Griffith, Arthur (1872–1922). Born in Ireland but worked in South Africa in the 1890s before returning to Dublin as a nationalist newspaper editor; founder of Sinn Fein, resigned presidency to de Valera, 1917; MP, 1918–22; acting president of the Dáil Éireann, 1919; imprisoned 1918, 1920–21; signatory of the Irish Treaty 1921; president of the Dáil, 1922.

Hankey, Maurice (1877–1963). Colonel in the Royal Marine Artillery; secretary to the Committee of Imperial Defence, 1912–38; secretary to the War Council, 1914–15, War Cabinet, 1916–18, House of Lords minister without portfolio, 1939–40; chancellor of the Duchy of Lancaster, 1940–41; paymaster general, 1941–42.

Jones, Thomas J. (1870–1955). Academic appointments in Scotland and Ireland; secretary, National Health Commission (Wales), 1912–19; deputy secretary to the cabinet under Prime Ministers Lloyd George, Bonar Law, Stanley Baldwin and Ramsay MacDonald, a strong supporter of Chamberlain's appeasement policies. Secretary and chairman of the Pilgrim Trust, 1930–45; vice-chancellor of the University of Wales, Aberystwyth.

King, William Lyon Mackenzie (1874–1950). Canadian deputy minister of
Labour before being elected Liberal MP (Ottawa) 1908; Canadian minister
of labour, 1909–11; Liberal leader, 1919; Canadian prime minister, 1921–
26; 1926–30; 1935–48.

Laurier, Wilfrid (1841–1919). Liberal MP, Ottawa, 1874–1919; Canadian
minister of inland revenue, 1877–78; Canadian prime minister, 1896–1911.

Law, Andrew Bonar (1858–1923). Born in New Brunswick but lived in
Scotland from age twelve; Conservative MP, 1900–23; parliamentary secretary, Board of Trade, 1902–05; Conservative house leader, 1911; secretary
of state for the colonies, 1915–16; chancellor of the exchequer, 1916–18;
lord privy seal, 1919–21; prime minister for seven months, 1922–23.

Long, Walter (1854–1924). Conservative MP, 1880–1921; president of Local
Government Board, 1900–05; chief secretary for Ireland, 1905; founded
the Union Defence League, the leading Anti–Home Rule organization,
1907–14; president of Local Government Board, 1915–16; secretary of state
for the colonies, 1916–19 (succeeding Bonar Law); first lord of the admiralty, 1919–21.

Macpherson, Ian (1880–1937). Liberal MP, 1911–18; Coalition Liberal,
1918–31; National Liberal, 1931–35; under-secretary of state for war,
1914–16; vice-president of Army Council, 1918; chief secretary for Ireland,
1919–20, minister of pensions, 1920–22.

Macready, Nevil (1862–1946). Commissioned 1881; general officer commanding Belfast, 1914; adjutant general, British Expeditionary Force,
1914–16; adjutant general to the Forces, 1916–18; commissioner of
Metropolitan Police, 1918–19; commanding in Ireland,1919–22.

McBride, Richard (1870–1917). Conservative member of the British
Columbia Legislature 1898–1915; premier, British Columbia, 1903–15;
agent general for British Columbia, London, 1915.

Mond, Alfred (1868–1930). Barrister who created Imperial Chemical
Industries; Liberal MP, 1906–23, 1924–28; joined Conservative Party, 1926;
first commissioner of works, 1916–21; minister of health, 1921–22.

Redmond, John (1851–1918). Irish Nationalist MP, 1881–1918; leader of the
Irish Nationalist Party (following Parnell).

Riddell, Lord (1865–1934). Solicitor; chairman of *News of the World*, 1903;
liaison officer between the government and the press, 1914–18; confidant
of Lloyd George.

Shortt, Edward (1862–1935). Liberal MP, 1910–22; chief secretary for
Ireland, May 1918–January 1919; home secretary, 1919–22.

Smuts, Jan Christian (1870–1950). Born in Cape Colony where he commanded Boer forces against the British, 1901; colonial secretary, Transvaal

1907; minister of defence, Union of South Africa, 1910–20; prime minister of South Africa, 1919–24, 1939–48; minister of justice, 1933–39.

Stevenson, Frances (1888–1972). Graduate of University of London; teacher; private secretary and mistress to Lloyd George, whom she married in 1943, becoming Countess Lloyd-George of Dwyfor in 1945.

Strathcona, Lord (born Donald Smith) (1820–1914). Rose through the Hudson's Bay Company to play leading roles in the Canadian Pacific Railway and Bank of Montreal. An independent Conservative MP, 1871–78, 1887–96; high commissioner for Canada to the United Kingdom, 1896–1914.

Notes

ABBREVIATIONS

CHAR   Churchill Archives, Churchill College, Cambridge, England
LAC   Library and Archives Canada, Ottawa
OA   Ontario Archives, Toronto
PA   Parliamentary Archives, London, England

INTRODUCTION

1 Clementine Churchill to Winston Churchill, 18 February 1921, in Soames, *Speaking for Themselves*, 231–2.
2 Churchill to Greenwood, 4 November 1922, Gilbert, *Churchill*, vol. 4, *Companion*, Part 3, Documents, April 1921–November 1922, 2117–18.
3 Buckner, *Canada and the End of Empire*, 3–4.

CHAPTER ONE

1 Gwyn, *John A: The Man Who Made Us*, vol. 1, 368.
2 Craick, "Sir Hamar Greenwood, Bar't.," 394.
3 *Oshawa Vindicator*, 18 July 1902.
4 Parliamentary Debates, House of Commons, Fifth Series, vol. 91, 22 March 1917, col. 2098.
5 *Globe and Empire*, 8 April 1920.
6 Galt to Macdonald, 10 June 1880; MacLaren, *Commissions High*, 43.
7 Roberts, *Salisbury*, 384.
8 *Toronto Daily Star*, 13 September 1924.
9 Ibid., 22 April 1911.

10 See Duncan, *The Imperialist*, chapter 9.

11 *Toronto Daily Star*, 13 September 1924.

12 Craick, "Sir Hamar Greenwood, Bar't.," 394.

13 *Saturday Night*, 16 May 1908, 4.

14 Sturgis, *Last Days*, 4 February 1921, 120.

15 Craik, "Sir Hamar Greenwood, Bar't.," 393.

16 *Toronto Daily Star*, 5 April 1920.

17 Ibid., 3 May 1920.

18 Berger, *Sense of Power*, 259–60.

19 *Toronto News*, 22 April 1911.

20 *Toronto Daily Star*, 5 April 1920.

21 Baldwin to Davidson, 8 September 1921, Williamson and Blake, *Baldwin Papers*, 55.

22 Craick, "Sir Hamar Greenwood, Bar't.," 394.

23 *Public Accounts of the Province of Ontario for the Year Ended 31 December 1893*, 225, and *Public Accounts ... 1894*, 237.

24 Charlesworth, *More Candid Chronicles*, 84.

25 Greenwood to R.L. McKinnon of Guelph, Ontario, 29 December 1894, OA, McKinnon Papers, MU 4756, no. 12.

26 Ferns and Ostry, *The Age of Mackenzie King*, 18.

27 Ibid., 22–3. The authors give no authority for this anecdote.

28 Dawson, *William Lyon Mackenzie King*, vol. 1, 34.

29 Diaries of William Lyon Mackenzie King, 9 March 1875, LAC, MG26 J13.

30 Ibid., 30 September 1895.

31 Greenwood, *Greenwood Tree*, 23.

32 Ferns and Ostry, *Age of Mackenzie King*, 27.

CHAPTER TWO

1   From an undated autobiographic note (1917?) in PA, LG/F/168/2/12.

2   Charlesworth, *More Candid Chronicles*, 88.

3   Greenwood, *Greenwood Tree*, 24.

4   *Toronto Daily Star*, 10 May 1921.

5   Quoted in *Saturday Night*, 9 January 1915, 3.

6   *Saturday Night*, 24 July 1897, 6.

7   Ibid., 23 April 1910, 8.

8   *Toronto World*, 3 April 1920.

9   Sifton to Strathcona, 26 July 1897; Hall, *Clifford Sifton*, vol. 1, 260.

10 *Toronto Globe*, 8 April 1920

11 Ibid.

12 Walker to Scott, 2 February 1907, LAC, RG 76, vol. 288, file 259109.

13 *Southport Visiter*, 12 November 1903.

14 *Toronto Globe*, 8 April 1920.

15 Hughes to Borden, 10 January 1914, LAC, MG 26 H, C 4362, vol. 147.

16 *Saturday Night*, 28 August 1915, 3.

17 *Toronto Globe*, 8 April 1920.

18 Ibid.

19 Charlesworth, *More Candid Chronicles*, 89–90.

20 "J.A.M.," *Toronto Star*, 8 January 1916.

21 Diaries of William Lyon Mackenzie King, 15 January 1906, LAC, MG 26 J 13.

22 Ibid., 28 May 1946.

CHAPTER THREE

1 Parliamentary Debates, House of Commons, Fourth Series, vol. 155, 6 April 1906, col. 922.

2 King to Greenwood, 10 January 1906, LAC, MG 26 J 1, vol. 5.

3 *Whitby Keystone*, 13 September 1906.

4 Greenwood to Churchill, 13 September 1906, Churchill Archives, CHAR 2/27/33 and 34.

5 Greenwood to King, 4 January 1907, LAC, MG 26 J 1, vol. 6.

6 Greenwood to Churchill, 15 January 1907, Williams, *Running the Show*, 335.

7 Hyman, *Elgin and Churchill*, 461.

8 *Saturday Night*, 23 February 1907, 17.

9 King to Amery, 2 April 1907, LAC, MG 26 J 1.

10 Speech of 27 July 1905, Porter, *The Nineteenth Century*, 356.

11 Greenwood to Laurier, 30 May 1907, LAC, MG 26 G, C 848, vol. 463.

12 Hyman, *Elgin and Churchill*, 214.

13 Greenwood to Laurier, 5 June 1907, LAC, MG 26 G, C 848, vol. 463.

14 Parliamentary Debates, House of Commons, Fourth Series, vol. 175, 13 June 1907, col. 1616.

15 McBride to Greenwood, 15 July 1907, Churchill Archives, CHAR 10/45.

16 Greenwood to Churchill, 16 July 1907, ibid.

17 Churchill to McBride, 17 July 1907, ibid.

18 Laurier to Elgin, 11 June 1907, LAC, MG 26 G, vol. 465.

19 Parliamentary Debates, House of Commons, Fourth Series, vol. 176, 21 June 1907, cols. 751–4.

20 Greenwood to Laurier, 1 May 1907, LAC, MG 26 G, C 848, vol. 463.

21 Laurier to Greenwood, 3 May 1907, ibid.

22 Wilson, *CB: A Life of Sir Henry Campbell-Bannerman*, 115; Jalland, "A Liberal Chief Secretary," 421–51.

23 Laurier to Greenwood, 3 June 1907, LAC, MG26 G, C848, vol. 465.

24 Laurier to Macpherson, 27 August 1907, LAC, MG26 G, 127981; Roy, *A White Man's Province*; Ward, *White Canada Forever*, 67.

25 Borden, *The Question of Oriental Immigration*, 9.

26 *Empire Club of Canada Speeches, 1907–1908*, 15–20; *Toronto Globe*, 14 September 1907.

27 Ormsby, *British Columbia*, 353.

28 Diaries of William Lyon Mackenzie King, 18 September 1907, LAC, MG26 J13.

29 Greenwood to Laurier, 25 March 1908, LAC, MG26 G, C860, vol. 511.

30 Laurier to Greenwood, 8 April 1908, ibid.

31 Ibid.

32 Whitney to Greenwood, 16 January 1908, OA, F5, MU3124, 8273270.

33 Greenwood to Whitney, 9 February 1908, ibid.

34 Ibid., 11 March 1908.

35 Greenwood to Burns, 8 June 1908, British Library, Ms. 46301, f 19.

36 Florence "Bryddie" Greenwood to Churchill, 18 August 1908, Churchill Archives, CHAR 1/73/35.

37 *Yorkshire Herald*, 18 October 1910.

38 Greenwood to Burns, 4 December 1909, British Library, MS 46301, f19.

39 King to Greenwood, 22 March 1910, LAC, MG26 J1, vol. 4.

CHAPTER FOUR

1 *Toronto Daily Star*, 6 December 1910.

2 Duncan, *The Imperialist*, chapter 28.

3 Parliamentary Debates, House of Commons, Fifth Series, vol. 21, 8 February 1911, col. 292.

4 Ibid., 9 February 1911, cols. 484–93.

5 *Canadian Annual Review*, 1911; *Toronto Daily Star*, 13 February 1911.

6 *Toronto Daily Star*, 13 February 1911.

7 *Toronto World*, 3 April 1920.

8 "Priest Who Lived Like a Hermit," *Hereford Times* and *Hereford Journal*, both of 3 June 1922.

9 "Outline of the Career and Services of Sir Hamar Greenwood," n.d., PA, LG/F/168/2/12.

10 Menzies, *As Others See Us*, 70.

11 Sylvester, *Life with Lloyd George*, 186.

12 Hague, *The Pain and the Privilege*, 105–6.

13 Author's conversation with Alexander Greenwood, 10 March 2008.

CHAPTER FIVE

1 W. Greenwood to Aitken, 6 July 1911, PA, BBK/A/212.

2 Aitken to W. Greenwood, 22 September 1911, PA, BBK/A/212.

3 Young, *Stanley Baldwin*, 42–3.

.4 *Canadian Club Speeches, 1911*; *Toronto Daily Star*, 9 October 1911.

5 Riddell, 14 April 1912, *More Pages from My Diary*, 52.

6 Parliamentary Debates, House of Commons, Fifth Series, vol. 36, 9 April 1912, col. 1437.

7 Parliamentary Debates, House of Commons, Fifth Series, vol. 39, 19 June 1912, col. 1775–80.

8 Amery to Bryddie Amery, 1 January 1912, Barnes and Nicholson, *Amery Diaries*, vol. 1, 84.

9 Parliamentary Debates, House of Commons, Fifth Series, vol. 54, 10 June 1913, cols. 1551–5.

10 Ibid.

11 *Times*, 13 and 14 June 1913.

12 R. Churchill, *Churchill, Companion Volumes*, vol. 2, part 3, 1509.

13 Northcliffe to Churchill, 12 August 1912, ibid., 1625–7.

14 Whitney to Borden, 15 August 1912, AO, F5, MU3124, B273280.

15 Churchill to the 118th meeting of the Committee of Imperial Defence, 11 July 1912, Tucker, *Naval Service of Canada*, vol. 1, 179.

16 Greenwood, *Canada as an Imperial Factor*, 247.

17 Greenwood to Churchill, 6 August, Churchill Archives, CHAR 13/20.

18 Brock and Brock, *H.H. Asquith: Letters to Venetia Stanley*, 20.

19 Bonham Carter and Pottle, *Lantern Slides*, 375; Rowland, *The Last Liberal Governments*, vol. 1, 269–70.

20 Greenwood to Churchill, 6 August 1913, Churchill Archives, CHAR 13/20/18–21 and 26–35.

21 Ibid.

22 Greenwood to King, 16 December 1913, LAC, MG26 J1, vol. 20.

23 King to Greenwood, 31 December 1913, ibid.

24 6 August 1913, Churchill Archives, CHAR 13/20.

25 R. Churchill, *Churchill*, vol. 2, 489.

26 Parliamentary Debates, House of Commons, Fifth Series, vol. 60, 23 March 1914, cols. 135–6.

27 Churchill, *The World Crisis*, vol. 1, 153.
28 Beaverbrook, *Politicians and the War*, vol. 1, 52.

CHAPTER SIX

1 Greenwood to Bryddie, 4 September 1914, Churchill Archives, AMEL/1/3/5. See also Johnson, "Liberal War Committee," 399–420.
2 Amery, *My Political Life*, vol. 2, 31.
3 *Toronto Globe*, 8 April 1920.
4 Craick, "Sir Hamar Greenwood, Bar't," 397.
5 Owen, *Tempestuous Journey*, 284.
6 Greenwood to Lloyd George, 10 January 1916, PA, LG/C/11/3.
7 Atkinson, *History of the South Wales Borderers*, 178.
8 *Saturday Night*, 28 August 1915, 4.
9 *Times*, 20 May 1953.
10 *Toronto World*, 18 March 1916.
11 Ibid., 16 August 1916.
12 "Outline of the Career and Services of Sir Hamar Greenwood," n.d., PA, LG/F/168/ 2/12.
13 Greenwood to Redmond, 15 September 1916, Finnan, *John Redmond*, 189.
14 Greenwood to King, 25 October 1916, LAC, MG26 J1, vol. 44.
15 Borden to Imperial War Cabinet, 23 July 1918, LAC, MG26 H.
16 Hurd and Hurd, *New Empire Partnership*, 253.
17 Beaverbrook, *Men and Power*, 43.
18 King to Greenwood, telegram, 7 December 1916, LAC, MG26 J1, vol. 44.
19 Parliamentary Debates, House of Commons, Fifth Series, vol. 91, 22 March 1917, col. 2098.
20 Parliamentary Debates, House of Commons, Fifth Series, vol. 92, 23 April 1917, col. 2113.
21 Margo Greenwood to Lloyd George, 13 November 1918, PA, LG/F/ 20/1/23.

CHAPTER SEVEN

1 Sir Frederick Smith to Lloyd George, 1 March 1919, PA, LG/F/94/1/63.
2 Storey to Chamberlain, 29 April 1919, PA, LG/F//7/2/30.
3 Law to Storey, 3 April 1920, ibid.
4 Storey to Law, 8 April 1920. PA, LG/F//7/2/30.
5 "Outline of the Career and Services of Sir Hamar Greenwood," n.d., PA, LG/F/168/2/12.

6 King to Greenwood, 11 July 1919, LAC, MG 26 J1, vol. 45.

7 Greenwood to King, 14 July 1919, ibid.

8 Greenwood to King, 3 January 1920, LAC, MG 26 J1, vol. 54.

9 Garro Jones, *Ventures and Visions*, 95.

10 Greenwood to Churchill, 22 September 1919, Churchill Archives, CHAR 16/12.

11 Riddell, *Diaries*, 30 August 1919, 288.

12 Ibid., 4 September 1919, 290.

13 Riddell, *Intimate Diary*, 6–7 September 1919, 123.

14 Stevenson, *The Years That Are Past*, 168.

15 Greenwood to Lloyd George, 23 December 1919, PA, LG/F/19/2/2.

16 Lloyd George to Greenwood, 27 March 1920, PA, LG/F/19/2/6.

17 Ibid.

CHAPTER EIGHT

1 Parliamentary Debates, House of Commons, Fourth Series, vol. 305, 10 May 1886, 587.

2 O'Brien, *Dublin Castle*, 420–1.

3 Hyam, *Elgin and Churchill*, 183.

4 Law speech at Blenheim of 27 July 1912, R. Churchill, *Churchill*, vol. 2, 469–70.

5 Lloyd George to F.E. Smith, 6 October 1913, Grigg, *Lloyd George, From Peace to War*, 124.

6 Laurier to an unidentified correspondent (possibly Greenwood) in London, 13 May 1916, O.D. Skelton, *Life and Letters of Sir Wilfrid Laurier*, vol. 2, 450n.

7 Greenwood to Redmond, 9 May 1916, National Library of Ireland, RED.MS.15192(5).

8 Stevenson Diary, 26 July 1916, PA, FLS/4/3.

9 Lloyd George to William Redmond, 6 March 1917, Fanning et al., *Documents on Irish Foreign Policy*, vol. 1, 181.

10 Parliamentary Debates, House of Commons, Fifth Series, vol. 92, 22 March 1917.

11 Riddell, *Diaries*, 356.

12 Stevenson Diary, 25 April 1917, PA, FLS/4/4.

13 Hancock, *Smuts*, vol. 1, 433 and 475–6.

14 Churchill, *The Aftermath*, 294.

15 Grigg, *Lloyd George: War Leader*, 466, 476.

16 Amery, *My Political Life*, vol. 2, 152.

17 Parliamentary Debates, House of Commons, Fifth Series, vol. 104, 9 April 1918.
18 Shea, *Voices and the Sound of Drums*, 22.
19 Minutes of the Cabinet Committee on Ireland, 9 May 1918, Jones, *Whitehall Diary*, vol. 3, 9.
20 Taylor, *English History 1914–1945*, 104.
21 O'Connor, *Memoirs of an Old Parliamentarian*, 77.
22 Hattersley, *Great Outsider*, n.p.
23 Wilson diary, 12 July 1920, Gilbert, *Churchill*, vol. 4, 456.
24 Spender to Scott, 23 August 1919, *Political Diaries of C.P. Scott*, 377.
25 Report of the Inspector General of the RIC, 9 May 1920, PA, BL/102/56.
26 Long to Macpherson and Long to Lloyd George, both of 21 May 1919, PA, LG/F/33/2/45.
27 Boyce, *Englishmen and Irish Troubles*, 46.
28 *The Nation*, 3 January 1920.
29 Amery, *My Political Life*, vol. 2, 228.

CHAPTER NINE

1 Jones, *Whitehall Diary*, 10 April 1919, vol. 3, 12.
2 Macready, *Annals*, vol. 2, 448–9.
3 Fisher to Lloyd George, Law, and Chamberlain, 12 May 1920, PA, LG/F/33/1/32.
4 Ibid, 15 May 1920, PA, LG/F/31/1/33.
5 Anderson to Greenwood, 20 July 1920. PA, LG/F/19/2/14.
6 Cope to Fisher, 17 June 1920, PA, LG/F/31/1/34.
7 *Times*, 3 April 1920.
8 Law to Greenwood, 17 April 1920, PA, BL/102/56.
9 Macready, *Annals*, vol. 2, 425.
10 Macready to Macpherson, 11 January 1919, Hopkinson, *Irish War of Independence*, 7.
11 Macready, *Annals*, vol. 2, 425.
12 Stevenson diary, 6 July 1921, PA, FLS/1/2/17.
13 Margo Greenwood diary, 9 January 1921 (in the possession of Alexander Greenwood).
14 Sturgis, *Last Days*, 30 April 1921, 167.
15 Churchill to Stamfordham, 13 May 1920, Gilbert, *Churchill*, vol. 4, *Companion*, part 2, July 1919–March 1921, 1096.
16 Duggan ("Periscope") *Last Days*, 150.

17 Sturgis diary, August 1920, PRO 30-59, quoted in Bowden, "The Irish Underground," 21.

18 Wheeler-Bennett, *John Anderson*, 57–8.

19 Saunderson to Long, 28 July 1920, Walter Long Papers, WRO 947/ 348, quoted in O'Halpin, *Decline of the Union*, 205.

20 French to Bonar Law, 4 April 1920, PA, BL/98/9/9.

21 Fisher to Bonar Law, 28 May 1920, PA, BL/102/56.

22 Anderson to Greenwood, 20 July 1920, PA, LG/F/19/2/14.

23 Macready to Law, 24 May 1920, PA, BL 102/56.

24 Roskill, *Hankey*, vol. 2, 153.

25 *Toronto Mail and Empire*, 28 March 1920.

26 Fanning, *Fatal Path*, 267.

27 Garro Jones, *Ventures and Visions*, 100.

28 Speech of Lloyd George to the electors of Sunderland, 7 November 1922, enclosure in Greenwood to King, 13 November 1924, LAC, MG 26 J 1, vol. 101.

29 Greenwood to Lloyd George, 30 December 1918, PA, LG/F/95/1/62.

30 Colmer, *Canada Club*, 98–9.

31 *Toronto Daily Star*, 13 September 1924.

32 Robinson, *Memoirs Wise and Otherwise*, 295.

33 Greenwood, *Greenwood Tree*, 26.

34 Papers of Leopold Amery, "Talk with Margo Greenwood," 16 April 1951, Churchill Archives, AMEL 8/74.

35 Stuart Menzies, *As Others See Us*, 62.

36 Jones, *Whitehall Diary*, vol. 1, 207.

37 Riddell, *Intimate Diary*, 378.

38 Stevenson diary, 17 January 1915, PA, FLS/4/1.

39 Keynes, *Essays in Biography*, 36.

40 Taylor, *English History, 1914–1945*, 131–2.

41 Sturgis, *Last Days*, 1 May 1921, 167–8.

42 Author's conversation with Alexander Greenwood, 10 March 2008.

CHAPTER TEN

1 Margo Greenwood to Stevenson, 6 April 1920, PA, FLS/4/5.

2 See p. 158.

3 Sturgis, *Last Days*, 1 May 1921, 168.

4 Ibid., 29 September 1920, 48.

5 Margo Greenwood to Stevenson, 6 April 1921, PA, FLS/1/2/16.

6 Stevenson diary, 24 May 1921, PA, FLS/4/7.

7 Amery Papers, "Talk with Margo Greenwood," 16 April 1951, Churchill Archives, AMEL 8/74.

8 Greenwood to Beaverbrook, 11 April 1920, PA, BLU/1/9/GREE 1.

9 *Times*, 15 April 1920.

10 *Times*, 10 May 1920.

11 Ibid.

12 Stuart Menzies, *As Others See Us*, 66.

13 Cabinet Conclusions 23/20, 26 April 1920.

14 Gilbert, *Churchill*, vol. 4, 454.

15 Roskill, *Hankey*, Hankey diary, 8 and 23 May 1920, vol. 2, 153.

16 Macready, *Annals*, vol. 2, 468.

17 Greenwood to Law, 12 May 1920, PA, LG/F/102/5/19.

18 Greenwood to Long, 20 June 1920, PA, BL/102/56.

19 Macready, *Annals*, vol. 2, 446.

20 Garro Jones, *Ventures and Visions*, 101–2.

21 O'Halpin, *Decline of the Union*, 204; see also Jackson, *Colonel Edward Saunderson*.

22 Memorandum by Macready to Stevenson, 25 May 1920, PA, LG/F/36/2/14.

23 Cabinet conclusions, 23/LOA, 26 April 1920.

24 Wilson diary, 1 June 1920, Boyce, *Englishmen and Irish Troubles*, 50.

25 Gilbert, *Churchill*, vol. 4, 453.

26 Jones, *Whitehall Diary*, 31 May 1920, vol. 3, 17.

27 Law to Greenwood, 11 May 1920, PA, BLU 103/4/3.

28 Amery, *My Political Life*, vol. 2, 228.

29 Shea, *Voices and the Sound of Drums*, 44–5.

30 Beaverbrook, *Decline and Fall*, 97.

31 Cope to Fisher, 17 June 1920, PA, BL/102/56.

32 Riddell, *Intimate Diary*, 11 June 1920, 202–3.

33 Macready to Irish cabinet committee, 18 July 1920, and cabinet document 24/109/f358.

34 Amery, *My Political Life*, vol. 2, 228.

35 Cope to Fisher, 17 June 1920, PA, BL/102/56.

36 Parliamentary Debates, House of Commons, Fifth Series, vol. 130, 22 June 1920, col. 2101.

37 Jones, *Whitehall Diary*, 31 May 1920, vol. 3, 18.

38 Macready to Greenwood, 17 July 1920, PA, LG/F/19/2/12.

39 Anderson to Greenwood, 20 July 1920, PA, LG/ F/19/2/14.

40 Macready to Greenwood, 17 July 1920, PA, LG/F/19/2/12.

41 O'Broin, *W.E. Wylie and the Irish Revolution*, 77.

42 Riddell, *Diaries*, 6 June 1920, 314.

43 Scott to Dillon, 20 January 1921, Hammond, *C.P. Scott*, 277.

44 Macready to Greenwood, 17 July 1920, PA, LG/F/19/2.

45 Jones to Lloyd George, 24 July 1920, *Whitehall Diary*, vol. 3, 31–2.

46 Riddell, *Intimate Diary*, 24 July 1920, 225.

47 Jones, *Whitehall Diary*, 31 May 1920, vol. 3, 26.

48 Parliamentary Debates, House of Commons, Fifth Series, vol. 132, 5 August 1920, col. 2695.

49 Ibid., cols. 2753–6.

50 Jones, *Whitehall Diary*, 31 May 1920, vol. 3, 35.

51 Sturgis, *Last Days*, 7 August 1920, 18.

52 Margo Greenwood to Lloyd George, 14 August 1920, PA, F/20/1/1.

53 Lloyd George to Law, 4 September 1920, PA, LG/F/19/2/20.

54 Sturgis, *Last Days*, 3 September 1920, 35.

55 Ibid., 13 September 1920, 39.

56 Ibid., 27 September 1920, 46.

57 Ibid., 7 October 1920, 52.

CHAPTER ELEVEN

1 Hopkinson, *Irish War of Independence*, 28. A systematic account with statistics of the killings on both sides is set out in Kee, *The Green Flag*.

2 Garro Jones, *Ventures and Visions*, 107.

3 Sturgis, *Last Days*, 18 August 1920, 24.

4 Riddell, *Intimate Diary*, 5 (?) September 1921, 319.

5 Macready Memorandum on Reprisals, [mid-October] 1920, PA, LG/F/10/3/7.

6 Churchill to Wilson, 18 September 1920, Gilbert, *Churchill*, vol. 4, *Companion*, Part 2, *July 1919–March 1921*, 1209.

7 Macready, *Annals*, vol. 2, 503–4.

8 Wilson Diary, 23 September 1920, Gilbert, *Churchill*, vol. 4, 460–1.

9 Amery Papers, "Talk with Margo Greenwood," 16 April 1951, Churchill Archives, AMEL 8/74.

10 H.A.L. Fisher diary, 24 September 1920, Gilbert, *Churchill*, vol. 4, 461.

11 Wilson diary, 1 July 1920, Callwell, *Field-Marshal Sir Henry Wilson*, vol. 2, 247–8.

12 Ibid., 29 September 1920, 263–4.

13 Cabinet notes, 2 June 1921, Jones, *Whitehall Diary*, vol. 3, 73.

14 Margo Greenwood to Sturgis, 3 October 1920, Sturgis, *Last Days*, 60.

15 Roskill, *Hankey*, Hankey diary, 5 October 1920, vol. 2, 196.
16 Fisher to Lloyd George, 16 November 1920, PA, LG/F/16/7/61.
17 Greenwood statement of 28 September 1920, PA, LG/F/16/8/2.
18 Greenwood speech of 30 September 1920, Bennett, *Black and Tans*, 86.
19 Ibid.
20 Jones, *Whitehall Diary*, 3 November 1920, vol. 3, 41.
21 Roskill, *Hankey*, 25 November 1920, vol. 2, 197.
22 Nicolson, *King George the Fifth*, 348.
23 O'Halpin, "Greenwood," 241.
24 Duggan ("Periscope"), *Last Days*, 155.
25 *Times*, 11 September 1948.
26 *Times*, 21 September 1948.
27 Montagu diary, 10 November 1920, Foy, *Michael Collins' Intelligence War*, 211.
28 Chamberlain, *Diary Letters*, 1 August 1920, vol. 2, 381.
29 Macready, *Annals*, vol. 2, 465.
30 Greenwood to Law, 25 September 1920, PA, BL/102/5/3.
31 Jones, *Lloyd George*, 189.
32 Ibid.
33 Stuart Menzies, *As Others See Us*, 64.
34 Coogan, *Ireland in the Twentieth Century*, 83.
35 Jones, *Whitehall Diary*, 13 October 1920, vol. 3, 40.
36 Gilbert, *Churchill*, vol. 4, *Companion*, Part 3, 462.
37 Ibid., 463.
38 Parliamentary Debates, House of Commons, Fifth Series, vol. 133, 20 October 1920, col. 948.
39 Riddell, *Intimate Diary*, 23 October 1920, 242.
40 Chamberlain, *Diary Letters*, 23 October 1920, vol. 1, 393.
41 Sturgis, *Last Days*, 26 October 1920, 60.
42 Greenwood to Henderson, 3 December 1920, PA, LG/F/19/2/27.
43 Fanning et al., "Notes on a Conference with the Governor General and President," 30 January 1924, *Documents on Irish Foreign Policy*, vol. 1, 263–4.
44 Parliamentary Debates, House of Commons, Fifth Series, vol. 134, 8 November 1920, cols. 828, 829.
45 Memorandum of the Secretary of State for War, 3 November 1920, in Townshend, *British Campaign*, 122.
46 Scott diary, 5 December 1921, Hammond, *C.P. Scott*, 284.
47 Hammond, *C.P. Scott*, 241.
48 Sturgis, *Last Days*, 11 November 1920, 69.
49 Ibid., 19 November 1920, 75.

50 Ibid., 26 November 1920, 81.
51 Ibid., 21 October 1920, 58.
52 Ibid., 26 November 1920, 81.
53 Parliamentary Debates, House of Commons, Fifth Series, vol. 135, 24 November 1920, col. 512.
54 *Times*, 25 November 1920.
55 Sturgis, *Last Days*, 29 November 1920, 84.
56 Parliamentary Debates, House of Commons, Fifth Series, 15 February 1921, vol. 138, col. 43.
57 *Times*, 14 and 29 December 1920.
58 Sturgis, *Last Days*, 4 November 1920, 65.
59 Greenwood to Lloyd George, 3 December 1920, PA, LG/F/19/2/27.
60 Margo Greenwood to Stevenson, 4 December 1920, PA, FLS/1/2/16.
61 *New York Times*, 6 May 1920; *Toronto Globe*, 7 May 1920.
62 Thomson to each of the five IRA targets, 9 November 1920, Churchill Archives, CHAR 2/111.
63 Greenwood to Bonar Law, 12 May 1920, PA, LG/F/102/5/19.
64 Riddell, *Intimate Diary*, 225.
65 Roskill, *Hankey*, Hankey diary, 18 September 1920, vol. 2, 190.
66 Garro Jones, *Ventures and Visions*, 107.
67 Roskill, *Hankey*, Hankey diary, 25 November 1920, vol. 2, 197.
68 Lloyd George to Greenwood, 2 December 1920, PA, LG/F/19/2/26.

CHAPTER TWELVE

1 Wheeler-Bennett, *John Anderson*, 71–2.
2 Greenwood to Lloyd George, 19 November 1920, PA, LG/F/19/2/23.
3 Sturgis, *Last Days*, 30 November 1920, 84–5.
4 Greenwood to Lloyd George, 3 December 1920, PA, LG/F/19/2/27.
5 O'Brien to Griffith, 14 December 1920, *Documents on Irish Foreign Policy*, vol. 1, 217.
6 Ibid.
7 Parliamentary Debates, House of Commons, Fifth Series, vol. 138, 15 February 1921, col. 44.
8 Hopkinson, *Irish War*, 188.
9 *Times*, 15 February 1921.
10 Roskill, *Hankey*, Hankey diary, 9 December 1920, vol. 2, 198.
11 Sturgis, *Last Days*, 12 December 1920, 89.
12 Ibid., 25 December 1920, 100.
13 Cabinet conclusions, 29 December 1920, 79A/20.

14 Ibid., 31 December 1920, 101.

15 *Times*, 1 January 1921.

16 The diary was in the possession of the late Alexander Greenwood.

17 Riddell, *Diaries*, 1 January 1921, 332.

18 Greenwood to Lloyd George, 31 January 1921, PA, LG/F/19/3/3, and Macready, *Annals*, vol. 2, 522.

19 Sturgis, *Last Days*, 9 January 1921, 108.

20 Ibid., 11 January 1921, 109.

21 Ibid., 12 January 1921, 112.

22 Margo Greenwood to Stevenson, 23 January 1921, PA, FLS/4/7.

23 Minutes of a meeting between Lloyd George and Bonar Law, 30 January 1921, Jones, *Whitehall Diary*, vol. 3, 49.

24 Hopkinson, *Irish War of Independence*, 7.

25 Sturgis, *Last Days*, 18 January 1921, 112.

26 Ibid., 20 January 1921, 113.

27 Ibid, 8 February 1921, 121.

28 Ibid., 20 January 1921, 114.

29 Ibid.

30 Margo Greenwood to Stevenson, 18 January 1921, PA, FLS/4/7.

31 *Times*, 24 January 1921, *Illustrated London News*, 29 January 1921.

32 Greenwood to Lloyd George, 26 January 1921, PA, LG/F/19/3/2.

33 Macready, *Annals*, vol. 2, 538.

34 Macready to Stevenson, 11 February 1921, PA, LG/F/36/2/16.

35 Sturgis, *Last Days*, 16 February 1921, 127–8.

36 Lloyd George to Margo Greenwood, 7 (?) February 1921, Sturgis, *Last Days*, 121.

37 Margo Greenwood to Sturgis, 18 February 1921, Sturgis, *Last Days*, 129.

38 Eric Geddes at Chequers, 14 February 1920, Jones, *Whitehall Diary*, vol. 3, 51.

39 Parliamentary Debates, House of Commons, Fifth Series, vol. 138, 15 February 1921, col. 42.

40 Crozier, *Impressions and Recollections*, 258.

41 Jones, *Whitehall Diary*, 15 February 1921, vol. 3, 53.

42 Churchill to Clementine Churchill, 15 February 1921, Soames, *Speaking for Themselves*, 230

43 Grigg, *Lloyd George: From Peace to War*, 321.

44 Clementine Churchill to Churchill, 18 February 1921, Soames, *Speaking for Themselves*, 232.

45 Parliamentary Debates, House of Commons, Fifth Series, vol. 138, 21 February 1921, col. 647.

46 Northcliffe to Kerr, 26 March 1921, Thompson, *Northcliffe*, 347–8.
47 Macready to Stevenson, 24 February 1921, PA, FLS/1/2/16, and
    LG/F/36/2/6.
48 Stuart Menzies, *As Others See Us*, 97.
49 Sturgis, *Last Days*, 25 February 1921, 132.
50 Crozier, *Impressions and Recollections*, 252.
51 *Times*, 22 February 1921.
52 Birkenhead, *Halifax*, 79–80.
53 Lloyd George to Greenwood, 25 February 1921, LG/F/19/3/4.
54 Sturgis, *Last Days*, 23 February 1921, 131.
55 Ibid., 23 February 1921, 132.
56 Jones to Stevenson, 21 March 1922, *My Darling Pussy*, 39.
57 Greenwood to Lloyd George, 3 April 1921, PA, LG/F/19/3/7.
58 Margo to Stevenson, 6 April 1921, PA, FLS/4/7.
59 Lloyd George to Greenwood, 21 April 1921, PA, LG/F/19/4/6.
60 Nicolson, *King George the Fifth*, 347.
61 Macready, *Annals*, vol. 2, 498.
62 Riddell, *Intimate Diary*, 368.
63 Thompson, *Northcliffe*, 350.
64 Sturgis, *Last Days*, 29 April 1921, 166.
65 Ibid., 30 April 1921, 167.

CHAPTER THIRTEEN

1 Hopkinson, *Irish War of Independence*, 188.
2 Sturgis, *Last Days*, 20 March 1921, 143.
3 Ibid., 15 April 1921, 158–9.
4 Ibid., 24 March 1921, 147.
5 Northcliffe to Kerr, 26 March 1921, Thompson, *Northcliffe*, 347.
6 Riddell, *Intimate Diary*, 2 April 1921, 289.
7 Sturgis, *Last Days*, 18 April 1921, 160.
8 Saunderson to Derby, 13 March 1921, R. Churchill, *Lord Derby*, 403
9 Sturgis, *Last Days*, 25 April 1921, 163.
10 Wheeler-Bennett, *Friends, Enemies and Sovereigns*, 151.
11 Cabinet notes, 27 April 1921, Jones, *Whitehall Diary*, vol. 3, 61.
12 Sturgis, *Last Days*, 1 May 1921, 167.
13 Ibid., 29 April 1921, 166.
14 Freddie Guest to Lloyd George, 9 March 1921, PA, LG/F/23/3/6.
15 Sturgis, *Last Days*, 1 May 1921, 167–8.
16 Margo to Stevenson, 3 May 1921, PA, FLS/1/2/16.

17 Greenwood to Lloyd George, 3 April 1921, PA, LG/F/19/3/7.
18 Greenwood to Lloyd George, 3 May 1921, PA, LG/ F/19/2/6, and 5 May
    1921, PA, LG/F/19/4/5.
19 Ibid., 3 May 1921, PA, LG/F/19/4/1.
20 Ibid., 4 May 1921, PA, LG/F/19/4/3.
21 Ibid., 5 May 1921, PA, LG/F/19/4/4.
22 Quoted in David McKittrick, "Echoes from the Past as Ulster's Old Foes
    Meet," *Independent*, 21 October 2014.
23 Greenwood to Lloyd George, 6 May 1921, PA, LG/F/19/4/6.
24 Sturgis, *Last Days*, 6 May 1921, 173.
25 Ibid.
26 Ibid., 7 May 1921, 173–4.
27 Riddell, 15 May 1921, Riddell, *Intimate Diary*, 298.
28 Jones, *Whitehall Diary*, 12 May 1921, vol. 3, 63–7.
29 Ibid.
30 Sturgis, *Last Days*, 11 May 1921, 176.
31 Greenwood to Lloyd George, 8 and 9 May 1921, PA, LG/F/19/4/1.
32 Sturgis, *Last Days*, 24 May 1921, 183.
33 Greenwood to Lloyd George, 11 May 1921, PA, LG/F/19/4/10.
34 Healy to Beaverbrook, 18 May 1921, Taylor, *Beaverbrook*, 187.
35 Churchill, *Aftermath*, 304.
36 Anderson to Greenwood, 18 June 1921, Boyce, *Englishmen and Irish
    Troubles*, 134–5.
37 Hoare to Beaverbrook, 13 June 1921, Beaverbrook, *Decline and Fall*, 282.
38 Scott, *Political Diaries*, 398.
39 Editorial comment by Keith Middlemas, Jones, *Whitehall Diary*, vol. 3, 74.
40 Ibid.
41 Smuts to Lloyd George, 14 June 1921, Jones, *Whitehall Diary*, vol. 3, 74–5;
    Nicolson, *King George the Fifth*, 350.
42 Stevenson diary, 18 June 1921, PA, FLS/4/7.
43 Greenwood's suggestions, most of which were incorporated in the final
    draft, are in PA, LG/F/19/5/3.
44 *Times*, 22 June 1921.
45 Jones, *Whitehall Diary*, 24 June 1921, vol. 3, 80.
46 Ibid., 78–9.

CHAPTER FOURTEEN

1 Greenwood to Lloyd George, 14 May 1921, PA, LG/F/19/4/12.
2 Sturgis, *Last Days*, 25 June 1921, 192.

3   Lloyd George to cabinet, 24 June 1921, Gilbert, *Churchill*, vol. 4, 665.

4   Sturgis, *Last Days*, 25 June 1921, 192.

5   Stevenson diary, 5 July 1921, PA, FLS/4/7.

6   Hancock, *Smuts*, vol. 1, 581.

7   Amery, *My Political Life*, vol. 2, 230.

8   Stevenson diary, 5 and 6 July 1921, PA, FLS/4/7.

9   Ibid., 11 July 1921, PA, FLS/4/7.

10   Greenwood to Lloyd George, 9 July 1921, PA, F/19/5/13.

11   Ibid., PA, F/19/5/13; Sturgis, *Last Days*, 10 July 1921, 201.

12   Sturgis, *Last Days*, 11 July 1921, 201.

13   Macready, *Annals*, vol. 2, 493.

14   Wilson diary, 12 February 1922, Gilbert, *Churchill*, vol. 4, *Companion*, part 3, April 1921–November 1922, 1771.

15   Stevenson diary, 14 July 1921, PA, FLS/4/6.

16   Ibid., 4 July 1921, PA, FLS/4/7.

17   H.A.L. Fisher diary, 24 July 1921, Gilbert, *Churchill*, vol. 4, 666.

18   Law to Jones, 30 July 1921, Jones, *Whitehall Diary*, vol. 3, 91. Jones provides an almost day-to-day account of the British correspondence with de Valera and the attitudes of various members of the cabinet, including Greenwood (90–125).

19   De Valera to Lloyd George, 10 August 1921, Jones, *Whitehall Diary*, vol. 3, 93.

20   Ibid.

21   Ibid.

22   Fisher to Lloyd George, 9 September 1921, PA, F 25/ 2/32. The British government released the correspondence to a generally welcoming press in August 1921 and published it in *Correspondence Relating to the Proposals of His Majesty's Government for an Irish Settlement*, cmd. 1502, 1921, I–IV.

23   Gilbert, *Churchill*, vol. 4, 667.

24   Cabinet notes, 7 September 1921, Jones, *Whitehall Diary*, vol. 3, 109.

25   Jones to Hankey, 9 September 1921, Jones, *Whitehall Diary*, vol. 1, 172.

26   Greenwood to Lloyd George, 29 October 1921, PA, LG/F/19/5/36.

27   Wheeler-Bennett, *Friends, Enemies and Sovereigns*, 151; other explanations are set out in, for example, Regan, *Irish Counter-Revolution, 1921–1936*.

28   Jones, *Whitehall Diary*, 29 October 1921, vol. 3, 149.

29   Scott, *Political Diaries of C.P Scott*, 28–29 October 1921, 402.

30   Stevenson diary, 17 January 1915, PA, FLS/4/1.

31   Beaverbrook, *Decline and Fall*, 100–3.

32   Churchill, *Aftermath*, 303.

33   Macready, *Annals*, vol. 2, 532.

34 Churchill, *Aftermath*, 316.
35 Riddell, *Diaries*, 16 January 1923, 385.
36 Campbell, *F.E. Smith*, 581.
37 Chisholm and Davie, *Beaverbrook*, 140
38 Stuart Menzies, *As Others See Us*, 277–8.
39 Cannadine, *Decline and Fall*, 334.
40 Cannadine, *Aspects of Aristocracy*, 148.
41 Stevenson diary, 27 July 1921, PA, FLS/4/7.
42 Chisholm and Davie, *Beaverbrook*, 180.
43 Taylor, *Michael Collins*, 153–4.
44 Greenwood to Lloyd George, 29 October 1921, PA, LG/F/14/9.
45 Scott, *Political Diaries of C.P. Scott*, 28 October 1921, 403; Fair, "Anglo-Irish Treaty," 141.
46 Gilbert, *Churchill*, vol. 4, 671.
47 Jones to Hankey, 6 December 1921, Jones, *Whitehall Diary*, vol. 3, 184.
48 Ibid.
49 Scott, *Political Diaries of C.P. Scott*, December 1921, 408.
50 Ibid., 5 December 1921, 411.
51 Duggan, ("Periscope"), *Last Days*, 187.
52 Leopold Amery Papers, "Talk with Margo Greenwood," 16 April 1951, Churchill Archives, AMEL 8/74.

CHAPTER FIFTEEN

1 Duggan ("Periscope"), "Last Days," 185.
2 Sturgis, *Last Days*, 8 June 1921, 186.
3 Amery Papers, "Talk with Margo Greenwood," 16 April 1951, Churchill Archives, AMEL 8/74; Amery, *My Political Life*, vol. 2, 230.
4 Barnett, *Collapse of British Power*, 185.
5 McMahon, *British Spies and Irish Rebels*, 63.
6 Stevenson diary, 17 January 1915, PA, FLS/4/1.
7 Macready, *Annals*, vol. 1, 198.
8 Beloff, *Imperial Sunset*, vol. 2, 317–18.
9 Campbell, *F.E. Smith*, 580–1.
10 Carson in the House of Lords, 14 December 1921, Campbell, *F.E. Smith*, 574.
11 *Times*, 14 December 1921.
12 Amery, *Diaries*, vol. 1, 276.
13 Garro Jones, *Ventures and Visions*, 101.

14 Ross to Greenwood, 7 December 1921, PA, LG/F/20/1. Another Irish
    public servant, C.J.C. Street, praised Greenwood in his instant history,
    The Administration of Ireland, 1920.
15 Churchill, *Aftermath*, 325.
16 Greenwood to Lloyd George, 29 December 1921, Gilbert, *Churchill*, vol. 4,
    Companion, part 3, April 1921–November 1922, 1706.
17 Borden to Beaverbrook, 9 October 1924, LAC, MG27, II, G1.
18 Greenwood to Lloyd George, 29 December 1921, PA, LG/F/20/1/1.
19 Scott to Margot Asquith, 31 August 1922, Scott, *Political Diaries*, 412.
20 Jones, *Whitehall Diary*, 2 June 1922, vol. 3, 208.
21 Shea, *Voices and the Sound of Drums*, 80.
22 Amery Papers, "Talk with Margo Greenwood," 16 April 1951, Churchill
    Archives, AMEL 8/74.
23 Tudor to Churchill, 22 October 1922, Gilbert, *Churchill*, vol. 4, 868.
24 Greenwood to King, 13 March 1922, LAC, MG26 J1, C 2245, vol. 74.
25 Colmer, *Canada Club*, 102.
26 Crawford, *Crawford Papers*, 30 May 1922, 421.
27 Ibid., 421–2.
28 Churchill, *Aftermath*, 307.
29 Beaverbrook to Rothermere, 12 February 1925, Gilbert, *Churchill*, vol. 5,
    Companion, part 1, 1922–1929, 389.
30 Riddell, *Diaries*, 385.
31 Diaries of William Lyon Mackenzie King, 19 October 1922, LAC,
    MG26J.
32 Ibid., 19 May 1944.
33 Crawford, *Crawford Papers*, 7 September 1922, 434.
34 Middlemas and Barnes, *Baldwin*, 112.
35 15 October 1922, Churchill Archives, AMEL 7/16.

CHAPTER SIXTEEN

1 Sturgis, *Last Days*, 9 May 1921, 175.
2 Stuart Menzies, *As Others See Us*, 65, 70.
3 Taylor, *English History*, 74.
4 Riddell, *Intimate Diary*, 378.
5 *Toronto Daily Star*, 26 October 1922.
6 Margo Greenwood to Stevenson, 31 October 1922, PA, LG/G/8/9.
7 Lloyd George speech in Sunderland, copy enclosed in a letter from
   Greenwood to King, 13 November 1924, LAC, MG26J3, vol. 101.

8 Churchill to Greenwood, 9 November 1922, Gilbert, *Churchill*, vol. 4, *Companion*, part 3, April 1921–November 1922, 2117–18. Winston Churchill wrote along similar lines of Greenwood's service in Ireland in *The Aftermath*, 325.

9 Jenkins, *Asquith*, 496

10 James, *Memoirs of a Conservative*, 138.

11 Powell, *Joseph Chamberlain*, 151.

12 Baxter, *Strange Street*, 174–5.

13 Beaverbrook, *Courage*, 223.

14 Young, *Stanley Baldwin*, 35.

15 Middlemas and Barnes, *Baldwin*, 238.

16 King to Amery, 17 July 1923, LAC, MG 26 J1; *Documents on Canadian External Relations, vol. 3*, 222.

17 Ibid.

18 Vance, *Maple Leaf Empire*, 133.

19 Kerr to Grigg, 15 April 1920, Butler, *Lord Lothian*, 79.

20 Wigley, *Canada and the Transition*, 214.

21 Parliamentary Debates, House of Commons, Fourth Series, vol. 139, 2 August 1904, 618.

22 Colmer, *Canada Club*, 102.

23 Diaries of William Lyon Mackenzie King, 2 August 1923, LAC, MG 26 J23.

24 Watts, *Baldwin*, 35.

25 Beaverbrook, *Courage*, 222–3.

26 Amery Papers, "Talk with Margo Greenwood," 16 April 1951, Churchill Archives, AMEL 8/74.

27 Larkin to King, 2 May 1924, LAC, MG 26 J1, C 2254, vol. 101.

28 Colmer, *Canada Club*, 105.

29 Greenwood to King, 16 July 1924, LAC, MG 26 J1, vol. 101.

30 King to Greenwood, 2 August 1924, ibid.

31 RCMP "O" Division report, 11 September 1924, LAC, RG 18, F1, vol. 3176.

32 *Toronto Daily Star*, 12 September 1924.

33 Darwin, *Oxford History of the British Empire*, vol. 4, 70.

34 Drummond, *Imperial Economic Policy*, 40.

35 *Toronto Daily Star*, 24 September 1924.

36 Diaries of William Lyon Mackenzie King, 20 September 1924, LAC, MG 26 J13.

37 Greenwood speech to the Royal Colonial Institute, London, 10 May 1929.

38 Greenwood to the President of the Central Cardiff Liberal Association, 4 October 1924.

39 Greenwood speech, "To the Parliamentary Electors of East Walthamstow," 27 October 1924, copy enclosed in a letter from Greenwood to King, 13 November 1924, LAC, MG26 J3, vol. 101.

40 Greenwood to King, 13 November 1924, LAC, MG26 J1, vol. 101.

41 Ibid.

42 Greenwood, quoted in Shawcross, *Queen Elizabeth*, 232.

CHAPTER SEVENTEEN

1 Gertrude Bell to her mother, January 1920, Wallach, *Desert Queen*, 249.

2 Mansfield, *British in Egypt*, 242.

3 Long, *British Pro-Consuls*, 126.

4 Amery, *My Political Life*, vol. 2, 307.

5 Margo Greenwood's private diary, in the possession of the late Major Alexander Greenwood.

6 Long, *British Pro-Consuls*, 109.

CHAPTER EIGHTEEN

1 Colmer, *Canada Club*, 109.

2 Diaries of William Lyon Mackenzie King, 18 October 1926, LAC, MG26 J23.

3 Amery to Byng, 3 July 1926, in Stacey, *Historical Documents of Canada*, 6.

4 *Prominent British Steelmakers*, 1938 (?), n.p.

5 Colmer, *Canada Club*, 114.

6 *Times*, 15 January 1932.

7 *Toronto Mail*, 7 May 1929.

8 Amery to the cabinet, 11 June 1929, Churchill Archives, AMEL 2/1/17.

9 Amery to Churchill, 11 June 1929, ibid.

10 Beaverbrook to Greenwood, 6 March 1929, PA, Beaverbrook Papers, Series B.

11 Margo Greenwood to Amery, 23 June 1929, Churchill Archives, AMEL 2/1/17.

12 Colmer, *Canada Club*, 117.

13 See chapter 13, p. 228.

14 Larkin to King, 19 September 1929, LAC, MG26 J1, C2247, vol. 78.

15 *Evening Standard*, "Diary," 4 and 6 May 1929.

16 *Diaries of Sir Robert Bruce Lockhart*, vol. 1, 24 November 1929, 109.

17 Chisholm and Davie, *Beaverbrook*, 292.

18 Lockhart diaries, vol. 1, 24 November 1929, 109.
19 Middlemas and Barnes, *Baldwin*, 662.
20 Camrose to Baldwin, 2 March 1932, in ibid., 671–2.
21 Amery Diaries, 29 February 1932, vol. 2, 237–8.
22 Ferguson to Bennett, 3 March 1932, in Oliver, *Ferguson*, 396.
23 Greenwood to King, 19 September 1935, LAC, MG25 J1, vol. 26.
24 Greenwood to Amery, 14 June 1933, Churchill Archives, AMEL 6/3/56.

CHAPTER NINETEEN

1 Greenwood to King, 20 October 1933, LAC, MG26 J1, vol. 196.
2 Hoare to Irwin, 15 July 1930, Gilbert, *Churchill*, vol. 5, 367.
3 Ibid., 336.
4 Darwin, "Third Political Empire," 80.
5 Ibid.
6 James, *Memoirs of a Conservative*, 394. Correspondence regarding India between Davidson and Greenwood is in PA, DAV/220-226.
7 *Report of the Joint Select Committee on Indian Constitutional Reform, 1933–1934*, 24.
8 James, *Churchill*, 230.
9 Middlemas and Barnes, *Baldwin*, 700.
10 Darwin, "Third Political Empire," 81.
11 Greenwood to King, 23 January 1937, LAC, MG26 J1, vol. 235.
12 King to Greenwood, 17 March 1937, ibid.
13 King to Greenwood, 6 October 1937, ibid.
14 Diaries of William Lyon Mackenzie King, 4 May 1937, ibid.
15 Greenwood to King, 2 July 1937, ibid.
16 Diaries of William Lyon Mackenzie King, 27 March 1938, LAC, MG26 J13.
17 Lloyd George in the *Daily Express*, 7 September 1936.
18 King to Greenwood, 6 October 1937, LAC, MG26 J1, C 3687, vol. 235.
19 Greenwood to Amery, various dates, Churchill Archives, AMEL 6/3/56 and AMEL 6/3/134.
20 Greenwood to Fourth International Advertising Convention, Glasgow, *Times*, 29 June 1938.
21 Greenwood to Chamberlain, 5 February 1938; *Times*, 9 February 1938.
22 Diaries of William Lyon Mackenzie King, 21 August 1943, LAC, MG16 J13.
23 King to Cody, 1 September 1938, LAC, MG26 J1, C 3732, vol. 250.
24 President Cody's speech, 2 September 1938, *University of Toronto Monthly*, 8 October 1938.
25 Greenwood speech, ibid.

26 *Globe and Mail,* 3 September 1938.
27 Greenwood to King, 10 September 1938, LAC, MG26 J1, C 3734, vol. 250.
28 Diaries of William Lyon Mackenzie King, 6 September 1938, LAC, MG26 J1.
29 Ibid.
30 Diaries of William Lyon Mackenzie King, 12 September 1938, ibid.
31 Diaries of William Lyon Mackenzie King, 24 October 1938, ibid.
32 Greenwood to King, 26 January 1939, ibid., vol. 250. Baldwin's lectures were published by University of Toronto Press as *The Falconer Lecturers* in 1939.
33 Greenwood to King, 27 June 1939, LAC, MG26 J1, vol. 268.
34 King to Greenwood, 17 August 1939, ibid.
35 *Times,* 9 December 1939.
36 James, *Memoirs of a Conservative,* 423.
37 Annual report for Dorman Long, 1939.
38 Greenwood to Dunn, 12 July 1940, LAC, MG26 J1, C4569, vol. 287.
39 King to Dunn, 20 July 1940, ibid.
40 Greenwood to Churchill, 11 May 1940, Churchill Archives, CHAR/20/11/54.
41 Greenwood to King, 11 September 1941, LAC, MG26 J1, C 4863, vol. 235.
42 Diaries of William Lyon Mackenzie King, 28 April 1944, LAC MG26 J13.
43 See chapter 15, p. 258.
44 Amery diary, 27 January 1942; Barnes and Nicholson, *Leo Amery Diaries,* vol. 2, 766.
45 Pickersgill and Forster, *Mackenzie King Record,* vol. 1, 663, 666; Greenwood to King, 12 May 1944, LAC, MG26 J1, vol. 361.
46 Parliamentary Debates, House of Lords, Fifth Series, vol. 135, 28 March 1935, col. 825.
47 Lockhart, *Diaries,* 207–8.
48 West, *Meaning of Treason,* 215.
49 Greenwood note of 30 November 1945, Churchill Archives, AMEL 7/39.
50 Duff Cooper, *Diaries, 1915–1951,* 18 December 1925, 397.
51 Greenwood to King, 26 July 1946, LAC, MG26 J1, C9170, vol. 404.
52 Montague Burton Archives, LAC, MG40-M51.
53 Diaries of William Lyon Mackenzie King, 18 June 1945, LAC MG26 J1.
54 King to Greenwood, 6 September 1946, LAC, MG26 J1, vol. 413.
55 *Parliamentary Debates, Lords,* 5 June 1946.
56 Greenwood to the Reverend Ralph Adye, 8 January 1947, Whitby (Ontario) Archives.

57 Diaries of William Lyon Mackenzie King, 14 September 1948, LAC MG26
   J1.
58 Stuart, *Opportunity Knocks Once*, 114.
59 Greenwood, *Greenwood Tree*.

CONCLUSION

1 Darwin, *Unfinished Empire*, 134.
2 Speech given in Liverpool, 1897, published in *Meetings Held during the Visit
   of the Prime Ministers of the Self-Governing Colonies, between June 12th and July
   5th, 1897* (London: British Empire League 1898).
3 Dafoe, *Laurier*, 34.
4 Hillmer, *Britain and Canada*, part 1, 6.
5 Greenwood, *Canada as an Imperial Factor*, 24.
6 Barnett, *Collapse of British Power*, 180–1.
7 Berger, *Sense of Power*, 127.
8 Trudeau, *Conversation with Canadians*, 6.

Bibliography

ARCHIVAL SOURCES

Leo Amery Papers, Churchill Archives, Churchill College, Cambridge.
Beaverbrook Papers, Parliamentary Archives, London (PA).
Winston Churchill Papers, Churchill Archives, Churchill College, Cambridge.
Greenwood Papers, Whitby Public Library, Ontario.
Alexander Greenwood papers and conversations, Nanoose Bay, British
   Columbia.
William Lyon Mackenzie King Papers, Library and Archives Canada, Ottawa
   (LAC).
David Lloyd George Papers, Parliamentary Archives, London (PA).
Ontario Archives, Toronto (OA).
Parliamentary Debates, House of Commons (Westminster).
Times; various other British and Canadian newspapers.

PUBLISHED WORKS

Ainsworth, John. *The Black and Tans and Auxiliaries in Ireland, 1920–1921:
   Their Origins, Roles and Legacy.* Paper presented to the annual conference
   of the Queensland History Teachers' Association, Brisbane, 12 May
   2001.
Amery, Leopold. *The Case against Home Rule.* London: N.p. 1912.
– *My Political Life.* 3 vols. London: Hutchinson 1953.
Atkinson, C.T. *History of the South Wales Borderers, 1914–1918.* London: Medici
   Society 1931.
Baldwin, Stanley Baldwin, Earl. *The Falconer Lecturers.* Toronto: University of
   Toronto Press 1939.

Banks, M.B. *Edward Blake, Irish Nationalist: A Canadian Statesman in Irish Politics, 1892–1907.* Toronto: University of Toronto Press 1957.

Barnes, John, and David Nicholson, eds. *The Leo Amery Diaries.* Vol. 1, *1896–1929.* London: Hutchinson 1980.

– *The Leo Amery Diaries.* Vol. 2, *1929–1945: The Empire at Bay.* London: Hutchinson 1989.

Barnett, Corelli. *The Collapse of British Power.* London: Eyre Methuen 1972.

Baxter, Beverley. *Strange Street.* New York and London: Appleton-Century 1935.

Beaverbrook, Lord. *Politicians and the War.* 2 vols. London: Butterworth 1928.

– *Courage: The Story of Sir James Dunn.* Fredericton: Brunswick Press 1961.

– *The Decline and Fall of Lloyd George.* London: Collins 1963.

Beloff, Max. *Imperial Sunset.* 2 vols. London: Methuen 1969.

Bennett, Richard. *The Black and Tans.* Staplehurst, UK: Spellmount 1959.

Berger, Carl. *The Sense of Power: Studies in the Ideas of Canadian Imperialism, 1867–1914.* Toronto: University of Toronto Press 1971.

– *The Writing of Canadian History.* Toronto: Oxford University Press 1976.

Bew, Paul. *Ireland: The Politics of Enmity, 1789–2006.* Oxford: Oxford University Press 2007.

Birkenhead, Lord. *F.E.: The Life of F.E. Smith, First Earl of Birkenhead.* London: Eyre & Spottiswoode 1960.

– *Halifax: The Life of Lord Halifax.* London: Hamish Hamilton 1965.

Blake, Robert. *The Unknown Prime Minister.* London: Eyre & Spottiswoode 1974.

– *An Incongruous Partnership: Lloyd George and Bonar Law.* Cardiff: Welsh Political Archive Lecture 1992.

Boghardt, Thomas. *Spies of the Kaiser.* Basingstoke: Palgrave Macmillan 2004.

Bond, Brian. *Survivors of a Kind: Memoirs of the Western Front.* London: Hambledon Continuum 2008.

Bonham Carter, Mark, and Mark Pottle, eds. *Lantern Slides: The Diaries and Letters of Violet Bonham Carter, 1904–1914.* London: Weidenfeld & Nicolson 1996.

Borden, R.L. *The Question of Oriental Immigration: Speeches (in Part) Delivered by R.L. Borden, M.P. in 1907 and 1908.* Toronto Public Library.

Bowden, Tom. "The Irish Underground and the War of Independence, 1919–1921." *Journal of Contemporary History* 8, no. 3 (1973): 3–23.

– *The Breakdown of Public Security: The Case of Ireland, 1916–1921, and Palestine, 1936–1939.* London: Sage 1977.

Bowman, Timothy. *Carson's Army: The Ulster Volunteer Force, 1910–1922.* Manchester: Manchester University Press, 2002.

Boyce, D.G. "How to Settle the Irish Question; Lloyd George and Ireland, 1916–21." In *Lloyd George, Twelve Essays*, edited by A.J.P. Taylor. London: Hamish Hamilton 1971.

– *Englishmen and Irish Troubles: British Public Opinion and the Making of Irish Policy, 1918–1921*. London: Jonathan Cape 1972.

– ed. *The Revolution in Ireland, 1879–1923*. Basingstoke: Macmillan Education 1988.

Boyce, D.G., and Alan O'Day, ed. *Ireland in Transition, 1867–1921*. London: Routledge 2004.

Brock, Michael, and Eleanor Brock, eds. *H.H. Asquith: Letters to Venetia Stanley.* Oxford: Oxford University Press 1982.

Bromage, Mary. *Churchill and Ireland.* Notre Dame, IN: University of Notre Dame Press 1964.

Brown, J., and Wm. Roger Louis, eds. *The Oxford History of the British Empire.* Vol. 4, *The Twentieth Century.* Oxford: Oxford University Press 1999.

Buckner, Phillip, ed. *Canada and the End of Empire.* Vancouver: University of British Columbia Press 2005.

Buckner, Phillip, and R.D. Francis, eds. *Canada and the British World.* Vancouver: University of British Columbia 2006.

Butler, J.R.M. *Lord Lothian.* London: Macmillan 1960.

Callwell, C.E. *Field-Marshal Sir Henry Wilson: His Life and Diaries.* London: Cassell 1927.

Campbell, John. *Lloyd George: The Goat in the Wilderness, 1922–1931.* London: Jonathan Cape 1977.

– *F.E. Smith, First Earl of Birkenhead.* London: Jonathan Cape 1983.

– *"If Love Were All": The Story of Frances Stevenson and David Lloyd George.* London: Jonathan Cape 2006.

Cannadine, David. *The Decline and Fall of the Aristocracy.* New Haven: Yale University Press 1990.

– *Aspects of Aristocracy.* New Haven: Yale University Press 1994.

Canning, Paul. *British Policy towards Ireland, 1921–1941.* London: Oxford University Press 1985.

Chamberlain, Neville. *The Neville Chamberlain Diary Letters.* Edited by Robert Self. 4 vols. Aldershot: Ashgate 2000.

Charlesworth, Hector. *More Candid Chronicles: Further Leaves from the Notebook of a Canadian Journalist.* Toronto: Macmillan 1928.

Chisholm, Anne, and Michael Davie. *Beaverbrook: A Life.* London: Hutchinson 1992.

Churchill, Randolph. *Lord Derby: "King of Lancashire."* London: Heinemann 1959.

Churchill, Randolph, and Martin Gilbert. *Winston S. Churchill: The Official Biography, 1874–1965*. Vols. 1–2. London: Heinemann 1966–67.

– eds. *Winston S. Churchill: Companion Volumes*. 13 vols. London: Heinemann 1966–2000.

Churchill, Winston. *The Aftermath*. London: Thornton Buitterworth 1929.

– *The World Crisis*. 6 vols. London: Cassell 1948–1954.

Clarke, Peter. *Hope and Glory: Britain, 1900–1990*. London: Penguin 1996.

Coates, Colin, ed. *Imperial Canada, 1867–1917*. Edinburgh: University of Edinburgh 1997.

Collins, Peter, ed. *Nationalism and Unionism: Conflict in Ireland, 1885–1921*. Belfast: Institute of Irish Studies, Queen's University of Belfast 1994.

Colmer, J.G. *The Canada Club (London)*. London: Committee of the Club 1934.

Coogan, Tim Pat. *Wherever Green Is Worn: The Story of the Irish Diaspora*. London: Hutchinson 2000.

– *Ireland in the Twentieth Century*. London: Arrow Books 2004.

Craick, W.A. "Sir Hamar Greenwood, Bar't." *Canadian Magazine*, March 1915.

Crawford, Lord. *The Crawford Papers*. Edited by John Vincent. Manchester: Manchester University Press 1984.

Crosby, Travis. *The Unknown Lloyd George: A Statesman in Conflict*. London: Tauris 2014.

Crozier, F.P. *Impressions and Recollections*. London: T. Werner Laurie 1930.

– *Ireland for Ever*. London: Jonathan Cape 1932.

– *The Men I Killed*. London: Michael Joseph 1937.

Dafoe, J.W. *Laurier: A Study in Canadian Politics*. Toronto: McClelland & Stewart 1968.

Dangerfield, George. *The Strange Death of Liberal England*. New York and London: H. Smith & R. Haas 1935.

Darwin, John. "Third Political Empire? The Dominion Idea in Imperial Politics." In *Oxford History of the British Empire*, vol. 4. Oxford: Oxford University Press 1999.

– *The Empire Project: The Rise and Fall of the British World System, 1830–1970*. Cambridge: Cambridge University Press 2009.

– *Unfinished Empire: The Global Expansion of Britain*. London: Bloomsbury 2012.

Dawson, R.M. *William Lyon Mackenzie King: A Political Biography*. Vol. 1. Toronto: University of Toronto Press 1958.

– *The Development of Dominion Status, 1900–1936*. London: Frank Cass 1965.

Documents on Canadian External Relations. Vol. 3, 1919–1925. Ottawa: Queen's Printer 1967 –.

Drummond, Ian M. *Imperial Economic Policy, 1917–1939: Studies in Expansion and Protection*. Toronto: University of Toronto Press 1974.

Duff Cooper, Alfred. *The Duff Cooper Diaries, 1915–1951*. London: Weidenfield & Nicolson 2005.

Duggan, G.C. ("Periscope"). "The Last Days of Dublin Castle." *Blackwood's*, August 1922, 137–90.

Duncan, Sara Jeannette. *The Imperialist*. Toronto: Copp Clark 1904.

The Empire Club of Canada Speeches, 1907–1908. Edited by J. Castell Hopkins. Toronto: Empire Club of Canada 1910.

Faber, David. *Speaking for England: Leo, Julian and John Amery*. London: Free Press 2005.

Fair, John. "The Anglo-Irish Treaty of 1921." *Journal of British Studies* 12, no. 1 (1972): 132–50.

Fanning, Ronan. *Fatal Path: British Government and the Irish Revolution, 1910–1922*. London: Faber & Faber 2013.

Fanning, Ronan, M. Kennedy, D. Keogh, and E. O'Halpin, eds. *Documents on Irish Foreign Policy*. Vol.1, *1919–1922*. Dublin: Royal Irish Academy 1998.

Ferns, H.S., and B. Ostry. *The Age of Mackenzie King: The Rise of the Leader*. London and Toronto: Heinemann 1955.

Finnan, Joseph P. *John Redmond and Irish Unity*. Syracuse: Syracuse University Press 2004.

Fitzpatrick, David. *Politics and Irish Life, 1913–1921*. Dublin: Gill & Macmillan 1977.

Foster, Roy. *Modern Ireland, 1600–1972*. London: Penguin 1989.

Foy, Michael. *Michael Collins's Intelligence War: The Struggle between the British and the IRA, 1919–1921*. Stroud, UK: Sutton 2008.

Gallagher, Frank. *The Indivisible Island*. London: Gollancz 1957

Gallagher, Frank, and Thomas P. O'Neill. *The Anglo-Irish Treaty*. London: Hutchinson 1965.

Gallagher, John. *The Decline, Revival and Fall of the British Empire*. Cambridge: Cambridge University Press 1982.

Garro Jones, George Morgan. *Ventures and Visions*. London: Hutchinson 1935.

Garvin, Tom. *Nationalist Revolutionaries in Ireland, 1858–1928*, Oxford: Clarendon Press 1987.

Gilbert, Martin. *Winston S. Churchill: The Official Biography. 1874–1965*. Vols. 3–8 (vols. 1 and 2 with R.S. Churchill). London: Heinemann 1968–1988.

– ed. *David Lloyd George*. Englewood Cliffs, NJ: Prentice Hall 1968.

Greenwood, Alexander. *The Greenwood Tree in Three Continents, or a Fertile Family of Five Centuries, 1487–1987*. Baltimore, MD: Gateway Press 1988.

Greenwood, Hamar. *Canada as an Imperial Factor*. London: Collins 1911.

Grigg, John. *Lloyd George: From Peace to War, 1912–1916*. London: Methuen 1985.
– *Lloyd George: War Leader, 1916–1918*. London: Allen Lane 2002.
Gwyn, Richard. *John A, The Man Who Made Us: The Life and Times of John A. Macdonald*. Toronto: Random House 2007.
Hague, Fion. *The Pain and the Privilege: The Women in Lloyd George's Life*. London: Harper 2008.
Hall, D.J. *Clifford Sifton*. 2 vols. Vancouver: U B C Press 1981.
Hammond, J.L. *C.P. Scott of the Manchester Guardian*. London: Bell 1934.
Hancock, W.K. *Smuts*. Vol. 1, *The Sanguine Years, 1870–1919*. London: Cambridge University Press 1962.
Hart, Peter. *The IRA and Its Enemies: British Intelligence in Ireland, 1920–21, The Final Reports*. Oxford: Oxford University Press 1998.
– *The IRA at War*. Oxford: Oxford University Press 2003.
Harvey, A.D. "Who Were the Auxiliaries?" *Historical Journal* 35, no. 3 (1992).
Hattersley, Roy. *The Great Outsider: David Lloyd George*. London: Little, Brown 2010.
Hillmer, Norman. *Britain and Canada in the Age of Mackenzie King*. Part 1, *"The Outstanding Imperialist": Mackenzie King and the British*. Lecture Series No. 4. London: Canada House 1978.
Holland, R.F., *Britain and the Commonwealth Alliance, 1918–1939*. Basingstoke: Macmillan 1981.
Holt, Edgar. *Protest in Arms: The Irish Troubles, 1916–1923*. London: Putnam 1960.
Hopkinson, Michael. *The Irish War of Independence*. Kingston and Montreal: McGill-Queen's University Press 2004.
Howland, O.A. *The New Empire: Reflections upon Its Origins and Constitution*. Toronto: Hart & Co. 1891.
Hurd, Percy, and Archibald Hurd. *The New Empire Partnership: Defence – Commerce – Policy*. Toronto: Briggs 1916.
Hyman, Ronald. *Elgin and Churchill at the Colonial Office, 1905–1908*. London: Macmillan 1968.
– *Britain's Declining Empire: The Watershed of the Empire-Commonwealth*. Cambridge: Cambridge University Press 2006.
Jackson, Alvin. *Colonel Edward Saunderson: Landlord Loyalty in Victorian Ireland*. Oxford: Clarendon Press 1995.
– *Home Rule: An Irish History, 1800–2000*. London: Phoenix Press 2003.
Jalland, Patricia. "A Liberal Chief Secretary and the Irish Question: Augustine Birrell, 1907–1914." *Historical Journal* 19, no. 2 (1976): 421–51.
James, Robert Rhodes. *Memoirs of a Conservative: J.C.C. Davidson's Memoirs and Papers, 1910–37*. London: Weidenfeld & Nicolson 1969.

– *Churchill: A Study in Failure, 1900–1939.* London: Weidenfeld & Nicolson 1970.

Jenkins, Roy. *Asquith, Portrait of a Man and an Era.* London: Collins 1964.

Johnson, Matthew. "The Liberal War Committee and the Liberal Advocacy of Conscription in Britain, 1914–1916." *Historical Journal* 51, no. 2 (2008).

Jones, Thomas. *Lloyd George.* London: Oxford University Press 1951.

– *Whitehall Diary.* Edited by Keith Middlemas. 3 vols. London: Oxford University Press 1971.

Kaut, William. *Ambushes and Armour: The Irish Rebellion, 1919–1921.* Dublin: Irish Academic Press 2010.

Kee, Robert. *The Green Flag: The Turbulent History of the Irish Nationalist Movement.* London: Weidenfeld & Nicolson 1972.

Kendle, J.E. "The Round Table Movement and 'Home Rule All Round.'" *Historical Journal* 11, no. 2 (1968).

Kenny, Kevin, ed. *Ireland and the British Empire.* Oxford: Oxford University Press 2004.

Kenny, M. *Germany Calling.* Dublin: New Island 2003.

Keynes, John Maynard. *Essays in Biography.* London: Hart-Davis 1951

Langton, H.H. "Mackenzie King, William Mulock, James Mavor, and the University of Toronto's Student Revolt of 1895." *Canadian Historical Review* 69, no. 4 (1988).

Lawlor, Sheila. *Britain and Ireland, 1914–1923.* Dublin: Gill & Macmillan 1983.

Leeson, D.M. *The Black and Tans, British Police and Auxiliaries in the Irish War of Independence, 1920–1921.* Oxford: Oxford University Press 2011.

Lloyd George, Frances. *The Years That Are Past.* Hutchinson: London 1967.

– *My Darling Pussy: The Letters of Lloyd George and Frances Stevenson, 1913–1941.* Edited by A.J.P. Taylor. London: Weidenfeld & Nicolson 1975.

Lockhart, R.H.B. *The Diaries of Sir Robert Bruce Lockhart.* London: Macmilllan 1973.

Long, C.W. *British Pro-Consuls in Egypt, 1914–1929: The Challenge of Nationalism.* London: Routledge Curzon 2005.

Longford, Lord (Frank Pakenham). *Peace by Ordeal.* London: Sidgwick & Jackson 1972.

Louis, William Roger, editor-in chief. *Oxford History of the British Empire.* 5 vols. Oxford: Oxford University Press 1998–99.

Lowe, W.J. "Who Were the Black and Tans?" *History Ireland* 12, no. 3 (2004).

Macardle, Dorothy. *The Irish Republic.* Dublin: Irish Press 1965.

MacDonagh, Oliver, and W.F. Mandle, eds. *Ireland and Irish-Australian Studies in Cultural and Political History.* London: Croom Helm 1986.

MacLaren, Roy. *Commissions High: Canada in London, 1870–1971.* Montreal and Kingston: McGill-Queen's University Press 2006.

Macready, Nevil. *Annals of an Active Life.* 2 vols. London: Hutchinson 1924.

Mansergh, Nicholas. *The Irish Question, 1840–1921.* London: George Allen & Unwin 1965.

– *The Commonwealth Experience.* 2 vols. London: Weidenfeld & Nicolson 1969.

Mansfield, Peter. *The British in Egypt.* London: Weidenfeld & Nicolson 1971.

Matthews, Kevin. Fatal Influence: The Impact of Ireland on British Politics. Dublin: University College Dublin Press 2004.

McBride, Lawrence. *The Greening of Dublin Castle: The Transformation of Bureaucratic and Judicial Personnel in Ireland, 1892–1922.* Washington, DC: Catholic University of America Press 1991.

McColgan, John. *British Policy and the Irish Administration, 1920–22.* London: Allen & Unwin 1983.

McDowall, D. *The Light: Brazilian Traction, Light and Power Company Limited.* Toronto: University of Toronto Press 1988.

McEwan, J.M. "Canadians at Westminster." *Dalhousie Review* 43, no. 4 (1963).

McKenna, Joseph. *Guerrilla Warfare in the Irish War of Independence, 1919–1921.* London: McFarland 2011.

McLaughlin, Robert. *Irish Canadian Conflict and the Struggle for Irish Independence, 1912–1925.* Toronto: University of Toronto Press 2013.

McMahon, Paul. *British Spies and Irish Rebels.* Woodbridge, Suffolk: Boydell Press 2008.

Middlemas, K., and J. Barnes. *Baldwin: A Biography.* London: Macmillan 1969.

Morgan, Kenneth. *David Lloyd George, Welsh Radical as World Statesman.* Cardiff: University of Wales Press 1964.

– *Lloyd George Family Letters, 1885–1936.* Cardiff: University of Wales Press 1973.

– *Consensus and Disunity: The Lloyd George Coalition Government, 1918–1922.* Oxford: Clarendon Press 1979.

Mosley, Oswald. *My Life.* London: Thomas Nelson 1968.

Nicolson, Harold. *King George the Fifth: His Life and Reign.* London: Constable 1952.

O'Brien, R.B. *Dublin Castle and the Irish People.* London: K. Paul, Trench, Trübner 1909.

O'Broin, Leon. *Michael Collins.* Dublin: Gill & Macmillan 1980.

– *W.E. Wylie and the Irish Revolution,* 1916–1921. Dublin: Gill & Macmillan 1989.

O'Connor T.P. *Memoirs of an Old Parliamentarian.* London: E. Benn 1929.

O'Farrell, Patrick. *England and Ireland since 1800.* Oxford 1975.

O'Halpin, Eunan. *The Decline of the Union: British Government in Ireland, 1892–1920.* Dublin: Gill & Macmillan 1987.

– "Greenwood." *Dictionary of Irish Biography*, vol. 4. Cambridge: Cambridge University Press 2009.

Oliver, W.G. *Howard Ferguson: Ontario Tory.* Toronto: University of Toronto Press 1977.

Ormsby, M.A. *British Columbia: A History.* Toronto: Macmillan 1958.

Owen, Frank. *Tempestuous Journey: Lloyd George, His Life and Times.* London: Hutchinson 1954.

Peatling, G.K. *British Opinion and Irish Self-Government, 1865–1925: From Unionism to Liberal Commonwealth.* Dublin: Irish Academic Press 2001.

"Periscope" [George Chester Duggan]. "The Last Days of Dublin Castle." *Blackwood's*, August 1922.

Petrie, Sir Charles. *Walter Long and His Times.* London: Hutchinson 1936.

Phillips, Alison. *The Revolution in Ireland, 1906–1923.* London: Longmans Green 1923.

Pickersgill, J.W., and D.F. Forster, eds. *The Mackenzie King Record.* Toronto: University of Toronto Press 1970.

Porter, Andrew, ed. *The Nineteenth Century.* Vol. 3, *Oxford History of the British Empire*, edited by William Roger Louis. Oxford: Oxford University Press 1999.

Powell, Enoch. *Joseph Chamberlain.* London: Thames & Hudson 1977.

Regan, John. *The Irish Counter-Revolution, 1921–1936.* Dublin: Liliput 2001.

Riddell, Lord. *Lord Riddell's Intimate Diary of the Peace Conference and After, 1918–1923.* London: Gollancz 1933.

– *War Diary, 1914–1918.* London: Nicholson & Watson 1933.

– *More Pages from My Diary.* London: Weidenfeld & Nicolson 1934.

– *The Riddell Diaries, 1908–1923.* Edited by J.M. McEwan. London: Athlone Press 1986.

Roberts, Andrew. *Salisbury: Victorian Titan.* London: Weidenfeld & Nicolson 1999.

Robinson, Henry. *Memories Wise and Otherwise.* London: Cassell 1923.

Roskill, Stephen. *Hankey, Man of Secrets.* 3 vols. London: Collins 1971–74.

Rowland, Peter. *The Last Liberal Governments.* 2 vols. London: Barrie & Rockliffe 1968, 1971.

Rowntree, Seebohm. *A Study of Town Life.* London: Macmillan 1901.

Roy, Patricia. *A White Man's Province: British Columbia Politicians and Chinese and Japanese Immigrants.* Vancouver: University of British Columbia Press 1989

– *The Oriental Question: Consolidating a White Man's Province, 1914–1941.*
Vancouver: University of British Columbia Press 2003.

Ryan, A.H. *Mutiny at the Curragh.* London: Macmillan 1956.

Savage, David. "The Parnell of Wales Has Become the Chamberlain of England: Lloyd George and the Irish Question." *Journal of British Studies* 12, no. 1 (1972).

Scott, C.P. *The Political Diaries of C.P. Scott.* Edited by Trevor Wilson. London: Collins 1970.

Seedorf, Martin. "The Lloyd George Government and the Anglo-Irish War, 1919–1921." PhD dissertation, University of Washington, 1974.

– "Defending Reprisals: Sir Hamar Greenwood and the 'Troubles,' 1920–1921." *Eire-Ireland* 25, no. 4 (1990).

– "Hamar Greenwood." *Oxford Dictionary of National Biography.* Oxford: Oxford University Press 2004.

Shannon, Catherine. *Arthur J. Balfour and Ireland, 1874–1922.* Washington, DC: Catholic University of America Press 1988

Shawcross, William. *Queen Elizabeth, the Queen Mother.* London: Macmillan 2009.

Shea, Patrick. *Voices and the Sound of Drums.* Belfast: Blackstaff Press 1981.

Skelton, O.D. *Life and Letters of Sir Wilfrid Laurier.* 2 vols. Toronto: S.B. Gundy / Oxford University Press 1921.

Skidelsky, Robert. *Oswald Mosley.* London: Macmillan 1975.

Soames, Mary, ed. *Speaking for Themselves: The Personal Letters of Winston and Clementine Churchill.* London: Black Swan 1999.

Spender, John. *The Life of the Rt. Hon. Sir Henry Campbell-Bannerman.* 2 vols. London: Hodder & Stoughton 1923.

Stacey, C.P. *Canada and the Age of Conflict.* Vol. 2, *The Mackenzie King Era.* Toronto: University of Toronto Press 1981.

– ed. *Historical Documents of Canada.* Vol. 5, *The Arts of War and Peace, 1914–1945.* Toronto: Macmillan 1972.

Stevenson, Frances L. *The Years That Are Past.* London: Hutchinson 1967.

– *Lloyd George, A Diary.* Edited by A.J.P. Taylor. London: Hutchinson 1971.

Street, C.J.C. *The Administration of Ireland, 1920.* London: Philip Allan & Co. 1921.

– *Ireland in 1921.* London: Philip Allan & Co. 1922.

Stuart, Campbell. *Opportunity Knocks Once.* London: Collins 1952.

Stuart Menzies, Amy (Amy Charlotte Bewicke; or "A Woman of No Importance"). *As Others See Us.* London: H. Jenkins 1924.

Sturgis, Mark. *The Last Days of Dublin Castle: The Mark Sturgis Diaries*. Edited by Michael Hopkinson. Dublin: Irish Academic Press 1999.

Sylvester, A.J. *Life with Lloyd George*. London: Macmillan 1975.

Taylor, A.J.P. *English History, 1914–1945*. Oxford: Clarendon Press 1965.

– *Beaverbrook*. London: Hamish Hamilton 1972.

– ed. *Lloyd George: Twelve Essays*. London: Hamish Hamilton 1971.

Taylor, Rex. *Michael Collins*. London: Hutchinson 1958.

Thompson, J. Lee. *Northcliffe: Press Baron in Politics, 1865–1922*. London: John Murray 2000.

Thompson, Neville. *Canada and the End of the Imperial Dream: Beverley Baxter's Reports from London through War and Peace, 1936–1960*. Toronto: Oxford University Press 2013.

Townshend, Charles. *The British Campaign in Ireland, 1919–1921: The Development of British Political and Military Policies*. London: Oxford University Press 1975.

– *The Republic: The Fight for Irish Independence*. London: Allen Lane 2013.

Trudeau, Pierre. *Conversation with Canadians*. Toronto: University of Toronto Press 1972.

Tucker, G.N. *The Naval Service of Canada*. 2 vols. Ottawa: King's Printer 1952.

Vance, Jonathan. *Maple Leaf Empire: Canada, Britain and Two World Wars*. Don Mills, ON: Oxford University Press 2012.

Wallach, Janet. *Desert Queen*. New York: Doubleday 1996.

Ward, Peter. *White Canada Forever: Popular Attitudes and Public Policies towards Orientals in British Columbia*. Kingston and Montreal: McGill-Queen's University Press 2002.

Watts, Duncan. *Stanley Baldwin and the Search for Consensus*. London: Hodder and Stoughton 1996.

Weale, Adrian. *Patriot Traitors, Roger Casement, John Amery and the Real Meaning of Treason*. London: Viking 2001.

West, Rebecca. *The Meaning of Treason*. London: Macmillan 1952.

Wheeler-Bennett, John. *John Anderson, Viscount Waverley*. London: Macmillan 1962.

Wigley, Philip. *Canada and the Transition to the Commonwealth, British-Canadian Relations, 1917–1926*. Cambridge: Cambridge University Press 1977.

Williams, Desmond, ed. *The Irish Struggle, 1916–1926*. Toronto: University of Toronto Press 1966.

Williams, Stephanie. *Running the Show: The Extraordinary Stories of the Men Who Governed the British Empire*. London: Viking 2011.

Williamson, P.A., and Edward Blake, eds. *Baldwin Papers: A Conservative States-man.* Cambridge: Cambridge University Press 2004.

Wilson, John. *CB: A Life of Sir Henry Campbell-Bannerman.* London: Constable 1973.

Wilson, Trevor. *The Downfall of the Liberal Party, 1914–1935.* London: Collins 1966.

Winks, Robin, ed. *The Oxford History of the British Empire.* Vol. 5, *Historiography.* Oxford: Oxford University Press 1999.

Winter, Brian. *Chronicles of a County Town: Whitby Past and Present.* Whitby, ON: Brian Winter 1999.

Winter, Ormonde de. *Winter's Tale: An Autobiography.* London: Richards Press 1955.

Wrigley, Chris. *Lloyd George.* Oxford: Blackwell 1992.

Young, G.M. *Stanley Baldwin.* London: Hart-Davis 1952.

Index